The Movement Reconsidered

The Movement Reconsidered, a collection of original essays by distinguished poets, critics, and scholars from Britain and America, sets out to show not only that realtions between Movement and other post-war British writers were more complex and nuanced than is usually suggested, but that the role these relations played in shaping the current literary scene has been misunderstood or undervalued. Other topics it examines include the origins of the grouping; the role of mediating figures such as Auden, Empson, and Orwell; the part the writers themselves played in promoting the grouping; the interlocking network of academics, journalists, and editors who aided them; and analogous developments in other fields, notably philosophy, politics, and language. The book's ultimate aim is to encourage readers to come to Movement writing with fresh eyes and to gain a fairer sense of its range and power.

The Movement Reconsidered

Essays on Larkin, Amis, Gunn, Davie, and Their Contemporaries

EDITED BY

Zachary Leader

OXFORD
UNIVERSITY PRESS

Great Clarendon Street, Oxford ox2 6dp

Oxford University Press is a department of the University of Oxford.
It furthers the University's objective of excellence in research, scholarship,
and education by publishing worldwide in

Oxford New York

Auckland Cape Town Dar es Salaam Hong Kong Karachi
Kuala Lumpur Madrid Melbourne Mexico City Nairobi
New Delhi Shanghai Taipei Toronto

With offices in

Argentina Austria Brazil Chile Czech Republic France Greece
Guatemala Hungary Italy Japan Poland Portugal Singapore
South Korea Switzerland Thailand Turkey Ukraine Vietnam

Oxford is a registered trade mark of Oxford University Press
in the UK and in certain other countries

Published in the United States
by Oxford University Press Inc., New York

British Library Cataloguing in Publication Data

Data available

Library of Congress Cataloging-in-Publication Data

The Movement reconsidered : essays on Larkin, Amis, Gunn, Davie, and their contemporaries/edited by
Zachary Leader. — 1st ed.
    p. cm.
Includes index.
ISBN 978-0-19-955825-4
1. English poetry—20th century—History and criticism. 2. Movement, The (English poetry)
I. Leader, Zachary.
PR605.M68M68 2009
821'.914091—dc22
    2008049521

Typeset by SPI Publisher Services, Pondicherry, India
Printed in Great Britain
on acid-free paper by the MPG Books Group, Bodmin and King's Lynn

ISBN 978-0-19-955825-4 (Hbk.)
ISBN 978-0-19-960184-4 (Pbk.)

2 4 6 8 10 9 7 5 3 1

ACKNOWLEDGEMENTS

I am grateful to Andrew McNeillie, Jacqueline Baker, Fiona Vlemmiks, Val Shelley, Tom Chandler, and Coleen Hatrick, of Oxford University Press, patient and efficient supporters of the book throughout. Thanks also to Rosemary Dear, who compiled the Index, and to Robert C. Ritchie and Susi Krasnoo, of the Huntington Library, San Marino, California, for hosting the conference out of which the book grew.

The original version of one essay, Craig Raine's 'Counter-Intuitive Larkin,' appeared in *Areté* 23 (Summer/Autumn 2007), 35-54. A short version of Terry Castle's article, 'The Lesbianism of Philip Larkin,' originally commissioned for this volume, appeared in *Daedalus* 136:2 (Spring 2007), 88-102. All the other essays in the book were commissioned for it and appear here for the first time.

I must thank the following for permissions: Jonathan Clowes, Ltd., for Kingsley Amis; Jeremy Crow, of The Society of Authors, Faber and Faber, Farrar Straus Giroux, and The Marvell Press, for Philip Larkin; Mike Kitay, Faber and Faber, and Farrar Straus Giroux, for Thom Gunn; Michael Schmidt and Carcanet Press, for Donald Davie; David Higham Associates, for Elizabeth Jennings.

Although every effort has been made to trace and contact copyright holders prior to publication this has not been possible in every case. If notified, the publisher will be pleased to rectify any omissions at the earliest opportunity.

CONTENTS

Introduction: Origins
and Ambivalences

Zachary Leader

When Oxford University Press invited Kingsley Amis to edit *The New Oxford Book of Light Verse* (1978), the successor to W.H. Auden's *Oxford Book of Light Verse* (1938), his friend Philip Larkin was almost as pleased as Amis. Larkin had previously been asked to edit the *Oxford Book of Twentieth-Century English Verse* (1973), successor to W. B. Yeats's *Oxford Book of Modern Poetry* (1936), and thought of his anthology partly as a challenge to modernism. He expected Amis's volume to be a comparable challenge. 'We shall have stamped our taste on the age between us in the end,' he boasted.[1] That this boast proved well-founded, even those who deplored Larkin's and Amis's taste have agreed. In volume 12 of the *Oxford English Literary History*, covering the period 1960 to 2000, the author, Randall Stevenson, declares that 'English literature was never more static than under the influence of the Movement. If the later twentieth century proved a difficult period for poetry, it was in large measure because it took so long to realize this, and move on.'[2] Moving on, though, was just what Larkin, Amis, and the other Movement writers—Thom Gunn, Donald Davie, Robert Conquest, Elizabeth Jennings, D. J. Enright, John Holloway, and John Wain—thought they were doing, even when deploring innovation and experiment. *Was* their influence, as critics like Stevenson claim, stultifying, retrogressive, a lament for 'England gone'? What, moreover, of

[1] In a letter of 14 April 1974 to J. Norton Smith, a colleague at Hull University, quoted in Andrew Motion, *Philip Larkin: A Writer's Life* (London: Faber and Faber, 1993), p. 434.

[2] Randall Stevenson, *The Oxford English Literary History*, Vol. 12: *1960–2000: The Last of England?* (Oxford: Oxford University Press, 2004), p. 270.

other familiar charges: that Movement writing is dry, academic, provincial, insular? These accusations, made by champions of modernism, also by their postmodern offspring, are often as extreme as the anti-modernist accusations that sparked them, as in Larkin's claim that Pound, Picasso, and Charlie Parker embody 'the two principal themes of modernism, mystification and outrage'.[3] In short, the debate between the two groupings is crude and needs refining. In recent years much attention has been devoted to individual writers associated with the Movement—principally Larkin, Amis, Gunn, and Davie. Given the literary-historical importance of Movement values and the relative neglect of some of its best works and writers, a more balanced reassessment is overdue.

Hence this book, which sets out to show not only that relations between Movement and other postwar British writers were more complex and nuanced than is usually suggested, but that the role these relations played in shaping the current literary scene is a complicated one. Other topics examined in the book are the intellectual origins of the Movement, including the role of mediating figures such as Auden, Empson, and Orwell; the role the writers themselves played in promoting the grouping (a role obscured by public disavowals); the interlocking network of academics, journalists, and editors who aided them; and analogous developments in other fields, notably philosophy, politics, and language. The approaches taken by contributors differ widely. Some concentrate on individual figures (Larkin, Amis, Davie, Gunn, Jennings), others on broad Movement themes or trends (common sense, for example, or clarity), others again on the scene or moment out of which the grouping grew. Several contributors—among them Anthony Thwaite, Karl Miller, Robert Conquest—knew at first hand the figures about whom they write; Robert Conquest was one of those figures.

Conquest, like all the Movement writers, denies or underplays joint activity or conscious affiliation. The Movement label was a journalistic contrivance; those grouped under it shared few common themes or preoccupations; their backgrounds were different; they barely knew each other.[4]

---

[3] Philip Larkin, *All What Jazz: A Record Diary 1961–1968* (London: Faber and Faber, 1970), p. 17.

[4] For what is still the most detailed weighing of these claims see Blake Morrison, *The Movement: English Poetry and Fiction of the 1950s* (Oxford: Oxford University Press, 1980), which also provides a detailed account of the origins of the grouping.

The first of these claims is incontestable. An anonymous leading article of 1 October 1954 in the *Spectator* entitled 'In the Movement' first identified the emerging writers of the new generation (those listed were Kingsley Amis, John Wain, Elizabeth Jennings, Thom Gunn, John Holloway, Donald Davie, D. J. Enright, and Iris Murdoch) as 'the Movement'. It was written by J. D. Scott, the paper's literary editor, following a period of lobbying and jockeying by, among others, Anthony Hartley, his assistant, in effect the magazine's poetry editor. Hartley was a friend of Wain's and 'vaguely'[5] knew Amis and Larkin at Oxford, where he'd read English at Exeter College (Amis, Larkin, and Wain had been at St John's). His first review for the *Spectator* appeared on 10 July 1953 and praised Amis's and Wain's contributions to *New Poems 1953*, a PEN anthology edited by Conquest, Michael Hamburger, and Howard Sergeant. Later that month, at Hartley's request, Amis submitted a poem to the *Spectator* ('Revenge'), which was published on 31 July. On 3 August Amis wrote to Larkin encouraging him to submit poems to Hartley, described as 'one of the Wain entourage so I'm sure he knows about you.'[6] Soon Larkin, Wain and Amis became regular contributors to the magazine, the latter two frequent London drinking companions of Scott, Hartley and the rest of 'the Spectator lot'. Six weeks before Scott coined the Movement label, Hartley published a review, again in the *Spectator*, entitled 'Poets of the Fifties' (27 August 1954). 'For better or worse,' he declared, 'we are now in the presence of the only considerable movement of English poetry since the Thirties.'

If the Movement label was bestowed by the *Spectator*, the grouping itself was identified earlier, initially on radio. In 1953 John Wain (Hartley's conduit to the new writers) was made producer and presenter of *First Reading*, a successor books programme to John Lehmann's *New Soundings*. Wain's objective, he later explained, was 'to move a few of the established reputations gently to one side and allow new people their turn.'[7] In the first programme of the series he pronounced the writers he would promote leaders of 'a new Elizabethan era', 'suspicious of anything that suggests sprawling or lack of discipline', interested in a tradition that looked beyond 'the last thirty years'.[8]

---

[5] Motion, *Philip Larkin: A Writer's Life*, p. 242.
[6] Kingsley Amis to Philip Larkin, 3 August 1953 (Bodleian).
[7] John Wain, *Sprightly Running: Part of an Autobiography* (London: Macmillan, 1962), p. 168.
[8] Quoted in Morrison, *The Movement*, p. 44.

After planting his standard, Wain broadcast a fifteen-minute extract from *Lucky Jim* (the bed-burning scene), a novel which hadn't yet been published, hadn't even secured a publisher, and was written by an author unknown to all but a handful of the programme's estimated 100,000 listeners. Hugh Massingham, radio critic of the *New Statesman*, deplored both the polemical tone and the content of the programme, complaining in an article of 18 July that 'there was something faintly ridiculous in treating young men, whom some of us have never heard of, with the solemnity that should be reserved for Mr. Eliot or Mr. Empson'.

Massingham's review sparked a lengthy controversy in the letters pages of the *New Statesman*, the very controversy Scott and Hartley hoped to whip up, or whip back up, fourteen months later in the *Spectator*. The controversy spread to other periodicals, including *Truth*, *Encounter*, and the *Times Literary Supplement*. In Larkin's words, the *First Reading* broadcasts 'got attacked in a very convenient way, and consequently we became lumped together'.[9] Larkin wanted no part of such lumping. As he wrote to Patsy Strang on 9 October 1954, 'People like Anthony Hartley and G. S. Fraser are very stupidly crying us all up these days: take my word for it, people will get very sick of us (or *them*; that is, Wain, Gunn, Davie, Amis).'[10] Amis's attitude to the controversy was more complicated. 'Jolly good about the John Wain programme isn't it?' he wrote to Larkin on 30 March 1953, after being asked to submit something to be broadcast.[11] In the midst of attacks on the programmes, Wain went off to Switzerland, to recover from a bout of TB. Amis wrote to him on 6 November 1953, conveying the latest news, beginning with George Scott's complaint in *Truth* that Stephen Spender, co-editor of *Encounter*, was ignoring a 'new renaissance' of writers:

> George Scott, as you may have seen or heard, gave the boys a write-up in a reply to Spender's reply to his attack on *Encounter*.... *Encounter* has been mauled on every side. It's a pity you're away; with you as

[9] 'A Conversation with Ian Hamilton,' in Philip Larkin, *Further Requirements: Interviews, Broadcasts, Statements and Book Reviews*, ed. Anthony Thwaite (London: Faber and Faber, 2001), p. 20.
[10] Philip Larkin to Patsy Strang, 9 October 1954, in Anthony Thwaite (ed.), *Selected Letters of Philip Larkin 1940–1985* (London: Faber and Faber, 1992), p. 230. Subsequent quotations from Larkin's letters are from this selection and cited within the text.
[11] Kingsley Amis to Philip Larkin, 30 March 1953, in Zachary Leader (ed.), *The Letters of Kingsley Amis* (London: HarperCollins, 2000), p. 313. Subsequent quotations from Amis's letters are from this edition and cited within the text, unless footnotes indicate unpublished correspondence.

general, the boys could move right into control. It occurs to me to try an old gag—more for my amusement than yours, I imagine:

JACK WAIN AND THE PROVINCIAL ALL-STARS

Wain (tpt, voc) directing Phil Larkin (clt), 'King' Amis (tmb), Don Davie (alto), Al Alvarez (pno), Tommy Gunn (gtr), George ('Pops') Fraser (bs), Wally Robson (ds).

> Drop me off at Reading/ Up the country
> Lay your racket/ Things ain't what they used to be
> It's the talk of the town/ How'm I doing hey hey

That Amis's gag might not have been to Wain's taste is suggested by a passage in a retrospective account of *First Reading* published in 1956: 'It doesn't behove me to talk about it, because I edited the series…[h]owever it is a fact that the very people who are now dominant were unknown before they became the centre of controversy in these six programmes.'[12] Though as sterling a foe of self-importance as of bullshit, Amis was willing to ally himself with Wain: 'the boys' suggests a genuine grouping, the prospect of their moving 'right into control' is only partly mocked. Later in the letter, after acknowledging simple egotism as a motive ('I want to get my name in the paper, too'), and lobbying on Larkin's behalf ('I know it's a bit of log-rolling, but he's the only man I know who I think readable enough'), Amis raises larger considerations. In response to Wain's reported threat to publish no poetry for five years, he reminds him that 'every inch of newsprint we can cover means less for K.R. [Kathleen Raine] and her pals; that's the way to look at it'. Not for another year, at the time of the *Spectator* leader, would misgivings about log-rolling surface, as in a letter to Larkin of 18 October: 'Well, what a load of bullshit all that was in the *Spr* about the new movt. etc. Useful up to a point, but the point is nearly here, I feel; someone should tell old GSF [G. S. Fraser] to pipe down a little before people think he's buggering all our arses.'

Larkin's resistance to Movement lobbying was only once breached, when in 1956 Amis inveigled him into collaborating on a series of parodies of Movement poets entitled 'All Aboard the Gravy Train: Or, Movements

---

[12] John Wain, 'The "Third" Man,' *Twentieth Century*, December 1956.

among the Younger Poets', under the pseudonym 'Ron Cain'. Amis tried and failed to place the parodies with *Encounter* and the *London Magazine* (they were not published until I came across them among his letters in the Bodleian and brought them to the attention of the *Times Literary Supplement*, which printed them on 5 May 2000).[13] That Amis was proud of the parodies is clear from a letter to Larkin of 24 September 1956: 'I send you All aboard the gravy train with a space for you to insert your poem if you care to…The only alteration in the texts I've made is to put "guessed" for "thought" in Wild ones, line 6. "Thought" clashes with "taught" a bit, it struck me. Agree? I must say the poems still strike me as good and bloody funny. Hope we can make some money out of them.'[14] Here and elsewhere in Amis's and Larkin's correspondence it is impossible to tell for certain—except for the poem Larkin eventually inserts—which parodies are his, which are Larkin's, and which are co-authored. 'Hope we can make some money out of them' certainly suggests collaboration, as does 'Agree?'

The 'Ron Cain' parodies, which mock friend and foe alike, are worth dwelling on for a moment, for the light they shed on their authors' mixed feelings about group identification. At the time of their composition, the Movement label had been firmly attached to two influential anthologies, despite the objections of both editors and a number of their contributors: *Poets of the 1950s* (1955), edited by D. J. Enright, and *New Lines* (1956), edited by Robert Conquest. When Amis's second novel, *That Uncertain Feeling* (1955), was published, it was reviewed, to his consternation, not just as a novel, but as a Movement novel.[15] By 28 September 1956, in a letter to Larkin, Amis was making clear his annoyance with group identification (perhaps in part because he knew Larkin's views): 'A bloody shame we can't tell them who we'd be rid of if we could. All except you and me, dalling.'[16] He seemed now to see merit in Evelyn Waugh's uncharacteristically sympathetic letter of 8 October to the *Spectator*, in response to Scott's leader: 'Please let the young people of today get on with their work alone and be treated to the courtesy

[13] They are printed as Appendix B in Leader (ed.), *The Letters of Kingsley Amis*, pp. 1141–5.
[14] KA to PL, 24 September 1956 (Bodleian); this letter appears in an abridged form, with this passage excised, ibid., p. 480.
[15] See Zachary Leader, *The Life of Kingsley Amis* (London: Jonathan Cape, 2006), pp. 355–6.
[16] KA to PL, 28 September 1956 (Bodleian).

of individual attention. They are the less, not the more, interesting, if they are treated as a "Movement".'

The parodies guy the self-advertising instincts of Movement writers but they also reinforce group identity. The parodied poets—Conquest, Davie, Gunn, Wain, Jennings, Enright and the authors themselves—are 'all aboard' (and presciently chosen, the poets to whom the label would stick); each of the parodies shares a common subject, a train journey; 'Movement' tics and traits are everywhere apparent, especially those singled out by the older generation, and involving class. Larkin's parody of himself, 'Poetry of Comings Back,' begins: 'The local snivels through the fields'; Amis's (in Empsonian triplets, like the Wain parody), self-mockingly titled 'Getting Somewhere', opposes 'five-star feeds...the concert hall' to 'Sandy's Caff and the Police Ball'. Stephen Spender, a particular Movement bugbear, characterized the rising generation as 'Lower Middle Brow', a 'movement' of 'teachers who, coming from the "red-brick" universities, resent being called "dons" '.[17] Hostility to Spender brought out feelings of solidarity even among the most independent-minded of Movement writers. Here is Robert Conquest to Amis, in a letter of 17 July 1956: 'chaps like Spender do regard us [as] clumping around the poetry columns in whacking great muddy boots and treading on fairy toes. (Perhaps you remember an early poem of his which had a line something like "My parents would not let me play with children who were rough". Well pull my plaits.)'[18] Thom Gunn's hostility to Spender, in 'Lines for a Book', resembles Conquest's: 'I praise the overdogs from Alexander | To those who would not play with Stephen Spender.'[19] The Amis/Larkin parody of Gunn, entitled 'The Wild Ones', begins: 'He watched the brutal boys pile off the truck.'

That Amis and Larkin sent the 'Ron Cain' parodies first to Spender at *Encounter*, then to John Lehmann at the *London Magazine*, is revealing in several respects. To begin with, it reinforces a point made by a number of contributors to this book, in particular those who were actually there: that literary allegiances in the 1950s, as at other times, were neither

[17] Stephen Spender, 'On Literary Movements,' *Encounter* (November 1953).

[18] Robert Conquest to KA, 17 July 1956 (Bodleian).

[19] From *Fighting Terms* (Oxford: Fantasy Press, 1954); later included in *The Sense of Movement* (London: Faber and Faber, 1957). Gunn suppressed 'Lines for a Book' in later editions of his poetry, though it was reprinted in A. Alvarez (ed.), *The New Poetry* (Harmondsworth, Middlesex: Penguin, 1962).

clear-cut nor stable. When he sent them the parodies, in September 1956, Amis was on good personal terms with both Spender and Lehmann. By instructing them not to disclose the authors' true identities, he and Larkin were including their detractors in a trick they hoped to play on their supporters. Both editors turned the parodies down, for reasons undisclosed, or unrecovered. Perhaps they simply didn't think much of them. Perhaps they recalled an earlier anonymous parody of Movement poets published in December 1955 in the *Spectator* itself ('"At the Poetry Reading", by Dr. Aloysius C. Pepper'). Perhaps they were worried about missing the boat (or train); in a review of 7 July 1956 entitled 'New and Healthy' in the *New Statesman*, Spender seemed almost aboard, calling *New Lines* 'promising'. After both editors rejected the parodies, Amis wrote to Larkin on 27 December 1956 urging him to send them to George Hartley of the Marvell Press, editor of the periodical *Listen*: 'We shouldn't get any money for them, but there's always a chance old Fraser will pontificate maladroitly about them and lay himself open.' The parodies were intended to mock both old guard foes, by exaggerating or caricaturing—playing up to—the qualities they deplored, and new guard friends, by luring them into disparaging 'Ron Cain' as tin-eared. Fraser may have been singled out here and elsewhere because of his age (he is 'Pops' Fraser in Amis's literary jazz combo) and Cadmus-like enthusiasm: he was an early champion both of the 'New Apocalypse' poets of the early 1940s and of the Movement poets who succeeded and deplored them.

Though the *Spectator* coined the label, and regularly published the most prominent of Movement writers, it was never the grouping's home or voice (it was too many other things as well). One didn't become identified as a Movement writer by writing for it, as one was identified as a 'Leavisite' by writing for *Scrutiny* or a 'New York Intellectual' by writing for *Partisan Review*. The instantiating medium was the anthology rather than the periodical, in particular the anthologies of Enright and Conquest, with their almost identical contributors and polemical introductions (Enright's anthology also contained brief prose prefaces by the poets themselves). Given prior controversy, the effect of both volumes, whatever their editors' intents, was to reinforce group identity. Conquest is as much his own man as a man can be, but he enjoyed collaborating with Amis, on poems, especially limericks, novels, and occasional bouts of literary politicking and mischief-making. He is to be believed when he says he consulted only personal preference in compiling

New Lines, just as he is to be believed when he says simple inquisitiveness rather than ideology motivated his beginning work as an historian of the Soviet Union.[20] But he would not have been unaware of the perceived politics of both sorts of work; he knew how the poets he preferred were being grouped.

The same is true for Enright, despite living in Japan while compiling *Poets of the 1950s*, a work alluded to but not discussed in the chapters that follow. Its subtitle is *An Anthology of New English Verse* and in the first paragraph of his introduction Enright identifies its 'subject' as 'the poetry written today by the younger generation in Britain'. This younger generation is represented by eight poets: Amis, Conquest, Davie, Holloway, Jennings, Larkin, Wain, and Enright himself. Unlike their immediate predecessors, these poets 'neither flog the dead horse of "Wastelanditis" nor fly to its sentimental opposite in a vain attempt to achieve a "New Romanticism" '.[21] Enright singles out 'The New Apocalypse' poets and Dylan Thomas for special censure, calling the former 'neither new nor apocalyptic', and deploring the latter's 'deficiency in intellectual conviction'.[22] He identifies William Empson and Robert Graves as the new generation's chief mentors. Its chief virtues are 'a fairly tough intelligence and an unwillingness to be deceived', 'moderation', and 'chastened common sense'.[23] The poets of the younger generation seek 'honesty of thought and feeling and clarity of expression', goals described as 'not easily to be achieved after they have been neglected, at least as literary virtues, for so long'.[24] That these goals and virtues were associated with the Movement, Enright knew full well, as is suggested at the end of the introduction:

> Some of the English periodicals are already talking of a poetic renaissance. Personally I should like to see more evidence of it before arriving at such a momentous conclusion. But there is undoubtedly a new spirit stirring in contemporary English poetry, and before long we should be able to define that spirit more accurately and in greater detail. This anthology should be considered as an interim report— not as the presentation of a 'movement' but as a presentation of

---

[20] See Leader, *The Life of Kingsley Amis*, p. 289.

[21] D. J. Enright (ed.), *Poets of the 1950s* (Tokyo: The Kenkyusha Press, 1955), pp. 1, 3.

[22] Ibid., p. 8 (both quotations).

[23] Ibid., p. 7 (for Empson and Graves) and pp. 14, 13 (for chief virtues).

[24] Ibid., p. 14.

selected poems by individual writers, some of whom share common attitudes.[25]

Weighed against Enright's caution is the fact that seven of the eight poets he selects were listed by Scott in his *Spectator* leader (the poet left out, oddly, was Larkin) and that all would appear months later in Conquest's *New Lines* (with the addition only of Thom Gunn). Conquest's introduction also shares a number of the views expressed in Enright's introduction, as Eric Homberger's chapter on *New Lines* suggests.

One final aspect of Movement origins, a suggested prototype of the grouping, is worth noting. At Oxford, Larkin, Amis, and five fellow St John's undergraduates formed a group they called 'The Seven', about which Larkin wrote an unpublished story. To Andrew Motion, Larkin's biographer, this group 'anticipated the principles that were more coherently described by The Movement in the 1950s'.[26] Movement principles are hard to discern in Larkin's story or in the recollections of mildly subversive raucousness, campery, and drunkenness from other group members. Only Norman Iles, with Larkin its moving spirit, has taken 'The Seven' seriously, identifying its purpose with its motto: 'SUMUS'. Sixty years later Iles explained the motto in a memoir in the *London Magazine*:

> 'We are' is an answer to 'You are not.' It was an answer to the Dean of the College, to academic learning, to our homes and parents, to the rules of society, and to the war itself. All these cried 'You are not.' 'We are,' we replied.
>
> In addition, it meant this. We are ourselves, whole, and will grow whole. We are greater than learning, intellect, logic, convention and desire to get on in life. It had the idea of ourselves as natural forces, growing as a flower does—or as a tree.[27]

The first of these paragraphs makes clear the universal character of the appeal which groups have to the young, of the difficulty of individual self-assertion in the face of adult or established authority (it also helps to

---

[25] Ibid., p. 15 [26] Motion, *Philip Larkin: A Writer's Life*, p. 69.

[27] Norman Iles, 'Our Group,' *London Magazine* (December 1999/January 2000), p. 26. Larkin's story is untitled, unfinished and undated, but Motion, in *Philip Larkin: A Writer's Life*, p. 64, conjectures a date of late 1941. It exists in a thirty-page handwritten manuscript among the Larkin papers in the Brynmor Jones Library in Hull.

account for youthul boasting and self-dramatization); the second suggests a specific historical model for 'The Seven,' that of the 'Auden Group' or 'Gang', including Christopher Isherwood, Spender, Cecil Day-Lewis, Edward Upward, and others. 'Let me earnestly advise you to *buy* "Lions and Shadows" ', wrote Larkin to Amis in 1943, of Isherwood's account of his and Auden's circle at Repton, also of a comparable circle at Cambridge: 'He is exactly like we are, and the story of his life at Cambridge and elsewhere is magnificent.'[28] Auden's poetry was a key influence on early Amis and Larkin, and an assertion like 'we are ourselves, whole, and will grow whole', recalls early Auden, whose poems aim to restore lost unity: between self and other, subject and object, conscious and unconscious, individual and society. Drinking and listening to jazz records, chief activities of 'The Seven,' are seen as serious or saving as well as fun, a way of 'losing the self'. The same can be said of joining a group. When Amis calls the Movement writers 'the boys' he hints at the adolescent character both of the needs that often underlie the joining impulse, and of the idealism and extravagance of group claims.

As many of the essays in this book make clear, the differences between the Movement writers widened over the years, but they were clear from the start, as the writers themselves recognized. Also clear from the start was how imperfectly Movement stereotypes fit Movement writers, even those thought of as central to the grouping. One source of these stereotypes was Amis's brief prose preface to the selection of his poems in the Enright anthology: 'nobody wants any more poems about philosophers or paintings or novelists or art galleries or mythology or foreign cities.'[29] When Enright received the draft of Amis's preface he wrote back in good-humoured protest from Japan, where the anthology was first published: 'it put paid to me, since practically everything I was writing at the time concerned Japanese cities.'[30] Hence the 'Ron Cain' parody of Enright, which begins: 'Paying off my rickshaw, I salute Mr. Hakagawa, | Who, in his capacity as station-master, bows in the train,' and ends with lines combining a swipe at English philistinism

---

[28] This letter is unfinished, unpublished, undated and found in the Brynmor Jones Library; in a subsequent letter, written on 19 October 1943, Larkin declares that he 'rejoices' that Amis has purchased, read and likes the book.
[29] Enright (ed.), *Poets of the 1950s*, p. 17.　[30] D. J. Enright to Zachary Leader, 26 May 2002.

(the view that abroad is always better, another Movement antipathy), fears of creative blockage, and an allusion to Keats on composition (so that the parody becomes a poem about poets, like a poem 'about philosophers or paintings or novelists'): 'When I reach the land where only dividends expand and blossom [i.e. England] | May my words come as naturally as leaves or their words [that is, the words of the Japanese passengers on the speaker's train, who "Chatter with the confidence of singing birds"].'

The Conquest parody also stresses qualities or characteristics Movement writers are meant neither to approve of nor possess. Conquest is the son of a well-born Virginian father and an English mother, was brought up in England and France, and educated at Winchester, the University of Grenoble, and Magdalen College, Oxford, where he read PPE. He was never Spender's chippy redbrick lecturer, nor any sort of 'little Englander' (an epithet often attached to Movement writers).[31] The title of the Conquest parody is 'To Hart Crane', whose death is the subject of one of Conquest's early poems; the train the speaker takes is American (an 'El'); what he reflects on is poetry; the places he refers to are foreign (Mexique Bay, the Hudson). The Thom Gunn parody also highlights supposedly non-Movement qualities. Those 'brutal boys' who pile off their 'truck' (not 'lorry') onto a troop-train are likened to 'Fresh meat the bully sun had handled raw', a line Ted Hughes might have written. Soon they learn not only to value 'white towered Argos' (not 'home') but the truth about battle, which is 'more than shooting from the hip' (a line which registers the characteristic self-awareness of Gunn's martial posturing). The ludicrous ending has 'Patroclus frying in the bloodsoaked jeep | And crew-cut Achilles two-timed on the sand'. Only the wondrous banality of the ending of the Wain parody (banality being another common charge against Movement writing) is as broad: 'Trains behind time are almost always late.' Here the mocked stereotype is upheld (appropriately, given Amis's sense of Wain as Movement 'general'), as it is in the Elizabeth Jennings parody, which also ridicules Movement abstraction: 'In trains we need not choose our company | For all the logic of departure is | That recognition is suspended; we | Are islanded in unawareness, as | Our minds reach out to where we want to be.'

---

[31] For Movement attitudes to 'abroad' and consequent accusations of 'little Englandism' see Morrison, *The Movement*, pp. 59–62.

Behind the banality mocked in the Wain and Jennings parodies lies a Movement anxiety acknowledged from the start. As Amis puts it in the Enright anthology, the great deficiency of the new poetry is 'meagreness and triviality of subject matter'.[32] This is a version of Jimmy Porter's complaint in John Osborne's *Look Back in Anger* (1956), about the absence of 'good brave causes', and is voiced by Enright as well (in the preface to the selection of his own poems), when he declares that 'particularly at the present time, we do need poetry that is *about* something'.[33] It derives in part from the Movement stress on moderation, its aversion to big themes and grandiose emotions, to some a product of postwar anxiety and exhaustion. Davie writes eloquently about the need for moderation, for Ismene over Antigone;[34] Conquest has spent a lifetime documenting the dangers of big thoughts, themes, systems. But the consequent impression that Movement poems are 'small' has had pernicious consequences, particularly for relations between British and American poetry. Today, according to the American poet Dana Gioia, 'most American readers are not only unfamiliar with current British poetry, but modestly proud of the fact'. Gioia, a student of Donald Davie at Stanford, attributes this prejudice not only to the perceived hostility of Movement poets to modernism ('the glory of American verse, the story runs') but to the 'intentionally minor' character of Movement poems. British poets, in thrall to Movement attitudes, are thought 'incapable, in short, of the broad vision and fiery passion of their American counterparts'.[35] The fairness of this charge is examined by several of the essays that follow.

Only one of these essays is about a woman, Elizabeth Jennings, a fact some will find unsurprising given the attitudes towards women expressed, for example, in the Amis–Larkin correspondence. But it could also be argued that as poets 'the boys' forwarded or embodied values conventionally gendered as feminine: modesty, decorum, restraint. In Romantic lyric, according to feminist accounts, heroic, isolated male speakers typically seek to control or transcend an erratic or unruly outer world, gendered as female. The male

[32] See Enright (ed.), *Poets of the 1950s*, p. 17.   [33] Ibid., p. 103.
[34] For Ismene over Antigone see 'Creon's Mouse' (1953), in Donald Davie, *Collected Poems* (Chicago: University of Chicago Press, 1990), p. 23; also the essay 'Hobbits and Intellectuals,' *Encounter* (October 1969).
[35] See Dana Gioia, *Barrier of a Common Language: An American Looks at Contemporary British Poetry* (Ann Arbor: The University of Michigan Press, 2003), pp. 1, x, 3.

speakers in Movement lyrics are often quite different, even when alone, contemplating the night sky, as in Larkin's 'Sad Steps,' which begins 'Groping back to bed after a piss'.[36] Then there's the subject matter of Movement writing. In Amis's preface to *The New Oxford Book of Light Verse*, he presents a definition of the genre that, as William H. Pritchard has suggested, neatly fits much of his own poetry. It also fits much of the poetry of other Movement writers, in particular Larkin, Conquest, and Gunn, in being 'realistic... close to the interests of the novel: men and women among their fellows, seen as members of a group or class in a way that emphasizes manners, social forms, amusements, fashion (from millinery to philosophy), topicality, even gossip'.[37] To the extent that Amis's description fits Movement writing, Movement writing could be thought of as feminine, as novels were once thought of as feminine (and sometimes still are, certainly in commercial contexts). In this regard, it is worth noting the gender balance of subsequent poetical groupings and anthologies claiming to herald or effect change or some new dispensation. In 1962, Al Alvarez edited a Penguin anthology entitled *The New Poetry*, partly aimed at countering Movement dominance. It contained no women poets (when revised in 1966 Alvarez added Sylvia Plath and Anne Sexton, two Americans). In 1982 Blake Morrison and Andrew Motion edited an influential anthology entitled *The Penguin Book of Contemporary British Poetry*. 'There are points in literary history when decisive shifts of sensibility occur,' they announce in the introduction. 'Such a shift of sensibility has taken place very recently in British poetry.'[38] Judging by the anthology's contributors list, this shift was mostly the work of men: only five of the twenty poets selected were women. A rival anthology, *Some Contemporary Poets of England and Ireland*, edited by Michael Schmidt and published by Carcanet in the same year, also selects twenty poets, only two of whom are women. It is hard to see the figure of two or even five out of twenty as much of an improvement, after a quarter of

---

[36] 'Sad Steps' is from *High Windows* (1974), reprinted in Philip Larkin, *Collected Poems*, ed. Anthony Thwaite (London: The Marvell Press and Faber and Faber, 2003), p. 144; for feminist accounts of Romantic lyric see, for example, Anne K. Mellor (ed.), *Romanticism and Feminism* (Bloomington: University of Indiana Press, 1988).

[37] Kingsley Amis, *The New Oxford Book of Light Verse* (Oxford: Oxford University Press, 1978), p. v; for Pritchard's suggestion, see 'Entertaining Amis', a review of Amis's *Collected Poems*, in *Essays in Criticism* 30:1 (January 1980), 58–67.

[38] Blake Morrison and Andrew Motion (eds.), *The Penguin Book of Contemporary British Poetry* (Harmondsworth, Middlesex: Penguin, 1982), pp. 11–12.

a century, over one out of eight or nine. Here, as in other respects, the common assumption is open to question or needs qualification. The contributors to this book hope that by testing or complicating such assumptions they will encourage readers to come to Movement writing with fresh eyes and to gain a fairer sense of its range and power.

1

'Still Going On, All of It': The Movement in the 1950s and the Movement Today

Blake Morrison

In his poem 'To the Sea', Philip Larkin describes a visit to a British seaside resort and marvels (an exclamation mark conveying his amazement) that its rituals are so little changed from those he knew as a child forty years earlier: 'Still going on, all of it, still going on!' The sea itself embodies this continuity, unchanging yet forever new: 'the small hushed waves' repeated fresh collapse'. Numerous British seaside towns today might prompt the same thought: how remarkable that their character should survive intact into the twenty-first century. But perhaps it's no less remarkable that Larkin's poem should still be read and enjoyed forty years after it was written. When he and the other Movement poets first emerged, sceptics dismissed them as ephemeral. Yet what the Movement achieved and stood for survive to this day.

By 'Movement'—to get the matter of definitions out of the way—I mean not just the nine poets (several of them also novelists) included in Robert Conquest's anthology *New Lines* but a set of values, or beliefs, to which these writers gave expression and which others in their generation, not necessarily writers, also shared: that's to say, a consensus we recognize as characteristic of Britain in the 1950s. The historical significance of this 'period style', in a

Britain emerging from the Second World War and entering the Cold War, is widely accepted. But the Movement is much less stranded in time and place than critics have allowed. It's undeniable that the term 'the Movement'— with a definite article and capital M—was created by chance, having been dreamt up one day in 1954 by the editor of the *Spectator* to get his magazine talked about.[1] And it's true that the Movement phenomenon was derided by many critics at the time, and disavowed by the participants themselves. It's also true that the identity of the Movement—for the most part, with the odd notable exception, white, Oxbridge-educated, heterosexual, middle-class, and male—has seemingly little to recommend it to the fashionable research areas of today. And true, too—one final concession—that the very name Movement seems ironic, given the immobility and sedentariness that old photos of the participants suggest: those pipes and spectacles, those tweed jackets, and (in John Wain's case) that proletarian flat cap. Yet the Movement has survived—not just because literary historians have allocated it a footnote, or because certain current practitioners are what we'd call Movement-like in their tone of voice or preference for regular rhyme and metre, nor even because the Movement embodies a spirit of Fifties-ness for which some people today are nostalgic. The Movement survives because Larkin and Amis in particular have left us with an indispensable body of literature—indispensable to our pleasure and understanding of the world, but indispensable too in its realism, honesty, and even courage.

Courage was not, I confess, the word that came to mind when I first began reading the Movement, in my early twenties, on my way home from a year's postgraduate work in Canada. At that point I was sated with Romanticism, having spent a year studying Blake, Yeats, and D. H. Lawrence, and I remember the shock of first encountering the Larkin persona, with his bicycle clips, and the rented room he'd taken over from Mr Bleaney, and his nose pressed to the glass watching others lead more exciting lives. Could something so timid and self-admittedly dull really be poetry, I wondered? My bemusement was sharpened by a sense of familiarity, since I found in Larkin, and more specially in Amis, attitudes I associated with my father (just a few years their senior) but which I had never come across in literature. In fact, I'd always thought my father the opposite of literature, but here, in books, were his tone and his idiom and his opinions.

---

[1] J. D. Scott, 'A Chip of Literary History', *Spectator*, 16 April 1977, p. 20.

Behind my interest in the Movement, I now see, lay a wish to come to terms with my father and his generation—to understand and do justice to them but also to get free of them and find my own way, not least as a poet. At the same time as I was completing my research on the Movement, Andrew Motion and I were beginning to compile an anthology—*The Penguin Book of Contemporary British Poetry* (1982)—which we hoped would make the same impact as *New Lines* had done, or A. Alvarez's *The New Poetry* (1962), in introducing a new generation of poets.

The supervisor for my PhD, at University College London, was Stephen Spender. It can't have been easy for Spender to supervise my research, given that he was the butt of many Movement sneers and jokes. ('I praise the over-dogs from Alexander | To those who would not play with Stephen Spender' went a poem by Thom Gunn.[2]) Perhaps it's no accident that Spender left UCL after my first year under his tutelage and even before that was, at best, perfunctory in his attentions to his pupil's work. But he did render one invaluable service, by taking me to lunch with Robert Conquest. In the 1950s, Conquest was the Big Daddy of the Movement, the worldliest and politically most sophisticated of its members, who not only corralled the others into an anthology and leapt to their defence whenever they were attacked by critics and rivals, but who was also a great raconteur, not least of bawdy poems, and a generous host. Conquest helped my research in numerous ways, and his book *The Great Terror* (1968), about the Soviet death-camps, remains one of the seminal historical works of the time.

Despite the help that he and others in the Movement gave me, I was sometimes conscious of feeling as Kingsley Amis's hero Garnet Bowen does in chapter 2 of *I Like It Here* (1958), when he wishes that Graham Greene would get on and die so that the annual lecture he gives on him doesn't have to be continually updated. It was safe to feel that kind of irreverence then, since most of the Movement writers were still in their fifties and actively producing new work. But within five years of my book on the Movement being published, Larkin was dead, and apart from Robert Conquest all the rest of the Movement—even the perpetually youthful Thom Gunn—have since followed him into the dark. In 1980 I couldn't have anticipated how quickly that would happen. But nor could I have guessed how much more

---

[2] Thom Gunn, 'Lines for a Book', *The Sense of Movement* (London: Faber and Faber, 1957), p. 30.

of the Movement there was to come, albeit posthumously. In those days, Larkin was represented by four slim volumes, and the only way to get more of him was to go to the Manuscripts Division of the British Library, which housed some of his notebooks. Now we have not only a *Collected Poems* (1988), in which Anthony Thwaite included eighty early poems as well as some late ones, but the *Early Poems and Juvenilia* (2005), in which Trevor Tolley adds a further 170. Having once looked as meagre a poet as Thomas Wyatt, say, Larkin now has the amplitude of Thomas Hardy. Andrew Motion's biography has altered our sense of the man, too, as have the letters. Zachary Leader's edition of Kingsley Amis's letters (and, subsequently, his biography) have performed a similar service for the Movement's finest novelist. Thom Gunn's candidly gay poems, and Aids poems, also postdate my book. The continuing public appetite for work by and about The Movement is evidence in itself that the Movement still matters. 'Still going on all of it', and no sign of a let-up half a century on.

Why is this? Primarily, as the Movement writers themselves would have wanted, it's because of the quality of work they produced; because—to put my cards on the table—Larkin is the greatest English poet of the second half of the twentieth century and Amis the greatest comic novelist; because Davie is the outstanding critic of his generation; and because Gunn, Davie, and Enright are all, in their different ways, considerable poets. But it's more than a matter of individual talent—which, after all, can always be said to transcend and transgress the work of the literary movement with which it is associated. The Movement also matters because its ideas about love, death, sex, marriage, God, gender, politics, and art are more fraught, complex and open to interpretation than they've been given credit for. Far from being mere 1950s little Englanders, the Movement authors have become strangely pertinent as history has since unfolded, as the age of Macmillan and Eisenhower and Cold War spy-games have passed through the age of Thatcher and Nixon and the revolutions of 1989 into the age of Blair and Bush and religious fundamentalism. Jake Balokowsky might see Larkin and his lot as 'old-style, *natural*, fouled-up guys', and Lisa Jardine proudly announce 'we don't tend to teach Larkin much now in my department of English'.[3] But those coming fresh to the Movement will find the group's preoccupations surprisingly pertinent today.

---

[3] Lisa Jardine, 'Saxon Violence', *Guardian*, 8 December 1992, p. 23.

I would like to look at three key elements in the Movement: its relationship to Modernism; its view of Abroad in general and America in particular; and its notion of 'neutrality'. And I want to show how these resonate in our own age.

It is fruitless trying to deny that anti-Modernism was an important part of the Movement. I have a stack of index cards, from the time of my research on the Movement, which assemble their many dismissive anti-Modernist remarks. Some of these were tactical: by arguing that Modernism had run out of steam, that 'Making it new' was old-fashioned, that the men of 1914 were now dead or geriatric, the Movement writers were advertising their own youthfulness. But four arguments they made are worth special mention. The first was social: Modernism was seen as elitist and haut-bourgeois, an arrogant rejection of the 'ordinary reader' and in effect of the Movement authors themselves. According to Packet, the fictional hero of two of D. J. Enright's novels, Lil, Albert, Bill, Lou, and May—characters from *The Waste Land*—are 'the kind of people among whom I was born and brought up', whereas Packet dismisses Stephen Dedalus (the archetypal Modernist artist-hero) as one of the most 'unpleasant characters in literature'.[4] There was also, secondly, the political issue, Pound, Lawrence, Eliot, and Yeats having flirted with far right ideas: 'The development from imagism in poetry to fascism in politics is clear and unbroken,' claimed Donald Davie.[5] I don't buy it in the least but it's an ingenious idea, based on the premise that a poem's orderliness, and its syntax, are a model of society, and that if they fragment, as they do in the *Cantos*, then destruction will follow in their wake. Third came the patriotic or nationalist objection that Modernism had destroyed a native line of English poetry, coming through Hardy, Housman, Edward Thomas, and the Georgians, much as the Great War had destroyed the flower of English youth. And finally, and most crucially, was the aesthetic objection, that Modernism broke the contract between a poet and his audience, a charge made with uncharacteristic crudity by Larkin in the introduction to his collection of essays *All What Jazz*, when he accused the likes of Pound, Picasso, and Charlie Parker of an 'irresponsibility peculiar to this

[4] D. J. Enright, *Heaven Knows Where* (London: Secker and Warburg, 1957) p. 51, and *Academic Year* (London: Secker and Warburg, 1955), p. 44.
[5] Donald Davie, *Purity of Diction in English Verse* (London: Chatto and Windus, 1952), p. 99.

century' for having busied themselves with 'the two principle themes of modernism, mystification and outrage'.[6] By contrast, Larkin's own descriptions of poetry are deliberately downbeat and homespun: writing is like knitting, he said, or 'like a slot machine into which the reader inserts the penny of his attention'.[7] Amis described his approach to fiction in a similarly bluff manner: 'what I think I am doing is writing novels within the main English language tradition. That is, trying to tell interesting, believable stories about understandable characters in a reasonably straightforward style: no tricks, no experimental foolery.'[8]

The Movement's hostility to certain aspects of Modernism was genuinely felt. And the attempts that have been made to deny it, and to present Larkin as a latter-day French Symbolist, on the grounds that he—or his alter ego Brunette Coleman—translated poems by Villon and Baudelaire, seem to me largely unconvincing. They're also unnecessary. It's clear from Larkin's letters, not least to Jim Sutton, how wide his reading of the Modernists was. There's his deep admiration for D. H. Lawrence, for example, and his schoolboy absorption of, indeed addiction to Auden—that is to say the early Auden, at his most Marxist and Freudian and subversive. It is true that Larkin was hostile to Eliot's idea that the modern poet needs to be aware of 'the mind of Europe' and can no longer depend on 'private admirations' for reading matter;[9] Larkin retaliated that, on the contrary, 'a style is much more likely to be formed by slipshod sampling'—and he ridiculed the idea that every new poem must somehow include all previous poems, 'in the same way that a Ford Zephyr has somewhere in it a Ford Model T'.[10] Yet anyone reading Larkin's 'Church Going', say, will notice how indebted it is to other poets (Hardy, Graves, Betjeman, Auden, Norman Cameron, Roy Fuller, and Robert Frost among them) and how profoundly it engages with Tradition, whether slipshodly sampled or not.

[6] Philip Larkin, *All What Jazz* (London: Faber and Faber, 1970), p.17.

[7] Larkin, quoted by Frances Hill, 'A Sharp-Edged View', *Times Educational Supplement*, 19 May 1972, p. 19, and in 'Speaking of Writing', *Times*, 20 February 1964, p. 16.

[8] Amis quoted in James Vinson (ed.), *Contemporary Novelists* (London: St James's Press, 1972), p. 46.

[9] Eliot, 'Tradition and the Individual Talent', in *The Sacred Wood* (1920; repr. London: Faber and Faber, 1997), p. 42.

[10] Larkin, 'Four Conversations: Interview with Ian Hamilton', *London Magazine* (November 1964), p. 71.

It is rather the same with Amis. His description of his fiction as telling 'interesting, believable stories about understandable characters in a reasonably straightforward style' isn't one which many people reading the late Amis would recognize. His last few novels—though he would hate the comparison—have something of Henry James about them: they're to be read not for their stories, but for the pleasure of a syntactically correct but far from straightforward prose style. Here, for instance, is an account of the feelings which Robin Davies, the young hero of *You Can't Do Both* (1994) has about his mother.

He was not the sort of boy to admit to loving his mother but quite often, like now, he experienced a surge of liking for her, not hard to feel for such a cheerful, nice-looking woman, nice-looking both in the sense of looking a nice old thing and quite pretty too, not so very old in fact, mid-forties perhaps, and with her mostly auburn hair and bright brown eyes declared attractive by that rigorous tribunal, an ad hoc selection of his schoolmates (who had had a look at her at speech days and other such functions). (chapter 1)

It is not just the length of that sentence, 96 words, that strikes me as unstraightforward, but the use of the word 'not' three times ('not the sort of boy who…not hard to feel…not so very old in fact'), the studiously self-qualifying tone of voice (suggestive of a mind anxious to get things exactly right), the add-on clauses, the subtle, snaking rhythm that allows these deliberations and self-corrections to be carried out, and then the final flourish of a parenthesis which detains us with the addition of one final piece of information, just as the sentence seems to be running out of steam. This is very typical late Amis. And though he sometimes takes pleasure in using this patient, painstaking prose while his ageing heroes deliver impatient, even malevolent observations on fellow members of the human race, there is no easy enforcement of prejudice. Here is Harry Caldecote, retired librarian, in *The Folks That Live on the Hill* (1990), on his way to see a woman friend:

It was true that almost any exploit would make a nice change from sitting in the Irving [Club] hour after hour feeling sixty, seventy-five, ninety as he had this afternoon while a very sociable fellow, known and feared all over London as one who told you about small-boat sailing, went on quite unforeseeably to tell him [Harry] about his financial work for the Conservative Political Centre and then, driven off that, about the by no means infrequent pianistic passages in Mozart's vocal writing, with a number of sung illustrations. (chapter 8)

Early Amis allowed Jim Dixon to speak with plain dismissiveness of 'Filthy Mozart'. Late Amis makes us work harder at discovering where his hero's prejudice lies. On the face of it, there's nothing repugnant about a 'very sociable fellow'; it's the phrase 'known and feared' that clues us in—that and the fact that he has to be 'driven off' his chosen conversational topic. In the context of Amis's known political views, a man who works for the Conservative Political Centre might merit authorial approval—but not when the work is 'financial' and the chap's leisure time interests are small-boat sailing and the 'by no means infrequent' (that quietly devastating double negative) pianistic passages in Mozart.

One of Amis's strengths as a novelist is an ability to detach himself from the views he held as a private citizen or which were attributed to him as a public figure. His 1984 novel *Stanley and the Women* is a case in point. The novel had difficulty in finding a US publisher, and aroused controversy in the UK, not so much because of Stanley's growing misogyny—directed against his wife, his ex-wife, and a trendy pseudo-Laingian psychiatrist—but because it was assumed Amis subscribed to it and was using Stanley to sound off. But Jake is his own man, not a mouthpiece. And if it's true that Amis's own experiences went into the book, not least the break-up of his marriage to Elizabeth Jane Howard and the insecurity and anger this provoked, the novel isn't autobiography. Towards the end, several characters, mostly but not exclusively male, concur that (*a*) all women are mad and (*b*) that Jake's wife Susan has inflicted an injury on herself partly to gain Jake's attention and partly to get his son by his first marriage committed to a mental hospital and out of the way. But there are as many women in the book who don't conform to type, and meanwhile the waywardness of the men, including Stanley himself, is problematic enough to make us wonder about the reliability of their judgement. In the *London Review of Books*, Marilyn Butler praised the novel for its 'compassionate' insights into misogyny and mental illness, on the ground that Stanley is being presented ironically, as a 'deconstruction' of the macho Amisian hero.[11] And though this is barking up the wrong tree, Butler is surely right to suggest that the prevailing tone in the book is one of 'scepticism'—what Stanley says and what the book says are two different things. A similar point might be made about the ending of *Jake's Thing*, where

[11] Marilyn Butler, 'Women and the Novel', *London Review of Books*, 7–20 June 1984, pp. 7–8.

Jake, in a spectacularly protracted, paragraph-long sentence, enumerates his many reasons for giving up on women: 'all according to him', the sentence ends, in case the innocent reader or prejudicial critic should suppose this the gospel according to Kingsley. A similar scepticism is present even in an early poem like 'A Bookshop Idyll', which first articulates but then subverts received opinion about the differences between men and women.

What I'm drawing attention to here is a willingness in the Movement to entertain prejudice but ultimately disown or evade it. This is not some desperate ploy to allow myself to enjoy Larkin and Amis despite their illiberal politics; it's to suggest that in their fiction and poetry they don't *assert* opinions but explore, dramatize, and finally transcend them.

This willingness to entertain prejudice, but then to rise above it, can also be found in the Movement's attitude to Abroad in general and to America in particular. It can't be denied there was a vein of anti-Americanism in Movement work, and indeed of simple ignorance. It's astonishing to reflect, for example, that Larkin never once visited America, despite the numerous invitations he must have received both as a poet and as a university librarian. (Indeed the furthest abroad he voluntarily travelled as an adult was to Paris, for a long weekend.) Perhaps the vastness of America frightened him. Many of his poems are about bumping up against fences and frontiers—against the limits of what it's possible to be or do, given our nature or the nature of existence. It seems he felt more comfortable on narrow ground—or within an island fastness (on holiday, he liked to visit islands, if they weren't too far from home). Certainly the hemmed-in, timorous, insular persona is a characteristic feature of the poetry which Larkin wrote in the early 1950s:

> Sometimes you hear, fifth-hand,
> As epitaph:
> *He chucked up everything*
> *And just cleared off*
> And always the voice will sound
> Certain you approve
> This audacious, purifying,
> Elemental move.

The poem, ironically entitled 'Poetry of Departures', goes on to celebrate the virtues of not-departing: sad or hateful though home might be, it is no worse—no more artificial—than taking off somewhere on impulse. It is easy to see why the poem would have struck a chord in an isolationist Britain still recuperating from the trauma of world war—a Britain in which foreign travel was positively discouraged, through the imposition of a £50 travel allowance. And perhaps it's no coincidence that the accusation of chucking up everything by clearing off was one which Larkin levelled against Auden, whose defection to the US in 1939 had, Larkin argued, resulted in a 'low-pressure non-serious element... directly traceable to his change of country'.[12]

Other Movement poets took the same line on Dylan Thomas, blaming America for destroying what was left of his talent (that talent being modest in the first place because he had come from Wales, so they would have argued). Nationalistic prejudice, like literary prejudice, can be a source of humour, and that's chiefly what this strand of the Movement was—like Larkin saying that he lived in Hull because he loved the idea of 'all the Americans getting on the train at Kings Cross and thinking they're going to come and bother me, and then looking at the connections and deciding they'll go to Newcastle and bother Basil Bunting instead'.[13] It would be a mistake to take the jokes too seriously. Amis—who did spend time in the US—said of New York that anyone who made a business of hating it was a creep and that anyone who could walk up Fifth Avenue on a sunny morning and not feel his spirits lift was 'an asshole' (a tribute in itself that he allowed himself to write 'ass' not 'arse'). Of the year he spent in Princeton he told Larkin that he had 'a very fine time indeed' and that the only reason for going back was to avoid the fate of Dylan Thomas and be able to write again, having devoted too much of himself to 'boozing and fucking harder than at any time at all. On the second count I found myself at it practically full-time.'[14] In effect Amis is saying that he loved America *too much*. Something similar might be said about his attitude to the war in Vietnam just a few years later: of twenty-three British intellectuals asked for their view, only he and Conquest declared support for US policy. One can hardly be more pro-American—or pro-the White House Administration—than that.

It is true Amis made sour remarks about American novelists, not least Bellow and Nabokov, and stuck up for English ones. But would Jim Dixon have been so eloquently, slangily denunciatory of Professor Welch and his

[12] Larkin, 'No More Fever', *Further Requirements*, ed. Anthony Thwaite (London: Faber and Faber, 2001), p. 159.

[13] Larkin, *Required Writing*, ed. Anthony Thwaite (London: Faber and Faber, 1983), p. 54.

[14] Zachary Leader (ed.), *The Letters of Kingsley Amis* (London: HarperCollins, 2000), p. 559.

phoney values without the example of J. D. Salinger, whose *Catcher in the Rye*, published three years before *Lucky Jim*, had popularized the anti-phoney stance? Would Philip Larkin have allowed himself to fire all his big guns at the end of 'Church Going' had he not read Robert Frost's poem 'Directive', which takes the same subject—a visit to a place fallen into disuse—and in its grandiloquent conclusion uses a strikingly similar phrase—a 'house in earnest' (Frost), 'a serious house on serious earth' (Larkin)? Would Gunn and Davie have loosened up as they did, casting off their tight-arsed Cambridge quatrains, but for reading William Carlos Williams, Charles Olson, Robert Creeley, and Robert Duncan—and but for spending part (in Gunn's case all) of their adult lives in California? (Gunn came to Stanford, to study with Yvor Winters, as early as 1954. Even before that, Winters's anthology, *Poets of the Pacific*, was one which Donald Davie—reviewing it in 1950—thought would point young English poets in a 'wholesome' direction.[15] Later Davie himself would come to Stanford, and write a sequence of Los Angles poems—and Gunn would settle in San Francisco.)

The Movement's insularity was as much a posture as its anti-Modernism. Indeed the two were intimately related. If the essence of Modernism was its crossing of borders and breaking down of cultural and linguistic barriers—as typified by *The Waste Land*, or by the closing credits to *Ulysses* ('Zurich, Paris, Trieste'), or by Auden and Isherwood moving to the US—the Movement emphasized the virtues of home: *I Like it Here*, as Amis's third novel has it. Being steadfastly British, indeed English (Scots, Irish, and Welsh writers were excluded), the Movement felt honour-bound to be critical of aspects of American life and art. But in the end it was too open-minded—too interested in its own good—to resist them. It certainly did not deplore, as Leavis and Richard Hoggart did, the effect of American 'materialism' on the fabric of English culture and working-class traditions. And whereas the resistance to Abroad—meaning Europe—was a resistance to the shorthand of the privileged classes ('nobody wants any more poems...about art galleries... or foreign cities' Amis famously said), going to America had entirely different connotations, America being the home of jazz, film, and, perhaps, the classless society.

---

[15] Donald Davie, *The Poet in the Imaginary Museum: Essays of Two Decades* (Manchester: Carcanet Press,1977), p. 5.

The usual effect on Brits of coming to the US (and this was truer still back in the 1950s) is, first, a feeling of liberation—from the constraints of social class and sexual inhibition—and, second, a sense of looking into the future and checking out how well it's working: we tend to think that what's happening in the US will later be happening in Britain. Unusually, perhaps, when Thom Gunn first moved to California the effect was rather the opposite—his mentor Yvor Winters seemed more old-fashioned and backward-looking than the tutors he'd had in Cambridge and acted as a brake to his movement: as Gunn later put it in an essay, Winters's advocacy of rule rather than energy 'pinpointed a certain irresponsibility, a looseness, a lack of principle—a promiscuous love of experience perhaps—which I know I need to keep going'.[16] That he did keep those going, and allow them an increasing role in his work, he owed to the wider circle of Californian acquaintance he gradually moved into: Isherwood was among those he came to know. Drugs and hot tubs and an uncovert gay culture released him too, and that sense of the Gunn persona opening himself to experience and shedding at least some of his English reserve is an attractive feature of his poetry. By contrast there is Roger Micheldene, the main protagonist of *One Fat Englishman* (1963), written after the year Amis spent in Princeton at the end of the 1950s. In Amis's early novels it is natural enough to conflate author and hero, and Roger Micheldene, the hero of this novel, is typically Amisian in that he drinks, philanders, and seethes with contempt for most of the Americans he encounters. But Micheldene is not Amis, as we infer from a striking passage when an American Anglophile, Atkins, challenges Micheledene on his prejudices:

Atkins now said pleadingly: 'Mitch, listen to me...I'd like to ask you something. Come on now, listen. Why do you hate us?'

'Hate you? How do you mean? I mean...'

'Why do you hate us? You do, don't you? You all do. Why? Why? What have we done to you? We didn't want to be world leaders. Last thing we wanted. We've never been imperialist? And yet you hate us? Why? We've never been colonialist. And yet you...'

'Oh, really,' Roger snapped.... 'Never been imperialist or colonialist? Why do you think places like California and Arizona and Florida and Puerto Rico and the rest have got those foreign-sounding names?...'

[16] Thom Gunn, 'On a Drying Hill: Yvor Winters', in *Shelf Life* (London: Faber and Faber, 1993), p. 210.

'Mitch, Mitch, Mitch,' Atkins broke through by degrees, 'I'm a horrible Anglophile. And you're trying to change me, boy.' (chapter 4)

The conversation brings to mind conversations conducted in the wake of 9/11, when many Americans asked themselves, perhaps for the first time: why does the rest of the world hate us so much? Roger Micheldene answers the question by pointing to America's imperial past, just as many British and European intellectuals since 2001 have answered it by pointing to America's imperial present, its oil hunger, its designs on the Middle East, its seeming indifference to global warming. But Micheldene does not come well out of the argument, even though Atkins, as a self-confessed Anglophile, is the kind of figure Amis hated almost as much as he did arrogant upper-middle class Englishmen. The numerous punishments inflicted on Micheldene—who is not granted the kind of sexual success Amis normally awards his heroes—is indicative of what the author thinks of him, or of his growing distance from his fictional creation, or, to use Marilyn Butler's term, of his scepticism. Any doubt over this is settled in the last words of the book's penultimate chapter, when Micheldene is told, devastatingly: 'you think that some of the people in this country don't like you because you're British. That isn't so. We're out of the redcoat era now, even if you aren't…It isn't your nationality we don't like, it's you.' (chapter 16)

If he were alive today we can guess that Amis the man would have approved of the invasion of Iraq; dismissed liberal anxieties about Guantanamo Bay as pissy Lefty cant; seen Bush and Blair (however much he disliked the latter's domestic policies) as defenders of democracy; and made light of the threat of global warming. In 1990 he wrote to Conquest that his son Martin was 'getting het up again over greenhouse effect and all that. I told him it was all lefty-trendy, a vacant spot for the Trots and assorted anti-West shags to go now that Marxism, etc, had packed up.'[17] Characteristic stuff. But Amis the novelist is harder to predict—there is always the possibility that characters whose political opinions he shares will turn out to be shits or bores; or the possibility that characters he dislikes will win out in arguments against those of whom he approves. Which is what is meant by the possibilities of fiction.

'A neutral tone is nowadays preferred,' wrote Donald Davie in his poem 'Remembering the Thirties', contrasting the politics of his generation of

---

[17] Leader (ed.), *Letters of Kingsley Amis*, p. 1090.

poets with the more *engagé* version of the Auden–Spender generation. 1950s Britain might not have been affluent but the war was over, the village squires were dead, mass unemployment had been banished, the British Empire had been surrendered, the Welfare State had been established to provide free education and health, and corruption and scandal seemed to have gone. 'There aren't any good brave causes left,' wails Jimmy Porter in *Look Back in Anger*, and Thom Gunn, defending his generation for its quietism, said something very similar: 'The agony of the time is that there is no agony.'[18] The later Gunn would have been less complacent. But for a time, until the Suez crisis, the Soviet invasion of Hungary and worries about nuclear war polarized British politics, neutrality was a seductive idea.

It is hard not to be struck by the parallels to the present. In the early 1950s, until Hungary, people talked of 'the end of ideology', just as through the 1990s, until 9/11, Francis Fukuyama was talking of the end of history. In the 1950s, the word 'Butskellism' summarized the temporary consensus between Left and Right, between R. A. Butler (Conservative) and Hugh Gaitskell (Labour); in the 1990s Tony Blair won a landslide election victory by rebranding the Labour Party as post-socialist and anti-trade union—to the point where 81 per cent of respondents to a 2004 opinion poll said that they found no important difference between the main political parties. Neutrality, consensus, consolidation, the end of ideology—the Movement slogans resonate in our own time.

Re-reading Movement poems and novels now, I'm struck by their equanimity—the way in which Movement protagonists ward off commitments (whether political, moral, or marital) and avoid taking sides. 'Loss of nerve' is one of the recurring motifs—according to Donald Davie, a willed, intentional loss of nerve, since holding one's nerve and standing up for something can be catastrophic: as he puts it in his poem 'Rejoinder to a Critic', 'How dare we now be anything but numb?' Of course it is not uplifting to see loss of nerve in action—to watch Jim Dixon kowtowing to Professor Welch, or to hear Larkin confess, in his poem 'Toads', that he lacks the guts to shout 'stuff your pension' ('I know all too well | that's the stuff that dreams are made on'). Not surprisingly, Movement writers sometimes turn on themselves in disgust for being weak and cowardly—or tie themselves in knots

---

[18] Gunn, letter to *London Magazine*, June 1957, pp. 65–6.

by trying to argue, as Larkin does, that if they're not as brave, colourful, sociable, adventurous or sexually active as they want to be, that's because 'fate' or heredity or God ('something hidden from us', anyway) has decreed it. And moreover—this is the premise of 'Poetry of Departures'—that whether we're audacious or timid, whether we stay home or swagger the nut-strewn roads, it all comes to the same thing, an artificial step backwards, and a life of reprehensible perfection. This is not a message one often hears in an age of anything-is-possible self-improvement. And yet by not being pumped-up or claiming too much for itself, the Movement produced a literature with which the fallible reader can sympathize. Its protagonists and personae are (in Auden's phrase) silly like us; they don't pose, or preen, or pretend to be better (or worse) than they are—and they don't slay dragons or vanquish the forces of Conformity and Mammon. The Beat Poets, coming along a few years later, offered a mode of rebellion which the anti-globalist young of today still find meaningful. But to the majority of us, there is more to identify with in the dilemma of Jim Dixon, forced to adapt to circumstances he dislikes, but confining his resistance to jokes, mimicry, and fantasies of violent retaliation (today he would doubtless be doing it by email).

And maybe there *is* something bold in the Movement's readiness to compromise, or own up to weakness, fallibility or ignorance, when—contemporary public life being what it is—all the pressure is to stand one's ground. Donald Davie attacked the Movement's hesitancy as a conversational gambit, a craven attempt to ingratiate itself with the reader through knowing winks and nods.[19] On the contrary, the hesitancy betokens a stunned admission of mysteries that pass all understanding and of truths that lie too deep to be articulated. Larkin has a poem called 'Ignorance' which seems to me exemplary in its self-confessed unknowing:

> Strange to know nothing, never to be sure
> Of what is true or right or real,
> But forced to qualify *or so I feel*,
> Or, *Well, it does seem so:*
> *Someone must know.*

'Someone would know, I don't' goes a line in 'Church Going', the great agnostic poem of the twentieth century, while 'Mr Bleaney' ends with a

---

[19] See Davie's essay, 'Remembering the Movement', reprinted in *The Poet in the Imaginary Museum*.

throwaway, seemingly syntactically unattached 'I don't know'. Larkin is not suggesting that he—or we—*surrender* to ignorance, but he is underlining how hard it is to achieve truth and understanding. (Perhaps it is this that explains the difference between him and Amis, at least as poets: whereas Amis the poet writes what he knows, with confidence, and that's what makes him a light verse poet, Larkin yearns for what he doesn't know, and that's what makes him a Romantic.) In 'Dockery and Son' Larkin does fight his way through to a wise if bleak summation, a big ending, one so powerful that it seems almost to stand independent of the rest, as if destined straight for the *Oxford Dictionary of Quotations*. But to get there, to earn the right, he proceeds through a series of stammers and hesitations ('Well it just shows | How much ... how little ...'), posing questions (there are seven of them in the poem's six stanzas), arguing with himself, offering partial answers then discounting them and checking back ('No that's not the difference, rather how ...'), going off on false tracks (with a run of three dots whenever he fetches up in a cul-de-sac or siding), and then changing register with a sudden image of sand-clouds—which blow from nowhere into a poem that until then has been scrupulously realist, urban and British in its geography—to signal the approach of something less cramped, a conclusion as bleakly moving as anything in Beckett:

> Life is first boredom then fear.
> Whether or not we use it, it goes,
> And leaves what something hidden from us chose
> And age, and then the only end of age.

It is crucial to make this point about hesitancy and self-doubt, equivocation and neutrality, because Larkin and Amis have been discredited in recent years for being men of extreme prejudice: fascists, racists, misogynists, misanthropes, and bigots of assorted kinds. Such an accusation would not survive a reading of, say, Amis's account of his second trip to the US, to Nashville, in 1967 (which is entirely taken up with revulsion against his hosts' demeaning of blacks) or his reaction to the *Satanic Verses* affair (unambiguously pro-freedom of expression, whatever he might have thought of Rushdie himself). But in any case, when they were not writing squibs, Larkin and Amis looked to literature as a place not to vent prejudice but to circumvent it, to play with it (as Amis does in his fiction) or to leave it behind (as Larkin does in his poetry). The most exalted moments in Larkin's poetry are those which bring us images of space, light, freedom, and transcendence, as at the end

of 'High Windows', where, having lifted his gaze beyond a world of moral
wrangling and fiddle-faddle about sexual morality, he sees 'the deep, blue air,
that shows | Nothing, and is nowhere, and is endless'. To Larkin this is what
poetry should be—a prejudice-free zone; a space for exploring ideas and feel-
ings, for entertaining doubts and mysteries, without any irritable reaching
after fact or finality. Call it Neutrality or Negative Capability, it is something
central to the Movement endeavour and of more lasting consequence than,
say, its war on metaphor or its treatment of class difference.

   In one respect, the matter of religious faith, or the lack of it, the scepti-
cism looks positively courageous—all the more so in these fundamentalist
times. 'Church Going' does its best to honour the seriousness of churches
but the speaker enters the 'accoutred frowsty barn' only when he is 'sure
there's nothing going on'. The later, less circumspect 'Aubade' dismisses reli-
gion as 'that vast moth-eaten musical brocade | Created to pretend we never
die'. Writing in a jauntier, more provocative spirit, Kingsley Amis—who
once characterized himself as a non-militant unbeliever, 'one of the com-
pany (large and rapidly growing, I hope) which says [with Empson]: "I think
the traditional God of Christianity very wicked" '[20]—takes on both God and
Jesus in his poetry. In 'The Huge Artifice', he writes in the tones of a book
reviewer disappointed to find the creator botching his masterwork through
brashness, 'authorial inexperience', vast gaps in sensitivity, and 'Concepts
that have not often been surpassed | For ignorance or downright nastiness'.
In 'New Approach Needed', he addresses Jesus on his cross ('You won't get
me | Up on one of those things'), urging him

> Next time, come off it
> And get some service in,
> Jack, long before you start
> Laying down the law:
> If you still want to then.
> Tell your dad that for me.

   I wonder how many magazine or newspaper editors would dare to pub-
lish that poem, were it submitted today. They might be willing to print a
Harold Pinter poem attacking US foreign policy—but a hatchet job on Jesus
and God? Both Amis and Larkin believed that our literary heritage would be

[20] See 'On Christ's Nature', in *What Became of Jane Austen* (London: Jonathan Cape, 1970), p. 229.

immeasurably poorer without religion, but that didn't moderate their atheism. According to Donald Davie's poem 'Creon's Mouse', the Movement assumption was that no one could or would 'be daring any more'. But from the perspective of the twenty-first century, the expression of non-conviction—or rather, of the conviction that scepticism, secularism, and liberalism are worth defending—*does* begin to look courageous in the extreme.

If I see that now, as I failed to in 1980, that is not just because times have changed but because I have; in Amis's terms, I'm less of a trendy-Lefty; in my own, I'm a lot older and a little wiser, and that makes me willing to acknowledge that Movement attitudes I used to think were supine—the caution and consolidation, the orderliness and rationalism, the neutrality and loss of nerve—have some value after all. These days as I read the Movement, Larkin and Amis in particular, I feel the same respect, regret, and belated love which I felt when my father died and which Kingsley Amis voices in the elegy to *his* father: 'I'm sorry you had to die | To make me sorry | You're not here now' ('In Memoriam W.R.A.'). But the good thing about the Movement is that the work is still there, and—far from shrinking in size or significance—grows larger as the years go by.

2

The 'Truth of Skies': Auden, Larkin and the English Question

Nicholas Jenkins

In memory of W. G. Moore

'Over millions of years', the philosopher Colin McGinn writes,

our eyes have evolved with the sky as their primordial companion.... the human eye
is as adapted to the sky as it is adapted to anything, limited as its viewpoint is. Clouds,
stars, and birds are among the objects the sky offers our visual system. We look up
into the sky and look at these objects, laid out before us in an infinitely expansive
medium, bounded only by the line of the earth's surface.[1]

Adapted to scrutiny of the atmospheric medium by, alike, ancient cultural
drives and biological necessities, our eyes can scan the sky with extraordin-
ary rapidity and efficiency, picking out significant details, discerning patterns
and contrasts, and registering subtle shifts in the sky's tones and hues. Indeed
human vision seems able to drink in the sky as if it were the primary arena
for which the faculty of seeing had been developed.

Moreover, or therefore, for tens of thousands of years the sky was the
home of the life-giving and life-taking deities, the sky gods, omnipotent

---

[1] Colin McGinn, *The Power of Movies: How Screen and Mind Interact* (New York: Pantheon, 2005), p. 25.
I owe a debt to McGinn, as well as to Claire Bowen, Alan Jenkins, Zachary Leader, and Blake
Morrison for shoring up both the prose and the ideas in this essay.

patrons (according to late Victorian and Edwardian anthropological studies) of those militaristic, nomadic peoples who overran the peaceable farming communities and established patriarchal religion. Dyaus Pitar was the 'Sky Father' in the Vedic religion, Zeus was the primordial Greek sky-god, Jupiter ruled the Roman sky. And, because the Gods overhead saw and knew everything, inspiration for poets and prophets was to be found in the sky. The path of the eagle circling in the heavens was Pindar's metaphor for sublime poetic flights.[2] The Muse Urania (the daughter of Zeus and the goddess of poetry *and* astronomy, the study of the night sky) descends for the poet at the start of *Paradise Lost*. In language full of ideas about height, loftedness, and ascent, Milton invokes her 'aid to my advent'rous Song, | That with no middle flight intends to soar | Above th' Aonian Mount'; he pleads with her who, 'Dove-like satst brooding on the vast Abyss', that 'What in me is dark' she 'Illumine, what is low raise and support; | That to the highth of this great Argument | I may assert Eternal Providence.'[3]

In the later part of the nineteenth century, physicists such as John Tyndall and Lord Rayleigh began a rigorous scientific study of the sky. But, once beyond the glow from the infernal cities which were springing up, the poetic notion of the sky remained one of an unsullied vista which was boundlessly sublime and beautiful.[4] In 'Of the Open Sky' in *Modern Painters*, probably the most influential piece of sky-writing for the modern English sensibility, Ruskin exalted J. M. W. Turner's ability to capture in paint the other-worldly *feeling* of the sky: 'still *spacious*, still infinite and immeasurable in depth... something which has no surface and through which we can plunge far and farther, and without stay or end, into the profundity of space.'[5] For Ruskin the 'truth of skies' is that they are timeless, historyless, and, blessedly, almost devoid of mere usefulness:

there is not a moment of any day or our lives, when nature is not producing scene after scene, picture after picture, glory after glory, and working still upon such

[2] Pindar, *Nemean Odes* 3, ll. 80–2 and 5, ll. 21, and *Olympian Ode* 2, ll. 86–8.

[3] *Paradise Lost* (1674), Book 1, ll. 12–25, in Milton, *Complete Poems and Major Prose*, ed. Merritt Y. Hughes (Indianapolis: Bobbs-Merrill, 1957), pp. 211–12.

[4] Tyndall was the person who finally explained the reason for the blueness of the sky—it is the result of light's 'selective scattering by molecules of the gases that make up the atmosphere'. See John Naylor, *Out of the Blue: A 24-Hour Skywatcher's Guide* (Cambridge: Cambridge University Press, 2002), p. 8.

[5] Italics in original; Ruskin, *Modern Painters* (1843), *The Works of John Ruskin*, vol. 3, ed. E. T. Cook and Alexander Wedderburn (London: George Allen, 1903), p. 348.

exquisite and constant principles of the most perfect beauty, that it is quite certain it is all done for us, and intended for our perpetual pleasure... [The sky] is fitted in all its functions for the perpetual comfort and exalting of the heart, for soothing it and purifying it from its dross and dust.[6]

Ruskin was a kind of bard of the Victorian sky, a place puritanically emptied of the interfering and capricious neo-classical deities and a revelation instead of the infinitely tender and capacious artistry of a benignly faceless Christian God. Gerard Manley Hopkins's receptiveness to the sky's grandeur was also especially strong. His notebooks, especially those from the 1870s, are filled with extraordinary descriptions of the sky, and especially of clouds. Hopkins was the poet of 'grey lawns cold where gold, where quickgold lies':

> Look at the stars! look, look up at the skies!
> O look at all the fire-folk sitting in the air!
> The bright boroughs, the circle-citadels there![7]

In 'The Starlight Night' the ecstatic vehemence of Hopkins's sky-love, his sense that the sky is indeed the 'home' of 'Christ and his mother and all his hallows', is spread between the tensions and compactions of the language and the ecstatic injunctions to 'look, look up'. The train of exclamation marks in his lines shines like darkly glowing traces left by the eyesight's repeated, rapturous sweeps upwards into the 'bright boroughs' of the sky. Hopkins's conceit of the 'bright boroughs' is profound, or lofty, because momentarily by 'look[ing] up' at the extraordinary wonder of the sky, we gain access to a feeling of height, to a sense of looking down from the sublime darkness of a mountaintop onto the glinting lights below. In the aftermath of Ruskin, Hopkins finds in the very act of looking up at the sky a redemptive moment, a moment of divine weightlessness and panoramic vision.

By the 1930s when a teenaged Philip Larkin began composing poems, the arbiters of modernity in poetry had recognized in Hopkins's *oeuvre* one of the most urgently intense bodies of 'modern' lyric writing. Addressing the elite audience of those 'who care' about such things, F. R. Leavis anachronistically welded

---

[6] Ibid., pp. 343–4. Virginia Woolf's description in her 1930 essay 'On Being Ill' of the 'Divinely beautiful' and 'divinely heartless' sky ('this endless activity, with the waste of Heaven knows how many million horse-power of energy, has been left to work its will year in, year out') draws heavily, and perhaps parodically, on Ruskin's rhetoric in *Modern Painters*.

[7] 'The Starlight Night', in *Gerard Manley Hopkins*, ed. Catherine Phillips (Oxford: Oxford University Press, 1986), pp. 128–9.

Hopkins into the canon of modern poetry by including a chapter on him in *New Bearings in English Poetry* (1932). There he aligned Hopkins with the fashionable modernist canon of 'Shakespeare, Donne, Eliot and the later Yeats' and, in a phrase glinting like a waved scalpel, he made Hopkins, along with Eliot and Pound, one of the triumvirate who 'together represent a decisive re-ordering of the tradition of English poetry'.[8]

Larkin's poetry draws on some of the same core energies found in Hopkins's work. Not least he is, like the earlier writer, an avid sky-poet. One can tell as much simply by recalling that Larkin's 1947 collection was titled *In the Grip of Light*. In fact, terms such as 'sky', 'air', 'night', 'light', 'clouds', 'rain', 'moon', and 'sun' are amongst the most frequently used nouns in his work. Each of these words outranks in frequency of appearance—by an impressive amount—words commonly supposed to be the typical furniture in a Larkin poem such as 'girl' or 'money' or 'work' or 'self'. The sky and the weather in Larkin's writing 'congregate endlessly', as he once wrote that 'any-angled light' would in a glass of water held up to sunlight.[9] References to the sky run from the weird, semi-surreal line in his early poem 'Street Lamps', 'night slinks, like a puma, down the sky', to the light that is 'pewter' in 'Dublinesque'. The melancholic line at the end of 'Money' describes 'churches ornate and mad | In the evening sun', while there is the 'moon thinned | To an air-sharpened blade' in 'Vers de Société' and the featureless sky 'white as clay, with no sun' in what was effectively Larkin's terminal poem, 'Aubade'. In the Dutch genre scene of 'The Card Players': 'Wet century-wide trees | Clash in surrounding starlessness above | This lamplit cave.'[10]

---

[8] Leavis, *New Bearings in English Poetry: A Study of the Contemporary Situation* (London: Chatto and Windus, 1932), pp. 171, 195. Leavis aside, the intense interest in Hopkins which sprang up in the 1930s in England is manifest in the appearance of a 2nd edn. of the 1918 Bridges' volume of Hopkins's *Poems* (1931), 3 vols. of Hopkins's correspondence (two in 1935 and one in 1938), as well as an edn. of his *Note-books and Papers* (1937) and E. E. Phare's *The Poetry of Gerard Manley Hopkins: A Survey and Commentary* (1933), the first academic monograph published on Hopkins's work. Small wonder, then, that Larkin would eventually call Hopkins one of the poets who 'have clearly helped to form the twentieth century poet's consciousness'. Letter of 20 Jan. 1966 to Dan Davin, in *Selected Letters of Philip Larkin: 1940–1985*, ed. Anthony Thwaite (New York: Farrar, Straus and Giroux, 1992), p. 380. Hereafter 'Larkin, *Letters*'.

[9] 'Water', in Larkin, *Collected Poems*, ed. Anthony Thwaite (New York: Marvell/Farrar/Straus and Giroux, 1989), p. 93. Hereafter, 'Larkin, *Poems*'.

[10] Ibid., pp. 178, 198, 181, 209, 177. 'Street Lamps' is from Larkin, *Early Poems and Juvenilia*, ed. A. T. Tolley (London: Faber and Faber, 2005), p. 22. Hereafter 'Larkin, *Early Poems*'.

In citing briefly from these poems I take my examples randomly and out of chronological sequence, hoping only to indicate the pervasiveness of the sky in Larkin's work. But I must also include in my list what is probably Larkin's best known 'sky poem', 'High Windows' (written in 1967):

> When I see a couple of kids
> And guess he's fucking her and she's
> Taking pills or wearing a diaphragm,
> I know this is paradise
>
> Everyone old has dreamed of all their lives—
> Bonds and gestures pushed to one side
> Like an outdated combine harvester,
> And everyone young going down the long slide
>
> To happiness, endlessly. I wonder if
> Anyone looked at me, forty years back,
> And thought, *That'll be the life;*
> *No God any more, or sweating in the dark*
>
> *About hell and that, or having to hide*
> *What you think of the priest. He*
> *And his lot will all go down the long slide*
> *Like free bloody birds.* And immediately
>
> Rather than words comes the thought of high windows:
> The sun-comprehending glass,
> And beyond it, the deep blue air, that shows
> Nothing, and is nowhere, and is endless.[11]

At a formal level the poem masterfully interlocks a set of numerically diverse structures: five stanzas, each stanza being of four lines, in a three sentence-long sequence. The sardonic use of verb of pure being, 'is' ('I know this *is* paradise'), in the final line of stanza one, is balanced against the final line of the last stanza where two exalted uses of the copula ('and *is* nowhere, and *is* endless') dramatize what Larkin wants to imagine as the inviolate, unchanging beauty of the sky. As so often, Larkin's formal zest and intricacy are ironic counterpoints to his thematic pessimism.

---

[11] Larkin, *Poems*, p. 165. Motion notes that the poem was written between Nov. 1965 and Feb. 1967. See Andrew Motion, *Philip Larkin: A Writer's Life* (New York: Farrar, Straus and Giroux, 1993), pp. 355, 371. Hereafter, 'Motion, *LWL*'.

This contrast between the poem's beginning and its ending underlines a basic dualistic division which structures the entire lyric. There is a longer first half, one which starts with a volley of first person verbal forms emphasizing the speaker's self-esteeming judgementalism: 'I see...[I] guess...I know'. This repetitiveness soon shifts direction, though, blending into the beautiful anthology of verb forms and tenses in which people are active rather than passive, acting rather than contemplating: 'she's | *Taking* pills...Everyone old has *dreamed*... gestures *pushed* to one side...everyone young *going* down the long slide'. The assertive, self-involved first 'half' ends with the 'thought' that 'forty years back' the speaker's younger self '*and his lot*' would have looked to an older person essentially like the couple do who have prompted the speaker's reflections now: '*He* | *And his lot will all go down the long slide* | *Like free bloody birds.*'

The epiphanic second half of the poem, smaller in terms of actual space but far more expansive emotionally, opens with the speaker not seeing or guessing or knowing but—in one of those Yeatsian swerves which are so typical of Larkin's work—moving into a state of receptive passivity. In this state, instead of *cogitating* on something the poet suddenly has a species of *vision*: 'Rather than words comes the thought.' Larkin's grammar subtly emphasizes the modulation: he reverses the normal 'subject followed by verb' sequence to a 'verb followed by subject' pattern. The visionary 'thought' is actually a visual memory: 'sun-comprehending glass, | And beyond it, the deep blue air.' This transition between the argumentative and imagistic halves of the poem is signalled too by the inward rhyming on which the poem pivots as if on the plates of a hinge—'*free bloody birds*' rhymes internally with 'Rather than words'. Rhymes can only exist between entities that are slightly dissimilar. The simile '*like free bloody birds*' leads, through what is strictly speaking a non-sequitur, to a thought about the realm of avian life (the 'deep blue air'). So what the rhyme suggests is that, as the poem builds towards its ending, it has moved from a rational to an associative mode.

H. G. Wells once recalled that Conrad would sometimes harry him about the deep subjects of books or authors: ' "what is this *Love and Mr. Lewisham about?*" ' he would ask Wells, or, 'wringing his hands and wrinkling his forehead, "What is all this about Jane Austen? What is there *in* her? What is it all *about?*" '[12] With the basic structure of 'High Windows' identified, the same

---

[12] Italics in original; Wells, *Experiment in Autobiography: Discoveries and Conclusions of a Very Ordinary Brain (Since 1866)* (1934; Boston: Little, Brown, 1984), pp. 527–8.

question occurs in relation to Larkin's sky-borne ending to his poem—'what is it all *about*?' The delusional 'thought' which someone 'forty years back' might have had about Larkin's speaker is that this young man's life must be 'paradise'. That was nonsense, just as the poem knows that Larkin's speaker is utterly wrong about the ease of the 'kids'' lives now. Why was the life of forty years ago not paradisal? The answer to the question comes in the form of a thought about the sky and its association with the emptiness and nothingness of death.

To find out what the poem is 'all *about*' therefore entails looking carefully at its sky. Larkin's sky has a special quality to it. For Ruskin, Turner's sky was miraculously like the real thing, 'something which has no surface and through which we can plunge far and farther, and without stay or end, into the profundity of space.'[13] The philosopher Maurice Merleau-Ponty talks in similar terms about the sky as a space which the mind enters into or fuses with:

When I contemplate the sky I am not *set over against it* as an acosmic subject; I do not possess it in thought, or spread out towards it some idea of blue such as might reveal the secret of it, I abandon myself to it and plunge into this mystery, it 'thinks itself within me', I am the sky itself as it is drawn together and unified, and as it begins to exist for itself; my consciousness is saturated with this limitless blue.[14]

But the post-war Larkin of a poem such as 'High Windows', while being obsessed with light and skies, never diffuses himself, never 'plunges' into the world above him in the way described by Merleau-Ponty. Instead Larkin's contemplated sky is a boundary, an emptiness, a mysterious vacancy, a border.

The final lines of 'High Windows' have a strong air of enigma about them, one which is perhaps subliminally heightened by the extreme closeness (only one letter different) of the compound 'sun-comprehending' to the more familiar term of 'uncomprehending'. And there is something uncomprehending about a literalistic reading of this poem. Clues to the poem's mystery come in such telling phrases as '*bloody birds*', and, at line endings, in such terms as 'forty years', '*sweating in the dark*', and '*having to hide*'. All evoke a

[13] Ruskin, *Modern Painters*, p. 348.
[14] Italics in original; *Phenomenology of Perception*, trans. Colin Smith (1945; London: Routledge and Kegan Paul, 1962), p. 214.

wartime world, the 'forty years' of the 1940s, a time of nighttime raids, darkness and terror. And the negative forms with which the poem ends— 'Nothing...nowhere...endless'—also hint at meanings which they conceal. Freud wrote that traumatic material only emerges into the patient's mind in negative form: 'the content of a repressed image or idea can make its way into consciousness on condition that it is *negated*. Negation is a way of taking cognizance of what is repressed.'[15] Here, Larkin's profounder subject emerges through negations. Larkin's youth, glancingly and obliquely recalled, was a period not of 'paradise' but of hell, a hell associated with the sky.

Nothing which moves us can be without a historical dimension. The challenge in interpreting this poem, like all of Larkin's work, is to go beyond the vague generality of identifying the sky as a mere image of non-being and to read Larkin's poem as describing a specific, focused experience. To rephrase the poem's own words, 'High Windows' is something about somewhere specific and finite. Such a reading moves Larkin from the embarrassing and unsatisfactory status of a 'wisdom poet' writing in universalizing terms about generalities of human experience. Instead, it lodges him in a richer, more meaningful historical context. To do this we need, above all, to 're-read' his skies and to see that they are not timeless but time-bound.

Celestial nature changed forever on or around December 1903. It was at that date, when, at the Wrights' hands, the sky was colonized by humanity. From a long perspective, it will probably look as if one of the most momentous developments during the twentieth century was humanity's unleashed drive to dominate, exploit and, finally, with the advent of global warming (such that, for example, the concentrations in the air of the greenhouse gas carbon dioxide are now at their highest levels in at least 650,000 years), to destroy the sky. That exploitation began with the first flight by a heavier-than-air vehicle. Everything else has quickly followed.

By the 1930s, the decade of Larkin's adolescence, the culture of aviation was firmly established in the artistic imagination. This was the first decade of moderately widespread public air travel. Literary historians such as Valentine Cunningham have described how the 1930s was also an era of intense air-mindedness amongst authors and painters. Auden, the primary young poet

---

[15] Italics is original; Freud, 'Negation' (1925), in *The Standard Edition of the Complete Psychological Works of Sigmund Freud*, vol. 19, trans. and ed., James Strachey *et al.* (London: Hogarth Press, 1958), p. 235.

for aspiring writers of Larkin's generation, wrote poems in the early 1930s which often adopted a high-angled, downward-looking or even an aerial viewpoint, analytically scrutinizing mundane phenomena below from a distant, sometimes actually airborne, position of power. But my emphasis here is not on a looking down but on a looking up. As the decade progressed, this is the perspective from which Auden's poems (and many other poems, novels, and paintings) began to observe.

In this, as he was in so many ways, Auden was representative of the period. The sky had an almost intrinsically poetic quality to Auden and to other 1930s authors: it was variously a kind of mirror, a source of beauty and fear, a vista that regularly loomed up in poems and novels which began in a purely horizontal dimension. But what thirties authors saw when they looked up was no longer what Yeats in lines about homecoming calls the beauty of 'customary skies'.[16] For writers, as for most other people in the 1930s, the air above them was suddenly alive in a different and newly dangerous way. This hypersensitivity to the sky had to do with widespread new fears about the dangers of military aviation. The perceptual changes created by the commercialization and militarization of airspace were momentous. They altered what the sky meant and how people in the 1930s thought and felt about it. The sky was suddenly mesmerizing because it was threatening. The conquered sky became a new version of the sublime space, of which Burke says, 'Whatever is fitted in any sort to excite the ideas of pain, and danger, that is to say, whatever is in any sort terrible, or is conversant about terrible objects, or operates in a manner analogous to terror, is a source of the *sublime*.'[17] The sky for the European world of the 1930s and the 1940s was sublime in this sense. Once it had been beautiful, then it became fascinatingly deadly. In understanding both Auden's and Larkin's poetry, to be aware this historical moment of culture within which they were both formed is especially important.

Stanley Baldwin, the Lord President of the Council and, in effect, the Prime Minister, gave the most famous expression of this fear of aerial bombardment when he announced to the House of Commons on 10 November 1932 that:

---

[16] 'Many a son and daughter lies | Far from the customary skies'. See 'In Memory of Alfred Pollexfen' in Yeats, *The Poems*, ed. Richard Finneran, rev. edn. (New York: Macmillan, 1990), p. 156.

[17] Italics in original; Burke, 'A Philosophical Inquiry into the Origin of our Idea of the Sublime and the Beautiful' (1757), part 1, sect. 7.

I think it is well also for the man in the street to realise that there is no power on earth that can protect him from being bombed, whatever people may tell him. The bomber will always get through.... The only defence is in offence, which means that you have got to kill more women and children more quickly than the enemy if you want to save yourselves. I mention that so that people may realise what is waiting for them when the next war comes.[18]

Thereafter, the British public, like that of most other nations in Europe, was haunted by the fear of rapid destruction from the air. Just how obsessing and 'dark' the sky had become for many people in England in the later 1930s can be gauged from an almost random survey of the period's periodicals and books. One cover of *The Listener* published in September 1937 shows a diagonal line of fighter planes, seen from below, looming into view against a background of clouds. The ominous headline (echoing Baldwin's words) reads: 'CAN THE BOMBER GET THROUGH?'[19] A year later, in Elizabeth Bowen's *The Death of the Heart* (1938), the heroine, Portia, is assembling a jigsaw puzzle of 'a magnificent air display' which at first seems to her beautiful. But soon, Bowen writes, the 'planes massing against an ultramarine sky began each to take a different symbolic form, and as she assembled the spectators she came to look for a threat or promise in each upturned face'.[20] The opening paragraph of Graham Greene's *Brighton Rock*, published in the same year as Bowen's novel, evokes both *Mrs Dalloway*'s sky-writing plane and Baldwin's bomber when it registers ominously 'an aeroplane advertising something for the health in pale vanishing clouds across the sky' while a man below realizes that he is going to be murdered.[21]

Artists too responded to the sky innovatively in the 1930s. For example, C. R. W. Nevinson, a veteran of aerial warfare in World War One, painted a number of pictures during the decade where the primary subject is a stark, almost hysterical horror at the prospect of death being dealt out from the air. Julian Trevelyan's pictures from 1939–40 show figures looking with apprehensive anguish into the sky. 'We all thought something was going to come from there,' Trevelyan said about this period.[22] And the painter Paul Nash

---

[18] Cited in 'Mr. Baldwin on Aerial Warfare', *The Times*, 11 Nov. 1932, p. 8.

[19] [Front cover], *Listener*, 15 Sept. 1937.

[20] Elizabeth Bowen, *The Death of the Heart* (1938; New York: Anchor, 2000), p. 237.

[21] Graham Greene, *Brighton Rock* (1938; Harmondsworth: Penguin, 2004), p. 3.

[22] 1973 interview, cited in David Mellor, 'British Art in the 1930s: Some Economic, Political and Cultural Structures', in Frank Gloversmith (ed.), *Class, Culture and Social Change: A New View of the 1930s* (Brighton: Harvester, 1980), p. 203.

commented similarly that by the end of the 1930s, that fear was universal: 'suddenly the sky was upon us all, like a huge hawk, hovering, threatening... I hunted the sky for what I dreaded in my imaginings.'[23] The sky was something difficult to face, or to tear one's eyes away from. The artistic and poetic imagination reached into the skies tentatively, uncertainly, with the kind of exploring delicacy of a hand groping for the light switch in a darkened room.

In the 1930s the conjoined subjects of the sky and death were so powerful that they are even sublimated into images which are not explicitly to do with aerial combat or bombing at all. For example, there is a light and space-filled photograph by Humphrey Spender, 'Wash on the Line', taken in Bolton in 1937, and ostensibly only of a scene in an alley where clothing strung on washing lines flaps as it dries in the open air. Spender made his image in the same year that Picasso painted *Guernica*, the first masterpiece of aerial warfare against civilians. In that context, the evidence of the violent gusts of wind in Spender's picture, the sight of the billowing pillows, of shirts and dresses filled out into strangely bloated, contorted, semi-human shapes and thrown wildly around, all read as if they were anxious, ghostly memories of Picasso's exploded bodies and tortured, skyward-staring faces.[24]

This sensitivity to the spaces above was an important inspiration for the period's poets. In the 1930s, even a cloudless sky seems to cast a kind of shadow onto the earth. By gazing down in 'Burnt Norton' (1935) T. S. Eliot's speaker finds himself watching the look of things being changed by the natural movements of the sky:

> So we moved, and they, in a formal pattern,
> Along the empty alley, into the box circle,
> To look down into the drained pool.
> Dry the pool, dry concrete, brown edged,
> And the pool was filled with water out of sunlight,
> And the lotos rose, quietly, quietly,
> The surface glittered out of heart of light,
> And they were behind us, reflected in the pool.
> Then a cloud passed, and the pool was empty.[25]

---

[23] Cited ibid., p. 203.

[24] For a reproduction of the photograph, see Deborah Frizzell, *Humphrey Spender's Humanist Landscapes: Photo-documents, 1932–1942* (New Haven: Yale University Press, 1997), plate 25.

[25] Eliot, *Complete Poems and Plays 1909–1950* (New York: Harcourt, Brace, 1952), p. 118.

The recurrence of the word 'pool', the description of which never seems ready to conclude, is an indication, in its flickering mutability, of the ceaselessly-altering nature of appearances on the earth's surface where everything that happens visually is constantly affected by the different kinds of light coming from the sky. (The same looking-down-to-see-up frame of reference occurs in a post-war context in Larkin's image of 'gull-marked mud' in 'Here'. The indentations made by the gull's feet are made visible by the reflected gleams of sunlight on the shiny, damp surface of the mud.[26])

In 1937 to 1938 Auden's poetry touched repeatedly on the presence of the sky from the perspective of the ground. Sometimes, its presence is overt. In one of the most famous sonnets from his and Isherwood's *Journey to a War* Auden's speaker stares upwards to watch air-raids overhead: 'the sky | Throbs like a feverish forehead; pain is real; | The groping searchlights suddenly reveal | The little natures that will make us cry.'[27] At other points in Auden's work, the prospect of aerial conflict is uncannier and more spectral. Thus, his responsiveness to the paintings of Breugel in late 1938 and the inspiration he found there for his poem 'Musée des Beaux Arts' about the doomed flyer Icarus, 'a boy falling out of the sky', illustrate how, in the 1930s, even an image created 500 years ago could seem, in cryptographic form, to express contemporary feelings of wonder and horror at the new, violent and sublime culture of the sky.[28]

Another late 1930s poem by Auden illustrates the point in detail. 'Dover' was written at the very height of Auden's early reputation in Britain and indeed was first published in *New Verse* in November 1937 in a special 'Auden Double Number'. The issue featured a photograph of the poet, a bibliography, a manuscript facsimile, essays on his work, and tributes from such diverse characters as Allen Tate, Graham Greene, and Dylan Thomas. Geoffrey Grigson, the periodical's editor, commented that 'One of the most frequent images used by Auden is the image of the frontier, the line between the known and the feared, the past and the future, and the conscious and everything beyond control.' He added:

[26] Larkin, *Poems*, p. 136.

[27] Auden, 'XIV' [from *In Time of War*] in *The English Auden: Poems, Essays and Dramatic Writings 1927–1939*, ed. Edward Mendelson (London: Faber and Faber, 1977), p. 256. Hereafter, '*The English Auden*'.

[28] Auden, 'Musée des Beaux Arts', ibid., p. 237.

'Auden lives very much in this frightening border territory (Dover is a border town).'[29]

Auden's 'Dover' mobilizes the intensely symbolic quality of the territory along the southern coast, vital to the iconography of Britain as an island apart, 'a precious stone set in a silver sea'. Auden mentions the 'historical cliffs' that mark the terminus of England and everything that, from an insular perspective, is, after a short watery hiatus, beyond the boundary. The poem imagines a series of concentric circles of which England is the centre: outside lie France, Europe, the world, all that terrifying open-ended space which Auden summarizes as 'the immense improbable atlas'.[30]

In later life Larkin dismissed 'Dover' as 'myopic'.[31] But ideas associated with seeing, though not sharp visual images, are a key to the poem's movement. It begins in a visually privative key by invoking darkness, concealment and obscured views: 'steep roads, a tunnel', the 'dominant Norman castle flood-lit at night', and the mournfully satiric images of the lighthouses 'that guard for ever the made privacy of this bay | Like twin stone dogs opposed on a gentleman's gate'.[32] After these circlings around the visual realm, the poem becomes fully ocular, so to speak, looking for two stanzas first through the eyes of the 'departing migrants' and then through the 'eyes of the returning' as people, the human waves, flood into and out of Dover harbour with a tide-like, lunar-influenced regularity and inexorability. Then, in the sixth stanza, the eye of the poem is drawn back into the town, registering voyeuristically, like the town's inhabitants themselves, the 'vows, the tears, the slight emotional signals' of the travellers and their well-wishers.

'Dover' lingers on this horizontal, land-based world until it describes soldiers, 'Fresh and silly as girls from a high class academy'. Capitalizing on this sudden abrupt metaphoric translation of men into women, Auden angles the poem into two entirely different dimensions, space as opposed to time, air as opposed to land.

[29] 'Auden as a Monster', New Verse, 26–7 (Nov. 1937), pp. 13–14. At the time when Auden wrote his poem, Dover was something of an artistic enclave. Various coteries of writers spent longish working holidays in this port in the 1930s, and it was the subject of various paintings made on commission, including one by William Coldstream's friend Graham Bell, secured for him from the IBM corporation by Sir Kenneth Clark.

[30] Auden, 'Dover', in The English Auden, p. 222.

[31] Larkin, 'Beyond a Joke' (1955) [review of Betjeman, A Few Late Chrysanthemums], repr. in Larkin, Further Requirements: Interviews, Broadcasts, Statements and Book Reviews 1952–85, ed. Anthony Thwaite (London: Faber and Faber, 2001), 147.

[32] Auden, 'Dover', in The English Auden, pp. 222–3.

> Above them, expensive and lovely as a rich child's toy,
> The aeroplanes fly in the new European air . . .
>
> High over France the full moon, cold and exciting
> Like one of those dangerous flatterers one meets and loves
> When one is very unhappy, returns the human stare.

In that airborne world, as Auden puts it in a strange, wholly monosyllabic line: 'the cry of the gulls at dawn is sad like work.' Auden's sky in 'Dover' is humanized and populated: he mentions the aeroplanes flying back and forth (and thus associated in their movements with the ships below that move people in and out of England), and the gulls whose plaintive cry is 'sad like work'. As if the new inhabitedness of the sky has overflowed from the literal to the figural, causing even the inorganic to become anthropomorphized, he writes that 'the full moon . . . returns the human stare'. Auden's poem builds to its air-dominated ending with planes, the sun, the moon, and gulls, with dawns and the dusk in which 'each one prays for himself'. Like a fading day, 'Dover' dwindles out: it has no resonant conclusions to astonish us with, the poem verbally fades into the darkness in the same way in which the night covers up the travellers and soldiers. The provisional quality of the conclusion, with its registration of 'temporary heroes' and its admission only that 'Some of these people are happy', makes us feel that time and history are bound to continue even though the poem has stopped.

We need to turn now to Larkin's own skies and, more particularly, to the skies which hang over the poetry he wrote at Oxford. But before doing so, I must confess to a small, accidental fascination with Larkin's career at Oxford University. It stems from my interest in a minor character in the Larkin story, purportedly one of the plagues of his life there, the Dean of St John's College at the time, W. G. Moore. Moore was evidently given the unenviable task of trying to exercise moral and practical control over the young, booze-fuelled, jazz-jarred Larkin. An extract from one of Larkin's wartime letters to Norman Iles grumbles: 'Moore called me into his room for a little straight talk on the evils of drinking. Until now he's just regarded me as a drunk sot, but my persistently good reports are beginning to shake him.'[33] Perhaps it is Moore whom Larkin is thinking about in 'Dockery and Son' (1963) when the

---

[33] Larkin, *Letters*, p. 49.

speaker recalls the escapades of his university years and how 'still half-tight |
We used to stand before that desk, to give | "Our version" of "these incidents
last night".[34] Moore is the butt of several comic exchanges between Larkin
and Amis in the 1940s. One letter from Amis to Larkin ends: 'Mr. Moore
would like to see you at a quarter past nine.'[35] And on a list of 'Twelve Bad
Men' which Amis compiled in 1946 for Larkin's perusal—it is in Zachary
Leader's edition of Amis's letters—alongside the names of 'bad men' such
as the clarinetist Woody Herman, the author of Beowulf, Chaucer, and the
popular novelist Warwick Deeping, there is the name of 'Moore.'[36]

Truly a heinous, sour, puritanical character by Larkin and Amis's accounts,
W. G. Moore was, as it happens, the present author's grandfather. It is curi-
ous to see just how different the same person can seem to different people.
For Larkin, W. G. Moore, like a humourless father, stood at the sinister apex
of the university's fun-prevention police. In my mind he is a benign grand-
father: all smiles, indulgence, a player of long games of cricket conducted
with a tennis ball, a poetry-lover, and, incidentally, the individual who gen-
tly introduced this writer to alcohol (in the form of Woodpecker cider).[37] He

[34] 'Dockery and Son', in Larkin, Poems, p. 152.

[35] The Letters of Kingsley Amis, ed. Zachary Leader (London: HarperCollins, 2000), p. 14.

[36] Ibid., p. 59.

[37] For brief details of the life of W. G. Moore (1905–78), see his obituary: 'Dr. W. G. Moore',
The Times, 3 Feb 1978, p. 16. He was also the model for the fictional detective Gervase Fen in the
novels that Larkin's Oxford friend Bruce Montgomery wrote under the pseudonym of 'Edmund
Crispin'. Fen was first introduced in The Case of the Gilded Fly (1944) and reappeared in eight further
crime novels that Montgomery published between 1944 and 1954, including the classic, The Moving
Toyshop (1946). Larkin writes a little further about Moore in this connection in 'Fen Country: Twenty-
Six Stories by Edmund Crispin' (1979), repr. in Larkin, Further Requirements, p. 124. Explaining there
that the name 'Gervase Crispin' in Michael Innes's Hamlet, Revenge! had given Montgomery the
first half of his detective's name and the second half of his pseudonym, Larkin continued that the
other half of the detective's name, 'Fen', 'evoked his Oxford tutor, W. G. Moore, by way of 'Lead,
Kindly Light' ('O'er moor and fen'). Fen reproduced much of Moore's appearance, and some of
his mannerisms, but the caricature was an affectionate one: in the last year of his life Bruce wrote
a tribute that was quoted at Moore's memorial service, for 'Fen' predeceased his creator by some
nine months only in 1978.

Like Eliot, Larkin was a poet mesmerized by names: instances include 'Warlock-Williams',
'Dockery', and 'Balokowsky'. One of his famous names is associated, as Moore was, with St John's
College, Oxford. Motion notes that Larkin's poem 'Mr. Bleaney', completed in Hull in the first half
of 1955 was originally titled 'Mr. Gridley' (LWL, pp. 247–8). Why the change? During Larkin's time
at St John's, there was a young physicist working at the college named Brebis Bleaney. Bleaney
(1915–2006), was an undergraduate at St John's from 1934–7 and earned a doctorate in physics in
1939. During the war Bleaney was working on radar techniques. He subsequently became first
Fellow and Tutor in Physics at St John's in 1947, and was later a Professor of Physics at Oxford.

was also, during the war-time period in Oxford when Larkin and all his co-conspirators were regularly being hauled before him, an air-raid warden.

The Oxford years (1940–1943) constitute the period when Larkin's obsession with Auden's poetry was at its zenith. Larkin had started reading Auden while he was a schoolboy in Coventry, and he continued to study Auden's poetry intensively when he arrived at Oxford. In this extract from an auto-biographical essay, written in 1943 but describing his enthusiastic response to Auden and Isherwood in Oxford in the autumn of 1940, Auden's visual power as a poet, figured in terms of a star, comes across as both life-giving and elevated (so much so that it becomes almost disabling):

Auden rose like a sun…It is impossible to convey the intensity of the delight felt…when a poet is found speaking a language thrilling and beautiful, and *describing things* so near to everyday life that their once-removedness strikes like a strange cymbal. We entered the land, books in hand, like travellers with a guidebook … *Poems, The Orators* and *Look, Stranger!* seemed three fragments of revealed truth…To read *The Journal of an Airman* was like being allowed half an hour's phone conversation with God.[38]

In the summer term of 1940 Larkin took a course of lectures on psycho-analysis with John Layard, a learned, eccentric figure (part anthropologist, part psychologist), who had strongly influenced Auden in Berlin at the end of the 1920s and who had remained a friend right up to the time when Auden left for the United States in 1939. Andrew Motion remarks that Layard was 'beguiling' to Larkin largely 'because of his association with Auden'.[39] 'The Village of the Heart', the collection which Larkin compiled in March 1940, took its title directly from a 1934 Auden sonnet. And Larkin's first poem to be published outside school or undergraduate circles, the sonnet 'Ultimatum', which appeared in the *Listener* in late November 1940, is paralysingly Audenesque, not least in its almost voluptuous sense of menace and doom:

> For on our island is no railway station,
> There are no tickets for the Vale of Peace,
> No docks where trading ships and seagulls pass.
>
> Remember stories you read when a boy
> —The shipwrecked sailor gaining safety by
> His knife, treetrunk, and lianas—for now
> You must escape, or perish saying no.[40]

[38] Cited in Motion, *LWL*, pp. 43–4.   [39] Ibid., p. 60.   [40] Larkin, *Early Poems*, p. 97.

Larkin was well aware of the Auden virus which he had caught by the time he reached university. 'Postscript: On Imitating Auden' from 1940 begins 'Imitating you is fairly easy'.[41]

He remained deeply under Auden's sway throughout the second half of that year, a fact remarkable because by the middle of 1940 Auden's reputation had started to suffer from innumerable assaults in Britain: the result of his apparent refusal to return home as the war went increasingly badly for the country. By the autumn of 1940, Auden had become a kind of poetic pariah in Britain. In late 1941, in the wake of Auden's journey to the United States and into poetic exile, the sociologist Tom Harrisson surveyed two years of wartime book publication in Britain for the journal *Horizon*. He came to an extraordinary conclusion: 'To judge from most war books,' he wrote, 'Britain is fighting this war to protect the world against Auden and Picasso, the Jews and any form of collectivisation.'[42] John Heath-Stubbs and Sidney Keyes were dominant undergraduates on the Oxford poetry scene in 1941. When they published in 1941 an anthology *Eight Oxford Poets* under the editorship at Routledge of Auden's old enemy Herbert Read, Heath-Stubbs and Keyes declared that the contributors are '*Romantic* writers' with 'on the whole, little sympathy with the Audenian school of poets'.[43] It was apparently on those grounds that Larkin's work was not included in the book.

Auden's influence on the young Larkin is apparent in many forms. For example, Larkin's earliest poems, the ones which he wrote at the end of his schooldays in Coventry and in his years at Oxford, show that his original sky-awareness was intrinsically connected both with the prosaic reality of seeing planes flying *and* with his experience of Auden's poetry. Indeed, the two subjects were inseparable. Instances include 'Street Lamps', quoted earlier, written in September 1939, where Larkin watches the night slink 'like a puma, down the sky' and hears 'the hours topple slowly past' until 'grey planes splinter the gloom at last'.[44] There is also 'Planes Passing' from 1940, where he writes (in pastiche of Stephen Spender's work as well as Auden's) about how 'The guns | Tap the slack drumhead of the sky | Where separate bombers

[41] Ibid., p. 127.   [42] 'War Books', *Horizon*, 4.24 (Dec. 1941), p. 420.
[43] Italics in original; cited in Tolley, 'Introduction' to Larkin, *Early Poems*, pp. xvii–xviii. See Motion, *LWL*, p. 45, for Larkin's dislike of Keyes.
[44] Larkin, *Early Poems*, p. 22.

crawl, | Leaving soft trails of sound'.[45] There are also 'Midsummer Night, 1940' with its 'angels yawning in an empty heaven' amongst 'Alternate shows of dynamite and rain' and the eerie Christmas 1940 poem: 'Out in the lane I pause: the night | Impenetrable round me stands, | And overhead, where roofline ends, | The starless sky | Black as a bridge.'[46] Other examples include the 1942 poem which begins 'As the pool hits the diver, or the white cloud | Gathers the plane scudding through the sky' and the 1943 poem, which Larkin published in *Oxford Poetry*, 'A Stone Church Damaged by a Bomb'.[47] In the latter, a dummy run for 'Church-Going', the aerial context is obvious: 'Planted deeper than roots, | This chiselled, flung-up faith | Runs and leaps against the sky.'[48]

Larkin may have continued to write Audenesque poems until as late as 1943. In retrospect, though, it is clear that Larkin's poetry of the Audenesque, epitomized by poems featuring a trafficked, populated sky, began slowly to come to an end on 14 November 1940. Here is Andrew Motion:

On 14 November 1940, at 7 in the evening, the German Luftwaffe bombed Coventry, dropping 500 tons of explosive, killing 554 people and seriously injuring 1,000 others. Large parts of the city were obliterated. The cathedral in which Larkin had been christened was ruined. Three-quarters of the car and aeroplane plant were destroyed. Two thousand homes were made uninhabitable. It was Hitler's first blitz on an English city—something Sydney [Larkin's father] had imagined might happen and which his family had always feared. When Larkin heard the news on the wireless in St John's he immediately turned to Noel Hughes, wondering what to do. Nothing, they decided: wait until word came from their families. But after two days, when still no news had arrived, they decided to go and see for themselves.[49]

In *Jill* Larkin gives a striking fictional version of the journey he made back to Coventry ('Huddlesford' in the novel). The episode begins with a powerful account of the way that the Blitz-era newspapers extracted 'every ounce of horror and pathos they could' from their stories and photographs of the

---

[45] Ibid., p. 84.   [46] Ibid, pp. 99–100, 137.   [47] Ibid., p. 181.   [48] Ibid., p. 200.

[49] Motion, *LWL*, pp. 47–8. Motion writes that the 'devastation continued to haunt [Larkin] for many years' after this first raid on Coventry (ibid., p. 49). Larkin's wartime letters contain multiple references to the destruction of large parts of his home city, all couched in the semi-humorous, pseudo-masochistic jargon in which he customarily wrote to friends (for example, the letters to Norman Iles of 16 Nov. 1940 and 16 April 1941, cited in ibid., p. 49). In the early autumn of 1942 Larkin would return early to Oxford for the Michaelmas quarter in order to serve as a college firewatcher (ibid., p. 79).

raid: 'The dominating picture showed an old man gazing fiercely up at the sky: it was captioned THEY'LL GET IT BACK!'[50]

When the novel's protagonist John Kemp arrives in post-raid 'Huddlesford' the sky is everywhere in his perceptions: 'Under the sour sky and occasional unwilling sun the streets seemed menacing.' And later:

The moon, by day a thin pith-coloured segment, hung brilliantly in the sky, spilling its lights down on to the skeletons of roofs, blank walls and piles of masonry that undulated like a frozen sea. It had never seemed so bright. The wreckage looked like ruins of an age over and done with.[51]

Once John discovers that his childhood house has survived this first wave of bombing, he makes his way back to the railway station and goes into a pub for some food and drink before starting the return journey to Oxford. Inside are the landlady and a group of six morose men. A conversation shudders into life, and the sky reference in it seals shut the Huddlesford air-raid passage by recalling the headline in the paper which John had seen before he started out from Oxford:

'I reckon they'll do this to everywhere,' said the young man, looking up again. 'Everywhere. There won't be a town left standing.'

His voice had a half-hysterical eager note as if he desired this more than anything.

'But they'll get it back, the papers say,' said the bowler-hatted man, wiping his nose.

Nobody spoke, sitting half-listening in the silence.[52]

Jill was written from around the summer of 1943 until the summer of 1944.[53] Read in the light of Larkin's earlier, Audenesque sky poetry, the novel's air-raids seem like a fiery expurgation of Auden's influence. As the end of the train ride approaches bringing Kemp back to Oxford, he reflects how the destruction

represented the end of his use for the place. It meant no more to him now, and so it was destroyed: it seemed symbolic, a kind of annulling of his childhood. The thought excited him. It was as if he had been told: all the past is cancelled . . . Now

[50] Larkin, *Jill: A Novel* (1946; London: Faber and Faber, 1975), p. 211. Hereafter 'Larkin, *Jill*'.

[51] Ibid., pp. 212, 215.   [52] Ibid., p. 218.   [53] Motion, *LWL*, pp. 106–7, 124.

there is a fresh start for you: you are no longer governed by what has gone before.[54]

Larkin wrote the novel's descriptions of the effects of aerial bombardment at a time which coincides almost exactly with the moment when Auden largely vanished as a presence in Larkin's poetry as also planes did, completely, from Larkin's skies.

Larkin's early poems such as 'Street Lamps' and 'Planes Passing' had described a 'Dover'-like populated, humanized sky filled with bombers and other planes, an Audenesque sky. But this work is categorized by Larkin scholars as his juvenilia. In Larkin's mature canon, in the four collections of poetry he published during his lifetime, the skies have been totally emptied of human presence—the word 'plane' does not appear once. In these post-war collections, flying is something which only birds, clouds, and oaths do. Such an absence, such a beautiful nothingness in the sky, is richly suggestive, especially since Larkin's early poems mention airborne craft with relative frequency. Larkin's later writing lavishes loving, lingering attention on these emptied skies—the 'deep blue air' which shows 'Nothing, and is nowhere, and is endless'. But their cleared, inhuman vistas are, for all their beauty, traumatically bare and pure.

Take the poem 'Here', composed in 1961, and made up of four eight-line stanzas which visually evoke Yeats's *ottava rima* poems ('Sailing to Byzantium', for example). The stanzas in Larkin's poem case are in fact more modestly constructed from two quatrains with, in each stanza, two contrasting rhyme-schemes. 'Here' follows a familiar modern arc for the topographic poem (very much as Auden's 'Dover' does too): it begins in Baedeker-like fashion with a description of the ways of getting to the place in question and follows with a survey of the centre of human activity, the town or city in question and the inhabitants of the town. Then, since Larkin's poem is about a town very near the sea, it pulls away from buildings and streets and towards the ocean and the sky. Since the topographic poem usually ends with a turn to nature, 'Here' concludes at the water's edge.

---

[54] *Jill*, 219. My reading of Larkin's exorcism of Auden from his poetry is at odds with the standard 'literary' explanation which stresses the visit of Vernon Watkins, with his enthusiastic advocacy of Yeats's work, to the English Club at Oxford in February 1943. But it is fair to say that Watkins's advocacy of the Irish poet's more vatic and nationalistic stance may have prepared Larkin's imagination to carry out the fiery anti-Auden rite of expurgation enacted in the Blitz scenes of *Jill* in the next year or so.

Larkin's poem was written some twenty-four years after Auden's 'Dover'. Those twenty-four years witnessed a world war whose decisive arena was the sky, and subsequently saw long-range commercial air travel become possible and then even relatively common. Larkin once praised Auden for making it possible to write about modern experience in poetry, and 'Here' lugubriously registers the merchandise of modern supermarkets and department stores: the 'Cheap suits, red kitchen-ware, sharp shoes, iced lollies, | Electric mixers, toasters, washers, driers' beloved of the 'cut-price crowd'. But, continuously 'Swerving east... to solitude' like the railway line with which the poem begins, 'Here' moves away from explicitly modern scenery to 'Isolate villages' and a margin of increasingly old-fashioned solitude. We probably expect 'Here', a poem written later in history than 'Dover', to be more familiar with and aware of everyday realities like travel through the air. Yet the reverse is the case: the earlier poem by Auden, with its peopled sky as well as its constant maritime traffic out of and into British waters, feels or seems more naturalistic and contemporary than the 'isolate' poem which Larkin wrote almost a quarter-of-a-century later.

'Here' initially hurtles forward: the first sentence of this 32-line poem ends mid-way through line 25, once the poem has arrived at the place to which the title refers. (The asymmetrical thematic shape prefigures the organization of 'High Windows', where prosaic actualities take up much of the space in the poem only to yield to a shorter visionary conclusion.) 'Here' is a world beyond the 'urban yet simple' inhabitants of Hull, beyond the weirdly surreal and sordid 'terminate and fishy-smelling | Pastoral of ships up streets, the slave museum, | Tattoo-shops'. But even before Larkin reaches his bleakly exciting confrontation with the elements, the sky has already been present in the poem at a subliminal level, first as something mentioned in passing, literally, 'solitude | Of skies and scarecrows', and then indirectly in a series of vistas and gleaming reflections: 'The piled gold clouds, the shining gull-marked mud'. The sky is the place towering over tall buildings and other structures, 'domes and statues, spires and cranes'. But the poem aspires to get beyond this crowded, built-up urban world, out into a more direct encounter with the emptiness which the sky contains. It ends in the silent and lonely world of the region known as Holderness. 'Here' finishes at dawn, with the speaker alone, looking east at the sun. In contrast to Auden's southern 'Dover', Larkin's north-eastern 'Here', reaches a terminus, rather than a point of departure, at its end. The emphatic, clinching finality of the last lines makes us feel that we have crossed into a place where time and travel have, at least for now, been transcended. This is the place of the poem's final stanza, the place of natural processes, fertility, vision, security, stasis:

> Here silence stands
> Like heat. Here leaves unnoticed thicken,
> Hidden weeds flower, neglected waters quicken,
> Luminously-peopled air ascends;
> And past the poppies bluish neutral distance
> Ends the land suddenly beyond a beach
> Of shapes and shingle. Here is unfenced existence:
> Facing the sun, untalkative, out of reach.[55]

Still, the difference between a crowded sky (Auden's) and an empty sky (Larkin's)—is that all there is to it? To paraphrase Conrad, 'What is all this really *about?*'

In an essay he wrote in 1948 Lionel Trilling commented that 'Every war breeds its traitors, for treason is bound up in the very idea of allegiance. But the recent war, with its fifth columns, collaborators, and quislings, was exceptional in the variety and extent of the treason it bred, and it brought the question of national allegiance to the forefront of our minds.'[56] This was never more evident than in the case of wartime poetry in England. Both Auden's and Larkin's work engaged profoundly with the 'question of national allegiance'. For both of them language and nationhood, and therefore poetry and nationhood, were interconnected.

From 'the start,' the scholar Benedict Anderson writes, 'the nation was conceived in language, not in blood'. Anderson sees nationality as a kind of organic, indeed almost bodily, element of human identity, as something not imposed on but actually constitutive of being: 'in the modern world everyone can, should, will "have" a nationality, as he or she "has" a gender.'[57] As a result, the sense of nationality, blurred or clear, reaches into the very pinnacles and turrets of the mind, and, it may be, into the skies of poetry.

---

[55] Larkin, *Poems*, pp. 136–7.

[56] Lionel Trilling, 'Treason in the Modern World' (1948), repr. in Trilling, *Speaking of Literature and Society*, ed. Diana Trilling (New York: Harcourt, Brace, Jovanovich, 1980), p. 230.

[57] Benedict Anderson, *Imagined Communities: Reflections on the Origin and Spread of Nationalism*, rev. edn. (London: Verso, 1991), p. 5.

The idea of the nation must also be *sustained* in language, not in blood. And perhaps the nation can be ended in language too. In the title poem to his 1940 collection *Another Time*, Auden wrote that:

> So many try to say Not Now,
> So many have forgotten how
> To say I Am, and would be
> Lost, if they could, in history.
>
> Bowing, for instance, with such old-world grace
> To a proper flag in a proper place,
> Muttering like ancients as they stump upstairs
> Of Mine and His or Ours and Theirs.

'Ours and Theirs', which only 'ancients' mutter about for Auden, are almost sacred terms for Larkin. This is why he and his friends reacted with incurious vehemence and lack of generosity to Auden's later work. For Larkin and other Movement writers, the 'question of national allegiance' became paramount, as, from a completely different angle, it was for Auden too. Amis wrote to Larkin in 1949: 'Talking of shit, I have read some of The [Age of] anxiety, by that crazy Awdontype, and find it Impossible piss plashing in pot, Shameful shagbaggery, and shite surely... The sooner he gets to be a yank the better.'[58] Compare the comments of John Wain, another writer associated, like Larkin, with the Movement. In his 1955 essay 'The Reputation of Ezra Pound', Wain wrote that for younger authors in the post-war period: 'The '30s were no use, at any rate as far as the main line was concerned, the Auden line: it was worn out even before it got smashed, and what smashed it decisively was not the war, but Auden's renunciation of English nationality.'

Responding in 1982 to a question about the Poet Laureateship, Larkin commented that 'Poetry and sovereignty are very primitive things' and that he 'like[d] to think of them being united in this way, in England'.[59] Thus Auden's great gestures—his severance of poetry and sovereignty, his renunciation of his status as an *English* poet—were almost treasonous to Larkin. In a 1960 review of Auden's *Homage to Clio*, Larkin bemoaned Auden's disappearance from the English scene in 1939. When that happened, Larkin claimed, Auden had 'lost his key subject and emotion... and abandoned his audience

---

[58] Letter of 9 March 1949, in *The Letters of Kingsley Amis*, p. 201.
[59] 'An Interview with [The] Paris Review' (1982), repr. in Larkin, *Required Writing*, p. 75.

together with their common dialect and concerns'. Larkin denigrated the 'individual and cosmopolitan path' that the later Auden had followed and offered more than a hint that Auden's homosexuality was the root-cause. He also denounced the poet's new non-English poetic language, calling it a 'wilful jumble of Age-of-Plastic nursery rhyme, ballet folklore, and Hollywood Lemprière served up with a lisping archness'.[60] (Larkin is rehashing here many of the same phrases he had first used to describe Auden's *The Shield of Achilles* in 1955.) In subsequent years, repeating this narrative, Larkin was reduced to nothing much more than name-calling, labelling the later Auden, the poet who had once risen in front of him 'like a sun', 'a ponderous windbag'.

Auden was fully aware of the stakes involved in his move to America. On Ischia in 1956 or 1957, he talked to an acquaintance about the case of Guy Burgess, one of the most notorious modern instances of British treachery, and one in which Auden had been tangentially involved. 'I know exactly why Guy Burgess went to Moscow,' he told his interlocutor.

It wasn't enough to be a queer and a drunk. He had to revolt still more to break away from it all. That's just what I've done by becoming an American citizen. You can become an Italian or French citizen—and that's all right. But become an American citizen and you've crossed to the wrong side of the tracks.[61]

At issue in Larkin's loathing of the later Auden, as in the manner in which Auden's later poetry migrates beyond the 'common dialect' of his English audience, is the question of national affiliation. That question also subtends the extraordinary emptying-out of Larkin's skies after 1943, the year when Larkin's devotion to Auden's poetry faded. In Larkin's poems the quiet and cold world of air, a huge void full of almost nothing, is a symbolic expression of a still deeper, more anguishing subject.

The sky is the place where the history of the modern English psyche was rewritten, because it was in the sky that some of the oldest and most significant images of national self-definition collided with modern realities. As early as 1908, before much sustained flying had been done (Blériot flew across the English channel the following year), H. G. Wells had written *The War in the Air* in which Bert Smallways gazes down at Manhattan from an

---

[60] 'What's Become of Wystan?'(1960), repr. ibid., pp. 126–7.
[61] Robin Maugham, *Escape from the Shadows: An Autobiography* (New York: McGraw-Hill, 1973), p. 193.

aeroplane before the apocalyptic conflict starts and gets 'glimpses that such disasters were not only possible now in this strange, gigantic, foreign New York, but also in London...that the little island in the silver seas was at the end of its immunity.'[62]

This was exactly how the advent of aviation was greeted in England. Indeed, by the 1930s this new vulnerability had become a national obsession. A typical volume of prognostications from the 1930s is *Our Future in the Air* by Brigadier-General P. R. C. Groves, published in London in 1935. Groves calls aviation 'the most portentous, physical phenomenon of our time'; asserts, perfectly accurately, that flight accelerates 'the replacement of national economies by a world economy' and that it revolutionizes 'the character of warfare'. For Britain, Groves writes, the military implications of air-power are that 'it has taken from the Navy and Army their characteristics as shields' and has 'deprived us of the inestimable advantage of our insular position'.[63] Or as Hitler himself menacingly put it in one of his speeches in October 1939, taunting Churchill by ridiculing Churchill's favourite 'island' metaphor for England,

guns with greater range will be drawn up, and on both sides the destruction will reach ever farther into the countryside. What cannot be reached by long-range projectiles will be destroyed by aircraft...And this struggle unto destruction will not remain restricted to the continent. No, it will reach across the Sea. There are *no more islands* today.[64]

The mandated structure of the typical modern English poem requires that a lyric build towards an epiphanic ending, often image-based, through which, like a sun rising behind clouds, some revelation of a deeper truth emerges. The meanings come in the ends. Larkin in particular is a master of such resounding endings. Christopher Ricks has mapped out the exquisitely calibrated conclusions to Larkin's poems and has explained the strategies by which his final lines can achieve the 'apophthegmatic weight of classical art'.[65] Ricks's main example is 'An Arundel Tomb' but his perception about Larkin's gift for

[62] Cited in Gillian Beer, 'The Island and the Aeroplane: The Case of Virginia Woolf', in Beer, *Virginia Woolf: The Common Ground* (Edinburgh: Edinburgh University Press, 1996), p. 151.

[63] P. R. C. Groves, *Our Future in the Air* (London: Harrap, 1935).

[64] My italics; Max Domarus, *Hitler: Speeches and Proclamations 1932–1945*, vol. 3: *The Years 1939 to 1940*, trans. Chris Wilcox (Würzburg: Domarus, 1997), pp. 1847–8.

[65] Ricks, 'Like Something Almost Being Said', in Anthony Thwaite (ed.), *Larkin at Sixty* (London: Faber and Faber, 1982), p. 121.

the decisive, clear-cut ending is also true of many other poems Larkin wrote. At the end of 'The Whitsun Weddings', for example, 'as the tightened brakes took hold, there swelled | A sense of falling, like an arrow-shower | Sent out of sight, somewhere becoming rain.' (Here is yet another Larkinesque sky and weather image, and again one subliminally linked with the war since Larkin told Jean Hartley that it came from a memory from 'a film he had seen as a young man during the war... the arrows fired by the English bowmen in Laurence Olivier's film of *Henry V*.'[66])

Ends and limits, which Larkin's poems such as 'Here' emphasize, demarcate space, giving it a shape, an inside and an outside. But when Auden looks up in 'Dover' and sees how 'expensive and lovely as a rich child's toy, | The aeroplanes fly in the new European air, | On the edge of that air that makes England of minor importance' he writes a poem with a deliberately indefinite structure. In Auden's poem the sun is setting on the whole notion of an 'island', as his next lines make clear: 'the tides warn bronzing bathers of a cooling star, | With half its history done.'[67] Auden's poem, no longer a self-contained entity with a clear perimeter, calculatedly fades out, as if reflecting the sense of a dwindling security in England itself, 'this little world,' no longer protected by 'a silver sea | Which serves it in the office of a wall'. By contrast, Larkin's poems, like little worlds, insist on strongly articulating their physical and metaphorical borders, especially in their endings. In 'Here' Larkin stands on Holderness and sees how the land, like his poem, firmly 'Ends' 'beyond a beach of shapes and shingle.' 'Here is unfenced existence,' the poem continues emphatically, 'Facing the sun, untalkative, out of reach.'

Unfenced existence is existence 'out of reach'. Out of reach of what? Of the jabbering 'cut-price crowd' in Hull? Of the earth-bound, gloom-ridden self, since the best experience of existence is in solitary contemplation of the empty sky? Yes, perhaps. But Larkin's poem contains a further suggestion. In fantasy, at dawn, at the spot where 'Ends the land suddenly beyond a beach', England is once again 'out of reach' of the machines which have destroyed the nation's traditional boundaries. England is, once more, 'isolate'; it is once more an island as long as this strongly-defined, well-wrought poem lasts. For the duration of 'Here', the nation's skies are once again empty.

[66] Motion, *LWL*, p. 288.   [67] Auden, 'Dover', in *The English Auden*, p. 222.

It would be wrong to counterpoint too sharply Auden and Larkin. Auden might be the weightless, rootless citizen of the world writing the death of the idea of England in his poetry and by the 1960s dramatizing himself as an 'air-borne instrument' who watches 'Dwindling below me on the plane, | The roofs of one more audience | I shall not see again'. But Larkin is not merely the subject of 'Her Majesty', the hermit of Hull, that 'Isolate city spread alongside water, | Posted with white towers,' who 'keeps her face Half-turned to Europe, lonely northern daughter, | Holding through centuries her separate place'.[68]

What is post-war England, this separate place, for Larkin? With sensitivity and finesse Larkin's writing preserves a little longer in literary form the sense of the nation's beauty distinctness, isolatic and value. But the brilliance of the holding operation only draws attention to the extremity of the situation which it confronts and tries to repress; the ghostly blanknesses of Larkin's skies are the signs of the erasures which the poet has made. Larkin's much-bruited melancholy expresses not so much a personal foible as a historical condition, a historical pessimism. Isolated by and in poetic language his England is a haunted, fading, twisted, melancholy world, perhaps not unlike the remote East-Anglian edge of England described by another tortured patriot, Benjamin Britten, in *Peter Grimes*. Larkin writes:

> It seems, just now,
> To be happening so very fast;
> Despite all the land left free
> For the first time I feel somehow
> That it isn't going to last,
>
> That before I snuff it, the whole
> Boiling will be bricked in
> Except for the tourist parts—
> First slum of Europe: a role
> It won't be hard to win,
> With a cast of crooks and tarts.
>
> And that will be England gone,
> The shadows, the meadows, the lanes,
> The guildhalls, the carved choirs.

---

[68] Auden, 'On the Circuit', in *Collected Poems*, rev. edn., ed. Edward Mendelson (1976; New York: Vintage, 1991), pp. 729–30; Larkin, 'Bridge the Living', *Poems* p. 203.

There'll be books; it will linger on
In galleries; but all that remains
For us will be concrete and tyres.

Most things are never meant.
This won't be, most likely; but greeds
And garbage are too thick-strewn
To be swept up now, or invent
Excuses that make them all needs.
I just think it will happen, soon.[69]

If we want to know when England 'started to go', and when a distinctively *English* poetry began to disappear for ever, the poems of both Auden and Larkin suggest that we should turn away from direct observation of the country and look at the history written into, and written out of, the skies.

[69] 'Going, Going', Larkin, *Poems*, p. 190.

3

Counter-Intuitive Larkin

Craig Raine

When I was Poetry Editor at Fabers in 1986, I published Barbara Everett's *Poets in Their Time—from Donne to Larkin*. Charles Monteith, the ex-chairman of Fabers—loveable, lazy, and anecdotal, lord of the late arrival and the long lunch hour—happened to read the chapter on Larkin's 'Sympathy in White Major'. Barbara Everett's argument turned on how much Larkin owed to Gautier's 'Symphonie en blanc majeur'. Charles was incredulous and dismissive. The very idea of 'Philip' being influenced by a foreign poet, he said, with a gentle smile that gradually broadened to show his well-spaced, tawny teeth, was 'ludicrous'. He had fallen for the propaganda—Larkin's bluff, insular, faux-xenophobic self-caricature. Several years before, John Fuller's Sycamore Press had published Larkin's imitation of Baudelaire's 'Femmes Damnées'. That rather gave the lie to Larkin's affectation of insularity, an insularity honed and practised and best illustrated by his answer to Ian Hamilton's question about foreign poetry. Larkin chose the simple ironical expedient of repetition in italics: *Foreign poetry?*[1]

Let me start with an easily understood example of the counter-intuitive in Larkin—'Dublinesque'. We know Larkin abominated the three Ps, Picasso,

---

[1] *Femmes Damnées* (Oxford: Sycamore Press, 1978); 'Foreign poetry?' quoted from a 1964 interview with Ian Hamilton, reprinted in Philip Larkin, *Further Requirements*, ed. Anthony Thwaite (London: Faber and Faber, 2001), p. 25.

Pound, and Charlie Parker, yet 'Dublinesque' is a poem written in free verse. Rare for Larkin. I have been wondering about the significance of Larkin's title 'Dublinesque'. What is the significance of the affix 'esque' here? Normally, it implies something characteristic, something typical, something expected, something formulaic. *Shandyesque*, for instance, something like *Tristram Shandy*—say, a whimsical digressiveness, or in Jane Austen's *Northanger Abbey* the ostentatious buttonholing of a fictive participant reader, not the abstract, token, frequently apostrophized reader of 'Gentle Reader' but someone to argue with, dissent from. At the end of chapter 5 of *Northanger Abbey*, Jane Austen launches an ironic defence of the novel—necessarily ironic because *Northanger Abbey* is an attack on the Gothic novel. Austen laments 'a general wish of decrying the capacity and undervaluing the labour of the novelist, and of slighting the performances which have only genius, wit and taste to recommend them.' She then follows Sterne's example in literalizing the implied reader of any novel. What Sterne does as a novelist is to underline, spell out, the conventions of the novel. Here is Austen aping his example. ' "I am no novel reader—I seldom look into novels—Do not imagine that *I* often read novels—It is really very well for a novel."—Such is the common cant.—"and what are you reading Miss —?" "Oh, it is only a novel!" replies the young lady; while she lays down the novel with affected indifference, or momentary shame…' This is Shandyesque. And it is no accident that Sterne is mentioned, name-checked, on the same page. My point, though, is this. You would never apply 'Shandyesque' to *Tristram Shandy*. That would be otiose, redundant, circular. The 'esque' form is adjectivally reserved for the imitation, whether conscious or unconscious. It is rather like the term 'realistic' which is reserved for imitations of reality, not reality itself. My late colleague, Tony Nuttall had a good example: false teeth are realistic. Real teeth are not.

Larkin's 'Dublinesque', then, is faintly fictive, not Dublin exactly, but Dublin as a literary topos—as we can see from the opening props—those 'stucco *sidestreets*' that make me sceptically alert to the grandeur of stucco in sidestreets. Pebble-dash is more like it. I associate stucco with Eaton Square, those dazzling Antarcticas of expensive whitewash. I quote from Wikepedia: 'due to its "aristocratic" look, baroque looking stucco decoration was used frequently in upper-class apartments of the 19th and early 20th century.' Those 'race-guides and rosaries' are laconic alliterative shorthand, too. They do the job perfectly—too perfectly, perhaps, because they come with a tinge of cliché. A deliberate tinge of cliché, I want to argue. Not quite the accordion for Paris, of course. Altogether subtler. But the two props work like autocomplete on a laptop. We have been here before. This is a short-cut. The two Rs, rosaries and race-guides, summon up the ould sod as surely as R&R would summon up Rest and Recuperation in an American context. And that stucco takes us into the past. This is historical Dublin, perhaps ambiguously prolonged into the present. The scene is anachronistic, or touched with anachronism, and somehow typical. Dublinesque, in fact.

I think we can deduce this from the clothes the mourning prostitutes are wearing: these are period, though they could just conceivably be 1960s and hippy. 'A troop of streetwalkers | In wide flowered hats, | Leg-of-mutton sleeves, | And ankle-length dresses.' The emphasis on clothes you might expect to find in Lawrence, but it is uncharacteristic of Larkin, this itemized wardrobe, and it is another indication that we are looking at the past—even as the poem also persuades us we are looking at the present. Partly because Larkin uses the present tense throughout: 'a funeral passes.'

Repetitions are always interesting in Larkin. Here, there are two. 'There is an air of great friendliness, | As if they were honouring | One they were fond of'. Again: 'A voice is heard singing | Of Kitty or Katy, | As if the name meant once | All love, all beauty.' Those 'as if's, two of them, tell us, inaudibly, at the frontiers of consciousness, that we are watching a simulation, a figment of the past. The first 'as if' is important, too, because it establishes that the dead person is also a streetwalker. It is explanatory. The 'as if' has the sense of 'because'. 'There is an air of great friendliness, | As if [because] they were honouring | One they were fond of'. The usual penumbra of doubt that accompanies 'as if' is muted here. Think about the expression 'As if' on its own. There it means 'completely unlikely'. The second 'as if'—'As if the name meant once | All love, all beauty'—is properly provisional. It isn't the case that the name meant 'All love, all beauty'. The person mourned is a tart. The all-important name is actually indefinite, is either Kitty or Katy. The poem doesn't know which. So 'Dublinesque' becomes a poem in the present and in the past, a poem with implicit strictures and reservations, a poem about sentimentality, actually, whose afflatus—'All love, all beauty' is phoney, *has* to be phoney—and yet demonstrates how powerful, how unstoppable sentimentality can be—and how close to sentiment it is. The last line of the poem overrides—and is intended to override—the reservations seeded everywhere before its sudden, undeniably moving advent.

I hope it is clear that in my non-Derridean way, I have just deconstructed 'Dublinesque'. Larkin is undeceived and deceived in equal measure. He connives at the deception. Connive: 3. To feign ignorance of or fail to take measures against a wrong, thus implying tacit encouragement or consent: The guards were suspected of conniving at the prisoner's escape. [Latin *connivere*, to close the eyes.]

We think Larkin is the unromantic, *l'homme moyen sensuel*, undeceived. But he is romantic. His yearning always gets under the wire, under the wary radar. The poetry is a form of smuggling, an exercise in hidden contraband.

Take 'Reference Back', the poem about Larkin playing jazz records and his mother listening. This poem shares with 'Dublinesque' a nympholepsy— specifically, the convenient idea that the past is a place far enough away for us to indulge the pretence that it is the location of something irrecoverable, something valuable, central even, but lost to us now. Nympholepsy: a frenzy for something unattainable.

'Reference Back' refers in its title to the past. The poem again has some interesting repetitions: '*That was a pretty one*, I heard you call | from the *unsatisfactory* hall | To the *unsatisfactory* room where I | Played record after record, idly, | Wasting my time at home, that you | Looked so much forward to.' Let me make the set-up absolutely clear. Larkin is upstairs in his room. His mother is calling up from the hallway. The room and the hallway are 'unsatisfactory' because the young Larkin is defeating the purpose of his visit, his 'time at home' that his mother had looked forward to. He isn't just wasting time, he's wasting his 'time-at-home', by being remote.

The micro-epiphany he records is 'the sudden bridge' between him and his mother created by their shared pleasure in King Oliver's *Riverside Blues*. The distant past of 'antique negroes', thirty years before, has impinged on the present. What is bridged is the gap between his mother's '*unsatisfactory* age' and Larkin's '*unsatisfactory* prime'. There are, then, four *unsatisfactory*s in 'Reference Back'. I think we can assume that Larkin thinks this near remembered past—when Larkin was in his prime, a condition immediately discounted here—was unsatisfactory.

It is the last stanza which puzzles me and which requires a certain amount of unpacking. 'Truly, though our element is time, | We are not suited to the long perspectives | Open at each instant of our lives.' That seems straightforward. At every moment, we can take the long view. But it doesn't suit us to do so. For two reasons. First, we are confronted by things completely lost: 'long perspectives' 'link us to our losses'. Second, and 'worse', is the consciousness of something, not lost, but depleted, *unsatisfactory*, when compared to its previous state: 'worse, | They show us what we have *as it once was*, | Blindingly undiminished…' Let's look at Larkin's title again: 'Reference Back.' Larkin, past his prime, is looking back on a younger Larkin in his unsatisfactory prime, remembering something he cannot remember and something he can remember. What he can remember is the spark that passed between him and his mother. What he cannot remember is King Oliver and his band recording *Riverside Blues*. Yet the syntax allows cunningly for both. 'And now | I shall, I suppose, always remember how | The flock of notes those antique negroes blew | Out of Chicago air into | A huge remembering pre-electric horn…' Repetitions again, this time of 'remember': 'I shall, I suppose, always remember'—what?—'a huge remembering horn'. A not-quite infinite regressus of memory, in which what is remembered is something remembering. And actually, Larkin cannot remember this because the recording took place only the year after he was born.

I know. Of course, what Larkin will 'always remember' is, in fact, 'the sudden bridge' the jazz made between him and his mother. 'And now | I shall, I suppose, always remember how | The flock of notes those antique negroes blew | Out of Chicago air into | A huge remembering pre-electric horn | The year after I was born | Three decades later made this sudden bridge | From your unsatisfactory age | To my unsatisfactory prime.' The object of the verb 'remember' is 'this sudden bridge'. But for a long syntactic moment, Larkin invites us quite deliberately to think he can remember the impossibly distant past. Why? Because in an imaginary past, sufficiently distant, beyond our ken, is the idea, the ideal. King Oliver isn't playing jazz simply. He is taking part in a miracle where a *flock* of notes is created out of thin air. For a second or two, Larkin seems to have witnessed this miracle. We have an idea of perfection even if we have never experienced it—and if we have to locate it somewhere, the past is the only place, since the present is 'unsatisfactory'. For Larkin the romantic can't quite see this perfection, which is presented to us oxymoronically: 'Blindingly undiminished.' How can he see it is 'undiminished' if its brightness blinds him? Again, though, the paradox is curiously weightless. What we are offered is something stupendous—something stupendous, something beautiful, erected on the slight remark *That was a pretty one.*

The poem insists on two contradictory positions. One, that the past is a convenient fiction where we can house our yearnings. Two, these yearnings were once actually fulfilled, in reality, in the past: 'as it once was'; 'we could have kept it so'. The syntax is affirmative even if the poem ends on a note of inevitable emotional entropy: 'just as though | By acting differently we could have kept it so.'

Sometimes in Larkin, the weighting of a poem can be deceptive, deliberately so. In 'Wild Oats', there are two girls, but only one of them, the 'friend in specs', is described intensively. The poem appears to be about Larkin's sclerotic emotions: 'an agreement | That I was too selfish, withdrawn, | And easily bored to love. | Well, useful to get that learnt.' There Larkin stands, heartless in the dock, as meagre as Camus's Meursault. 'Wild Oats' is an ironic title: there is nothing wild in this notation of emotional failure with its drolly observed ragged endgame: 'Parting, after about five | rehearsals.'

Initially, the poem seems to be an account of duffers like that given to Jenny Bunn by Graham McClintoch in Kingsley Amis's *Take a Girl Like You*. You'll remember that Graham kisses Jenny and she responds politely. Graham immediately picks up on the lack of ardour, the subtle rebuff, and unburdens himself of a credo (chapter 14) that divides the world into the attractive and the unattractive. Jenny is attractive, Graham is unattractive. 'You can't imagine,' he tells her, 'what's it's like not to know what it is to meet an attractive person who's also attracted to you, can you? [A fine obstacle course: the Amis prose style already in its hobbled stride.] Because unattractive men don't want unattractive girls, you see. They want attractive girls. They merely *get* unattractive girls. I think a lot of people feel vaguely when they see two duffers marrying that the duffers must prefer it that way. Which is rather like saying that slum-dwellers would rather live in slums than anywhere else.'

All of Larkin's focus and attention seems concentrated on the failure of two duffers to marry. We are given the inventory of emotional failure, item by item: 'Wrote over four hundred letters, | Gave a ten-guinea ring | I got back in the end [In the end! The phrase adumbrates an elided struggle of competing mulishness], and met | At numerous cathedral cities | Unknown to the clergy.' In so far as the other girl appears, her demeanour is tinged with amused contempt: 'I believe | I met beautiful twice. She was trying | Both times (so I thought) not to laugh.' Then Larkin reveals that he has kept two snapshots of beautiful in his wallet—snapshots he describes as 'unlucky charms'. Unlucky charms: a wry throwaway, a bathetic inversion of 'lucky charms'. The tone is undramatic, downbeat, *ironic*, but the import is otherwise. The import is romantic. Why has Larkin kept the two snaps? They are introduced as an afterthought—by way of being by the way. But they are freighted with mute significance. The true significance of the snaps is to be found in the first stanza, where Larkin's unromantic, comic delivery—'the whole shooting match'—deliberately masks his deep romantic involvement. It is easy to miss its significance. 'Faces in those days sparked | The whole shooting match off, and I doubt | If ever one had like hers.' *And I doubt | If ever one had like hers.* He is smitten. 'But it was the friend I took out.' Despite this, he goes on being smitten—hence the snapshots in the wallet and hence the failure of the relationship with the friend. They may have an 'agreement | That I was too selfish, withdrawn, | And easily bored to love', but Larkin, the poem whispers—barely audibly but unmistakably—is already deeply, helplessly, inextricably in love with the other girl, the 'bosomy rose with fur gloves on'. Andrew Motion's biography supplies probable prototypes, but I don't think particular identifiable individuals will unlock the poem, which is written out of a central emotional conviction—a belief in romantic love itself.

In Tom Stoppard's play *The Real Thing*, the hero Henry explains to his wife Annie how he knows that she is having an affair with Billy: 'I know it's him. Billy, Billy, Billy, the name keeps dropping, each time without significance, but it can't help itself. Hapless as a secret in a computer. Blip, blip, Billy, Billy.'[2] Something like this happens in the essays in *Required Writing* (1982).

There Larkin periodically gestures towards his core belief in romantic love. At the end of his essay on Housman, for example: 'For as Housman himself said, anyone who thinks he has loved more than one person has simply never really loved at all.'[3] (Where did Housman say this? Archie Burnett, the Housman scholar, tells me that on p. 449 of Grant Richards's *Housman 1897–1936* (2nd Impression 1942) there is a biographical reminiscence of Joan Thomson, daughter of Sir J. J. Thomson, Master of Trinity from 1918 to 1940: 'Housman would not tolerate the idea that it was possible for a man truly to love more than one woman in his life; anyone who considered that he had done so had simply never really loved at all'.)

---

[2] Tom Stoppard, *The Real Thing* (London: Faber and Faber, 1982), Act 2, scene 10.
[3] From 'All Right When You Knew Him,' a review of Richard Perceval Graves, *A. E. Housman: The Scholar-Poet* (1979), in Larkin, *Required Writing*, p. 265.

In 'Big Victims', he quotes the opening to Emily Dickinson's 'My Life had stood—a Loaded Gun— | In Corners—till a Day | The Owner passed—identified— | And carried Me away' and comments: 'This is romantic love in a nutshell.' At the end of his piece on Hardy's poetry, he praises Hardy's directness. In fact, he is also praising Hardy's romantic temperament: 'He can often be extremely direct. "Not a line of her writing have I, not a thread of her hair." Donne couldn't be more direct than that.'[4]

In 'Wild Oats' Larkin isn't direct at all. He is deceptive, deliberately devious. There is a secret narrative, an implied romantic narrative, overlaid by the cover story about an unsatisfactory relationship that dwindled to a pedestrian conclusion—a cover story told with rueful ironic humour. The title is typical—at once an ironic joke about prudence and tameness, and at the same time a signal inviting us to look at the edges of the too neat story, where wild oats grow.

'An Arundel Tomb' famously ends with this endorsement of romantic love: 'What will survive of us is love.' Donne couldn't be more direct than that. But this famous last line is famously qualified with reservations: 'Our almost-instinct almost true.' We are invited to look in two directions at once. Like 'Dublinesque', 'An Arundel Tomb' is a liminal poem existing at the precise border where sentimentality and sentiment meet. Conventional wisdom has it that, after *The North Ship*, Larkin shed the influence of Yeats, the old spellbinding tenor. Away went the elaborate bow ties and on came the bicycle clips. What actually occurred was that Yeats went undercover. He was wearing a wire and Larkin was still tuned to his master's voice. One of those double hearing aids was in fact an ear-piece. It isn't that Larkin is belting out lines like 'Life scarce can cast a fragrance on the wind' (from 'Nineteen Hundred and Nineteen') or 'Was there another Troy for her to burn?' ('No Second Troy').But the *sense*, the romantic heft, is often plangent, as it is in 'Wild Oats'. Andrew Motion identifies Jane Exall as the 'bosomy rose' but I think the real prototype is Maud Gonne, the fugitive love of Yeats's life.

'An Arundel Tomb' is a much loved Larkin poem that describes a characteristic arc, one shared with 'High Windows' and 'Sad Steps', of prose to passion—an idea I shall return to. But I think 'An Arundel Tomb' rather over-valued. It is basically iambic with slippage. There are some finely judged

---

[4] For 'Big Victims,' see ibid., p.193; for the Hardy quotation and Larkin comment see 'The Poetry of Hardy,' ibid., p.176.

metrical effects. For instance, the last two lines of the first stanza: 'Side by side, their faces blurred, | The earl and countess lie in stone, | Their proper habits vaguely shown | As jointed armour, stiffened pleat, | [And here the metre relents, marking a shift in the tone, a hint of potential irony] And that faint hint of the absurd—| The little dogs under their feet.' Nothing would have been easier for Larkin than to re-establish his metre by writing 'beneath' for 'under'. The ceremonial tone and formal sentiment find their objective correlative in the armour and the *stiffened* pleat. There is a starchiness hereabouts that would accommodate 'beneath' for the more workaday word, 'under'. Additionally, the couple's faces are 'blurred' and their clothing 'vaguely shown': what we feel here is distance rather than intimacy. With the dogs, though, our ears should warn us that instability is in the offing.

There are similar delicate metrical effects in the second stanza which supplies the detail around which the poem gathers its meaning. The earl is holding the countess's hand. Again, it is the last two lines of the stanza that subtly vary the metre. At the same time, though, the rhymes are banal and contrived for no obvious reason other than incompetence. 'Pre-baroque' and 'shock' is good, but 'until', 'still', and 'and' are posted like look-outs at the end of the line. Every one a kind of cliff-hanger clinging by its fingernails. They are not integral to their lines and they are obtrusive and feeble. 'Such plainness of the pre-baroque | Hardly involves the eye, until | It meets his left-hand gauntlet, still | Clasped empty in the other; and | [here the metre shifts with beautiful appropriateness] One sees, with a sharp tender shock | His hand withdrawn, holding her hand.' The shock lodges itself in the ear also.

I think Larkin, as happens quite often—and this, too, is Yeatsian—finds it difficult to thread his thought through the rhyme scheme. There can be two results. Murky exposition or enfeebled rhymes. Larkin knew this and says (in his interview with John Haffenden) that 'technically it's a bit muddy in the middle—the fourth and fifth stanzas seem trudging somehow, with awful rhymes like voyage/damage'.[5] The third stanza begins to test Larkin's skill. 'They would not think to lie so long.' He begins with this lightly archaic construction, meaning the monument was never meant to last this long. 'Such faithfulness in effigy | Was just a detail friends would see: | [that is,

[5] From a 1981 interview with John Haffenden, reprinted in ibid., pp. 57–8.

a detail only friends would see in their living memories| A sculptor's sweet commissioned grace | Thrown off in helping to prolong | The Latin names around the base.' As readers, we have to keep at bay unhelpful readings like the idea that the hand-holding is merely a piece of sculptural eking out. The real sense is that friends who remembered the couple would relish this tribute to their love. The sculptor is responsible, it is part of his metier, an inspired touch, but pure professionalism, 'sweet commissioned grace', part of a project to memorialize the dead couple, to ensure their names (in Latin round the base) live on a little longer. So Larkin cunningly vacillates. We are touched. We are touched by a touch of the artist. It isn't innocent.

The next three stanzas are social history. In its way, 'An Arundel Tomb' is a political poem. Larkin records his implicit verdict on the present—in an aurally clumsy phrase—'An unarmorial age'. The difficulty of these stanzas is their difficulty—the inept conduct of Larkin's argument. 'They would not guess how early in | Their supine stationary voyage | The air would change to soundless damage.' I am unsure what this third line means: 'The air would change to soundless damage.' What follows helps a little, since it describes particular social change: the break between aristocracy and their tenants. We can work out, too, that the inability to read Latin is intended by the lines 'How soon succeeding eyes begin | To look, not read'. So 'soundless damage' must be damage to the social fabric. Why is it 'soundless', though? The 'air' must mean, slightly bafflingly, the general social 'atmosphere', what's in the air. 'Soundless' presumably carries the implication that the changes—damage from the earl and countess's point of view—were effected without violent revolution. But I freely confess that the line is gnomic as far as I am concerned.

Motion tells us that the sculpture was damaged in the Reformation and Civil War and that the hand-holding is a later addition by Edward Richardson in the nineteenth century—to disguise the damage. However, Larkin did not know this when he wrote the poem, but, as Motion puts it, 'subsequently'.[6] In any case, none of this gets into the poem, though you might deduce a reference to the Reformation in the perhaps contrasted 'soundless damage'.

The succeeding stanza is clearer, and has some nice touches (that 'bright | Litter of birdcalls') but the rhymes are again fabricated. Look what they do to

⁶ Andrew Motion, *Philip Larkin: A Writer's Life* (London: Faber and Faber, 1993), p.274.

the integrity of Larkin's lines. 'Of time. Snow fell, undated. Light.' The next line is: 'Each summer thronged the glass. A bright.' 'Breadths' and 'paths' is a satisfying rhyme, but it comes at a cost. The 'lengths and breadths | Of time' is a strikingly empty phrase. The *breadth* of time it took to write this essay. See what I mean?

The penultimate stanza is smoke and mirrors more than it is cogent syntax. 'Now, helpless in the hollow of | An unarmorial age, a trough | Of smoke in slow suspended skeins | Above their scrap of history, | Only an attitude remains.' I have no idea what this means. About thirty years ago, I reviewed the first night of Harold Pinter's *No Man's Land* for the *New Statesman*. I was the summer stand-in for Benedict Nightingale. Two months later, I was introduced to Harold Pinter at a party. 'Ah yes,' he said, 'you reviewed my play. Very good.' In fact, as I explained to him, I had chosen one of two possible interpretations of *No Man's Land*—neither correct, I now think— because of restrictions on words. I wanted to know if I was right. The words were hardly out of my mouth, when Pinter's hand reached into his inside jacket pocket, retrieved a pair of sunglasses and put them on. 'Search me, squire,' he said. These lines of Larkin seem to me more difficult than Pinter's play—another P to add to Pound, Parker, and Picasso. The earl and countess are lying in a hollow. Is the hollow the same thing as the trough of smoke? That seems more unlikely than likely, because the trough is said to be above their scrap of history. But I really don't know how to interpret 'the hollow of an unarmorial age'. Nor can I make much of the 'smoke in slow suspended skeins'. It is an evocation of the unarmorial age, but more evocative than precise. Is it Larkin's idea of the industrial revolution? You almost wonder, desperately, if the couple haven't been made into a gift ashtray. I admit defeat, but the responsibility, the blame, is Larkin's.

Andrew Motion's biography tells us that Larkin wrote on the end of the manuscript draft: 'Love isn't stronger than death just because statues hold hands for 600 years.' Larkin is consciously refuting *The Song of Solomon* 8: 6: 'for love is strong as death.' And logically that—'Love isn't stronger than death'—is the enforced conclusion of the poem. 'Time has transfigured them into | Untruth.' There is, apparently, no way around this. It fills the doorway like a bouncer saying 'I'm afraid *not*, sir. If I could just stop you there, sir.' It is reinforced by another denial: the earl and countess didn't mean it. I take it this isn't a reference to the Victorian repairs, but the primacy of the sculptor's role. 'The stone fidelity | They hardly meant...' Thereafter, though, the qualifications are themselves qualified. *Prove* is a very strong verb and almost cancels the almosts in 'Our almost-instinct almost true'. It again becomes a question of weighting. The last line has all the force of a last line. It simply overrides the prior qualifications so that we, and Larkin, enjoy the afflatus unqualified. It is an indulged poetic fiction. When we speak about poetic justice we mean something perfectly balanced, where the offence and its punishment are exactly matched. This poetic fiction is perfectly balanced between complete endorsement and careful reservations. It is a curious form of co-existence, a two-state solution, where each exists independently of the other. Like the duck–rabbit in Gestalt psychology, you can't hold the two interpretations simultaneously. They alternate.

Sometime in the early 1980s, the drama editor at Fabers, Frank Pike, went to visit Larkin on Faber business. This involved staying the night in Hull—as it still does—so Larkin had the task of entertaining Frank. After a Chinese meal, Larkin took Frank to an amateur boxing match. As the boxers bobbed and weaved, feinted, dodged, ducked, pawed distantly at each other, Larkin turned to Frank and said lugubriously: 'Only connect.' Referring, of course, to E. M. Forster's hallowed liberal-humanist nostrum from chapter 22 of *Howards End*: only connect the prose and the passion. In Forster's novel, the passion is represented by the Schlegels while the prose is represented by the Wilcoxes. It isn't quite this simple, however, because Forster takes some pains to complicate what might seem a trite polarity. Helen and Meg Schlegel are passionate enough, but their pedantic brother, Tibby, displays a donnish slightly inhuman frigidity. And Meg Schlegel can see that people like Henry Wilcox, business people, the sons of Martha, have a saving *usefulness*: 'If the Wilcoxes hadn't worked and died in England for thousands of years, you and I [Meg says to her censorious sister] couldn't sit here without having our throats cut. There would be no trains, no ships to carry us literary people about in' (chapter 9). Remember, it is Henry who has saved Howards End from destruction.

Forster's polarity between prose and passion and their conflation are clearer in *The Longest Journey*. Forster fuses them in the famous scene when Rickie goes back into the arbour to retrieve his sandwiches and finds the bully Gerald (with the body of a Greek athlete and the face of an English one) locked in an embrace with Agnes. Forster conflates prose (those mislaid sandwiches) and passionate love. 'But they [Agnes and Gerald] had got into heaven, and nothing could get them out of it. Others might think them surly or prosaic. He [Rickie] knew... and so in time to come when the gates of heaven had shut, some faint radiance, some echo of wisdom might remain with him outside' (chapter 3). The same conflation, the same instinct shows itself in Virginia Woolf, who inherits it from Forster. This is a famous hybrid sentence from chapter 17 of *To the Lighthouse*, concerning, not sandwiches, but Mrs Ramsay's *boeuf en daube*: 'It partook, she thought—helping Mr Bankes to a specially tender piece—of eternity.'

This tradition, this fusion of the banal and the brilliant, is picked up by Larkin. Only connect the down-to-earth with the dazzling; the hedging, the hesitation, with the high romantic. We've seen this fusion at work in 'Wild Oats' and 'Reference Back'. I'd like now, if I can carry your scepticism with me, to look at Larkin the secular mystic—what you might call the Marriage of Heaven and Hull. 'It partook, she thought—helping Mr Bankes to a specially tender piece—of eternity.' Bear that sentence in mind.

The last stanza of 'Solar' can serve as a starting point. Andrew Motion quotes the stanza on its own—an unconscious act of criticism and improvement. Shorn of its inferior preceding stanzas, its power is enhanced.

> Coined there among
> Lonely horizontals
> You exist openly.
> Our needs hourly
> Climb and return like angels.
> Unclosing like a hand,
> You give for ever.

The sun as an image of self-sufficiency, of singleness married to inexhaustible generosity, to perpetual open-handedness. What is given is the coin of itself. We don't need the reference to Jacob's Ladder to sense the religious dimension. The anthropomorphism of the sun is crucial to this, too. There is something here that is fearless and generous that we might be tempted to worship. I am interested in the word 'unclosing'. Larkin partly chooses this word rather than the more obvious 'opening' because he has already used 'openly' only eight words earlier. The other reason for choosing 'unclosing' is that it strongly suggests its opposite, 'closing'—more than 'open' suggests 'shut'—and the contrast enhances the generosity. There is a moment in Scott Fitzgerald's *Tender is the Night*, when the novelist describes the Divers' beach in the south of France: 'The hotel and its bright tan prayer rug of a beach were one.' Fitzgerald and Larkin are playing with a cliché, a figure of speech, literalizing and transfiguring it. Sun worshippers both. The stale hyperbole is invigorated and brought to blazing life. From the prose of Ambre Solaire to solar energy. 'High Windows' starts with prose and ends with passion. The poem is a radical tonal journey from the coarse to the exalted. 'When I see a couple of kids | And guess he's fucking her' to 'and is nowhere and is endless'. So many of Larkin's poems are about the gap between the ideal and the real—'Essential Beauty' being the *locus classicus*.

'High Windows' seems a relatively simple poem about solipsism, the prison of the self. In Michael Frayn's early philosophical book, *Constructions*, his image for the mind is a suitcase—a suitcase capable of containing everything except itself.[7] In 'High Windows', each generation sees its own limitations and *idealizes* the subsequent generation—because it can't escape itself. Larkin's generation is unhappy, but previous generations could see the release from fear of God and guilt about sin. Larkin, in his turn, idealizes the present younger generation for their sexual liberation. The idealism is actually ignorance turned inside out and Larkin's image for this is high windows—of the kind that let in light but which are too high to see through and discover what is on the other side.

The last stanza nevertheless isn't purely ironic—though it is 'nowhere', a species of fiction, a non-existent alternative. It is also a vision of heaven—hinted at in the fourth line: 'I know this is paradise'. By the end this means more than sensual 'bliss'. That bliss is desecularized and given 'real' spiritual content.

I want to make an analogy with le Corbusier's chapel at Ronchamps, la Chapelle de Notre Dame du Haut. There is a side altar there of solid concrete, a giant inverted ingot, with a simple white linen runner on top of it. Behind the altar is a kind of chimney, a whitewashed tunnel reaching up to the sky. But all you can see from the inside is the downward flood of light. And though the source is unseen, you can see the light's intensity grows higher up. It is the perfect metaphor for spirituality.

Larkin's poem has a tightening rhyme scheme (with only one duff rhyme) that mirrors the poem's growth in intensity. The last lines are both negative and promissory. 'The sun-comprehending glass' offers both understanding of the sun and physical containment of the sun. The glass shows—after a

[7] Michael Frayn, *Constructions* (London: Wildwood House, 1974), p. 63.

line-break freighted with suspense—nothing, and is nowhere, and is ironic, even bathetic, while at the same time it promises an infinity that is 'endless'. And the final word casts its spell on the other words, 'nothing' and 'nowhere' so they become not empty but cleansed of physical reality. A nirvana for the non-believer.

I want to turn now to 'The Explosion', which, like 'Solar' turns partially on a bit of subtle, semi-conscious wordplay—this time, blow-up and blown up, explosion and enlargement as in the Antonioni film *Blow Up*, with David Hemmings and Vanessa Redgrave. 'The Explosion' is written in trochees, rather uncertainly for the first two undecided lines: 'On the day of the explosion | Shadows pointed towards the pithead.' The first conversational line isn't obviously trochaic, but becomes so in retrospect. The second would be more pronouncedly trochaic if Larkin had written: Shadows pointed to the pithead. Obviously, then, he begins by wanting to finesse the Hiawatha metre. It soon establishes itself and forces on Larkin some contrived, awkwardly maladroit locutions: 'Coughing oath-edged talk and pipe-smoke.' Oath-edged, like the beards and moleskins, locate the poem in the elastic past, where reality is more permissible and permeable, as in 'Dublinesque'. And I believe that 'The Explosion' toys, quite seriously, with the mystical, leaving a trail of Christian trace elements. Those 'tall gates standing open' are at once the colliery gates and also perhaps those heavenly gates evoked by Forster in *The Longest Journey*. On its own, this detail would count for nothing, of course, but the touches accumulate. 'At noon, there came a tremor . . . sun, scarfed as in a heat-haze, dimmed.' In the conventional narrative, this is barely plausible. Why should an underground explosion, that 'tremor', cause the sun to dim? We are surely looking at a quasi-Calvary: Luke, Matthew, and Mark all record an eclipse of the sun from the sixth to the ninth hour. What Koestler called *Darkness at Noon*. In Luke 23: 45 we read: 'And the sun was darkened, and the veil of the temple was rent in the midst.' Doesn't Larkin conflate the veil and the eclipse? 'Sun, | *Scarfed* as in a heat haze, dimmed.' And consider the second line. Even on a strictly secular reading, it is ominous: 'Shadows pointed towards the pithead.' Why would those shadows be 'pointing'? It reads like an omen. And to me 'pithead' suggests a near-miss—'godhead'—but only retrospectively, when all the other evidence is in. The evidence, though, is inconclusive. It is meant to be inconclusive, to exist at the periphery of our vision, at the far borders of our disbelief. We are addressing an aura, an inexplicable suggestion.

And then Larkin's poem risks unclosing its hand to show us what might be there. The italicized sixth stanza alludes to two different passages in the Bible. *'The dead go on before us, they* | *Are sitting in God's house in comfort,* | *We shall see them face to face —'* The third Epistle of St John v.14 is actually an excuse for not writing more: 'But I trust I shall shortly see thee, and we shall speak face to face…' The other Biblical passage is that standby at weddings, 1 Corinthians 13: 12, the passage about the importance of charity/love and the imperfection of human knowledge: 'when I was a child, I understood as a child, I thought as a child: but when I became a man, I put away childish things. ‖ For now we see through a glass, darkly; but then face to face: now I know in part; but then shall I know even as I am known.' Neither passage is an exact match for the words in the poem. The best match is Richard Francis Weymouth's New Testament of 1903, an idiomatic translation into everyday English from the text of 'The Resultant Greek Testament' by R. F. Weymouth. This reads: 'For the present we see things as if in a mirror, and are puzzled; but then we shall see them face to face. For the present the knowledge I gain is imperfect; but then I shall know fully, even as I am fully known.' Of course, Larkin is covered. He's quoting from the chapel walls.

The point is, though, that Larkin should now be so direct in his religious citation. Before, we were given elusive allusion, evocation. To conclude, Larkin protects himself with hearsay—'It was said'—but (*mot juste*) wishes on his readers a miracle, a poetic miracle perhaps, but one containing the idea of the resurrection of the body. 'Wives saw the men of the explosion ‖ Larger than in life they managed— | Gold as on a coin, or walking | Somehow from the sun towards them.' This miracle, of invulnerability to bodily injury, is epitomized in the unbroken eggs—which are an index of its impossibility, its imaginative fragility; which are also perfect because they particularize one person, one individual, so we see him face to face, as it were. It isn't true. It is an idealization: 'larger than in life they managed.' The traditional halo is assimilated to a face on a gold coin. But the unbroken eggs are the telling, the clinching, the circumstantial detail on which the poem ends.

Finally, I'm going to stretch your tolerance a bit by poking behind the opening poem in *High Windows*—'To the Sea'. This is obviously a kind of companion piece to 'Show Saturday'—the celebration of an English rite, something specifically and eternally English going on: 'Still going on, all of it, still going on.' Compare 'Show Saturday': 'Regenerate union. Let it always be there.' In addition, though, 'To the Sea' is also like 'The Explosion'—the opening poem, like the closing poem, is ghosted by eternity. The interpretative key is the line 'the miniature gaiety of seasides'. Why 'miniature'? Partly because the seaside is 'under the sky', 'crowded under the low horizon' as if it were squashed and miniature by contrast. But it is 'miniature' mainly because Larkin is returning to his childhood where everything seems smaller than it did at the time. Not just going to the seaside after a long time. In reality, there is nothing miniature about the seaside itself. You go to your old classroom and squeeze into your old desk. He is going back in time a bit like Alice entering Wonderland. He is an adult actually revisiting his childhood. It's a bit like the skewed mysticism of 'Burnt Norton'—at once impossible and obvious.

The first line—'To step over the low wall that divides'—tells us a great deal. It is a low wall but it also *seems* low now that Larkin has grown up. He once described childhood as a 'forgotten boredom' but here it is vivid and welcome. A species of time-travel has been accomplished. An ordinary miracle.

It partook, she thought—helping Mr Bankes to a specially tender piece—of eternity. Or consider A. E. Housman writing to Arthur Pollard on 17 January 1923 about the death of Moses Jackson. This is high romanticism, this is unblunted passion at its most direct: 'Now I can die myself: I could not have borne to leave him behind me in a world where anything might happen to him.' The next day, 18 January 1923, Housman writes to Grant Richards, his publisher: 'I am told that the Brighter London Society are printing Lovat Fraser's illustrations to *A Shropshire Lad* on calendar covers.'[8] The prose and the passion coarsely connected—as they are in life, always.

[8] See Archie Burnett (ed.), *The Letters of A. E. Housman*, 2 vols. (Oxford and New York: Oxford University Press, 2007).

4

The Lesbianism of Philip Larkin

Terry Castle

'Love various minds does variously inspire,' wrote Dryden in *Tyrannic Love*, but for many of us true sexual eccentricity remains difficult to comprehend.[1] We still don't have the words. Granted, in most modern liberal societies, you can use the term 'gay' or 'straight' and people will know (or think they know) what you mean. But anything more convoluted than plain old *homosexual* or *heterosexual* can be hard to grasp. (*Bisexual* doesn't help much: many sensible people remain unconvinced that this elusive state of being even exists.) For a while I've kept a list in my head of famous people whose sexual proclivities I myself find *inexpressible*—so odd and incoherent I can't begin to plumb their inner lives. Greta Garbo, Virginia Woolf, T. E. Lawrence, the Duke of Windsor, Marlon Brando, Simone de Beauvoir, Michael Jackson, and Andy Warhol have been on the list for some time; Condoleeza Rice may join them soon. Futile my attempts to pigeon-hole such individuals: they seem to tran-scend—if not nullify—conventional taxonomies.

Pious readers of course will already be spluttering: *how presumptuous to 'label' someone else's sexual inclinations!* The truth is, however, Everybody Does It, and the psychological insight gleaned in the attempt—especially with regard to spectacular deviations from the norm—can enhance one's day-to-day

[1] A version of this essay appeared previously in *Daedalus: Journal of The American Academy of Arts and Sciences*, 136:2 (2007).

comprehension of other human beings. When it comes to understanding the very greatest writers and artists, some empathetic conjecture regarding the psychosexual factors involved in creativity would seem to be a necessity. Would life be better if Wilde had not raised the issue of Shakespeare's sexuality in 'In Praise of Mr. W.H.'? If Freud had not explored the homoerotic themes he found in the works of Michaelangelo and Leonardo da Vinci? Half-baked their conclusions can seem to us now but Wilde and Freud initiated a kind of discussion with innumerable social and intellectual ramifications.

And hard it is, or so I will maintain in this essay, to approach the work of Philip Larkin (1922–1985)—considered by many the greatest English poet of the second half of the twentieth century—without acknowledging *his* particular brand of sexual eccentricity. If less inscrutable than, say, the fey, mannikin-like Duke of Windsor, Larkin still presents a formidable challenge to the erotic taxonomist. The quintessential Establishment poet—he was offered the Poet Laureateship in 1984—Larkin is usually thought of as a straight, if not blokish, man of letters. He portrays himself as such in numerous poems. Not in any vainglorious way: on the contrary, the rhetorical pose usually cultivated—indeed now regarded as typically 'Larkinesque'–is that of shy (if sardonic) English bachelor: reclusive, timid, physically unattractive to women, envious of other men's romantic successes. At its most poignant to be 'Larkinesque' is to feel excluded from the family life and ordinary sexual happiness granted to others. ('For Dockery a son, for me nothing.') The dominant note is one of settled privation: of having lost out at the very start in the suave game of couples and coupling. For those who love Larkin, this rueful evocation of sexual loneliness, tempered always of course with subtle intransigence and a wildly uncensored wit, is just what they love him *for*—the best and choicest part of his imperishable sing-song:

> Sexual intercourse began
> In nineteen sixty-three
> (Which was rather late for me)—
> Between the end of the *Chatterley* ban
> And the Beatles' first LP.[2]

[2] 'Annus Mirabilis', in Philip Larkin, *Collected Poems*, ed. Anthony Thwaite (New York: Farrar, Straus and Giroux, 2004), p. 146. All further quotations from Larkin's poems are taken from this edition, with the exception of the 'Brunette Coleman' poems. The latter have been published separately in *Trouble at Willow Gables and Other Fiction 1943–1953*, ed. James Booth (London: Faber and Faber, 2002).

Despite tiresome over-quotation the rhymes never go stale; nor do they lose their odd power to console. Yet the point remains: however bleak the (real or imagined) erotic life, Larkin's 'normality' would seem to be a given. As the poet has his frustrated stand-in say in 'Round Another Point'—an unpublished *débat* between two young men on the subject of women, sex, and marriage from 1951—'I want to screw decent girls of my own sort without being made to feel a criminal about it.'[3]

Since the poet's death, however, some unexpected kinks in the Larkin persona have come to light. Pixillating indeed was the revelation, in Andrew Motion's 1993 biography, that the bespectacled author of *The Whitsun Weddings* was an avid, even compulsive, consumer of lesbian porn—especially the kind involving frolicking English schoolgirls in gym slips and hockey pads.[4] But downright electrifying was the news that after finishing his final term at St John's College, Oxford, in 1943, the young poet, then 21, had spent several months writing such stories himself under the pseudonym 'Brunette Coleman'. Brunette was in fact a full-blown comic persona: the imaginary sister of Blanche Coleman, the platinum-blonde leader of a forties 'All-Girl' swing band in whom the jazz-loving Larkin took both a musical and prurient interest. Unlike her real-world sister, the fictional Brunette was supposedly tweedy, bookish, and sentimental—a prolific author of Angela-Brazil-style schoolgirl novels and one of those mawkish middle-aged English lesbians whose imperfectly suppressed homosexuality is plain to everyone but themselves. Her works, it seemed, were an odd mixture of the lecherous and the dotty. Amazingly enough the Brunette manuscripts had survived, Motion disclosed, and were to be found along with other unpublished works in the Larkin archive at the Brynmor Jones Library, Hull University, where Larkin had served with great distinction as Head Librarian for almost thirty years.

Sensing curiosity—or at least titillation—among Larkin readers, Faber, Larkin's long-time publisher, made the complete Brunette *oeuvre* available in a 2002 volume called *Trouble at Willow Gables and Other Fiction 1943–1953*, edited by James Booth. 'Brunette's' literary corpus, it turned out, consisted of five works: *Trouble at Willow Gables* and *Michaelmas Term at St. Bride's*—two fully elaborated parody school stories, full of games mistresses, mash notes,

---

[3] Booth (ed.), *Trouble at Willow Gables*, p. 492. Subsequent page references to the volume are bracketed in the text.

[4] Andrew Motion, *Philip Larkin: A Writer's Life* (London: Faber and Faber, 1993), pp. 86–96.

and lubricious hijinks after lights out; *Sugar and Spice*, a set of fey Sapphic poems modelled (with suitable langour) on the 'Femmes damnées' poems in Baudelaire's *Les fleurs du mal*; *Ante Meridien*, a fragment of autobiography in which Brunette reminisces about her Cornish childhood in the blowsy she-male manner of Daphne du Maurier; and 'What Are We Writing For?'—an artistic manifesto, supposedly composed at the instigation of her live-in pro-tegée, 'Jacinth', wherein Brunette defends the genre of popular girls' school fiction against 'penny-a-liners' who flout the time-honoured rules of the form. Brunette's lucubrations were clearly significant to Larkin: in printed form, they run to nearly 300 densely-packed pages and along with his jazz writings, could be said to represent, however risibly, the otherwise costive Larkin's most fluent and sustained literary endeavour.

It's hard, of course, to keep the usual scholarly po-face. Why—at the very outset of Larkin's estimable career—this protracted muddy detour across the playing fields of Lesbos? A post-adolescent liking for scabrous fun is one thing, but what inspires an ambitious young poet, already sizing up his chances in the great literary game, to impersonate at such length—and with such conspicuous *dedication*—a leering, half-mad, sapphistically-inclined author of books for girls? The editor of the *Girls' Own Paper*, last heard from in 1956, has yet to address the question.

Conservative poetry-lovers have been displeased by the whole business. In 'Green Self-conscious Spurts', a stunningly humourless piece about Larkin's early work recently in the *TLS*, Adam Kirsch dismisses the posthumous pub-lication of *Trouble at Willow Gables* as 'strictly unnecessary, and potentially dam-aging to [Larkin's] reputation'.[5] As punishment for such prissiness—not to mention the frigid little blast of homophobia—Kirsch should no doubt be required to sit on it and rotate. But one also wants to disagree with him pro-foundly. Yes, Larkin was a peculiar wanker and the Brunette Coleman phase seedy to say the least. Larkin *knew* he was a wanker: wankerish-ness was an essential component in the Hermit of Hull mystique. (Not for nothing did Larkin sometimes sign letters 'Furtive Lurking'.) In 'Posterity', the mock-heroic plaint in which he imagines his future biographer, 'Jake Balokowsky', a tenure-grubbing American academic, disparaging him after his death, Jake is heard describing his 'old fart' subject's secret sex-hangups thus:

---

[5] Adam Kirsch, 'Green Self-Conscious Spurts', *Times Literary Supplement*, 13 May 2005.

> Oh, you know the thing,
> That crummy textbook stuf from Freshman Psych,
> Not out of Kicks or something happening—
> One of those old-type *natural* fouled-up guys.

Just so: they foul you up, your mum and dad.

Yet the Brunette phase speaks volumes, I think, about the paradoxical process by which Philip Larkin became 'Larkinesque'—modern English poetry's reigning bard of erotic frustration and clammy (if verse-enabling) self-deprecation. Homosexual women have long been associated with sexual failure and fiasco: Sappho grieves for her faithless girls; Olivia loses Viola; Sister George is cuckolded and killed off. In *The Well of Loneliness*, Radclyffe Hall's classic lesbian potboiler from 1928—a book I'm convinced Larkin knew well and to which I will return to at the end of this essay—the luckless heroine, a supposedly famous writer, is rebuffed by everyone she cares about and ends up suicidal and alone. The girl-loving women of Western literature are *femmes damnées* indeed: sterile, rejected, forced to endure a perpetual Baudelairean hell of humiliation and psychic abuse. 'Brunette Coleman', spinster-sapphist-*cum*-panto-dame, no doubt seemed a marvellous comic invention in 1943—exactly the sort of Monty-Pythonish alter ego a young poet-cynic might exult in. Yet by impersonating her so fully and strangely the young Larkin was also, I would argue, plumbing his own well of loneliness: gaining imaginative and emotional purchase on an ever-deepening sense of sexual alienation. The literary results would be beautiful, witty, and original but it was a sad business nonetheless. What begins in play ends in *tristesse*, or so the lives of the poets teach us, and the 'trouble at Willow Gables' was enough to be getting on with for a sensitive soul named Larkin.

It seems important to emphasize from the start the *lesbianism* of the Larkin persona. Unconvincing, in my view, is the attempt of Larkin scholars to explain away the Brunette fantasy by associating it (vaguely enough) with male homoeroticism. In his introduction to *Trouble at Willow Gables*, James Booth suggests that when Larkin began composing the Brunette material he 'was not far from his own days as a shy "homosexual" schoolboy' and still 'undirected' in his sexuality. By impersonating Brunette Larkin was simply 'working out', even seeking to exorcize, residual homoerotic feelings for *boys*, left over from his experiences at King Henry VIII School, the Coventry grammar school he attended from 1930 to 1939. The Willow Gables milieu,

Booth claims, 'is not fundamentally different from that of the implicitly homosexual boys' school of Isherwood's *Lions and Shadows* or Julian Hall's *The Senior Commoner*, both of which Larkin read and admired at the time'. The last-mentioned even contains a scene, he notes, in which one senior boy asks another if a reportedly winsome member of the junior school is 'a brunette'.[6]

Yet the theory depends—rather too patly in my opinion—on a view that male and female homosexuality are, libidinally speaking, but two sides of the same coin and that one can automatically stand in for the other. The adolescent Larkin may well have had feelings for other boys but the somewhat hackneyed biographical storyline applied here—After 'Normal' Schoolboy Crushes British Male Writer Goes Straight and Stays Straight (More or Less)—strikes me as a bit cursory and cartoonish, and not only because it has been attributed over the years, with a broad brush indeed, to everybody from Robert Graves and Siegfried Sassoon to Evelyn Waugh, David Garnett, Cyril Connolly, Stephen Spender, Graham Greene, and (indeed) Larkin's friend, Kingsley Amis. Larkin himself claimed to be bewildered by his evolving fantasy life: 'Homosexuality', he wrote to Amis on 7 September 1943, 'has been completely replaced by lesbianism in my character at the moment—I don't know why.'[7]

[6] Julian Henry Hall, *The Senior Commoner* (London: Martin Secker, 1934).

[7] Cited by Motion, p. 86. Despite the fact that he includes other letters to Amis on closely related topics—some from the same month—Larkin's editor Anthony Thwaite omits the 7 September letter in his *Selected Letters of Philip Larkin 1940–1985* (New York: Farrar, Straus & Giroux, 1993).

Though Larkin shared Brunette's *oeuvre* with male friends—Amis, above all—I'm not sure men had much to do with it. To be interested in lesbianism is, de facto, to be interested in *women*—in liking women and thinking about women, in thinking about women liking other women, and in liking to think about women liking other women. And just as there are women whose particular psychosexual idiosyncracy it is to hanker obscurely after homosexual men—'fag hags' in rude parlance—there are likewise men, otherwise seemingly heterosexual, who become oddly transfixed by homosexual women. (No slang term exists for such men but hordes of lesbians can testify to their existence. Ernest Hemingway was one of the more boorish, if good-looking, examples of the type.) The sheer connoisseurship, even pedantry, that Larkin brought to the Sapphic theme—not to mention the curious crystallization of his own nascent poetic identity around that of Brunette—suggests exactly this sort of unusual yet generative symbolic investment.

Larkin's preoccupation was from the start a profoundly literary one. It is hardly overstating the case to describe the young Larkin as an ardent reader, first of all, of popular girls' school fiction—a genre notorious since the late nineteenth century for its barely sublimated Sapphic inflections. His knowledge of 'this exciting field of composition' (as Brunette calls it) seems to have been freakishly extensive, taking in everyone from Charlotte Brontë to Angela Brazil. Not for Larkin the sophisticated artistry of Brontë, however, or indeed Colette, whose cheerfully salacious *Claudine* novels perhaps constituted, around the turn of the century, the aesthetic apotheosis

of the genre. Larkin's tastes were at once more juvenile and downmarket. Continental knowingness was *de trop*: he preferred the ostensibly innocent works produced by earnest female hacks for 14- or 15-year-old girls. Thus Dorothy Vicary's *Niece of the Headmistress* (1939) and Nancy Breary's *Two Thrilling Terms* (1944) were special favourites; as Booth notes, Larkin owned copies of both. But to judge by the Brunette writings, he was acquainted with a truly startling number of other girls' school stories too—Brazil's *The Jolliest Term on Record*, *The Fortunes of Philippa*, and *A Pair of Schoolgirls*; Dorita Fairlie Bruce's popular *Dimsie Moves Up* (1921) and *Dimsie Moves Up Again* (1922); Elsie J. Oxenham's *The Abbey Girls Win Through* (1928); Phyllis Matthewman's *The Queerness of Rusty: A Dinneswood Book* (1941); Joy Francis's *The Girls of the Rose Dormitory* (1942); and Judith Grey's *Christmas Term at Chillinghurst* (1942), among others.

No doubt the fixation had its lubricious dimension. In a 1945 letter to Amis, Larkin describes a conversation in which he and Bruce Montgomery planned a fanciful 'little library of short novels' each of which was to focus on a different 'sexual perversion'. The labours were to be divided between them according to personal preferences. 'Dropping ONANISM as too trite', he writes, '[Montgomery] put in a claim for SADISM and SODOMY (male) while I bagged LESBIANISM and ANAL EROTICISM. He brought up MIXOSCOPY, and we discussed for some time PAEDERASTY and what I call WILLOWGABLISMUS.' ('Neither of us', the letter continues, 'had much feeling for BESTIALITY or MASOCHISM, though we goodnaturedly undertook them, one each. But I forget which.')[8] By 'WILLOWGABLISMUS' Larkin no doubt refers to the kinky schoolgirl sex-play so often featured in the male pornographic imagination. James Booth suggests that of all the school stories he had read, Larkin especially favoured the Vicary book, *Niece of the Headmistress*, because it has 'an unusually legible erotic subtext'.

Yet what Larkin appears to have prized about the girls' school story was not so much any outright kink as an odd, overall, seemingly *unintended* suggestiveness: the comic way that novelists like Vicary and Bruce managed to set up titillating situations without ever seeming to be aware that they were doing so. Larkin took obvious delight in such obtuseness and in just how eas-

---

[8] Letter of 9 July 1945. In Thwaite (ed.), *Selected Letters*, p. 103.

ily a prurient reader might convert a supposedly nice story into a naughty one. 'Nice' and 'naughty' indeed seem to have been curiously proximate categories for him, as a famous Larkin anecdote suggests. In the introduction to the 1963 reprint of *Jill* (1946)—the first of the two 'serious' novels he published immediately following the Brunette phase (*A Girl in Winter* is the other)—Larkin describes a letter from Kingsley Amis, written just after *Jill*'s publication, in which Amis reported seeing a copy of *Jill* in a seedy Oxford bookshop lodged 'between *Naked and Unashamed* and *High-Heeled Yvonne*'. As Larkin explains, it was most likely the reputation of his publisher, Reginald Ashley Caton, the 'mysterious and elusive proprietor of the Fortune Press', that had won *Jill* its place on the X-rated shelf. Caton 'divided his publishing activity between poetry and what then passed for pornography', Larkin writes, 'often of a homosexual tinge', and *Jill*'s own dust jacket bore adverts for such intriguing titles as '*Climbing Boy, Barbarian Boy, A Diary of the Teens by A Boy*, and so on'.

The image of the chaste *Jill* indecently wedged in between works of a less decorous nature no doubt appealed to Larkin-the-librarian's subversive side. (One can't help thinking how much time he must have spent reshelving misplaced books early in his career.) But it also indicates how permeable the conceptual boundary between the 'polite' and the 'pornographic'

sometimes was for him. The modes were as it were thrust up against one another—pressed embarrassingly together, like two strangers in a crowded Underground train—and when the action involved schoolgirls, the one kind of writing, embarrassingly enough, could all too easily morph into the other. In fact the more sentimental and old-maidish the story writer's attitude, the more the fictional *mise-en-scène*—that supercharged realm of prefects, pashes, and meet-you-in-the-cloakroom-Elspeth intrigue—seemed to lend itself to obscene embellishment.

At first glance the Brunette Coleman writings might be thought to promote exactly this kind of salacious comic dissonance. The 'proximity' ploy works perhaps most effectively in 'What Are We Writing For?'—Brunette's supposed artistic manifesto. This Dame Edna-ish little treatise is a satiric mini-masterpiece—in a class, I think, with works by Wodehouse, Waugh, or Grossmith. Ostensibly a call for a more scrupulous regard to craft—Brunette chastises 'slovenly' sister novelists for dashing off stories 'with the radio playing and a cigarette in the mouth'—it exposes, fairly flagrantly, its spinster-author's sublimated obsession with the school story's homoerotic conventions. Thus Brunette's quasi-neoclassical aesthetic strictures: *no stories set in day schools* (scenes of nocturnal conspiracy, illicit biscuit-eating, and pajama-clad hair-stroking are essential, she argues, to the 'excitement' of the genre); *no episodes set outside the school* (too reminiscent of tiresome boy–girl 'Adventure' stories), and above all, *few, if any, male characters:*

The essence of the story we are writing is that 'our little corner' becomes a microcosm. I cannot stress strongly enough the need for the elimination of all irrelevancies. There must be no men, no boy cousins, no neighbouring boys' schools, no (Oh, Elsie J. Oxenham!) coeducation. Uncles and fathers must be admitted with the greatest circumspection. And as for fiancés and husbands (Oh, Elsie J. Oxenham!)—they are so *tabu* that I hardly dare mention the matter.[9]

Brunette recommends instead a sequestered all-girl milieu. 'a closed, single-sexed world, which Mr Orwell would doubtless call a womb-replica, or

---

[9] 'What Are We Writing For?' in Booth (ed.), *Trouble at Willow Gables*, p. 269.

something equally coarse' (269). A handsome 'Jehovah'-like headmistress should be in charge—one who delivers awards and punishments publicly, in accordance with a clearly defined moral code. ('If it is forbidden to eat biscuits after lights out, though not a sin, then the heroine and her chums can do it: but if it is downright wicked to let the air out of the tires of the centre forward's bicycle to prevent her from reaching the match, then this crime must be reserved for the villainess, and the rest of the school must speak in hushed tones about it.') Head Girls, in turn, are to be 'beautiful, strict and fair'—especially when required to administer 'thrashings'—and villainesses demonstrably wicked:

Remember Satan, and Iago, and Lady Macbeth! Let the villainess be vicious and savage: let her scheme to overthrow game captaincies and firm friendships, and spread slackness through the Hockey XI! Let us…remember the dictum of Baudelaire: 'There are in the young girl all the despicable qualities of the footpad and the schoolboy.' Alas! it is only too true! (259–60)

Finally, the writer must seek to imbue her narrative with 'body' and 'fervour'. 'Vast webs of friendships, hatreds, loyalties, indecisions, schemings, plottings, quarrellings, reconciliations, and adorations must arise: incredible self-torturings and divided allegiances must lie behind that white, strained little fourth-form face. And behind all must stand the school itself—the rooms, the dripping trees, the crumbling stone fountain, the noise of water in the pipes as the Early Bath List undress' (270). In the juvenile bosom of a Dimsie or Millicent, the emotions of Phèdre or Andromache.

Yet oddly enough, despite being supposedly written by Brunette her-self, neither *Trouble at Willow Gables* or *Michaelmas Term at St. Bride's* holds to such Homo-Rhapsodical Unities. Like Dorita Fairlie Bruce's *Dimsie* novels, Brunette's fictions share the same *dramatis personae*: a heroine named Marie Moore, whose older sister Philippa is 'Captain of the School' and a leather-belt fetishist; Myfanwy, the devoted 'chum' with whom Marie is often seen cuddling; Margaret, a secret gambling addict who prefers off-track betting to more usual schoolgirl pursuits; Hilary Russell, aesthete, lesbian seductress-in-training and supposed 'villainess'; and Mary Beech, the hulking, slightly moronic captain of the hockey Second XI who is the principal object of Hilary's lascivious wiles. In *Trouble at Willow Gables*, the main action revolves around a mysterious theft: someone has stolen five pounds intended for the new Gymnasium Fund (an endowment sponsored by one 'Lord Amis') and only after various mix-ups and false accusations is the perpetrator identified. In *Michaelmas Term at St. Bride's*—a sequel of sorts— Marie, Myfanwy, and the rest are seen adjusting, somewhat imperfectly, to their first term at St Bride's, a fictional Oxford women's college rather like Somerville or St Hugh's. Larkin uses different surnames in the second tale: 'Marie Moore', interestingly enough, becomes 'Marie Woolf', and her sister 'Philippa Woolf'.

A certain slapstick porniness surfaces, to be sure, at various points in both stories. When the Fourth Form gets rambunctious while undressing for bed in *Trouble at Willow Gables*, a plump prefect named Ursula restores order by 'sweeping up and down the lines of beds' flicking offenders with a leather belt—

She had considerable skill in doing this, and there was a hasty scuffling and strip-ping and knotting of pyjama cords as she toured from girl to girl like a well-made Nemesis. Myfanwy returned to her bed with as much dignity as was compatible with a stung bottom: Marie's head was buried in the pillow (24).

In *Michaelmas Term at St. Bride's*, after a wild argument-cum-wrestling match with her older sister (Philippa the belt fetishist) poor Marie ends up 'lying face downwards on Philippa's silken knees', her 'velvet skirt folded neatly round her waist', while Philippa administers a dreadful 'thrashing' using one of the thirty-seven 'exotic' belts in her collection—one sporting 'a curious metal buckle, which Philippa rightly adjudged would add an awful sting to the lashes' (191).

A Summons from the Mistress.

Yet such questionable moments apart, one can't help noticing how curiously *un*-erotic the 'Brunette' stories are—how often they seem merely diffident and strange. For a would-be pornographer, even a very softcore one, the young Larkin seems painfully lacking in seigneurial aplomb. Titillating situations fizzle; characters one might expect to deliver some smutty business—the jaded Hilary for example—turn out to be surprisingly maladroit. In *Willow Gables* the single schoolmate Hilary succeeds in bedding (the racing-form addict Margaret Tattenham) is hers only through blackmail and the lovemaking is never described. The overall mood is one of *tristesse*—as when Hilary, oppressed by her inability to land her main prey (Mary Beech) during an intimate late-night tutoring session, succumbs to the mopes as soon as Mary leaves her room:

Lighting a cigarette, she stretched herself on the sofa, rubbing her cheek caressively on the cushion Mary had warmed, and murmuring idiotically to herself: 'She was here, and is gone. The young lioness was here and is gone . .' After that she undressed slowly, munching a biscuit, and read *Mademoiselle de Maupin* in bed till a very late hour. (28)

The fact that Larkin describes the thwarted prefect as feeling—rather unappetizingly—like a 'jelly newly tipped out onto a plate', adds another element of anti-climax to the scene.

In *Michaelmas Term at St. Bride's*—Brunette's supposed 'Oxford' sequel—the absence of 'WILLOWGABLISMUS' is even more pronounced. Most of the

Willow Gables characters, it's true, reappear: Hilary is again on the scene ('large as life and twice as unnatural'); likewise Mary Beech (now called Burch), who discovers to her horror upon arriving for her 'fresher' term at St Bride's, that she will be sharing rooms with her former persecutor. Marie, Myfanwy, and Philippa also return, the last-mentioned with collection of leather belts intact. In the fine old nice-turned-naughty tradition of *Willow Gables* Philippa at one point even welcomes her little sister into her college rooms clad only in 'socks and nail varnish'.

But the Oxford setting changes everything—not least of all because *men*, odious men, now intrude upon the action. Compared with *Trouble at Willow Gables, Michaelmas Term* is spectacularly plotless: in one of several aborted story-lines Marie tries to 'cure' Philippa of her belt fetish through a sort of Freudian shock-therapy involving worms. But for the most part 'Brunette' seems unable to do much but fling her *Willow Gables* characters, haphazardly, into the new mixed-sex environment. In so doing she necessarily flouts the very '*tabu*' marked in 'What Are We Writing For?' as fundamental to the girls' school genre: that no male character ever penetrate the all-female 'womb-replica' of the school. Can the famed university on the Isis in fact be considered a 'school' in the Angela Brazil sense? Even the redoubtable Dorothy Sayers twigged it: Oxford could hardly be mistaken for a lesbian hothouse.

This contradictory turn is dire and bewildering—especially since the men of *Michaelmas Term* are singularly unpleasant and intrusive—clammy chaps of the sort British tabloids are wont to refer to as 'sex-pests'. Not even hardened tribades like Hilary Russell can avoid them. The perplexing relationship Hilary develops over the course of the fragment with the 'Creature'—a tall, weak-eyed, chronically doleful male undergraduate who after being 'thrashed hollow' by her in a game of table-tennis becomes her abject swain—is emblematic. Despite the abuse heaped on him—Hilary likes to 'minimize his masculine qualities' and make him cry—the 'Creature' pursues her with masochistic ardour, asserting at every turn that 'in a previous existence [she] had been a Roman empress, who had personally chastised a Christian slave, of whom [he] was a reincarnation' (166). Hilary seems to tolerate his damp-palmed presence: not only does she allow the 'Creature' to ply her with cocktails, theatre tickets, and expensive meals at the Randolph, she's even willing on occasion to let him 'inspect, reverently, the strength of her muscles'.

Yet this oddly stagnant relationship—like other boy–girl unions in the sequel—seems to destroy whatever minimal narrative coherence *Michaelmas Term* might be said to possess. Larkin-as-Brunette seems unsure what to do with his rapidly multiplying quasi-heterosexual couples and the story breaks off abruptly in a welter of half-hearted 'metafictional' incidents. (When Marie finds Pat—the school skivvy from *Trouble at Willow Gables*—tending bar in an Oxford pub and asks her why she isn't still working at the school, Pat replies: 'That story's over now, Miss Marie, [...] Willow Gables doesn't exist anymore.') Significantly, the 'Creature's' love-dream remains unrequited at the breaking-off point: we last see him alone in the same pub's infernal 'Smoke Room', soddenly 'picking out in an incompetent fashion a negro twelve-bar blues' (230).

Much could be said about *Michaelmas Term at St. Bride's*, particularly—as I'll suggest in my conclusion—in connection with *Jill*, the extraordinary autobiographical novel, also set at Oxford, that Larkin began writing in 1943, shortly after abandoning the Brunette persona. But perhaps the tale's most immediately striking feature is the transparent, almost algebraic way it announces Larkin's poetic identification with what might be called the 'Sappho-position'—that of sex-starved, ugly, erotically luckless pseudo-man. One is hardly surprised to read in Motion's biography that as a St John's undergraduate Larkin was himself soundly 'thrashed' in a game of table tennis by an Amazonian friend named Hilary; or that in letters to male friends he referred to the young woman to whom he was briefly and unhappily engaged in 1950—Ruth Bowman—as the 'School Captain'. (Panic-stricken, he rescinded his proposal after three weeks.) Like Brunette, the Creature is no doubt a self-inscription. In fact the two *personae* seem oddly to interact, if not merge, at the end of *Michaelmas Term*. The same pub in which the Creature plays his feckless tune—or so the metafictional Pat tells Marie—was once frequented by 'the woman that writes all these books'. ('Haven't you ever met her, Miss Marie? I saw her once. She used to come in here and drink. Very tall she was, and beautifully dressed.') The Creature is nothing less than a ludicrous quasi-male Brunette—studious, melancholic, rapidly balding (as Larkin himself was by the mid-1940s), partial to alcohol, jazz, and adolescent girls.

Watching the Creature's slotting into the 'Sappho position' one senses, rather more ominously than in *Trouble at Willow Gables*, the self-critical, even self-punishing aspect of Larkin's cross-sex identification. At the deepest level the poet's affinity with female homosexuality was a bleak one and perhaps could not have been otherwise. Love between women, after all, is hardly an unexplored or uncontroversial theme in mainstream Western literature. (That it has likewise been a central trope in the history of pornography for almost two millennia goes without saying.) Over the centuries a host of writers have broached the topic: not just Sappho, obviously, but also Ovid, Juvenal, Martial, Ariosto, Shakespeare, Ben Jonson, Donne, Dryden, Aphra Behn, Pope, Fielding, John Cleland, Diderot, Sade, Laclos, Maria Edgeworth, Coleridge, Gautier, Baudelaire, Emily Dickinson, Balzac, Verlaine, Maupassant, Zola, Swinburne, Hardy, Henry James, Wedekind, Proust, Strindberg, Colette, H.D., Ronald Firbank, Amy Lowell, Cather, Stein, Woolf, Katherine Mansfield, D.H. Lawrence, Rosamond Lehmann, Radclyffe Hall, Djuna Barnes, Daphne Du Maurier, Dorothy Sayers, Elizabeth Bowen, Wyndham Lewis, Hemingway, William Carlos Williams, Lillian Hellman, Graham Greene, Marguerite Yourcenar, Sartre, de Beauvoir, Elizabeth Bishop, Jane Bowles, Iris Murdoch, and many others. However oddly assorted, most of these writers have depicted lesbianism voyeuristically and/ or satirically; many have expatiated on its supposedly morbid psychological effects. The past fifty years, it is true, have brought forth more sympathetic treatments—and not just from lesbian writers. Still, lampoon, defamation, and a peculiar kind of lascivious disparagement remain dominant rhetorical modes.[10]

What almost all of the works in the Western lesbian canon share—including even the more worldly or forgiving—is a sense of the *unviability* of female same-sex love. To yearn for a woman, it would seem, is to fall victim to an *amor impossibilis*—to lose oneself in a sterile, unwholesome, usually fatal enterprise. Even the most selfless attachments will be nullified. Passionate Sappho, alas, set the pattern: watching her former beloved simper on the wedding dais with her new husband—as in 'Peer of the Gods', the celebrated Fragment 31—the poet becomes dizzy, breathless, and fears she will expire from the pain. Yet the logic of the *amor impossibilis* operates just as harshly elsewhere. When the cross-dressing Rosalind is reunited with her lover Orlando

---

[10] For more examples and discussion, see the Introduction to my recent compilation, *The Literature of Lesbianism: A Historical Anthology from Ariosto to Stonewall* (New York: Columbia University Press, 2003). The anthology itself provides numerous samples of works in the Western 'sapphophobic' tradition.

in *As You Like It*, Phebe, the gullible shepherdess who has fallen in love with her, is fobbed off on oafish Silvius. In Balzac's *The Girl with the Golden Eyes*, both the wicked Marquise de Réal and Paquita, her female lover, end up stabbed to death at the end of the tale. The eponymous heroine of Swinburne's lurid *Lesbia Brandon* (1877) expires in agony, worn out by unnatural practices. In both Wedekind's *Lulu* and Berg's opera, the lesbian Countess Geschwitz, hopelessly besotted with the *femme fatale* of the title, is murdered by Jack the Ripper in the drama's final scene. And in *The Fox* (1929), one of several campy lucubrations on female homosexuality by D. H. Lawrence, Banford, the more childish and charmless member of a quasi-lesbian couple, is abandoned by her companion for a man and crushed by a falling tree. Radclyffe Hall, as usual, trumps everyone in the Utter Misery Department: after four hundred pages of rejection, insult, and sexual frustration Stephen Gordon—mannish heroine of *The Well of Loneliness*—not only loses her lover to a man, but succumbs at novel's end to 'the terrible nerves of the invert'. She is last seen lurching suicidally through Paris from one squalid dyke bar to another.

Nowhere is the doomed nature of female same-sex love more explicit, finally, than in what one might call (*pace* Brunette) the School Story for Grown-Ups: the explicitly homoerotic tale—often female-authored and autobiographical—set in a girls' boarding school or college. Enough of these 'serious' school fictions exist to constitute a distinct subgenre of lesbian writing: Colette's *Claudine à l'école* (1900), Gertrude Stein's *Q.E.D.* (1903), Henry Handel Richardson's *The Getting of Wisdom* (1910), Clemence Dane's *Regiment of Women* (1915), Christa Winsloe's *The Child Manuela* (source for the classic 1933 German cult film *Mädchen in Uniform*), Antonia White's *Frost in May* (1933), Dorothy Strachey's *Olivia*, Lillian Hellman's *The Childrens' Hour*, May Sarton's *The Small Room*, Muriel Spark's *The Prime of Miss Jean Brodie* (1961), and Violette Leduc's *Thérèse and Isabelle* (1964) are only some of many. These 'adult' school narratives are almost always dysphoric in tendency. Some, like Dane's *Regiment of Women* and Strachey's *Olivia*, are toxic little tales of female-on-female abuse: a charismatic teacher seduces a susceptible young student and then turns on her; an older and more sophisticated girl entangles one younger or more naive in an 'unhealthy' friendship. In other works, as in *The Fox*, the homoerotic bond between two female characters is destroyed by an intruder-male. Thus in Dorothy Baker's melodramatic *Trio* (1948), the student-heroine, seduced by an unsavoury female French professor—a specialist in nineteenth-century 'decadent' verse!—is saved from a life of *Fleurs du mal* perversion by a strapping young fellow who falls in love with her and threatens the professor with exposure. The latter, understandably dismayed, shoots herself at novel's end.

The repetitive, ruthlessly end-stopped pattern is clear, and for Larkin the bad news plainly resonated. In the literature of the *amor impossibilis*—the brutal and bittersweet narratives of lesbian desire—Larkin found, I believe, a doom-laden prediction of what was to become the central and most painful theme of his imaginative and emotional life: *no girls for you.* The pain of the discovery was no doubt sublimated, covered over with misogyny and a lot of schoolboy smuttiness; it would likewise be transformed soon enough into a matchless poetic endeavour. But however much he intended the Brunette *oeuvre* as collegiate spoof—an experiment, egged on by Amis, in the higher prurience—he could not help castigating his own deepest longings: *You wish to be loved? Dream on, mate: you will fail—pathetically—while real men succeed. Better not to bother. Drink, listen to jazz; write poems; accept privation as your lot.* Pretending to be a middle-aged invert named Brunette was a bookish young man's way of neutering himself at the starting-gate—of announcing second-tier status and yielding in advance to the competition. No Enormous Yes, or even a Tiny Yes, in the Larkin love-and-sex game: sadness, loss, and loneliness—the original Sapphic hat-trick—seemed from the beginning the main thing on offer.

How far from Brunette, burbling spinster-sapphist, to the chilled-to-the-bone speakers of 'Mr. Bleaney' or 'The Whitsun Weddings'?

> Struck, I leant
> More promptly out next time, more curiously,
> And saw it all again in different terms:
> The fathers with broad belts under their suits
> And seamy foreheads; mothers loud and fat;
> An uncle shouting smut; and then the perms,
> The nylon gloves and jewellery substitutes,
> The lemons, mauves, and olive-ochres that
> Marked off the girls unreally from the rest.

In his Introduction to *Trouble at Willow Gables*, Larkin's editor Booth suggests that the Baudelaire knock-offs in *Sugar and Spice*—the 'slim sheaf' of verses attributed to Brunette—are already recognizably Larkinesque in mood and manner: 'Technically', he proposes, the Brunette poems are 'among the

finest poems Larkin wrote during the decade, with an assured delicacy of
tone far beyond anything in *The North Ship*.' He cites the opening lines of 'The
School in August'—

> The cloakroom pegs are empty now,
> And locked the classroom door,
> The hollow desks are dim with dust,
> And slow across the floor
> A sunbeam creeps between the chairs
> Till the sun shines no more.

—and notes how closely they anticipate the 'empty rooms' in such charac-
teristic Larkin poems as 'Home is So Sad', 'Friday Night in the Royal Station
Hotel', and 'The Old Fools'.[11] One has to agree: against all expectation, the
Brunette poems are spare, elegiac, ominously good. Above all, somewhat
anachronistically, they display the mature poet's weary autumnal sense of
Ubi sunt:

> Who did their hair before this glass?
> Who scratched 'Elaine loves Jill'
> One drowsy summer sewing class
> With scissors on the sill?
> Who practised this piano
> Whose notes are now so still?
>
> Ah, notices are taken down,
> And scorebooks stowed away,
> And seniors grow tomorrow
> From the juniors today,
> And even swimming groups can fade,
> Games mistresses turn grey.

The echo in the last line here of Pope's *Rape of the Lock*—'But since, alas! frail
Beauty must decay, | Curl'd or uncurl'd, since Locks will turn to grey'— is
apposite, for Larkin's sense of erotic alienation, of gauche unsuitedness for
carnal love, rivals the eighteenth-century poet's. What other pair of English
writers have felt themselves so bitterly excluded from 'sugar and spice and
everything nice'?

[11] Booth (ed.), *Trouble at Willow Gables*, p. xvii.

There's Amis-style mischief too of course—as in 'Ballade des Dames du Temps Jadis', a Villon pastiche to which 'Brunette' appends instructions for reading the poem aloud. The opening quatrain, we learn—

> Tell me, into what far lands
> They are gone, whom once I knew
> With tennis-racquets in their hands,
> And gym-shoes, dabbled with the dew?

—is to be delivered '*with a sense of "old, unhappy, far-off things"*.' Another should be read '*lingeringly*'; and another, '*with something of "the monstrous crying of wind"*—*Yeats, of course*'. As for the bittersweet *envoi*, it requires a '*rising to, and falling from, an ecstasy of nostalgia*'.

Yet looming up too in silhouette, like a tall evening shadow cast forward in time—the solitary witness of masterworks to come:

> A group of us have flattened the long grass
> Where through the day we watched the wickets fall
> Far from the pav. Wenda has left her hat,
> And only I remain, now they are gone,
> To notice how the evening sun can show
> The unsuspected hollows in the field,
> When it is all deserted.

('Fourth Former Loquitur')

One doesn't want to make the Brunette oeuvre sound more sanitary than it is. Though no Humbert Humbert or Henry Darger, Larkin played his Sapphic game in part to camouflage what many will still regard as an unwholesome preference for underage girls. Fourteen- and 15-year-olds—beyond the nymphet stage but still lissome and luscious—seem to have been the target demographic. In *Trouble at Willow Gables*, when Hilary Russell deliquesces over Mary Beech's 'shell-like ears', 'tawny hair', and 'bare white ankles emerging from woolly slippers', one can't help but sense—somewhat queasily—the storyteller's own preoccupation with the barely pubescent:

Hilary thought, as so often before she had thought, that there was nothing so beautiful in the world as a fourteen-year-old schoolgirl: the uncosmetic'd charm depended on the early flowering into a quiet beauty of soft, silken skin, ribboned hair, print dresses, socks and sensible shoes and a serious outlook on a world limited by puppies, horses, a few simple ideas, and changing Mummy's book at Boots'. How anyone could regard the version of six years later as in any way superior beat Hilary to a frazzle: it was preferring a painted savage dressed in bangles and skins, chockfull of feminine wiles, dodges, and other dishonesties directed to the same degrading sexual end, to a being who lived a life so simple and rounded-off in its purity that it only remained for it to be shattered—as it was. (84)

The mock-heroic rhetoric used to monumentalize such fixations—'Hilary had a vision of [Mary] embodying the purity of youth, dressed in white tennis things and haloed with a netball stand, surrounded, like a goddess of plenty, with hockey-sticks, cricket-pads, and other impedimenta'—does not entirely obviate the rather nasty wet-dream quality.

That said, for me at least, the lubriciousness is okay—and stays okay—when I consider what it led to. I don't mean only Larkin's poetry. It would take a far longer essay than this one to begin to measure the greatness of Larkin's novel *Jill*—perhaps the most exquisite and self-lacerating male-authored English fiction of the postwar period. Let me conclude with a Sappho-philic postscript on this, my favourite of his works—one seldom given the attention it deserves, even by otherwise devout Larkin-lovers.

By *self-lacerating* I simply mean honest and self-revealing to a shocking, painful, poetic degree. True, Larkin always insisted that the story of John Kemp, a shy scholarship student from the Midlands who arrives at Oxford in wartime and becomes disastrously obsessed with the schoolgirl cousin of his roommate's girlfriend—had little connection with his own university experiences. Critics and biographers have been careful not to press the question. (It is amazing how solicitously Larkin is still treated by prominent members of the British poetry establishment—as if he were a delicate maiden aunt in need of protection by those younger and indeed sexually more robust.) In the preface to the 1975 reprint of *Jill* Larkin obfuscated the matter quite brilliantly by suggesting that if readers of the novel *had* confused him with John Kemp it was because they mistakenly assumed that he, like his protagonist, was lower-middle-class and thus representative of the emerging Oxbridge meritocracy of the postwar period. Such was not the case, claimed Larkin: Kemp, his character, indeed has a bursary, but 'thanks to my father's generosity, my education was at no time a charge on public or other funds, and all in all my manner of life is much the same today as it was in 1940—*bourgeois*, certainly, but neither *haut* nor *petit*. Perhaps in consequence I may receive a few more degrees of imaginative credit for my hero's creation'.[12]

Readers of 'Brunette Coleman' may sense a certain disingenuousness here. The autobiographical aspect of *Jill* is glaring, it seems to me, and signalled above all by Larkin's flagrant recycling (and darkening) of his Willow Gables material. In *Jill's* central and strangest sequence, the otherwise timid Kemp—hoping to impress Christopher, his crass and carousing roommate—tells him (falsely) that he, Kemp, has an adorable younger sister named Jill. When Chris expresses mild curiosity Kemp begins embellishing wildly. Jill and he have always been very close, he explains: 'She's fond of poetry—that line. And it's funny, she's very sensitive. She had a great friend at school called Patsy—Patsy Hammond. They were really awfully thick. Then a year ago she went back to school as usual after the holidays and found that Patsy had gone to America with her people and wasn't coming back again. She was awfully cut up: hardly wrote for weeks' (117). Chris asks what school and Kemp promptly fabricates one: 'Willow Gables, the place is called. It's not very big' (118).

Christopher will evince no further interest in Kemp or his supposed sibling—he's cynically pursuing a rather fast young woman named Elizabeth—

[12] Philip Larkin, Introduction (1975), rpt. in *Jill* (Woodstock, NY: The Overlook Press, 1984), pp. 18–19. All further *Jill* references are to this edition.

but Kemp, shunned by Chris and his friends over the next weeks, becomes increasingly obsessed with his non-existent 'sister':

[She] was fifteen, and slight, her long fine dark honey-coloured hair fell to her shoulders and was bound by a white ribbon. Her dress was white. Her face was not like Elizabeth's, coarse for all its make-up, but serious-looking, delicate in shape and beautiful in repose, with high cheekbones: when she laughed these cheekbones were most noticeable and her expression became almost savage. (135)

Kemp is overtaken by a compulsion to picture 'Jill' before him:

She was a hallucination of innocence: he liked to think of her as preoccupied only with simple untroublesome things, like examinations and friendships, and, as he thought, each minute seemed to clarify her, as if the picture of her had been stacked away waiting in his mind, covered with dust, until this should happen. He spent hours filling up sheets of writing paper [...] with her address and name, repeated at all angles in different hand (some intended to be her own) and hesitant attempts to draw her face. But he soon stopped this last activity, because every line her drew merely obscured the picture in his own mind, and he had to stop and wait for it to reform. (135–6)

The fantasy 'Jill', one can't help noticing, is an almost exact replica of the 'uncosmetic'd' schoolgirl admired by Hilary Russell in *Michaelmas Term*. And soon enough, Pygmalion-like, Kemp has begun writing a story about her. In this strange twelve-page tale-within-a-tale Kemp imagines 'Jill' at Willow Gables, shortly after the departure of Patsy Hammond. Jill is lonely and falling in love from a distance, it seems, with another girl, a tall and introverted prefect named 'Minerva Strachey', whose air of dignified solitude intrigues the heroine. The story breaks off abruptly: Jill's father dies suddenly and when she returns to school following his funeral, she is met at the station by Minerva, who has been sent by the headmistress to accompany her back in a cab. Minerva is sympathetic but distant, and when Jill, sadly overwrought, declares she hates school, has no friends, and wants to be like Minerva—'able to get on without anyone else'—the prefect rebuffs the obvious overture. '[Jill] saw that Minerva had indicated that her detachment, even though it was admired, must still be respected; that loneliness was not to be abandoned at the first chance of friendship, but was a thing to be cherished in itself' (148).

This last appalling notation—that 'loneliness' is to be cherished in itself—might be said to encapsulate the zero-sum vision of the mature Larkin. For

Kemp, of course, solitary fantasy leads to a kind of self-obliteration: he sees an attractive young schoolgirl in an Oxford bookshop; imagines, uncannily, that she is his 'Jill' come to life; and starts stalking her in an inept yet sinister fashion. When he finds out that she is the fifteen-year-old cousin of Christopher's girlfriend Elizabeth and that her name is *Gillian* he simply becomes all the more infatuated. At the end of the fiction, having drunkenly tried to kiss Jill/Gillian on the stairwell outside a party in someone's rooms—to which he has not been invited—the hapless Kemp is excoriated by Elizabeth, punched in the face by Christopher, and thrown into a freezing fountain by a gang of loutish revellers. He is last seen, having succumbed to pneumonia, abject and feverish in the Oxford infirmary—dimly conscious that 'the love [he and Jill] had shared was dead'. Confused 'whether she had accepted him or not', Kemp can see 'no difference'—alarmingly—'between love fulfilled and love unfulfilled' (243). By contrast, Christopher and Elizabeth—jolly, spoiled, and sedate—are seen on the book's last page setting off for London where they plan to consummate their affair.

Might Kemp's suffering be construed as *lesbian* in nature? No summary of *Jill* can convey the powerful sympathy with which Larkin treats his hero or indeed the viciousness and venality of the book's other characters. Like Patricia Highsmith in her *Ripley* novels Larkin is unnervingly adept at making Kemp's secret longings seem comprehensible if not oddly benign. Kemp may be a sociopath—or not. ('With his fair hair and pale face he looked like a fanatic, but his eyes were not bright enough', 161). Yet everyone else is so much worse. Gillian the schoolgirl remains a cipher, but the ghastly Chris and Elizabeth are like a pair out of Shakespearean tragedy: they would do well in *Macbeth* or *King Lear*. *Jill*'s world is one in which the milk of human kindness has permanently soured.

And time and again Larkin makes the lesbian subtext impossible to miss. The aborted connections in the embedded school tale—Jill and Patsy, Jill and Minerva—provide a homoerotic matrix of course for Kemp's own doomed infatuation: even before seeing Gillian, he already inhabits his own private Willow Gables, a dream-world of impotence, fear, and impinging loss. (Psychologically speaking, the interpolated tale seems at once uncanny and overdetermined: it is as if Kemp both wants to *have* Jill and to *be* Jill.) Yet striking too the book's other invocations of the *amor impossibilis*. Noticing Gillian for the first time in the crowded bookshop Kemp falls into a lyric reverie positively Sappho-like in tone: 'It was her hair, the colour of dark viscous honey, her serious face, her wild high cheekbones' (156); 'the sight of her awkward girl's body afflicted him with a fearful longing, like some call of destiny' (157). Later, sitting impatiently through a comic film in an Oxford cinema because Gillian is in the theatre across the street with Elizabeth and Chris and he wants to spy on her when she comes out, Kemp, like a sort of downmarket Sidney, experiences precisely those symptoms of love-anguish itemized—so momentously for English poetry—in Sappho's Fragment 31:

The enormous shadows gesticulated before him and he sat with his eyes shut, hearing only the intermittent remarks of the characters and the sounds of the action. It was curious how little speech there was. A squalling childish voice said something and everyone laughed: this was followed by a long interval of banging, scraping, and rending, interspersed with studiedly familiar noises—the tinkling of glass against decanter, the slamming of a car door. He opened his eyes for a moment, saw a man and a girl driving through the country, and shut them again. When he thought of Jill being so near, only across the street, with people he knew, yet where he was not with her and could not see her, his breath came faster and a curious physical unease affected him and he wanted to stretch. (177–8)

Nor does Larkin ignore the English Sappho, the charm-impaired Radclyffe Hall.[13] The word 'loneliness' resounds throughout *Jill*, ever more numbingly. One's sense of the repetition is largely subliminal: one feels it as a sort of low-level textual *headache*. Yet every now and then Larkin sets the word off talismanically—as when Kemp watches 'Jill' ride away on her bicycle after seeing her for the first time in the bookshop:

He stopped under a tree, looking this way and that. And if he found her name and address, what then? He would not dare to approach her again after his rudeness that afternoon. All that would remain for him to do would be to discover her real life, to follow her about and not be noticed, to make lists of the clothes she wore and the places she went to, to make her the purpose of his life once more, now that he had just begun sniffing enviously again at the society of Christopher Warner and Elizabeth Dowling. In this quest his loneliness would be an asset: it would be mobility and even charm. (159)

[13] The gym mistress at Willow Gables, one notes, is named 'Miss Hall.'

Later, having discovered her identity and waited in vain to see her, he feels 'hollow with grief, as if there were *a great well of aloneness* inside him that could never be filled up' (180; my italics). A case could even be made, I think, that *Jill*'s tragi-buffoonish next-to-last scene—the tossing of the drunken Kemp into the fountain—is a kind of mock-heroic literalization of Hall's title: Kemp finds his own well of loneliness, bathetically, in the middle of a college quadrangle, above which 'stars [march] frostily across the sky' (236).

Can Philip Larkin be forgiven? In a startling rant after *Trouble at Willow Gables* was posthumously published in 2002, a female critic for the *Guardian* sent Larkin to 'the back of the class'—first for writing porn she felt wasn't 'saucy' enough, and then, somewhat unfairly, for having been glum, bald, and bespectacled. (In case anyone wondered, women can be as nasty about men as men can be about women.) The fact that since his death he had been exposed as a 'man with…urges' struck her as 'pretty funny', the critic revealed, for 'after all, with skin the colour of soft curd cheese and his curranty eyes blinking out from behind a couple of jam-jar bottoms, Larkin was hardly made for sex. The first time Monica Jones clapped eyes on the man who was to be her lover for more than three decades, she turned to her companion and said: "He looks like a snorer".'[14]

Now from what I have written one perhaps might conclude—wrongly— that the adult Larkin had no sex life at all. Such was not the case, as Motion's biography made absorbingly clear in the 1990s. Yet the description above of Larkin as the 'lover' of Monica Jones for over three decades produces a somewhat distorted image, I reckon, of both poet and work. Though obviously of long duration, the intimacy with Jones, a lecturer at the University of Leicester and subsequently Larkin's literary executor, does not strike one as primarily eros-driven. Nor indeed do the poet's other somewhat sketchy affairs—including an elderly fling with Betty Mackereth, his secretary at the Bryn Jones Library in the 1970s. Judging by photographs, none of these girlfriends was either young or conventionally beautiful; not a single 'Jill' among them. On the contrary—especially to the lesbian eye—several have a curiously mannish 'Brunette' look. With 15-year-olds out of the running, it would seem, Larkin made do with his own little crew of middle-aged spin-

[14] Rachel Cooke, 'Larkin Takes a Beating', *The Guardian*, 21 April 2002.

sters. The 'loaf-haired' Betty—risibly described as such in the poem 'Toads Revisited'—looks like a rangy, somewhat weather-beaten games mistress. And so, one might add, did Larkin's mother Eva—another 'Larkinesque' brunette to whom he remained devoted all his life.

Yet whatever the 'real' circumstances, what matters is the inner life. I have to say I find the dysphoric sense of self—and of the erotic—revealed in Larkin's poetry rather more sympathetic than the comments of erstwhile critics. Who is to judge who is 'made for sex' and who isn't? A lack of pulchritude does not always spell carnal frustration: Jean-Paul Sartre was pretty hideous—Larkin an Adonis in comparison—but in Sartre's case a troll-like physiognomy seems not to have diverted him from a lengthy career as the Casanova of the Left Bank. What differs, obviously, is whether one has the necessary full-forwardness and *esprit*—especially when social conventions, rightly or wrongly, set up barriers to fulfilment. Philip Larkin was as 'made for sex' as anyone else, it seems to me, which is not to say it came to him easily. In the character of 'Brunette Coleman' he created someone whose loneliness, obliquely observed, mirrored his own—indeed, *was* his own. Was he entirely aware what he was doing? Perhaps not. But he knew enough to know he needed her—needed to smoke her cigarettes and write her stories, to dream of Willow Gables in her company, and in the waywardness of her desire find a way into his own.

5

Kingsley Amis: Against Fakery

James Fenton

'Thou hast it now,' says Banquo at the beginning of Act Three: 'King, Cawdor, Glamis, all | As the weird women promised; and yet I fear | Thou playedst most foully for't.' And, quite apart from the petty level of rivalries over the trivial sorts of recognition, most poets have a strong professional sense of when their colleagues and predecessors are playing most foully for some advantage. Just as actors are, among themselves, the most devastating critics of their fellow actors, because they can see only too easily how cheaply certain effects were achieved that may well have wowed an innocent audience, so poets are alert to what smacks of trickery. And they feel there is a sort of double injustice when a particular kind of shamming succeeds, first because it is shamming, and second because it happens to be precisely the kind of shamming that the rest of us like to feel we have forsworn.

But it may happen, deplorable though it is to have to admit it, that a certain degree of fakery helps things along, that a liberal application of bogusness in art is a way of priming the pump. For instance, only a part of what a conductor does on the podium may be aimed at the orchestra; the rest could be a way of winning over the audience, of prompting their emotions, guiding their understanding and eliciting their admiration. Particular gestures of the concert pianist may serve no function as far as the making of the music is concerned, but may usefully say to the crowd: what I've just played was very difficult and has taken it out of me; please show your appreciation in the usual way. Fellow conductors or rival pianists may watch in horror while these subtle or gross appeals are made, but have to admit that, nevertheless, the performance in the strict sense—the actual production of the notes—was superb. A splendid result may be achieved by dishonest means. In a just world this shouldn't happen, but whoever said this was a just world? And besides, the audience is already on its feet.

In one of his Oxford lectures, Seamus Heaney, always a most generous critic, tried to characterize the poetry of Dylan Thomas without turning nasty. 'I have the impression,' says Heaney, 'that negative criticism of Dylan Thomas's work is more righteous and more imbued with [a] kind of punitive impulse than is usual...It often seems less a matter of the poet's being criticised than of his being got back at, and my guess is that on these occasions the reader's older self is punishing the younger one who hearkened to Thomas's oceanic music and credited its promise to bring the world and self into cosmic harmony.'[1]

Well, yes, there is that. There is the sense of having been cheated, if the older self discovers that what had been puzzled over, long and hard, was 'meaningless, windy trash'. The young self was trusting, and that is not something to be ashamed of. Heaney has a telling phrase about Thomas. He says that 'too often in the *Collected Poems* the largeness of the utterance is rigged'.[2] And he calls him, using a term from Patrick Kavanagh, a 'bucklepper'—'one who leaps like a young buck. The bucklepper...is somebody with a stereotypical sprightliness and gallivanting roguery, insufficiently self-aware and not necessarily spurious, but still offering himself or herself too readily as a form of spectator sport...an image of the Celt as perceived by the Saxon...'[3]

But imagine for a moment the possibility that, without being a bucklepper, Thomas would never have got going at all. Imagine that a part of the charm comes from the spuriousness, as it certainly does with the early Yeats:

> I will arise and go now, and go to Innisfree,
> And a small cabin build there, of clay and wattles made:
> Nine bean-rows will I have there, a hive for the honey-bee,
> And live alone in the bee-loud glade.

> ('The Lake Isle of Innisfree')

---

[1] 'Dylan the Durable', in Seamus Heaney, *The Redress of Poetry* (London: Faber and Faber, 1995). pp. 136–7.
[2] Ibid., p. 134.   [3] Ibid., p. 125.

Of course there is the question how long is a row of beans, but *nine* bean-rows seems an awful lot of beans.

Nobody surely thought when they first read this poem that Yeats was actually planning to do as he said: up sticks from London and learn the art of building in clay and wattle. It was a poem after all, and what was expected from this kind of poem was a beautiful sort of phoniness. The poet counts on our indulgence, from the very first line, with its shocking secular appropriation of 'I will arise and go to my father and say unto him, Father I have sinned, etcetera,' to the last, 'I hear it in the deep heart's core.'

What we like about the 'Deep heart's core' (a phrase lifted and adapted from Blake's 'The Smile') is what we like about the termination of the first stanza, the 'bee-loud glade'. It's a matter of the beautiful deployment of vowel sounds on three successive accented syllables. And, yes, it is possible to share a profound desire to return to nature, but there is nothing deep about the frivolous, unrealistic proposal Yeats actually makes in his opening stanza.

Most of us agree with Marianne Moore that there ought to be, in poetry, a place for the genuine; it's galling to have to admit that there's a place for the phoney as well. And the Movement poets perhaps put themselves at something of a disadvantage if a refusal of phoniness turned into a refusal to risk a gesture. If there is sometimes more than a hint of bitterness about them, that might be partly to do with the feeling of having held back. It takes a little historical sympathy to understand that bitterness today when a great deal of the windy poetry of the 1940s has been forgotten, so that we don't notice, in the Movement poets, what is being renounced in favour of what, today, might seem modest virtues. Two people can look at the same evidence. The first sees in it a splendid rejection of the false. The second detects a reluctance to get going, an inability to take on the role of poet.

I am reminded of Richard Burton who, though blessed with everything required of a classical actor—looks, voice, nobility of demeanour—seemed as the years passed not to respect himself as a thespian. *His* fantasy, his Lake Isle of Innisfree, was the academic life. In such a role he thought he might achieve full self-respect, but, when wearing makeup and tights...not. He once described making a film in which he refused to wear costume from the waist down. It was the ultimate budget film, and all the long shots were taken from the cutting room floor of somebody else's epic. The scenes in which Burton appeared were exclusively close-ups. So he could keep his everyday

pants on throughout the shoot. And that is what he did. He still wanted to be
a great actor, but he was no longer prepared to wear the tights.

Something of this uneasiness may be found, but very carefully negotiated,
transmuted, in certain poems of Philip Larkin's, where it seems as if in order
to get to the beautiful moment, like the beautiful moment in the last stanza
of 'High Windows', you have to pass through the very ugly first stanza: you
have to pay a little ugliness tax. And it is usually made clear in mature Larkin
that the sort of indulgence I have mentioned as being expected by a Yeats
or a Dylan Thomas is neither expected nor desired. The poetry seeks to be
unaffected and immune to mockery. It is not supposed to play most foully
for advantage.

Yeats is there at the outset, of course, in *The North Ship* (1945), Larkin's first
collection. Here is Larkin in the grip of Yeats, in a poem called 'Ugly Sister':

> I will climb thirty steps to my room,
> Lie on my bed;
> Let the music, the violin, cornet and drum
> Drowse from my head.
>
> Since I was not bewitched in adolescence
> And brought to love,
> I will attend to the trees and their gracious silence,
> To winds that move.

Thirty steps, perhaps a magical number, like the nine bean-rows. I will arise,
I will climb, I will *attend* to the trees, a ceremonious future tense of a cere-
monious verb. But Yeats is in Larkin an influence to be overcome. Yeats,
Auden, Graves, Thomas—all of them figured large in the shared world of
the young Larkin and the young Kingsley Amis, but all of them would have
figured in ways very different from today. Auden, for instance, meant the
pre-war Auden, but I doubt very much whether the categories of pre- or
post-war Auden (which were for Larkin's generation so controversial) have
much force today.

Unease about the pretension involved in writing poetry at all is something
one expects to find in young poets—manifesting itself in violence, obscenity
perhaps, and mockery. Yet the violence and obscenity of Larkin's poetry, the
ugliness tax, is a feature of the later works, and in the case of Amis there are
parodies written towards the end of his life—parodies is perhaps not quite
the right word, *sinkings* of poems, which you would expect to find from a
younger, anxious pen, as for instance the 'impromptu' squib 'Equal Made':

> Only the actions of the just
> Smell sweet and blossom in their dust,
> Which does the just about as much
> Good as a smart kick in the crotch.[4]

What is being sunk here, by means of the title and the quotation in the first two lines, is one of the old stalwarts of school anthologies, James Shirley's *Dirge*. Shirley is one of the Cavalier poets, and this song comes at the end of a drama written in 1659, long since forgotten except in this context, called *The Contention of Ajax and Ulysses for the Armour of Achilles*.

Actually this is just the sort of poem that Amis liked, or came to like better as he despaired of the poetry and in general the art of his day. It is normally called 'Death the Leveller'. Here are the first and the last stanzas:

> The glories of our blood and state
>   Are shadows, not substantial things;
> There is no armour against fate;
>   Death lays his icy hand on kings;
>   Sceptre and crown
>   Must tumble down
> And in the dust be equals made
> With the poor crooked scythe and spade.

And the last:

> The garlands wither on your brow,
>   Then boast no more your mighty deeds;
> Upon death's purple altar now,
>   See where the victor-victim bleeds;
>   Your heads must come
>   To the cold tomb;
> Only the actions of the just
> Smell sweet, and blossom in their dust.

You will see that the Amis sinking lines ('Which does the just about as much | Good as a smart kick in the crotch') do not in fact subvert Shirley's meaning. Shirley never implies that living on through the memory of your just deeds does you yourself any good after your death. He says simply that that is all there is—no mention of the resurrection of the body in this classicizing dirge.

---

[4] All quotations from Amis's poems are from *Collected Poems: 1944–1979* (London: Hutchinson, 1979).

Another poet Amis sends up is Walter de la Mare (1873–1956), once again a figure often encountered in the classroom of former days, and one, as the textbooks say, 'unaffected by fashion'—meaning thereby that he set his face against modernism, as can be seen in this poem, called 'When I lie where shades of darkness'. Needing to look this up recently, I found I had no text of it, having never got round to buying a complete De la Mare. But it was immediately available on the internet, having been one of a group of favourite poems read, not long before, at the memorial service for an Oxford biologist. The poems chosen for this occasion included another by de la Mare, 'Very old are the woods', an extract from Tennyson's 'In Memoriam', Shakespeare's 'Fear no more the heat of the sun', Tennyson's 'Break, break, break', and Housman's 'Tell me not here, it needs not saying'.

This kind of ad hoc memorial service anthology, featuring poems that have something of the quality of a talisman or a motto, can give us an insight into the popular life of poetry. The funeral poem is a burgeoning rather than a dying form, as is its equivalent for wedding services. Often it is a replacement for biblical texts, meeting a secular need for a solemn utterance. It is by no means immune to fashion, since Auden's 'Stop all the clocks' began to feature at funeral services, and in anthologies that cater for such occasions, only after the film *Four Weddings and a Funeral*, just as his 'September 1939' spread on the internet after 9/11.

Amis was very interested in this kind of poetry, and in 1978 produced an anthology called *The Faber Popular Reciter* whose purpose was to bring together poems which had once, that is before the Second World War, been 'too well known to be worth reprinting...they were learned by heart and recited in class, or performed as turns at grown-up gatherings; they were sung in church or chapel or on other public occasions. Some were set as texts for classical translation, an exercise that gives you an insight hard to achieve by other means: the fact, noted by my fellows and me, that Mrs Hemans's "Graves of a Household" went into Latin elegiacs with exceptional ease encourages a second look at that superficially superficial piece.'[5]

Amis assumed that most of what he was talking about had gone, partly because poetry was not learnt by heart at school any more, and partly because the occasions for standing up and reciting a poem, as opposed to quoting it among friends, had vanished. But as we have seen this is no longer the

[5] Amis (ed.), *The Faber Popular Reciter* (London: Faber and Faber, 1978), p. 15.

case: any of the poems read at my Oxford biologist's memorial service could, with a slight shift in criteria, have figured in his anthology. One that does is Tennyson's 'Break, break, break'. Another is 'Death the Leveller'—the poem Amis mocks. But Amis thought that 'a poet of our own day cannot write like that—in fact, during the 1930s this entire literary genre quite suddenly disappeared, never to return'.[6]

He was wrong up to a point, and a part of what he had overlooked was the abiding influence of figures such as Walter de la Mare, who not only was held in sufficient esteem (Companion of Honour, Order of Merit) to be buried in St Paul's Cathedral, but had also, in addition to his own poetic example, made such anthologies as *Come Hither*, a 'collection of rhymes and poems for the young of all ages' (1923) which lived on, and which is rich both in the kind of largely Victorian poetry Amis was talking about, as well as in folk poetry and all sorts of verse that happened to be out of literary fashion at the time.

Here is the de la Mare poem Amis parodied:

When I lie where shades of darkness
Shall no more assail mine eyes,
Nor the rain make lamentation
    When the wind sighs;

How will fare the world whose wonder
Was the very proof of me?
Memory fades, must the remembered
    Perishing be?

Oh, when this my dust surrenders
Hand, foot, lip, to dust again,
May these loved and loving faces
    Please other men!

May the rusting harvest hedgerow
Still the Traveller's Joy entwine,
And as happy children gather
    Posies once mine.

Look thy last on all things lovely,
Every hour. Let no night
Seal thy sense in deathly slumber

[6] Ibid., p 18.

> Till to delight
>
> Thou have paid thy utmost blessing;
> Since that all things thou wouldst praise
> Beauty took from those who loved them
> In other days.

The diction is antiquated for its day, although not as bizarre a take on the antique as we find in early Pound. The expression is, to my ear, often awkward, as if the poet really was having some difficulty in negotiating the chosen form. What of the message?

De la Mare says that when we face death we should not surrender to the temptation to wish that everything and everyone should cease with us. We should take a final delight in what we are bidding farewell to, remembering that we inherited these objects of beauty from others who delighted in them—as it were, we inherited our love of the autumn hedgerow. It did not originate with us. Also, we should be glad that those who survive us will themselves become objects of delight to others.

These are sentiments that have a meaning. They may be hard things to meditate upon when we are dying, but the poem had obviously been something that had stayed in the Oxford biologist's mind, embodying, perhaps, an aspiration: this is what it would be to die well.

Now here is Amis's version, which is called 'Shitty':

> Look thy last on all things shitty
> While thou'rt at it: soccer stars,
> Soccer crowds, bedizened bushheads
> Jerking over their guitars,
>
> German tourists, plastic roses,
> Face of Mao and face of Ché,
> Women wearing curtains, blankets,
> Beckett at the ICA,
>
> High-rise blocks and action paintings,
> Sculptures made from wire and lead:
> Each of them a sight more lovely
> Than the screens about your bed.

The worst things he can think of—modern art and architecture, revolutionary youth culture, sport, rock music, German tourists, artificial flowers, pretentious women—not one of them is as ugly as the knowledge of imminent death. The point being made, once again, leaves the point being made by Walter de la Mare unscathed.

Amis returns to the attack, in the pendant to 'Shitty' which is called 'Lovely':

> Look thy last on all things lovely
>   Every hour, an old shag said,
> Meaning they turn lovelier if thou
>   Thinkst about them soon being dead.
>
> Do they? When that 'soon' means business,
>   They might lose their eye-appeal,
> Go a bit like things unlovely,
>   Get upstaged by how you feel.
>
> The best time to see things lovely
>   Is in youth's primordial bliss,
> Which is also when you rather
>   Go for old shags talking piss.

It hardly needs saying that de la Mare was not in the least implying that these lovely things will seem lovelier to you in your death agonies, but never mind: de la Mare thinks you should bless the world as you leave it, and Amis says you won't be feeling like that sort of mental activity when you are dying; it is in youth that we tend to fall for poetry that proposes such rubbish. And so this poem, with its warning that death is going to be absolutely horrible, is part of a dialogue with Larkin, whose 'The Old Fools' asks of the old the rhetorical question 'Why aren't they screaming?'

Well, the purpose of parody is as often to celebrate as to destroy the original. But what we see here and in the introduction to the *Faber Popular Reciter*, products of Amis's increasing tendency to rant in his later years, is the result of an uneasiness about popular poetry, very similar to that of George Orwell, from whose 1942 essay on Kipling the idea for an anthology of what Orwell calls 'good bad' poetry derives. Amis alludes to Orwell's point that 'there is a great deal of good bad poetry in English, all of it, I should say, subsequent to 1790'. He names several examples, half of which Amis includes in his reciter, adding that 'one could fill a fair-sized anthology with good bad poems, if it were not for the significant fact that good bad poetry is usually too well known to be worth reprinting'. Decades later Amis realized that this was no longer the case.

What Amis doesn't quote is the next, to my mind faintly repulsive, passage in Orwell:

It is no use pretending that in an age like our own, 'good' poetry can have any genuine popularity. It is, and must be, the cult of a very few people, the least tolerated of the arts. Perhaps that statement needs a certain amount of qualification. True poetry can sometimes be acceptable to the mass of the people when it disguises itself as something else. One can see an example of this in the folk-poetry that England still possesses, certain nursery rhymes and mnemonic rhymes, for instance, and the songs that soldiers make up, including the words that go to some of the bugle-calls. But in general ours is a civilisation in which the very word 'poetry' evokes a hostile snigger or, at best, the sort of frozen disgust that most people feel when they hear the word 'God'.[7]

Orwell was trapped in a circular chain of reasoning here. However much he wishes to champion Kipling, he cannot see his poetry as good. For when any poem becomes popular he suspects that if it is popular it must be bad. Amis, around about the period of the *Popular Reciter*, ran a little poetry column in the *Daily Mirror* whose purpose was precisely to recommend the virtues of poetry to a working-class audience, so he cannot have entirely agreed with Orwell on this point.

Nevertheless there is some residue of Orwell's circular thinking in him. He includes Gray's Elegy, for instance, and a beautiful section of Tennyson's 'In Memoriam', and some pieces by Blake, in a book about which he says: 'Perhaps popular poetry, outside the accidental contributions of poets whose critical esteem rests on other achievements, can never be anything but what George Orwell called good bad poetry.' From this, I conclude that if Amis (like Orwell) really liked a poem he too began to distrust it. Popular poetry disappeared in the 1930s, and could never return because a popular poet

would almost certainly lack in the first place the required skill and application. Should he possess these, he would even so find himself using a dead style and forms. Clarity, heavy rhythms, strong rhymes and the rest are vehicles of confidence, of a kind of innocence, of shared faiths and other long-extinct states of mind. The two great themes of popular verse were the nation and the Church, neither of which, to say the least, confers much sense of community any longer. Minor themes, like admiration of or desire for a simple rustic existence, have just been forgotten. The most obvious cause of it all is the disintegrative shock of the Great War.[8]

And indeed it is with the poetry of the Great War that the volume ends—but not with what we think of now as war poetry par excellence—that is

---

[7] 'Rudyard Kipling,' in *George Orwell: Essays*, ed. John Carey (London: Everyman, 2002), p. 408.

[8] *Faber Popular Reciter*, p. 18.

anti-war poetry (Owen, Sassoon, Ivor Gurney). The volume ends with Rupert Brooke's 'The Soldier', Alan Seeger's 'I have a rendez-vous with death', and Julian Grenfell's 'Into Battle':

> In dreary, doubtful waiting hours,
>   Before the brazen frenzy starts,
> The horses show him noble powers;
>   O patient eyes, courageous hearts!
>
> And when the burning moment breaks,
>   And all things else are out of mind,
> And only joy of battle takes
>   Him by the throat and makes him blind,
>
> Through joy and blindness he shall know,
>   Not caring much to know, that still
> Nor lead nor steel shall reach him, so
>   That it be not the Destined Will.
>
> The thundering line of battle stands,
>   And in the air Death moans and sings;
> But Day shall clasp him with strong hands,
>   And night shall fold him in soft wings.

I can almost see Kingsley Amis, as he concludes his volume with such verses, bursting with laughter at the provocation he anticipates, for he knows perfectly well that the reader will find these sentiments deplorable. In his introduction he has called Rupert Brooke's 'The Soldier' 'one of the greatest poems of our century'. So he wants to shock. I might add that de la Mare's anthology, *Come Hither*, which is organized thematically, has a section on war which does display, although published in 1923, this prelapsarian quality, without perhaps glorying in war as Julian Grenfell did, yet managing to include even Owen and Sassoon without making them seem particularly anti-war in the now familiar sense.

Popular poetry can no longer be written, good poetry can never be popular, war poetry can no longer praise war, poetry can no longer be written with clarity, strong rhythms and rhymes: there is a great deal of lamenting here. One is reminded of Larkin's view, very much shared by Amis, that jazz was a music of the past, that the well of jazz had essentially been poisoned by Charlie Parker. Amis often talked on this subject, and sometimes wrote letters to the Saturday radio jazz programmes, out of the same dismay. He composed a parody of a famous Betjeman poem that was itself a light-hearted tribute to Thomas Hardy. Amis's tribute to Hardy's tribute to Betjeman is called 'Brunswick Blues':

> Bongo, sitar, 'cello, flute, electric piano, bass guitar,
> Training orchestra, Research Team, Workshop, Group, Conservatoire,
> *Square Root, Nexus, Barbaresque, Distortions, Voltage*—bloody row,
> For Louis Armstrong, Mildred Bailey, Walter Page and Sidney Catlett lie in
> Brunswick Churchyard now.

> Trumpets gelded, drums contingent, saxophones that bleat or bawl,
> Keyless, barless, poor-man's Boulez, improvising on fuck-all,
> Far beyond what feeling, reason, even mother wit allow,
> While Muggsy Spanier, Floyd O'Brien, Sterling Bose and Henry Allen
>   lie in Decca churchyard now.

> Dead's the note we loved that swelled within us, made us gasp and stare,
> Simple joy and simple sadness thrashing the astounded air;
> What replaced them no one asked for, but it turned up anyhow,
> And Coleman Hawkins, Johnny Hodges, Bessie Smith and Pee Wee Russell
>   lie in Okeh churchyard now.

The music of our youth is dead. The poetry we once fell for turns out to be piss. What strikes one is the penchant shared by Larkin and Amis for premature mourning. Here's another poem about disillusionment with music, this time classical music: César Franck's Symphony in D minor:

> 'That slimy tune,' I said, and got a laugh,
> In the middle of old Franck's D minor thing:
> The dotted-rhythm clarinet motif.

> Not always slimy. I thought, at fifteen,
> It went to show that real love was found
> At the end of the right country lane.

> I thought that, like Keats and the rest of them,
> Old Franck was giving me a preview of
> The world, action in art, a paradigm.

> Yes, I know better now, or different.
> Not image: buffer only, syrup, crutch.
> 'Slimy' was a snarl of disappointment.

Perhaps this is the moment to note how much work, in Amis's poetry, is done by conversational idiom. In this case, we get over a worryingly pretentious reference to a Belgian composer's most famous work by calling it a

D minor thing rather than symphony. Whether twice calling the composer Old Franck helps dispel the feared pretentiousness, I doubt. Still, ' "Slimy" was a snarl of disappointment' is swift and concentrated and brings us back to what Heaney was saying about Dylan Thomas—in attacking him we punish our younger self.

We have so far chiefly encountered, in Amis, poems about poems or the writing of poetry—a characteristic legacy of the Movement. Amis wrote in his first collection, *A Case of Samples,* one of the best known of these, called 'A Bookshop Idyll':

> Between the GARDENING and the COOKERY
> Comes the brief POETRY shelf;
> By the Nonesuch Donne, a thin anthology
> Offers itself.
>
> Critical, and with nothing else to do,
> I scan the Contents page,
> Relieved to find the names are mostly new;
> No one of my age.
>
> Like all strangers, they divide by sex:
> *Landscape near Parma*
> Interests a man, so does *The Double Vortex,*
> So does *Rilke and Buddha.*
>
> 'I travel, you see', 'I think' and 'I can read'
> These titles seem to say;
> But *I Remember You, Love is My Creed.*
> *Poem for J.,*
>
> The ladies' choice, discountenance my patter
> For several seconds;
> From somewhere in this (as in any) matter
> A moral beckons.
>
> Should poets bicycle-pump the human heart
> Or squash it flat?
> Man's love is of man's life a thing apart;
> Girls aren't like that.
>
> We men have got love well weighed up; our stuff
> Can get by without it.
> Women don't seem to think that's good enough;
> They write about it,

And the awful way their poems lay them open
   Just doesn't strike them.
Women are really much nicer than men:
   No wonder we like them.

Deciding this, we can forget those times
   We sat up half the night
Chockful of love, crammed with bright thoughts, names, rhymes,
   And couldn't write.

It was the fate of this poem to be remembered for its patronizing depiction of women's poetry, not for the rueful coda that was supposed to cast doubt upon everything said hitherto.

Another of these programmatic poems about poetry is 'Here is Where', a short lyric critical of a rather easy sort of deployment of natural landscape in verse. The first stanza is a quote from an imaginary poem, then the authorial voice intrudes:

Here, where the ragged water
Is twilled and spun over
Pebbles backed like beetles,
Bright as beer-bottles
Bits of it like snow beaten,
Or milk boiling in a saucepan...

Going well so far, eh?
But soon, I'm sorry to say,
The here-where recipe
Will have to intrude its *I*,
It's main verb *want*,
Its *this* at some tangent.

What has this subject
Got to do with that object?
Why drag in
All that water and stone?
Scream the place down *here*,
There's nobody *there*.

The country, to townies,
Is hardly more than nice,
A window-box, pretty
When the afternoon's empty;

> When a visitor waits,
> The window shuts.

What is being proposed here is a rather radical act of self-abnegation. It is saying to city-dwelling poets don't fill out your poems with descriptions of nature that are, let's face it, of no great interest or consequence to you. What matters is what you really want, not this stock background.

However if we take the last two poems together an awful lot of poetic subject-matter is being placed out of bounds: don't write poems whose purpose is to show off your acquaintance with foreign lands, or to blind us with philosophy or your superior reading habits. Don't lay your heart bare in such an embarrassing way. Don't blather on about nature. Add to that a paradoxical acceptance of claims made on behalf of modernism (after the Great War it became inappropriate to write a certain kind of poem) and he's in danger of making the whole enterprise impossible.

Here is an unusual poem for Amis: it found its way into the *Penguin Book of Homosexual Verse*.[9] It describes something I believe new to poetry, which is 'situational homosexuality'—same-sex relations arising principally out of the restricted situation, rather than having their chief impulse in personal preference. It's called 'An Ever-Fixed Mark'—but it is not, for once, getting at Shakespeare or some other poet:

> Years ago, at a private school
> Run on traditional lines,
> One fellow used to perform
> Prodigious feats in the dorm;
> His quite undevious designs
> Found many a willing tool.
>
> On the rugger field, in the gym,
> Buck marked down at his leisure
> The likeliest bits of stuff;
> The notion, familiar enough,
> Of 'using somebody for pleasure'
> Seemed handy and harmless to him.
>
> But another chap was above
> The diversions of such a lout;

---

[9] Ed. Stephen Coote (London 1983).

Seven years in the place
And he never got to first base
With the kid he followed about:
What interested Ralph was love.

He did the whole thing in style—
Letters three times a week,
Sonnet-sequences, Sunday walks;
Then, during one of their talks,
The youngster caressed his cheek,
And that made it all worth while.

These days, for a quid pro quo,
Ralph's chum does what and with which;
Buck's playmates, family men,
Eye a Boy Scout now and then.
Sex is a momentary itch,
Love never lets you go.

The boy who is after sex chooses well, it appears, since he selects partners who have no objection to being 'used for pleasure'. The boy who falls seriously in love has unfortunately chosen the school tart, who in future life is indeed going to become a prostitute. But that's love, whereas the other situational homosexuality essentially evaporates, leaving in later married life—and here the poem exhibits a liberalism which would be likely to get it into trouble in Britain today nothing more than an occasional passing attraction to a Boy Scout.

Like Larkin, he was not a prolific poet. The 150-odd pages of the *Collected Poems 1944–1979*, indeed, look compact beside the 300-plus of the Collected Larkin. Amis deferred to Larkin as a poet, and his work takes on an extra interest as an accompaniment to Larkin's. The two friends shared so much, in addition to their horror of transience, their evident fear of death, their disenchantment with art, their brutal way with conversational idiom.

Amis's 'A Reunion', evoking a gathering of old soldiers, is one of his most sober and extensive achievements, and belongs in the same category as Larkin's 'Show Saturday'—pictures of an England not yet gone for good. It ends with a tribute to the 'Small kinds and degrees of love'—the old camaraderie between soldiers—seen from the perspective of old age:

Disbandment has come to us
As it comes to all who grow old;
Demobilised now, we face

What we faced when we first enrolled.
Stand still in the middle rank!
See you show them a touch of pride!—
Left-right, left-right, bags of swank—
On the one-man pass-out parade.

A note immediately beneath these lines tells us that all characters and details in this poem are fictitious, but the voice, the idiom, the fears, and the stab at fortitude—all these are authentically authorial.

6

Philosophy and Literature in the 1950s: The Rise of the 'Ordinary Bloke'

Colin McGinn

For most of the history of Western philosophy, the views of the 'common man' were not held in high esteem. Such a man may be populous, he may even be powerful, but he is not astute about fundamental matters. When it comes to philosophical insight, a caste system is in force: an elite group of trained philosophers stands in judgement over the shallow errors of the hordes of the philosophically uneducated, criticizing and correcting. The common man knows nothing—or nothing worth knowing—about Truth, Reality, Goodness, and Beauty. Nowhere is this attitude more pronounced than in the philosophy of Plato. In Plato's system the run of mankind is hopelessly in thrall to the world of sensory appearance, cut off from the real world of eternal Platonic forms; the common man (or woman: but women didn't get much of a look-in) lives a life of delusion, tricked by the senses, stunted in intellect. The famous analogy of the cave illustrates this Platonic disdain for how the common man sees things. He is like a man imprisoned in a dark cave, seeing only the flickering shadows of real things, convinced that this is the whole world, while outside the cave there is a more robust reality of which he is lamentably unaware. Only the rigorously trained philosopher, sequestered at birth, bombarded with mathematics, steeped in esoteric doctrines, can ascend to knowledge of this higher reality, eventually perceiving the 'sun' itself, the Form of Goodness.[1] For Plato, these cave dwellers are rather like cave men in our modern sense (though Plato knew nothing, of course, of our troglodytic prehistory): men of ignorance, rough-minded, riddled with error, small of soul. Philosophy alone, as an esoteric discipline, can release us from this natural veil of ignorance, and it is available only to a fortunate few. Those trips of Socrates around the marketplace, interrogating the Athenian man about town (Glaucon, Thrasymachus, et al.), are exercises in humiliation for the intellectual pygmies he so patiently exposes for the ignorant twits they are—notwithstanding their initial confidence when Socrates steps up to chat a while. The common man exists to be corrected, not consulted.

Later Greek philosophy kept up the pressure and the disdain, particularly in the form of scepticism. Zeno (it was thought) had already demonstrated that motion is unreal, despite its appearance to our uncritical senses, but later Greek scepticism insisted further that our senses are so prone to illusion, our intellects so easily led astray, that nothing of any consequence could seriously be said to be known. The Pyrrhonic sceptics even went so far as to suggest that *all* judgement should be suspended, so hopelessly inept is the human mind. The common man may take himself to know this or that simple thing, but the philosopher, from his superior vantage point, can see that all such claims are baseless. What is called common sense is just so much stabbing in the dark with a blunt instrument (human intelligence). Nor did such extreme scepticism disappear with the Greeks: in one form or another it persisted through to the time of Montaigne, Descartes, Locke, Berkeley, and Hume.[2] For these philosophers, common sense is all false conviction and faulty inference. Hume, notoriously, questioned our ordinary beliefs in persisting objects, the self, causation, and induction. It was generally assumed, indeed, that the common man's conviction that he is in contact with a world of material things that exist independently of his senses cannot withstand even casual scrutiny. Philosophers took to

[1] See Plato's *Republic*, any edition.
[2] See Richard Popkin, *The History of Scepticism* (Oxford: Oxford University Press, 2003) for a detailed account of scepticism through the ages.

referring to this commonsensical belief as 'naïve realism', condemning it by its very name. Naïve, confused, deluded: that is the natural state of the common man, without philosophy to keep him in line. (The Scottish realist Thomas Reid was an exception to this general point of view, defending the common man on such questions as whether we really see things around us, as opposed to ideas in our own minds. He is a forerunner to the reevaluation of the common man that was to take place during the course of the twentieth century.)

The twentieth century did not begin with the rehabilitation of the common man's view of things. Philosophy took the 'linguistic turn' with Frege, Russell, and Wittgenstein, but the language they were interested in was mathematical language, primarily, not the kind spoken by that man on the Clapham omnibus we were later to hear so much about. These linguistic philosophers regarded ordinary language as a defective instrument, unsuitable for serious purposes. It may serve our everyday needs but as a system for Representing Reality it was sorely lacking. It treats 'exists' as a predicate, for example, like 'red' and 'square', but logical analysis had revealed that it can be no such thing. In Russell's Theory of Descriptions, saying things like 'the king of England is bald' is logically quite misleading, because phrases beginning 'the . . . ' are not really 'denoting phrases' at all, but disguised conjunctions of statements of existence and uniqueness; ordinary language here badly misrepresents its own logic. What we need, as a substitute for ordinary language, with all its blemishes and pitfalls, is an 'ideal language' that can be constructed only by experts in mathematical logic. This language will be intelligible only to an elite minority—being composed of specially invented symbols combined according to mathematically precise rules (this was to be no universal Esperanto). Russell and Whitehead's *Principia Mathematica* (1910–13) laid down this rigorous formal language, which looks like no natural language you've ever seen; it is an early version of what is now called the Predicate Calculus. It is not a language that the common man could hope to master, except by special training, let alone use for everyday purposes.

Wittgenstein's *Tractatus Logico-Philosophicus* (1921) was also concerned with the form of an ideal language. He writes: 'Language disguises thought. So much so, that from the outward form of the clothing it is impossible to infer the form of the thought beneath it, because the outward form of the clothing is not designed to reveal the form of the body, but for entirely different purposes.'[3] Accordingly, we need to construct a new language that does transparently reveal the form of thought. The language of the common man misleads us about the true structure of thought, and hence about the nature of reality. Wittgenstein, like Russell, was an aristocrat, and the idea that a logical aristocracy was needed to set ordinary language straight came naturally to both men. Just as there are aristocratic manners and interests, so there must be an aristocratic language that is accessible only to the privileged few—the intellectual aristocracy that has the time and leisure to master an ideal logical language constructed for essentially impractical ends. This is not to be a language for getting and doing, but for passive contemplation of reality in its essential structure, removed from the grubby details of everyday life. It was to be a language of thought, not of work; of reflection, not action.

But all this began to change as the century reached its midpoint. Suddenly the common man began to seem like not such a bad sort of chap, once you took the trouble to get to know him. There was something bracingly down to earth about him. His time-tested workaday language came to be admired and cited. His no-nonsense common sense gained respect for its robust simplicity. The philosophical champions of this heretofore despised species included: G. E. Moore, the later Wittgenstein, J. L. Austin, A. J. Ayer (with some qualifications), Gilbert Ryle, and P. F. Strawson, among others. In Oxford and Cambridge, in particular, the ordinary bloke found vocal support among professional philosophers: his thought and language were welcomed there—if not his actual presence. Moore was in the vanguard, holding up his hands and declaring that he thereby *knew* there was an external world, since he had two examples of it in front of him; in addition, he stubbornly found Hegel perplexing. But it was the Wittgenstein of the *Philosophical Investigations* (1953) who insisted most strongly on the merits of common sense and ordinary language over traditional metaphysics and formal languages, thus repudiating the esoteric doctrines and ideal languages of the *Tractatus*. He writes: 'We are under the illusion that what is peculiar, profound, essential, in our investigation, resides in its trying to grasp the incomparable essence of language. That is, the order existing between the concepts of proposition, word, proof, truth, experience, and so on. This order is a *super*-order between—

---

[3] Ludwig Wittgenstein, *Tractatus Logico-Philosophicus*, trans. D. F. Pears and B. F. McGuiness (London: Routledge & Kegan Paul, 2001), section 4.002.

so to speak—*super*-concepts. Whereas, of course, if the words "language", "experience", "world", have a use, it must be as humble a one as that of the words "table', "lamp", "door".[4] Or: 'Here it is difficult as it were to keep our heads up,—to see that we must stick to the subjects of our everyday thinking, and not go astray and imagine that we have to describe extreme subtleties, which in turn we are after all quite unable to describe with the means at our disposal. We feel as if we had to repair a torn spider's web with our fingers' (section 106). Again: 'When philosophers use a word—"knowledge", "being", "object", "I", "proposition", "name"—and try to grasp the *essence* of the thing, one must always ask oneself: is the word ever actually used in this way in the language-game which is its original home?—What we do is bring back words from their metaphysical to their everyday use' (section 116). The *Investigations* begins by describing a trip to the grocer's shop to buy apples and examines what might be uttered there; it goes on to consider a pair of builders humping slabs around and shouting 'Slab!' to each other; it compares words to tools in a toolbox—hammer, nails, screwdriver, etc. Throughout, the concrete use of ordinary language is emphasized, not any supposed abstract mirroring relations between propositions and facts—still less the hidden ideal language that calls for discovery or construction by the aristocratic logical expert. Ordinary language is declared just fine as it is, thank you very much: it serves its pragmatic purpose well and it cannot be made subject to critique from on logical high. It is, in fact, a precious commodity, not to be messed with lightly, not to be underestimated.

Concurrently with this new-found respect for the everyday, we have the development of logical positivism, spearheaded into Britain by A. J. Ayer in *Language, Truth and Logic* (1936). Positivism combined respect for science with disrespect for traditional metaphysics. All that highfalutin stuff that had dominated Western thought since Plato was just so much nonsense, words put together to sound meaningful but actually meaningless. In its British incarnation, the respect for science became a respect for common sense; after all, common sense is what metaphysics had always heaped scorn upon. The insistence on verifiability as a test of meaning is, in effect, the restriction of sense to what can be practically affirmed—to what our ordinary faculties

---

[4] Ludwig Wittgenstein, *Philosophical Investigations*, trans. Elizabeth Anscombe (Oxford: Basil Blackwell, 1958), section 97. Section numbers for later references are indicated in the text.

of perception and inference can discern, as opposed to what Platonically refined Reason can descry beyond the sensory veil. The common man can see and hear, and this is all we need to apprehend reality. There is no special intellectual faculty possessed only by the metaphysical expert ('intuition'). Positivism trades in the transcendent for the tangible.

Austin is perhaps the most extreme of the major figures to discover the virtues of plain thinking, the vernacular, and what people ordinarily say in specific situations. He also introduced a novel element into philosophical discourse: humour. Let me be more exact: ridicule—of the pompous, windy, carelessly abstract, and pretentious. His paper titles tell it all: 'The Meaning of a Word', 'How to Talk—some simple ways', 'Unfair to Facts', 'A Plea for Excuses', 'Ifs and Cans', 'Three Ways of Spilling Ink'.[5] None of that 'Critique of Pure Reason' inflatedness, self-importance, only-for-the-initiated. Austin was intensely interested in the actual workings of speech in concrete situations, especially those acts of speech in which something is achieved instead of being merely stated (what he called, with misgivings, the 'performative' utterance: things like saying 'I apologize' and *thereby* apologizing). He was also, like the Scottish realist Reid, resolutely unconvinced of the empiricist position that we do not really see and touch material objects but only the sense-data that exist in our minds; he saw no good reason, that is, to reject 'naïve' realism.[6] And he was famously dedicated to the dictionary as a tool of philosophical analysis, even using it as a basis for his weekly Saturday morning meetings. But, above all, Austin pioneered a style of writing philosophy that might be described as the common man on steroids: colloquial, devoid of 'isms', witty, punchy, fastidious—yet super-literate. He wrote philosophy as if it were a glass of cold water thrown in the face of the fevered posturing of traditional philosophical discourse. Here is a typical Austin passage, from the beginning of 'A Plea for Excuses' (1956–7):

I shall try, therefore, first to state *what* the subject is, *why* it is worth studying, and *how* it may be studied, all this at a regrettably lofty level: and then I shall illustrate, in

---

[5] Austin's papers are collected in *Philosophical Papers* (Oxford: Oxford University Press, 1961).

[6] Austin attacks the sense-datum theory of perception in *Sense and Sensibilia* (Oxford: Oxford University Press, 1962). Oxford philosophers of this period were strong admirers of Jane Austen, to whose *Sense and Sensibility* John Austin was obviously alluding—a literary and philosophical convergence of sorts. For Austin, Ayer was not 'sensible' about sense and sensibilia, being an opponent of commonsense realism, and he comes in for wittily ruthless criticism.

more congenial but desultory detail, some of the methods to be used, together with their limitations, and some of the unexpected results to be expected and lessons to be learned. Much, of course, of the amusement, and of the instruction, comes in drawing the coverts of the microglot, in hounding down the minutiae, and to this I can do no more here than to incite you. But I owe it to the subject to say, that it has long afforded me what philosophy is so often thought, and made, barren of—the fun of discovery, the pleasures of co-operation, and the satisfaction of reaching agreement. (175)

Later in the same essay, speaking fondly of *field work* in philosophy, Austin writes: 'How much it is to be wished that similar field work will soon be undertaken in, say, aesthetics; if only we could forget for a while about the beautiful and get down instead to the dainty and the dumpy' (183). Concerning his neologism 'performative' he makes this tart remark: 'You are more than entitled not to know what the word "performative" means. It is a new word and an ugly word, and perhaps it does not mean anything very much. But at any rate there is one thing in its favour, it is not a profound word' (233). At the close of this paper he leaves us with these sobering words:

And is it complicated? Well, it is complicated a bit; but life and truth and things do tend to be complicated. It's not things, it's philosophers that are simple. You will have heard it said, I expect, that over-simplification is the occupational disease of philosophers, and in a way one might agree with that. But for a sneaking suspicion it's their occupation. (252)

Perhaps my favourite Austin sentence begins 'Unfair to Facts' (1954): 'This paper goes back to an old controversy between Strawson and me about truth' (154). I like it because of its aggressive plainness: he isn't going to let the ancient and revered topic of Truth slow his no-nonsense stride. The paragraph continues: 'Of course comments on comments, criticisms of criticisms, are subject to the law of diminishing fleas, but I think there are here some misconceptions still to be cleared up, some of which seem to be still prevalent in generally sensible quarters' (154). Those are the quarters we definitely want to find ourselves camped in: not to be 'sensible' is, for Austin, the most grievous of failings in a philosopher. Austin is a man who likes his prose straight and spiky, with zero uplift, and nothing in the way of inflation. It is philosophy with the hot air knocked unceremoniously out of it.

We can sum up the trends I have been sketchily enumerating as follows. Sometime around the middle of the twentieth century, and arguably a bit earlier, a philosophical mood took hold that regarded itself as breaking with the past, both stylistically and substantively. Certain intellectual values characterized this new mood: clarity, tough-mindedness, descriptive accuracy, attention to linguistic fact, down-to-earthness, anti-obscurantism, celebration of the ordinary, respect for common sense, hatred of pretentious nonsense. Above all, I would say, the mood was one of *debunking* those elements of the tradition that seemed empty, frivolous and foolish—and especially pretentious. The merely scholastic was deplored, and authority could no longer be cited to establish a position. We must write philosophy in the vernacular and pay scrupulous attention to the vernacular. Short words were good; bluntness was prized. We shouldn't engage the philosophical tradition on its own terms but work to deflate it—show it to be phony, vacuous. It needed to be replaced with something more robust, more particularistic, and more rooted in the familiar. The primary question should be: *how do we actually speak?* And, I might add: *what do we actually think?* Not: *what would an ideal language be like?* And: *how can we develop a perfect conceptual scheme?* Because maybe what we actually say and think, as ordinary people, has more depth and truth to it than what philosophers can dream up in an effort to improve on the language and thought that has served mankind well for thousands of years. We jolly well *can* see tables and chairs and make contact with other minds—despite all the fancy philosophical arguments that purport to show that we are confined to our own private sense-data. And we really *do* have free will, despite what those sceptical philosophers have maintained in the past. The cave dwellers so derided by Plato are actually a lot shrewder than philosophers have traditionally allowed. The job of the philosopher should be to make explicit what is implicit in common sense and ordinary language, to give a perspicuous account of our ordinary modes of speech and thought—not to criticize and condemn these modes.

How might these mid-century philosophical developments have affected the literary writers of the Movement? Two plausible lines of influence may be conjectured. First, Ayer's *Language, Truth and Logic* was a widely discussed and influential work, the contents of which would, at least in rough outline, be known to any intelligent reader of the period. As Blake Morrison writes in *The Movement*:

Further intellectual support of this kind [favouring the kind of unmusical poetry sometimes advocated by Donald Davie] came, if somewhat less directly, from the Logical Positivist school of philosophy, a school which was enjoying such prestige in the early 1950s that it was spoken of as 'the official English philosophy of the time'. The most influential work of English Logical Positivism was A. J. Ayer's *Language, Truth and Logic*, first published in 1936, and re-issued in a revised edition in 1946. Appealing to 'empiricism', 'verification' and 'analysis', Ayer's book was a jauntily confident attack on metaphysics. It maintained that 'no statement which refers to a reality transcending the limits of all possible sense-experience can possibly have any literal significance'; that 'the philosopher has no right to despise the beliefs of common sense', and that 'the mystic, so far from producing propositions which are empirically verified, is unable to produce any intelligible propositions at all'. In 'Mr Sharp in Florence', Davie talks of being 'grounded and ground in logic-chopping schools', and most of the Movement were acquainted with Ayer's work. Even if not fully conversant with the specialized philosophical problems in *Language, Truth and Logic*, they could admire its general temper. (p. 158)

Anglicized positivism could be said to constitute the philosophical temper of the times, even for non-specialists, and the Movement writers seem to share many of the values it espoused. We might, indeed, say that they instantiated a parallel movement naturally labelled *literary positivism* (the leading tenets of which I shall describe shortly). In fact, Ayer and Kingsley Amis knew each other quite well and were neighbours for a while (though they later disagreed over communism).

The second possible influence stems from the intellectual atmosphere at Oxford during the time Kingsley Amis and Philip Larkin were students there. Although I have no direct evidence for this, it seems inconceivable that these two adventurous students of English literature would have been completely insulated from the very lively developments in philosophy that were being hatched mainly at Oxford, particularly by Austin and Ryle. David Lodge, in his introduction to *Lucky Jim*, comments on Amis's 'new tone' as follows: 'The style is scrupulously precise, but eschews traditional 'elegance'. It is educated but classless. While deploying a wide vocabulary it avoids all the traditional devices of humorous literary prose—jocular periphrasis, mock-heroic literary allusion, urbane detachment. It owes something to the 'ordinary language' philosophy that dominated Oxford when Amis was a student there. It is a style continually challenged and qualified by its own honesty, full of unexpected reversals and underminings of stock phrases and stock responses, bringing a bracing freshness to the satirical observation of everyday life.'[7] Lodge is surely right about this; and a reading of Austin's

---

[7] Lodge's introduction to *Lucky Jim* is to the 1992 Penguin edition, to which all my page numbers refer. The quotation in the text is on p. vi.

papers together with Amis's novel confirms the determination of both men to write in a fresh way that implicitly rebukes the calcified style of traditional practitioners. Both want to let ordinary ways of speaking breathe freely and flex their muscles. Every sentence Austin and Amis write is an oblique criticism of more 'affected' ways of writing (and thinking). Truth and honesty are their overriding values, not profundity and uplift. Austin is saying: 'Yes, philosophy can be written like this, colloquially, despite its remoteness from the style of Kant or even Russell, and to do so makes for greater verisimilitude.' Amis is saying: 'Yes, literature can be written like this, colloquially, despite its remoteness from traditionally "literary" models, and to do so makes for greater verisimilitude.' Both writers are aiming for truthfulness, transparency, clarity—and these can be achieved only by giving ordinary speech the respect it deserves. We don't need a *special language* in order to do philosophy or to express literary themes; we just need to deploy ordinary language with sufficient rigour and honesty (and talent, it goes without saying).

With these general points in mind, let me now have a look at *Lucky Jim*. The title itself tells us a lot about the literary values that animate the work: this is to be a plain spoken, almost nondescript, piece of writing, about a bloke called Jim, who was quite lucky. If we thought the title unassuming, the verse with which Amis prefaces the story is wilfully crude and unliterary:

> Oh, lucky Jim,
> How I envy him.
> Oh, lucky Jim,
> How I envy him.
> OLD SONG.

The challenge is to make literature out of these apparently unpromising materials. How can stripped-down ordinary speech be made into art? But before I get to that, let me first deal with a philosophical question raised by the novel, or at least a philosopher's question. One of the main characters of the story is named Bertrand (Professor Welch's odious son, a painter of sorts and Dixon's romantic rival), and there was of course a famous philosopher of that name alive and well and knocking around England at the time *Lucky Jim* was being composed, viz. Bertrand Russell. Amis must have noticed the coincidence, and the name was rare enough then that hardly anyone else bore it (nor is it a very 'cool' name). Can we read anything into Amis's choice here? So far as I can see, the two Bertrands have nothing of significance in common at all; so it can hardly be that Amis's character is intended as a satirical dig at the celebrated (and in some circles reviled) philosopher. Perhaps the name simply struck Amis as one of those silly names that upper-class people sometimes foist on their children, suggested by Bertie Russell, but not in any way meant to reflect him. Yet many readers would think of Russell when they first encountered Amis's character. Maybe the very contrast between the two Bertrands was something Amis wanted to bring out—with one Bertrand the evil twin of the other? I see no grounds here for supposing any deeper connection. The name is funny in itself, and maybe that's enough. Certainly, though, the contrast between 'Bertrand' and 'Jim' is intended to signal a cultural divide, between the effete and the sturdy, the privileged and the self-made (or self-making)—and not just a divide but a conflict. The two are, more than anything, *linguistic* enemies. Jim clearly hates the way Bertrand talks, and so obviously does Amis.

Jim Dixon is an academic of sorts, teaching in a provincial university. He has written an article entitled *The Economic Influence of the Developments in Shipbuilding Techniques, 1450 to 1485*, which he is trying to have published (his reappointment depends on it). He reflects: 'It was a perfect title, in that it crystallized the article's niggling mindlessness, its funereal parade of yawn-inducing facts, the pseudo-light it shed on non-problems... "In considering this strangely neglected topic," it began. This what neglected topic? This strangely what topic? This strangely neglected what?' (14–15). I think Austin would have enjoyed this passage, with its blunt ridicule and clever use of the vernacular. Here the ordinary bloke inside Dixon is rebelling against the dully conventional academic, with his self-inflated style and his willingness to 'play the game', no matter how trivial the game may be. Later on the same page he observes that 'the thing's worth could be expressed in one short hyphenated indecency'—*bull-shit*, presumably: and 'bullshit' is certainly one of the terms the Movement writers would happily apply to the kind of literature they despised. If Austin were capable of uttering such an indecency (which may be doubted), I suspect he would apply it to the kind of windy ponderous philosophy he likewise despised, or at least wanted to escape from in his own work.

But Dixon's disapproval of his own work is as nothing compared to the disdain he feels for the pretensions of the incompetent and fatuous Professor Welch—with his recorder music, his madrigals, and his 'musical weekends'. Welch is the archetype of meaningless sound—noise that carries neither sting nor solace, but is merely irritating. Welch can't even manage to say what is false; he can hardly finish a sentence, let alone complete a coherent thought. He is, above all, *evasive*—not comprehensible, not straightforward, not honest. He is contrasted with such unpretentious people as the barmaid Dixon studies (Amis's word): 'He thought how much he liked her and had in common with her, and how much she'd like and have in common with him if she only knew him' (25). The word 'common' occurs twice, not accidentally, and the sentiment expressed is both truthful and put with maximum clarity and plainness; and it's a sentiment that pierces. The common person is identified as a source of 'sober veracity' (Amis so characterizes Dixon's very first utterance in the book, namely 'I don't know, Professor.'). Clearly, we have a thematic opposition between the forces of bombastic bullshit, on the one hand, and the quieter voice of simple declarative truthfulness, on the other. Mr Michie, Dixon's rather-too-keen would-be student, intimidates his reluctant teacher: 'One of the things he knew, *or seemed to* [my italics], was what scholasticism was. Dixon read, heard, and even used the word a dozen times a day without knowing, though he seemed to' (28–9). The clear implication here is that no one else knows either: it's just a pretentious word people throw around to sound impressive—one of those 'isms' of which Austin so disapproved. But at least Dixon has the honesty to admit it, at least to himself. His fear: not to know what he means by what he says (compare positivism). (Actually, in philosophy—I don't know about literary studies—it has quite a precise meaning, referring to the philosophy produced in the Middle Ages and influenced strongly by Aristotle.)

One of Amis's most subversive tricks in the novel is to use sentences that sound almost ungrammatical, as if the colloquial has tripped itself up, but which when studied closely reveal their formal rigour. Many examples could be given, but I select more or less at random such choice items as these: 'Bertrand's jaws snatched successfully at a piece of food which had been within an ace of eluding them' (40); 'He smiled among his beard, from which he now began brushing crumbs' (40); 'It was from this very bottle that Welch had, the previous evening, poured Dixon the smallest drink he'd ever seriously been offered' (59); 'The piece was recognizable to Dixon as some skein of untiring facetiousness by filthy Mozart' (63); 'People who wore clothes of that sort oughtn't to mind things of this sort, certainly not as much as Margaret clearly minded this thing' (77); 'Naming to himself the two substances of which he personally thought Bertrand a mixture, Dixon said:

"In what way?" ' (138); 'It should be possible for the right man to stop, or at least hinder, her from being a refined gracious-liver and arty-rubbish-talker' (142). No one would call these sentences conventionally 'elegant', but there is a wit and clarity to them that sends them straight into the brain. They dare the reader to find fault, but emerge victorious from scrutiny; much as Austin fires bolts of the vernacular at his reader and challenges him or her to detect an infelicity. There is nothing 'free form' about these writers; they are as rigorous grammatically as anyone could be. But they reject the usual pieties about what 'good style' is, and hence what good taste is, reinventing the conversational. They write a kind of stiffened smart demotic—spinal, not cerebral, prose.

Another notable aspect of Amis's novel is its respect for the obvious: just because everyone knows something is no reason to suppose it not to be true. The same idea permeates the ordinary language philosophy of post-war Oxford. We must not always be on the hunt for the surprising and disorienting; sometimes we need the obvious truth—what every person with any common sense knows quite well. Thus we have this famous passage from *Lucky Jim*: 'Christine was still nicer and prettier than Margaret, and all the deductions that could be drawn from that fact should be drawn: there was no end to the ways in which nice things are nicer than nasty ones' (243). The philosopher would describe this proposition as analytic: that is, its truth simply follows from its meaning. Nice things are nicer than nasty things just because of what these words *mean*. Yet even analytic truths—the most obvious truths of all—can be forgotten or occluded, especially when in the grip of ideology or moralistic zeal. Jim feels he *ought* to like Margaret more, but the plain fact is that Christine is just a lot nicer in every way—looking, talking, and kissing. It is also quite obvious that Gore-Urquhart, Jim's eventual benefactor, is an intelligent, discerning, ethically solid individual—despite his absurd-sounding name and his general poshness (which Jim might be expected, mindlessly, to hate). But the reader's easy prejudice against him, itself a stock response, can get in the way of appreciating his obvious virtues. Sometimes the obvious isn't so obvious, when a cloud of cliché and bias gets in the way. The novelist may need to render the obvious transparent and vivid—just as the philosopher sometimes needs to (Moore's 'I know I have two hands'). One of Dixon's virtues is that the obvious is not lost on him: he sees it, and can even act on it. He knows very well, for example, that Professor Welch is a complete drip and dud—in whose power he unfortunately lies.

I must also mention an interesting behavioural trait of Jim Dixon's: his propensity to make funny faces in times of emotional pressure. Early on in the novel, Dixon, in 'conversation' with Professor Welch, 'tried to flail his features into some sort of response to humour. Mentally, however, he was making a different face and promising himself he'd make it actually when next alone. He'd draw his lower lip in under his top teeth and by degrees retract his chin as far as possible, all this while dilating his eyes and nostrils.' These facial contortions function as sub-verbal soliloquies for Dixon: they express his state of mind, for himself and his reader, without having to resort to language. Here communication dips below the merely colloquial and recruits the body to convey the intended message. Wittgenstein would have approved, because of his emphasis on the relations between the verbal and the non-verbal: we have other communication systems than language, and these make their way into our communicative exchanges. Dixon's 'shot-in-the-back' face conveys volumes, despite its primitive nature. When language seems inadequate to the expressive task, pulling your face seems like the only way to get it out. And don't people pull their faces all the time as a means of communication? A smile, a frown, a grimace, a wince, a wink—all this is talking with your face. Amis is here reminding us of how primitive human expression can be; not just the speech act, the Austinian performative, but the bodily act, the face as 'text'. Amis is hyper-aware of the intricacies of speech, phonetic and social, as Austin also tried to be, and Dixon's face talk is just another aspect of that interest. In general, Dixon seems uncomfortable with ordinary speaking (witness his disastrous lecture on 'Merry England'), but with his face he can express himself perfectly. No form of communication is simpler and more natural.

Jim Dixon, provincial lecturer, medieval historian, blunt talker, girl chaser, boozer, cigarette smoker, occasional liar, bed destroyer, face puller: behind him, improbably enough, stands the gaunt figure of Ludwig Wittgenstein, returning us to our common 'language games' and the ordinary life into which those are woven—with J. L. Austin and A. J. Ayer standing close by to applaud the unschooled opinions of the common man as against the old-style philosopher. Lucky Jim, we envy him.

I have said nothing so far in this essay about the social and political changes that characterize the period we are considering, particularly the social mobility that resulted from a more widely available higher education. The ordinary bloke, after all, is apt to be a working-class bloke by origin, however far he may have advanced by means of the educational ladder. This strand in the story is no doubt easy to detect in the literary history of twentieth-century Britain, but in the philosophical strand it is virtually invisible. Certainly, none of the major philosophical figures who promoted the common man—Wittgenstein, Moore, Ayer, Austin, Ryle, and other Oxbridge philosophers—were remotely working class; I doubt they even talked much to the ordinary bloke, despite their professed respect for his linguistic practices (this was a theoretical not a practical respect). Still, many of them supported the kinds of political change that led to a better life for working-class people (such as my own family). My view is that the kinds of intellectual and artistic developments with which I have been concerned are largely self-propelled, not the offshoots of social and economic forces. I think that the philosophy and literature of the period affected each other, but I doubt that these developments were caused by broader historical events. It may be true, however, that the *reception* of the new style of philosophy, and of the Movement as a literary fashion, owed something to the broader social changes taking place at the time—as opposed, that is, to their *generation*. There were just more educated people around who shared this general outlook. Maybe without this expanding audience the Movement might not have had such success; and just possibly the parallel philosophical movement tapped into the same pool of new readers—those who wanted their philosophy straight (or as straight as philosophy can be). At any rate, there was a kind of convergence of the intellectual/artistic and the social/historical during this period—as the ordinary bloke (and soon blokette) came into his (her) own, stepping into the bright light from out of the cave.

What of the subsequent period? This is a large subject, but let me approach it briefly from a personal angle. I never knew Wittgenstein or Austin, but I did know Ayer quite well. He was a supporter of mine in the early days, and we got along just fine. But he didn't approve of my later philosophical tendencies—particularly as they emanated from trends in America (he especially disliked the views of Saul Kripke). I think he felt I'd betrayed the truths he had spent his life working to establish: to him I was reverting to views that he thought had been blown out of the water long ago by himself and his fellow positivists (such as a belief in metaphysical necessity). This was a bit of a strain between us, though we got along personally well enough. I can't help noting a parallel here with Amis's view of his son's writing: Kingsley didn't approve of the kind of writing Martin was doing—which was influenced by models from abroad, chiefly America. He thought, perhaps, that his work had shown the fatuity of the kind of 'literary' writing practised by Nabokov, for example, which Martin much admires (as do I). True, Ayer's objection to me was not stylistic, it was doctrinal; but in literature the distinction between style and substance isn't so clear (style reflects literary *doctrine*). Ayer and Amis felt they had staged a successful revolution, only to find younger practitioners going back to the bad old ways—and those they felt especially close to. The truth, though, I think, is that we absorbed their excellent lessons, with due gratitude, but then enriched them with other materials, correcting their understandable excesses. We still like the ordinary bloke, but we also want to see him striving for self-improvement—maybe even reading some of the classics. We want to see our man on the Clapham omnibus with a volume of Plato in his hands, his eyes wide.[8]

---

[8] I'd like to thank Zachary Leader and Martin Amis for useful comments.

7

'The Virtues of Good Prose': Verbal Hygiene and the Movement

Deborah Cameron

This chapter will consider the nature and significance of the Movement writers' ideas about language. It will not, however, analyse the language of their poetry and fiction in an effort to bring to light the underlying ideas or implicit theories revealed by their literary practice. Rather it will examine some of the other writings—the critical works, essays, reviews, and letters—in which several of them chose to express their views on language directly, explicitly and often at some length.

It should be acknowledged, of course, that not all the Movement writers were equally engaged or interested in the kind of linguistic commentary that interests me here. Philip Larkin's published writing, for instance, contains only a few passing comments, made mainly in reviews of other poets or in answer to questions put to him by interviewers. Yet for some of the writers—Donald Davie, Kingsley Amis, and to a lesser extent D. J. Enright—language was a significant preoccupation, and one they returned to repeatedly.

The most sustained and theoretically sophisticated contribution to this strand in the Movement's writing was made by Donald Davie, who published a number of scholarly books on literary and poetic language.[1] The best known of these works, *Purity of Diction in English Verse*, has sometimes been described (though the validity of the description is disputed) as a linguistic manifesto for the Movement.[2] Kingsley Amis read and admired *Purity of Diction*,[3] but his own writings on language are less theoretical. They belong to what historians of English call the 'complaint tradition', an anecdotal genre in which writers since medieval times have worried about abuses of language and lamented declining standards.[4] In addition to the scathing comments that recur in his private letters, Amis made numerous public interventions denouncing both what he saw as the widespread misuse of English and the lack of respect for authority and rules which he held largely responsible for it. Along those lines, in 1969 both he and Robert Conquest contributed to the 'Black Papers' on education, a series of polemical attacks on the 'permissive' educational orthodoxy of the time.[5] Later, Amis published essays in both the 1980 and 1990 editions of a collection called *The State of the Language*.[6] (Their titles—respectively, 'Getting it wrong' and 'They can't even say it properly any more'—give a fair indication of what he took the state of the language to be.) Towards the end of his life, he found another outlet for his concern about standards of usage when he accepted an invitation to compile a new version of Henry Fowler's classic usage guide *The King's English*.[7] D. J. Enright, though less active than Amis, showed a comparable concern with the use and abuse of language in his edited collection on euphemism, *Fair of Speech*, and in a collection of his own essays, *Fields of Vision*[8].

[1] Donald Davie, *Purity of Diction in English Verse* (London: Routledge, 1952); Donald Davie, *Articulate Energy: An Inquiry into the Syntax of English Poetry* (London: Routledge, 1955); Donald Davie, *The Language of Science and the Language of Literature, 1700–1740* (London: Sheed and Ward, 1963).

[2] Davie suggested this himself in an afterword in 1966.

[3] Amis praised *Purity of Diction* in a letter written to John Wain in November 1953. See Kingsley Amis, *The Letters of Kingsley Amis*, ed. Zachary Leader (London: HarperCollins, 2000), p. 342.

[4] For an outline of the English complaint tradition, see James Milroy and Lesley Milroy, *Authority in Language: Investigating Language Prescription and Standardization* (London: Routledge, 1998).

[5] C. B. Cox and A. E. Dyson (eds.), *Fight for Education: A Black Paper* (London: Critical Quarterly Society, 1969); C. B. Cox and A. E. Dyson (eds.), *Black Paper Two: The Crisis in Education* (London: Critical Quarterly Society, 1969). The title 'Black Paper' is a satirical allusion to the term 'White Paper', which in Britain denotes an official policy document setting out the basis for a piece of legislation the government intends to introduce.

[6] Christopher Ricks and Leonard Michaels (eds.), *The State of the Language* (London: Faber & Faber; 1980; 2nd edn., 1990).

[7] Kingsley Amis, *The King's English: A Guide to Modern Usage* (London: HarperCollins, 1997).

[8] D. J. Enright (ed.), *Fair of Speech: The Uses of Euphemism* (New York: Oxford University Press, 1986); D. J. Enright, *Fields of Vision: Essays on Literature, Language and Television* (Oxford: Oxford University Press, 1989).

It would be hard to argue that as a group these writers had a unified or coherent linguistic theory; indeed, it would be hard to argue that about any one of them, even Davie, whose most serious engagement with linguistic theory—*Articulate Energy*—was undertaken in an attempt to show that current theories of poetic syntax were reductive and finally inadequate. What can be argued, however, is that the Movement writers shared, and in some cases articulated very powerfully, an important subset of mid-twentieth-century concerns about language. I will suggest that the significance those concerns held for Movement writers can be related not only to the general climate of their time and place, but also to some of the particularities of their social and political position. I will consider, too, how their concerns about language might relate to certain much-discussed aspects of their literary practice: for instance, their anti-experimentalism, their championing of an intelligible poetic syntax and diction, their tendency to embrace a kind of Englishness that has been labelled 'provincial', meaning both non-metropolitan and non- or anti-cosmopolitan, their anti-intellectualism and cultural conservatism.

The Movement writings I discuss in this chapter are most aptly placed in the category of metalinguistic discourse and practice which has been labelled *verbal hygiene*,[9] an umbrella term denoting all the discourses and practices through which people attempt to 'clean up' language and make it conform to their ideals of what it should be. In literate societies, the most culturally pervasive forms of verbal hygiene tend to be standardization and prescriptivism, that is, the imposition and subsequent policing of rules of correctness in grammar, vocabulary, spelling, and pronunciation. But this is only one of the forms verbal hygiene can take. Others include, for instance, purism (the attempt to purge languages of 'foreign' elements); the regulation of obscene or offensive language; campaigns for plain language or spelling reform; the suppression or conversely the cultivation of minority languages such as Welsh and Basque; or, in complete contrast, the promotion of artificial languages like Esperanto. What these various practices have in common is that they are based on value-judgements: they combine common-sense beliefs about what languages are and how they work with evaluations of some language varieties or ways of using language as functionally, aesthetically, or morally superior to others.

---

[9] See Deborah Cameron, *Verbal Hygiene* (London: Routledge, 1995).

All cultures and communities practise forms of verbal hygiene: though beliefs and practices vary cross-culturally and historically, no linguistic ethnographer or historian has ever come across a group of people whose capacity for acquiring and using human language was not accompanied by a capacity for reflecting and making value judgements on it. Another defining feature of verbal hygiene is that these judgements are seldom if ever *only* about language. When people (especially professional linguists) complain about the triviality of popular linguistic obsessions—the disproportionate reactions prompted by split infinitives or misplaced apostrophes—they miss the point that verbal hygiene debates have a deeper symbolic dimension. Language in these debates is not just literally itself, it is also a metaphor for other things: a perceived lack of order in language is apprehended as symptomatic of deeper disruptions to the social and moral order, and putting language to rights becomes a surrogate for putting the world to rights.

This way of conceptualizing language is strongly evidenced in Movement writings on the subject. Consider, for instance, the passage in Davie's *Purity of Diction* which links Ezra Pound's abandonment of prose syntax in the *Cantos* to his sympathy for the fascism of Mussolini:[10]

it is impossible not to trace a connection between the laws of syntax and the laws of society, between bodies of usage in speech and in social life, between tearing a word from its context and choosing a leader out of the ruck. One could almost say, on this showing, that to dislocate syntax in poetry is to threaten the rule of law in the civilised community. Once one has seen this connection between law in language and law in conduct, observations about the nature of language take on an awful importance...

The connection Davie finds it 'impossible not to trace', between 'law in language and law in conduct', is at the root of all verbal hygiene. But while language-users in all times and places may share Davie's understanding of the connection as 'natural', the particular ways in which they make the connection are not natural but ideological, historically and socially constructed. In the following discussion of the Movement and verbal hygiene, the questions I want to ask are about the effects of time, place, and allegiance (social, political, and literary) on their thinking about language and its relationship to the social and moral order. What discourses on that relationship would

---

[10] Davie, *Purity of Diction*, pp. 99–100.

have influenced the Movement writers, growing up when and where they did? What questions about language were significant in that context, and how did the Movement writers respond?

One connection between linguistic and social order which has been both salient and ideologically loaded in Britain for several centuries is the link between language and social class. It is one of the commonplaces of discourse about the Movement that most of the writers associated with it had non-elite class origins. These were often remarked on by early commentators, who connected the Movement's emergence with the meritocratic educational policies of the 1940s, which enabled clever boys from unprivileged backgrounds to attend state grammar schools, or win scholarships to private schools, and then go on to Oxbridge. This in fact was a continuation of a much older story; and that story may have a bearing on the conservatism and prescriptivism which is one prominent strand in the Movement writers' writing about language.

As the historian Eric Hobsbawm has argued, the advent of compulsory education in England in the late nineteenth century benefited the lower middle-class more than any other, because it opened up to the children of artisans and tradesmen the opportunity to move up into the professional class.[11] By studying assiduously and passing examinations they could compete for entry to the professions and the colonial service. As Hobsbawm also points out, success in this endeavour was particularly strongly linked with mastery of the standard language. 'The classes which stood or fell by the official use of the written vernacular,' he says, 'were the socially modest but educated middle strata.'[12]

This helps to explain one of the most consistent findings of sociolinguistics, the empirical study of socially conditioned variation in language-use which has now been going on for about forty years: that in class-stratified societies, the people who show the greatest investment in elite linguistic norms, and who are most active in promoting those norms by both precept and example, are typically not members of the elite class itself, but people located more towards the middle of the social hierarchy. In both Britain and the US,

[11] Eric Hobsbawm, *Nations and Nationalism since 1780: Programmes, Myths, Reality* (Cambridge: Cambridge University Press, 1990).

[12] Ibid., p. 117.

it is lower middle-class speakers, and upwardly-mobile working-class ones, who are most likely to insist on all the shibboleths and nice distinctions that prescriptivists identify with 'correct' standard English usage, and to lead linguistic changes in the direction of prestige norms. Their identification with those norms may even prompt them to use prestige linguistic variants with a higher frequency than most members of the class whose usage they are supposedly emulating—a phenomenon sociolinguists call 'hypercorrection'.

The ideological investment of the 'socially modest middle strata' in linguistic correctness, which had begun in the late nineteenth century, was reinforced and made more explicit by developments that occurred in the sphere of education shortly after the first world war—in time to affect the schooling received by the Movement writers. During the 1920s there was an intense debate on the teaching of English in England's schools: as R. B. McKerrow remarked in a 1921 pamphlet, 'one of the minor results of the Great War has been a revival of the interest taken by educationalists and the general public in the historical study of English literature and of the English language'.[13] More accurately, that interest was prompted by anxieties arising from the extension of the franchise to all men and most women in 1918. Moderate commentators saw the newly enfranchised working classes as barbarians needing to be civilized if they were to function as good citizens; less moderate commentators saw them as class warriors and communists in the making. The remedy was felt to lie in educating them to know and cherish their cultural heritage, and so fostering a sense of British national identity that would transcend allegiances based purely on class.

The English language and its literature were central to this project. Both the 1921 Newbolt Report on English teaching in schools and an influential text by one of the Newbolt Committee members, George Sampson, titled *English for the English*, viewed English teaching as a means to resolve the dangerous tensions between social classes.[14] It would achieve this partly by extending to working-class children the same opportunities for social mobility that their lower middle-class counterparts had been able to make use of since the 1880s,

[13] R. B. McKerrow, *A Note on the Teaching of English Language and Literature* (Pamphlet no. 49, English Association, London, 1921).

[14] Henry Newbolt, *The Teaching of English in England: Being the Report of the Departmental Committee Appointed by the President of the Board of Education to Enquire into the Position of English in the Educational System of England* (London: HMSO, 1921); George Sampson, *English for the English*, rev. edn. (London, 1925).

but it would also work by promoting an idea of 'culture' that could in prin-
ciple be shared by all classes. As Sampson put it, 'though a common school
is impracticable, a common basis of education is not. The one common basis
of the common culture is the common tongue'.[15] The Newbolt report, simi-
larly, wanted English lessons to do the job of 'linking together the mental life
of all classes'[16] and eliminating what it called 'the difference between educated
and uneducated speech, which at present causes so much prejudice and diffi-
culty of intercourse on both sides'.[17] Newbolt was critical of the public schools
(in the British context this, of course, means elite private schools) for margin-
alizing English by comparison with Greek and Latin, and so failing to offer a
vision of culture that was accessible to the whole nation.

The Newbolt report is most often cited by language historians as the
document that inaugurated the long and still ongoing verbal hygiene
movement to eradicate, by means of schooling, the non-standard dialects
of the urban working class. But in that aim, unrealistic then as now,
Newbolt clearly did not succeed; its main effect was rather to consolidate,
and to institutionalize in the educational practice of schools serving the
middle strata (state grammar schools and the less elite private schools)
the ideological belief that mastery of proper English holds the key to
upward mobility and social status. The Movement writers were among the
beneficiaries of this approach to education: they were sufficiently successful
at school to be admitted to study English at the elite universities of Oxford
and Cambridge, and a number of them later taught English at universities
in Britain and overseas.

But the efforts of non-elite speakers to attain and display linguistic mastery,
however successful they appear, are apt to be accompanied by some degree of
insecurity and ambivalence. For these speakers, knowing what is 'correct' lin-
guistically speaking is not only, as it is for the elite class, a mark of 'distinction'
in the sense Bourdieu uses the term;[18] it is the very foundation of their claim

---

[15] Sampson, *English for the English*, p. 39.
[16] Newbolt, *The Teaching of English*, p. 15.   [17] Ibid., pp. 22–3.
[18] Pierre Bourdieu, *Distinction: A Social Critique of the Judgement of Taste*, trans. Richard Nice (London:
Routledge, 1984). 'Distinction' means the kind of good taste or aesthetic judgement which is often
taken as a mark of individual discernment, but which in Bourdieu's analysis is really the product
and symbol of social distinctions between classes. Tastes in art, food, language, etc., are not just
personal preferences, but display the 'cultural capital' people have acquired (or in the case of the
less privileged, have not acquired) through their upbringing and education.

to be part of the class that possesses distinction. Constant vigilance is necessary, since any lapse may threaten their achieved status by revealing their socially modest origins. This is what underlies the 'hypercorrect' behaviour of lower middle class speakers; it may also develop the sensitivity to small linguistic differences which was manifested in, for instance, Amis's talent for verbal mimicry and Larkin's ability, recalled by his friends, to slip chameleon-like into the register of whoever he was corresponding with.

At the same time, ambivalence may be engendered by the lurking suspicion that 'real' distinction will forever elude those not born to it: that the kinds of cultural capital your parents and teachers encouraged you to invest in will turn out in the end to be less valuable than they promised, because less valued by the people whose taste and judgement really count. D. J. Enright dramatizes this ambivalence in one of his Faust Book poems, *Mephistopheles addresses the working class*:

'And your children's children
Shall learn how to spell correctly
How to pen a neat and legible hand
And to read good books

They shall be granted scholarships
And shall suffer therefrom
But they shall succeed in their time
Where their forefathers might not try

And they shall then discover
That correct spelling is held cheap
That the best people hire scriveners
And books are no longer read

Doffing their smocks and overalls
Your children's children
Shall go out to meet the world
And find themselves attired in last year's fashions
(For all things change and remain much the same)
And all the world shall ignore them
As hitherto.'[19]

It might seem counter-intuitive to suggest that the Movement writers were in thrall to the linguistic standards of a class elite, since they, or some of them,

---

[19] D. J Enright, *Collected Poems 1987* (Oxford: Oxford University Press, 1987), pp. 230–1.

are famous for the opposite tendency—their open disdain for the kind of cultural capital that traditionally marks distinction, like a taste for Mozart or foreign poetry. But the evidence suggests that they were much less iconoclastic in their attitudes to language. On the contrary, they were conformists who displayed their linguistic capital ostentatiously, and in some cases (the most striking is that of Amis, who in other spheres was a tireless and fearless puncturer of elite cultural pretension) became prominent public critics of linguistic 'permissiveness'.

In that connection it is interesting to compare Mephistopheles's address to the working class with what Enright says *in propria persona* in his introduction to *Fair of Speech*:

Those who complain about the misuse of language, however temperately, are bound to be accused of elitism or [more hurtful] priggishness or [most hurtful] ignorance of how language lives and grows—freely, vigorously, paying no heed to pedants and purists.... I have noticed that it is generally intellectuals who take the breezy view, whereas the poorly educated, who respect the education they never got, would like some guidance in matters of language usage, even a degree of firm prescription.[20]

This passage exemplifies what had become, by the 1970s, a very common kind of verbal hygiene rhetoric, denouncing the linguistic irresponsibility of 'intellectuals'—though the writer was often, as here, someone who might reasonably be considered an intellectual himself. Essentially, Enright is accusing those who have risen to elite status through education of pulling the ladder up behind them by denying to the non-elite the 'firm prescription' that produced their own facility with standard English. The same line of argument featured in the Black Papers on Education, and it returned to prominence during the Thatcher era, when it was favoured by conservatives advocating a 'back to basics' approach.[21] It is the common sense of a

---

[20] Enright, *Fair of Speech*, pp. 1–2.

[21] Examples from the 1980s include John Honey, *The Language Trap: Race, Class and the Standard English Issue in British Schools* (Middlesex: National Council for Educational Standards, 1983), and John Marenbon, *English Our English: The New Orthodoxy Examined* (London: Centre for Policy Studies, 1987). Unlike the Black Papers, both these texts were commissioned and published by organizations overtly linked to the Conservative Party (the NCES was a conservative educational pressure group, while the CPS, a right-wing think-tank, was particularly influential during the Thatcher era). Their call for what Enright dubs 'firm prescription' was heeded by the designers of the national school curriculum, instituted by the Conservative government in 1988, and the prescription has if anything become even firmer under the Labour government which came to power in 1997. In short, the prescriptive arguments of Amis, Conquest, and Enright were and are both conservative and mainstream.

community in which lower middle-class linguistic values and interests have achieved hegemonic status. In it we hear the voice of someone whose education went so far and no further: it allowed them to master all the nuances of prescriptive correctness, but did not give them the means (or the desire) to question the underlying logic and thus the legitimacy of the prescriptions, nor to wonder, as Mephistopheles does in the poem, about their true exchange value in the real social world.

It is difficult to think of any other subject that prompts highly educated people to take pride in this kind of 'ours not to reason why' attitude, to recommend unquestioning obedience to even the most trivial and arbitrary commandments, and to feel justified in expressing publicly what would in other contexts be seen as unacceptably snobbish and bigoted judgements. Because of the ideological belief that the norms of correct usage can be mastered by anyone prepared to make the effort, linguistic prejudices remain expressible where the class or ethnic prejudices they are often in fact surrogates for would not be. Kingsley Amis frequently exploited this in polemical pieces, demolishing the credentials of whoever he was attacking with an opening sneer at some misspelt word or misplaced apostrophe. People who did not share his own knowledge of and regard for the rules were 'berks'.

But Amis had another set of targets, 'wankers'—people whose great linguistic sin was not incorrectness but affectation. Opposition to affected, pretentious, obscure, and unintelligible usage is the other major strand in the Movement's writing on language; indeed, for many commentators it is their most characteristic attitude, and also the one that most clearly differentiates them from their modernist predecessors. This might seem to complicate the argument that the verbal hygiene practised and promoted by Movement writers was conservative and elitist, reflecting the ideological investment in linguistic mastery which had been cultivated in people of their class and generation by the educational and social system. How does that conservatism and elitism fit with their much-discussed championing of the familiar, intelligible, and accessible over the strange, obscure, and difficult—of a poetry with what Davie, quoting T. S. Eliot, called 'the virtues of good prose'[22]:

[22] The phrase appears in T. S. Eliot, 'Poetry in the 18th century', reprinted in *From Dryden to Johnson: A Guide to English Literature*, ed. Boris Ford (London: Penguin, 1956), p. 273.

Davie is not the only Movement writer to use prose as a reference point when discussing poetic language. In a letter to an American critic written in 1958, Amis says of himself and the other Movement poets: 'All we really have in common is a desire to write sensibly . . . we all try to write poems that are intelligible in the sense that they can be paraphrased'—which presumably implies, rendered in prose.[23]

It is hard to read these sentiments without hearing in the background the voice of George Orwell championing the notion that good writing is not only intelligible but transparent, like a pane of glass: you should ideally be able to see straight through the words to the underlying meaning or content they were, or should have been, chosen to convey. 'Let the meaning choose the word and not the other way about' is Orwell's overarching principle in his 1946 essay 'Politics and the English Language', which is also an ideological defence of plain and intelligible prose and a warning about the political dangers of linguistic obscurity, whether willed or inadvertent.[24] This argument, of course, had a particular resonance at the time it was made by Orwell, just after the Second World War. In relation to the contemporary phenomenon of totalitarianism, Hitler's and then Stalin's, certain observations on the nature of language did indeed take on, as Davie puts it, an 'awful importance'. Language, it appeared, could be deliberately corrupted for political ends and used to manipulate on a mass scale. In his essay and in his fictional exploration of the same theme in *Nineteen Eighty-Four*, Orwell produced what it would not be an exaggeration to call the most influential verbal hygiene texts of the entire twentieth century—certainly in English, and possibly in any language. The linguists James and Lesley Milroy in their history of the English complaint tradition credit Orwell with having inaugurated a new strand of linguistic complaint, distinctively modern in the sense that the underlying concern is no longer about class divisions *per se*, but about the threat posed to societies by ideological extremism and conflict.[25]

There seems little doubt that the Movement writers were influenced by Orwell's views on language. Those views are referred to directly and

---

[23] Amis, *Letters*, p. 525.

[24] George Orwell, 'Politics and the English Language' [1946], in Sonia Orwell and Ian Angus (eds.), *The Collected Essays, Letters and Journalism of George Orwell, Vol. IV: In Front of Your Nose, 1945–1950* (Harmondsworth: Penguin, 1968).

[25] Milroy and Milroy, *Authority in Language*.

approvingly by Enright in *Fair of Speech* and by Amis in his letters; and it is tempting to read them into Davie's remarks on Pound's syntax, quoted earlier, which depend for their plausibility on the reader's willingness to make not just any old connection between linguistic and social order, but more specifically the connection Orwell had made between the systematic dismantling of ordinary language and the ability of tyrants to bend whole populations to their will by destroying truth, logical reasoning, and the possibility of dissent. Orwell was not writing about poetic or literary language—a point he explicitly emphasizes in 'Politics and the English Language'—but something very like his argument about the corruption of political discourse becomes in Davie's linguistic criticism a stick to beat modernism with. The deliberate difficulty of modernist poetry is represented as an anti-democratic break with long-established traditional speech-ways, and in the case of fractured syntax, with logical thought. For Davie, these tendencies in language had their political correlate in fascism.

Modernism is also beaten with this stick, among others, in a much more recent work of criticism, John Carey's *The Intellectuals and the Masses.*[26] Carey argues that intellectuals during the period he considers (1880–1939) sought to set themselves apart from the despised vulgar masses by promoting forms of literary and other artistic practice which could only be understood and enjoyed by a small elite—a move prompted by the advent of universal suffrage, mass literacy, and the attendant fear of proletarian political and cultural ascendancy. That might lead us to ask whether the Movement writers' linguistic values embody a reaction against modernist elitism, interpretable partly in terms of their own non-elite class origins, and partly also in terms of the political and cultural climate in which these writers were formed— the post-war climate which was, for understandable reasons, so receptive to Orwell's brand of language criticism. But if we look more closely at comments made by the Movement writers on the theme of linguistic corruption, we might conclude that matters are more complicated.

It is a mistake to view Orwellian language criticism in general as unequivocally democratic or anti-elitist. It could be argued that a certain kind of elitism was always latent in Orwell's own texts (a point I will return to below);

---

[26] John Carey, *The Intellectuals and the Masses: Pride and Prejudice among the Literary Intelligentsia, 1880–1939* (London: Faber, 1992).

but in addition, as those texts became increasingly disembedded over time from the political context in which they were produced, the ideas they popularized began to be deployed in new ways. In particular, those ideas were appropriated to bolster conservative and elitist critiques of mass culture.

Anxiety about the corrupting effects of the popular mass media is a recurring theme in the Movement writers' language criticism. When I quoted Enright above on the irresponsibility of intellectuals taking a 'breezy' view of linguistic standards, I omitted a sentence: 'Yet the policy of laissez faire with its complacent appeal to the past ignores the unprecedented factors at work today, in particular the effects of television, a forcing-bed of change, coinage and corruption, such as we have never known before.'[27] Kingsley Amis in 1974 wrote a letter to the *Daily Telegraph* musing on 'the political distribution of corrupters and preservers of our language'. He granted that conservatives had no monopoly of good writing, but suggested that the main source of corruption was the illiteracy fostered by misguided left-wing educational policies: the effect, he asserted, was 'to render users of English more vulnerable to the admittedly damaging assaults of Madison Avenue'.[28]

Such sentiments point to the elitism that is always latent in Orwellian verbal hygiene. The problem is not, or not just, the overt distaste for television or advertising; more fundamentally, it is the way the writer positions himself and his audience, as intellectually superior to the great mass of the population. Writers in this vein are never worried about the malign effects of television, advertising, or political propaganda on themselves: it is always some less intelligent, less educated Other who is liable to be taken in by manipulative language. The Orwellian critic and his implied reader are assumed to have the sophistication to see through the circumlocutions and euphemisms; only 'they', the simple masses, are susceptible to manipulation.[29]

For a language critic like the later Kingsley Amis, the corruption of English has reached the point of no return; most people, especially if they

---

[27] Enright, *Fair of Speech*, p. 2.   [28] Amis, *Letters*, p. 763.

[29] It is perhaps worth noting that there is no very good evidence for this supposition, however logical it may seem to the extensively educated. Some linguists researching the way people process media messages have found that on the contrary, working-class subjects are more likely than their middle-class counterparts to interpret pronouncements made by politicians and other authority figures sceptically, as attempts to manipulate or conceal. See for instance Kay Richardson, 'Interpreting Breadline Britain', in Ulrike Meinhof and Kay Richardson (eds.), *Text, Discourse and Context* (London: Longman, 1994).

had the misfortune to be born after 1945, are too ignorant or too stupid to follow Orwell's injunction to 'let the meaning choose the word'. Amis has a particular preoccupation with the supposed loss of semantic distinctions which results, in his view, from speakers using words in ways that destroy their proper etymological sense. Ultimately this leads to a situation in which meaning can no longer be conveyed with any precision, a point Amis elaborates in his contribution to the 1990 edition of *The State of the Language*:

> We seem to be moving... towards a social and linguistic situation in which nobody says or writes or probably knows anything more than an approximation to what he or she means and on the hearer's or reader's part nothing more is expected or could be recognised.... [W]e seem to have arranged things, with the powerful back-up of an incomprehension-fostering educational system, to make any approach to precision more difficult, rarer and less apparently important than ever before, and at an increasing rate.[30]

Remarkably similar views had been expressed more than twenty years earlier by W. H. Auden, in the T. S. Eliot Memorial lectures he delivered in 1967 and subsequently published as *Secondary Worlds*. Auden too attributed what he explicitly called 'the corruption of language' to the growth of mass education and mass media, but he was even more explicit than Amis about where and when the rot set in. 'Until recently', he observed,

> most people spoke the language of the social class to which they belonged. Their vocabulary might be limited, but they learned it at first-hand from their parents and neighbours, so that they knew the correct meaning of such words as they did use and made no attempt to use any others. Today I would guess that nine-tenths of the population do not know what 30 percent of the words they use actually mean.[31]

Amis's tone may be less patrician, but his message is the same: if we care about language and precision in language, we must regret the social process which has given so many speakers aspirations above their linguistic station.

Amis speaks of the 'corrupters and preservers' of language, but not of its improvers or renewers; it is often said of the Movement that their attitude to poetic language was self-consciously conservative, with the emphasis on consolidation rather than innovation, whereas the modernist attitude was

---

[30] Kingsley Amis, 'They can't even say it properly any more', in Christopher Ricks and Leonard Michaels (eds.), *The State of the Language* (London: Faber, 1990), p. 459.

[31] W. H. Auden, *Secondary Worlds* (London: Faber & Faber, 1968), p. 127.

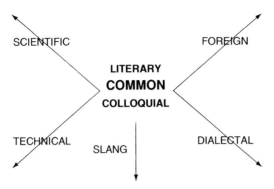

Figure 1 The structure of English vocabulary, as represented in Murray's Introduction to the *New (Oxford) English Dictionary on Historical Principles*

the reverse. But here too matters are arguably more complex, prompting me to raise the question of how far the Movement poets practised in their poetry the kind of verbal hygiene they, or some of them, preached in their punditry.

In Figure 1 I reproduce the famous diagram of the structure of the English lexicon which appeared in James Murray's introduction to what is now the *Oxford English Dictionary*.[32] Murray explains that the core of English is a 'common' vocabulary, shading at one end of the spectrum into a more 'colloquial' register and at the other into a more 'literary' register, though in neither case is the boundary with 'common' English sharply drawn. Then on the periphery we have other kinds of vocabulary, which are not part of or continuous with the common stock: scientific and technical terms, foreign terms, dialect, and slang.

This diagram also appears in Robert Crawford's *Devolving English Literature*, where it is used to make the argument that modernist writers like Pound, Eliot, and Joyce achieved their characteristic linguistic effects by 'combining

---

[32] The first edition of the OED was known as the *New English Dictionary on Historical Principles*, but Murray's original introduction, including the diagram reproduced here, was incorporated into the expanded and retitled second edition which is still in use among scholars (pending the completion of the comprehensively revised 3rd edition which is currently in preparation, and partially available on-line). See James A. H. Murray, 'Introduction', in John Simpson and E. S. C. Weiner (eds.), *The Oxford English Dictionary*, 2nd edn. (Oxford: Clarendon Press, 1989), p. xi.

the materials on the outer edges…rather than simply rearranging the common pool with the literary and colloquial'.[33] As Crawford rightly points out, that was as much a matter of making use of the more demotic forms of English—slang and non-standard dialect—as of injecting obscure high-culture references from science or foreign languages. He goes on to argue that the Movement's use of demotic diction, especially Larkin's, owed much to the modernist example. We might say of the Movement poets that they got their characteristic effects using a smaller subset of the lexical categories in the diagram: in Crawford's terms they did favour 'rearranging the common pool with the literary and colloquial', but the use they made of the colloquial produces effects more striking than mere rearrangement. As Crawford suggests, the way Larkin plays obscenity or coarseness off against the gentility of 'common' standard English used by some ordinary speaker in some mundane situation, 'Groping back to bed after a piss', for instance, has quite similar functions to, say, the mixing of dialect with 'higher' registers in *Ulysses*.

Crawford views English literary modernism as a provincial movement, led by people who came from outside the centres of English culture and whose linguistic practice reflected a desire to challenge the authority of those cultural centres over English. He sees the Movement, whose members, though English, were also from outside the cultural centre, more as part of that tradition than as a decisive break with it.

To the extent they were active language critics or verbal hygienists, the Movement writers by and large were not original or radical: they shared the anxieties and defended the language ideologies that were commonplace in their time and their social milieu. But one must be cautious about generalizing. Some Movement writers were more interested than others in reflecting explicitly on linguistic questions, and some of those who were interested spoke with more than one voice. The voice of the poet and the voice of the pundit did not necessarily coincide; even when the same individual was both, it is not always clear that one took direction from the other.

[33] Robert Crawford, *Devolving English Literature* (Oxford: Clarendon Press, 1992), p. 270.

8

'An Instrument of Articulation': Empson and the Movement

Deborah Bowman

When William Empson was first introduced to the younger poet and critic John Wain,

he hailed him: 'Hello, young man, I'm told you imitate me.' Wain replied, 'Imitate you? Why, I invented you!'—a reply which Empson said 'quite won my heart'.[1]

Wain's reply sounds like Tweedledee teasing Alice over the sleeping Red King: 'Why, you're only a sort of thing in his dream!'[2] It suggests a world in which allusions come first, sources afterwards.On the other hand, when asked in 1970 about his poetic influence, Empson replied: 'Oh, I think that's long over. I shouldn't think I've influenced a poet for twenty years, thank God for it'; his tone is that of a reformed character looking back on a misspent youth, lending the verb 'influence' a peculiarly active character, as if influencing poets were a sort of anti-social behaviour you might indulge in and then grow out of, like

[1] Cited in John Haffenden, *William Empson II: Against the Christians* (Oxford: Oxford University Press, 2006), p. 352.

[2] Lewis Carroll, *Through the Looking-Glass, and What Alice Found There*, in *The Annotated Alice: The Definitive Edition*, ed. Martin Gardner (London: Allen Lane, 2000), pp. 129–273 (p. 189).

happy-slapping.[3] This complicated relationship had been captured in 1954 by Patric Dickinson's parody, 'At the Villa Nelle', which concluded: 'That the young have taken Empson for a master | One cannot but regard as a disaster'; Dickinson's poem, like Wain's and Empson's conflicting claims, raises questions not only about who is master but about what might be involved in the 'taking'; in other words, who is doing what to whom?[4] Such questions, always necessary in discussions of influence, are particularly relevant in the case of Empson's influence on those poets usually described as belonging to the Movement.

That G. S. Fraser was protesting, in 1956, that 'the degree to which Mr. Empson is the sole dominant influence over the newest group of the young can be much exaggerated', demonstrates the extent to which Empson's influence on the poets of the early to mid 1950s was at the time considered as such.[5] However, as many of those young poets were, or later became, academics, their lectures, tutorials, and publications, as well as their poems, gave them in turn the opportunity to 'invent' their poetic and critical predecessor for posterity; Wain, for example, had made an earlier attempt to master the situation when he wondered whether an article he published in 1950 'was responsible for starting the astonishing vogue of [Empson's] poetry which has produced so many diminutive Empsons in the last five years' (not a vogue 'for', but 'of', as if the interest has produced new waves of the original).[6] Reading Robert Conquest's popular and influential anthology New Lines, it's certainly easy to spot the fashionistas. The signs are often scattered lines and phrases, but as they accumulate, they create not only a catalogue of allusions and borrowings, but a recognizable style. So D. J. Enright's 'He could not think that the land was wholly waste' catches a tune from Empson's villanelle 'Reflection from Anita Loos' ('No star he aimed at is entirely waste'); Donald Davie's 'No ripening curve can be allowed to sag' hums the same line under its breath, and in another of his poems the

[3] Christopher Norris, David B. Wilson, and John Haffenden, 'An Interview with William Empson', in *Some Versions of Empson*, ed. Matthew Bevis (Oxford: Clarendon Press, 2007), pp. 289–319 (p. 295).

[4] 'At the Villa Nelle', *Encounter* 3: 1 (July, 1954), 63.

[5] 'Preface', to *Poetry Now: An Anthology*, ed. G. S. Fraser (London: Faber and Faber: 1956), pp. 15–27 (p. 23).

[6] John Wain, in D. J. Enright (ed.), *Poets of the 1950s: An Anthology of New English Verse* (Tokyo: Kenkyusha, 1955), pp. 90–1 (p. 91), referring to his essay 'Ambiguous Gifts: Notes on the Poetry of William Empson' (1949), in Wain, *Preliminary Essays* (London: Macmillan, 1957), pp. 169–80.

lines 'No knife can stick in history or the id, | No cutlass carve us from the lime of fate' keep the rhythm of and derive their motif from Empson's whole stanza:

> Christ stinks of torture who was caught in lime.
> No star he aimed at is entirely waste.
> No man is sure he does not need to climb.[7]

Davie condenses the sounds of three lines into two: his anaphora and end-stopping shadow Empson's, and the words 'carve' and '*lime*' almost repeat the trick of making 'caught in *lime*' become '*climb*'; but while Empson's rhyme extracts its own sounds from the trap to put together a whole word, Davie's sound-pattern can't make the connection without referring to the earlier poem. Conquest's 'Humanities' returns to the same source, his lines 'It takes a whole heart's effort to see all | The human plenum as a single ens' borrowing their flexible strength from the movement of Empson's last stanza: 'It gives a million gambits for a mime | on which a social system can be based' ('plenum', here, can't help but recall the title—though only that— of Empson's poem 'Plenum and Vacuum').[8] Wain also reflects on Empson's 'Anita Loos,' but as with many of these grace-notes, his line—'Love rules the world, but is the world subdued?'—is a subdued imitation, keeping the assonance but cleaning up the syntax and rhythm and losing the naughty slipperiness of the original: 'Love rules the world but is it rude, or slime?'[9] Wain's 'An Eighth Type of Ambiguity' declares its debts at the same time as it claims to go one better than Empson's famous volume of criticism *Seven Types of Ambiguity*, but its repayments fall short: 'When love as germ invades the purple stream | It splashes round the veins and multiplies,' are lines which messily but painlessly ape the elegant wasting of the villanelles 'Missing Dates' ('Slowly the poison the whole blood stream fills') and 'Villanelle' ('My heart pumps yet the poison draught of you').[10] In the same way, Wain's line 'So when she heard him speak out loud and clear' tries to draw strength it

---

[7] D. J. Enright, 'The Wondering Scholar', in *New Lines: An Anthology*, ed. Robert Conquest (London: Macmillan, 1956), hereafter *NL*, pp. 62–3 (p. 62); Donald Davie, 'Cherry Ripe: On a Painting by Juan Gris', and 'Too Late for Satire', in *NL* pp. 67–8 (p. 67), pp. 68–9 (p. 69); William Empson, *The Complete Poems of William Empson*, ed. John Haffenden (Harmondsworth: Penguin, 2000), hereafter *CP*, p. 85.

[8] Conquest, 'Humanities', in *NL*, pp. 79–80 (p. 79); *CP*, pp. 85, 14.

[9] 'Don't let's spoil it all, I thought we were going to be such good friends', in *NL*, p. 89; *CP*, p. 85.

[10] 'An Eighth Type of Ambiguity', in *NL*, pp. 90–1 (p. 90); *CP*, pp. 79, 33.

doesn't earn from Empson's 'It was a reprieve | Made Dostoyevsky talk out queer and clear'; the cliché 'loud and clear', and the familiar 'speak out,' are precisely what Empson *didn't* write, and why we hear so distinctly the queer clarity of his line.[11]

For the poets of *New Lines*, then, Empson is both master and remastered, as Conquest's introduction to the volume suggests:

Some years ago Mr John Wain advocated the methods of Mr William Empson in poetry . . . And soon a number of young poets were following Empsonian and similar academic principles . . . As a starting point for Mr. Wain and others this was a not unreasonable way of learning the first lesson—that a poem needs an intellectual backbone. But that it became merely a fashionable formula among the young is unfortunate. Intellectual frameworks can be filled out with bad materials as well as good, and Empsonianism has been almost as much a vehicle for unpleasant exhibitionism and sentimentality as the trends it was designed to correct . . . At least the Empsonian fashion is an improvement on its predecessors.[12]

Although Conquest complains that Empson's style has been reduced to 'merely a fashionable formula', the ease with which his paragraph slips from the name through the quality ('Empsonian') to the practice ('Empsonianism') suggests that he's comfortable with this shimmy, and that his problem isn't with the reduction of Empson's poetic example to an 'intellectual framework', but only its subsequent use. Empson isn't the only influence mentioned in the introduction to this anthology—he's preceded by George Orwell, and followed by W. B. Yeats, Robert Graves, Edwin Muir, and W. H. Auden—but he is the only influence to be so deployed and so deplored. Orwell 'exerted . . . one of the major influences on modern poetry'; 'the general recognition of Yeats . . . is reflected in a considerable debt of matter and method'; Graves and Muir 'have their echoes', and Auden 'casts an obvious shadow': nothing, though, is Orwellian, Yeatsian, Gravesian, Muirish, or Audenesque.[13] When Conquest remarks that the Movement poets don't have 'the Auden tendency', Auden's name remains intact and he keeps his tendency to himself; the phrase 'the Empsonian fashion' is grammatically identical but spreads the poet into a thinner, stickier adjective.[14] The trick isn't just Conquest's; in a review of *Oxford Poetry 1954*,

---

[11] *NL*, p. 89; *CP*, p. 80.   [12] *NL*, pp. xvi–xvii.   [13] *NL*, pp. xv, xvii.   [14] *NL*, p. xviii.

Hilary Corke had named 'Mr Eliot, Mr. Auden, Mr. Spender' as 'masters' of the new poets, but had gone on to discuss at some length 'a "school", known generally as "the Empsonians" ', or the ' "Empsonian" movement'.[15] Enright deplores 'Wastelanditis', but Empson's is again the only *personal* name he labels as an order and a disorder: 'the Empsonian school of poetry' and ' "Empsonianism" ' both appear in the same introduction; Fraser prefaces his 1956 collection *Poetry Now* with a mention of 'the neo-Empsonian tone', Empson again singled out for adjectival treatment.[16] The practice is persistent: Blake Morrison, nearly twenty-five years later, defends the Movement from identification with 'second-rate Empsonianism' (to say something is 'second-rate' is already to have taken it for granted) and finds that the Movement poets were 'appropriately...called "Empsonian" ', indicating, but not explaining, their 'characteristic Empsonian technique'.[17] This habitual distinction of Empson's influence on the Movement from that of other literary predecessors dissolves his identity and agency into an aspect of something or someone else. He's at once insubstantial and contagious; the real William Empson disappears, but the suffix '-ian' indicates something 'of, or belonging to'; to refer, as Conquest does, to 'the Empsonians', moves the writers in question further away from their master, but at the same time places them more completely under his influence.[18]

This was undoubtedly the case for those poems which do little more than snatch a phrase from Empson. Other works from *New Lines*, however, borrow more successfully because what's lent is also a turn of thought. Enright's 'On the Death of a Child', for example, is moved by looking back to these lines from Empson's 'Aubade':

> Tell me more quickly what I lost by this,
> Or tell me with less drama what they miss
> Who call no die a god for a good throw,

---

[15] Hilary Corke, 'The Bad Old Style', *Encounter* 4: 6 (June 1955), 20–6 (pp. 21, 22).

[16] 'Poetry in England Today', in Enright (ed.), *Poets of the 1950s*, pp. 1–15 (p. 7.); Fraser, *Poetry Now*, p. 25.

[17] Blake Morrison, *The Movement: English Poetry and Fiction of the 1950s* (Oxford: Oxford University Press, 1980), pp. 7, 118, 26.

[18] All such definitions are from the *Oxford English Dictionary* (*OED*), 2nd edn (Oxford: Oxford University Press, 1989); Robert Conquest, interview with William Baer, in William Baer, *Fourteen on Form: Conversations with Poets* (Jackson, MS.: University Press of Mississippi, 2004), pp. 120–36 (p. 124).

> Who say after two aliens had one kiss
> It seemed the best thing to be up and go.[19]

Here is Enright:

> For it will not do
> To hiss humanity because one human threw
> Us out of house and home. Or part
> At odds with life because one baby failed to live.
> Indeed, as little as its subject, is the wreath we give—
> The big words fail to fit. Like giant boxes
> Round small bodies.[20]

Enright's passionate distance here, the combination of gritted teeth and trembling lip, comes from a deliberately anatomizing look at cause and effect which puts the homely phrase 'house and home' alongside the cold accounting of 'one human...one baby'; it gets this sudden shiver from recalling Empson's pedantically precise 'two aliens had one kiss' (the ghost of which hovers like a sigh over Enright's 'hiss'). At the end of a love affair in Japan, and the beginning of a war, Empson's poem zooms out until the 'I' and 'she' of his earlier stanzas are vanishingly tiny, his monosyllables generalizing to a point of disappearance; Enright tries to achieve the same grip on his domestic tragedy, but by using a similarly exact turn of descriptive phrase to focus on the painful littleness of this particular grief, keeping the memory of the earlier poem, which set intimate details of love and loss against the different passions and losses of international conflict, at the back of its mind.

Empson's 'Aubade', a kind of distended villanelle, takes the two refrains 'It seemed the best thing to be up and go' and 'The heart of standing is you cannot fly', and tests their strength against increasingly large predicaments, from what to do in the event of an earthquake, to the difficulty of a relationship between people of different nationalities, to that difficulty when their countries seem to be approaching war with each other, to how one should act in the World War itself. None of these circumstances is exactly articulable or extricable from the others, and they all have a bearing on and bear down upon the lovers of the poem, so that the refrains, as they alternate at the

---

[19] 'Aubade', in CP, pp. 69–70 (p. 70).   [20] NL, p. 57.

ends of stanzas, and repeat their rhymes through the poem, take up in turn an increasingly large and complicated burden:

> It seemed the best thing to be up and go.
>
> The language problem but you have to try.
> Some solid ground for lying could she show?
> The heart of standing is you cannot fly.[21]

A rhyme-scheme which is both enclosed (in the stanza's *aba* pattern) and cross-rhymed (in the *b aba* pattern which cuts across it) fences in and encroaches upon a dilemma; the ambiguities of 'solid ground', 'lying' and 'fly' expand to include both literal and figurative meanings. The aphoristic, translatorese tone of the refrains lends them, as the poem continues, a massive solidity and air of universal and inescapable truth; between them, they fit all situations, from personal to global, including escape, inspiration, paralysis and stoutheartedness. You might mutter them as curses or repeat them wryly as the parts of your life fall into place after place.

In recalling Empson's 'Aubade', the poem Enright is deliberately not looking back to is Dylan Thomas's 'Refusal to Mourn the Death, by Fire, of a Child in London', and its superficially similar avowal from the poet that he will 'not murder | the mankind of her going with a grave truth'.[22] Thomas's poem, as Empson wrote,

tells us that Dylan Thomas *isn't* going to say something … [T]he child was killed in an air raid, and … Dylan Thomas won't say so because he is refusing to be distracted by thoughts about the war from thoughts about the child herself [23]

Enright, conversely, is refusing *not* to be distracted from 'humanity' by 'one human', and does so by thinking back to a poem which thinks about both in its defining refrains; 'it will not do' is an old-fashioned chiding in a poem which comes after Empson, and after the war, and is trying to keep both in mind in order to keep a stiff upper lip. This could easily stand as a fable

---

[21] *CP*, p. 69.

[22] Dylan Thomas, 'A Refusal to Mourn the Death, by Fire, of a Child in London' (1946), in *Collected Poems 1934–53*, ed. Walford Davies and Ralph Maud (London: Phoenix, 2003) pp. 85–6 (p. 86).

[23] William Empson, 'To Understand a Modern Poem: "A Refusal to Mourn the Death, by Fire, of a Child in London", by Dylan Thomas' (1947), in Empson, *Argufying: Essays on Literature and Culture*, ed. John Haffenden (London: Hogarth Press, 1988), pp. 382–6 (p. 383).

about the displacement of Thomas, as representative of the romantic 1940s, by classical Empson, the cool-headed 1930s man; it would illustrate what Conquest meant when he contrasted 'Empsonianism' with 'the trends it was designed to correct'. But although Enright's poem is a story of sorts, it isn't emblematic in that way. In his shaky, unevenly-stressed lines, so unlike Empson's strong pentameter, its writer isn't 'taking Empson for a master', or even 'mastering' him, but using the perspective lent by allusion to master his situation, with what Empson called 'our strong and critical curiosity about alien modes of feeling, our need for the flying buttress of sympathy with systems other than our own'.[24] For similar reasons, Edwin Muir disputes the generally accepted resemblance between Empson and the Movement poets, whose writing 'is very unlike Mr. Empson's... He moves us by the spectacle of a shocking struggle for control. In his followers the control is almost complete; the passion is stifled.'[25] Muir may be right to point to the importance of formal control, both in Empson's poetry and that of the Movement, but Enright's poem shows his generalization to be too sweeping.

Perhaps the reason the Movement is so often thought of as a collection of 'Empsonian' fashion-victims is because Empson's influence has been repeatedly cast as a matter of merely formal features, a 'framework', in Conquest's phrase, to be 'filled out'. Fraser declared that among the new poets of the decade 'certain metrical forms had an unusual prestige... notably two, borrowed from Mr. Empson: the villanelle... and *terza rima*'.[26] Dickinson's parodic villanelle bears out this claim, relying on its form as an automatic allusion to Empson; Amis advanced a similarly limited definition when he agreed that he was often 'Empsonic', deciding 'not to write another poem in 10-syllable lines, 3-line stanzas, for another ten years'.[27] Hilary Corke ridiculed 'Empsonian' poems 'serve[d] up in *villanelle* or *terza rima*', marking a clear separation of form and content.[28] Even much later, Morrison sum-

---

[24] 'Where the Body is...' (1927), in *Empson in Granta: the book, film & theatre reviews of William Empson originally printed in the Cambridge magazine Granta 1927–1929* (Tunbridge Wells: The Foundling Press, 1993), pp. 31–2 (p. 32).

[25] Edwin Muir, 'Neat, Muted and Despondent', *Observer* (14 October 1956), 18.

[26] Fraser, *Poetry Now*, p. 23.

[27] Kingsley Amis, letter to Robert Conquest, 16 April 1954, cited in Zachary Leader, *The Life of Kingsley Amis* (London: Jonathan Cape, 2006), p. 190.

[28] Corke, 'The Bad Old Style', p. 22.

marizes the 'characteristic Empsonian technique' as a formal charge: '*terza rima*, heavy end-stop, a blend of colloquialism and literary allusion', together with 'ingenious metaphors...ambiguities...clever-clever word-plays'.[29] Conquest criticized the 'well-constructed dry bones' of this 'Empsonian' style; Empson distanced himself from this tendency by emphasizing that his own 'narrow talent...isn't nearly as narrow as what turns up when somebody imitates it; that does feel very narrow'.[30]

However, as Fraser suggests, Movement poets could also display a different narrowness, 'some sense of constriction, indefinable but inhibiting'; the 'stifled' expression to which Muir referred.[31] It is a commonplace that Movement poetry doesn't actually move very far, and as in Enright's 'On the Death of a Child', where 'the big words fail to fit. Like giant boxes | Round small bodies', its writers often rehearse, in the variously-sized containers of their poems and within the tight rhymes of 'Empsonian' terza rima, villanelle, and refrain, their various coercions and limitations. Discussing 'the very rigid form' of his villanelle 'Missing Dates', Empson remarks that 'the difficulty of writing a villanelle is to stop it dying as it goes on', but adds that 'my villanelles sound very stiff and rather like tombstones—but they are intended to'.[32] As Ezra Pound notes, 'the villanelle can...achieve its closest intensity...when...the refrains are an emotional fact, which the intellect, in the various gyrations of the poem, tries in vain and in vain to escape'; as in the refrains of Empson's 'Aubade', this is what Muir calls a 'struggle', but it's a way of articulating, not an elaborate carapace for invertebrate gush.[33] Empson's refrains *are* an emotional fact, they don't *contain* one.

In *Articulate Energy: An Inquiry into the Syntax of English Poetry*, Davie emphasized the importance of syntax in poetry as, ideally, 'an instrument of articulation,

---

[29] Morrison, *The Movement*, pp. 118, 26.

[30] Conquest, in Enright (ed.), *Poets of the 1950s*, pp. 31–3 (pp. 32–33); 'Literary Opinion', BBC broadcast, 20 October 1954, cited in John Haffenden, *William Empson I: Among the Mandarins* (Oxford: Oxford University Press, 2005), hereafter *AM*, pp. 374–5.

[31] Fraser, *Poetry Now*, p. 27.

[32] *The Poems of William Empson*, ed. Peter Duval Smith, BBC Third Programme, 15 December 1952 recording DLO 19754/A); *Contemporary Poets Reading Their Own Poems*, British Council (National Sound Archive, British Library: 10226 WR); *Morris Gray Poetry Reading*, Harvard University, 13 April 1973 (PR 6009.M7 A6x 1973), both cited in *CP*, p. 345.

[33] Ezra Pound, 'Lionel Johnson', in *Literary Essays of Ezra Pound* (London: Faber and Faber, 1954), pp. 361–70 (p. 369).

a way of establishing relationships' both within the poem, and between the poem and the rest of the world.[34] For Davie, a poem should not be

a world, like the world of a symbolist poem, 'closed and self-sufficient, being the pure system of the ornaments and the chances of language'. It takes on meaning only as it is open to another world…Its syntax articulates not just itself, not only its own world, but the world of common experience.[35]

'Empsonianism', as it was invented by many of the Movement poets, made Empson's attention to form into just such an exclusive interest in 'the ornaments and the chances of language'. The protagonist of Wain's novel, *Hurry on Down*, repeats to himself a line by Empson, but corrupts it so that 'And I a lover twist what I abhor' becomes successively 'And twister I, abhorring what I love', 'And I a whore, abtwisting what I love', and 'Love eye and twist her and what I abhor'; his operation takes from the real Empson, and takes after Wain's idea of Empsonianism, and its repetitive inventions caricature the line's original elliptical obliquity into a parody of itself.[36] The painful articulations of Enright's poem begin to show, however, how the formal care with which Empson was associated could provide what Conquest aptly terms 'backbone' and 'a skeleton': an integral structure and support whose articulations enable and restrict movement. In this sense, Empson's form can do the job of Davie's ideal syntax. This goes beyond 'imitation': the influence of both Empson's 'narrow' poetry and his criticism—which turns and returns to the idea of 'what may indeed be the fundamental commonplace of poetry, a statement of the limitations of the human situation'—can be felt in the most eloquently limited articulations of the Movement.[37]

Philip Larkin's, for instance. In the fashionable sense, Larkin is the least 'Empsonian' poet of the Movement, and the statement which prefaces his poems in *Poets of the 1950s* contains no mention of Empson or the tics of style then associated with him. What Barbara Everett calls Larkin's 'wilfully modest' writing has always put on an aggressively plain-man attitude: 'I make a

---

[34] Donald Davie, *Articulate Energy: An Inquiry into the Syntax of English Poetry* (1955), in *Purity of Diction in English Verse and Articulate Energy* (Harmondsworth: Penguin, 1992), pp. 179–359 (p. 191).

[35] Ibid., p. 353.

[36] Wain, *Hurry on Down* (1953; repr. Harmondsworth: Penguin, 1979), pp. 29–30, 120, 252.

[37] Empson in conversation with Christopher Ricks, *The Review* 6 and 7 (June 1963), reprinted in *CP*, pp. 115–25 (p. 118); *Seven Types of Ambiguity*, 3rd edn., rev., (1953; repr. Harmondsworth: Penguin, 1995), hereafter *Types*, p. 96.

point of not knowing,' he asserts, 'what poetry is or how to read a page or about the function of myth.'[38] But as Everett goes on to argue, things aren't that simple, as 'Larkin's great art is to appear to achieve the literal while in fact doing something other'.[39] One of the other things he is doing (and he does so particularly when his writing considers 'something other') is being, in his own way, Empsonian.

Looking back on his undergraduate days at Oxford with Larkin, Amis recalled that everyone he knew had read Empson's first work of criticism, *Seven Types of Ambiguity*, and relished its enumerations of the multiple meanings of words and phrases: 'the feeling of illumination it gave, of helping you see things in poetry you had no idea were there—10 different reasons why Shakespeare's "bare ruined choirs" in Sonnet 73 was an appropriate phrase'.[40] Larkin's poem 'To My Wife' should be seen in this light, as the prospect of a choice prompts a catalogue of ambiguous expressions which flaunt and flirt with alternatives:

> Choice of you shuts up that peacock-fan
> The future was, in which temptingly spread
> All that elaborative nature can.
> Matchless potential! but unlimited
> Only so long as I elected nothing;
> Simply to choose stopped all ways up but one,
> And sent the tease-birds from the bushes flapping.
> No future now. I and you now, alone,
>
> So for your face I have exchanged all faces,
> For your few properties bargained the brisk
> Baggage, the mask-and-magic-man's regalia.
> Now you become my boredom and my failure,
> Another way of suffering, a risk,
> A heavier-than-air hypostasis.[41]

The poem shimmers with possibilities. To close a 'peacock-fan' is to furl the fan-like tail of a peacock, and snap shut a fan made of its feathers—one is

---

[38] Barbara Everett, 'Philip Larkin: After Symbolism', in Everett, *Poets in Their Time: Essays on English Poetry from Donne to Larkin* (London: Faber and Faber, 1986), pp. 230–44 (p. 243); Larkin, 'Statement', in Enright (ed.), *Poets of the 1950s*, pp. 77–8, reprinted in Larkin, *Required Writing: Miscellaneous Pieces 1955–1982* (London: Faber and Faber, 1983), hereafter *RW*, p. 79.

[39] Everett, 'Larkin's Edens', in Everett, *Poets in Their Time*, pp. 245–57 (p. 245).

[40] 'Bare Choirs' [review of *Argufying*], *Sunday Telegraph*, 29 November 1987, cited in *AM*, pp. 3–4.

[41] 'To My Wife', *LCP*, p. 54.

'elaborative nature' in its evolved plumage, the other in its tendency to accessorize—and this ends both mating rituals and their coy preambles, as the theatrical 'properties' of one night's performance collapse into the more everyday characteristics and belongings with which the groom chooses to live for good. 'Potential' is superbly 'matchless' only as long as you remain properly without a love 'match'; 'simply to choose' describes the mere act of selection, and hints at the less complicated life it initiates; the 'tease-birds' sent 'from the bushes flapping' are other likely lasses flushed out by a definite rejection, and a reminder that the proverbial smugness of the phrase 'a bird in the hand is worth two in the bush' ignores how you might feel as you watch the other ones get away.

'To My Wife' seems at first like a poem influenced by Auden, not Empson: the sonnet has the same rhyme-scheme as Auden's 'Who's Who', and the rhythm and syntax of its penultimate line echo 'In Memory of W.B. Yeats' ('A way of happening, a mouth.').[42] But the dwindling stresses in the last three lines—five, then four, then three—narrow the poem down to focus on its last, cumbersome, puzzling word, which then opens out, teasingly, into a spread of potential meanings. The following definitions of 'hypostasis', from the *OED*, fit Larkin's context:

1. *Medicine*. Sediment, deposit.
2. Base, foundation, groundwork, prop, support.
3. *Metaphysics*. That which subsists, or underlies anything; substance: (*a*) as opposed to qualities, attributes, or 'accidents'; (*b*) as distinguished from what is unsubstantial, as a shadow or reflection.
4. Essence, principle, essential principle.
5. *Linguistics*. The citing of a word, word-element, etc., as an example, a model.

'My Wife' is, then, (1) the dregs of wooing, sinking 'heavier-than-air' to the bottom of the glass; traditionally, a support; (2) an all-too-substantial presence; (3) (*a*) emerging from the coquettish attributes of courtship and (*b*) the flitting shadows of earlier flirtations; (4) a supposedly 'essential principle' of the groom's future life; (5) a blank 'model' cited, the title 'My Wife'. The word asks for its senses to be teased out: its multiple meaning puts an end to a list of five definitions, thrown in breathlessly, each adding to the last. But these interpretations don't lead anywhere; they sign and seal the poem's end. The carefulness

---

[42] W. H. Auden, 'Who's Who' and 'In Memory of W. B. Yeats', in *Collected Poems*, ed. Edward Mendelson, rev. edn. (London: Faber and Faber, 2007), pp. 126, 247–9 (p. 248).

of its selection, the adjustments of the adjectival hyphens like shock-absorbers, the exact fit of the long word into the short line and its slow, deliberately mispronounced completion of a polysyllabic rhyme as the last piece in the sonnet's jigsaw all combine to show that this isn't a bad choice because it's careless, but because it's a choice: this, in this poem, is what everything comes down to.

The sonnet contains a further coercion in its rhyme-scheme, as the cross-rhymes of the octave give way to the envelope-rhyme of the sestet; it is alluring to begin with, as the lack of rhyme leads you on through the as-yet-matchless line-endings 'faces', 'brisk' and 'regalia', but then as they find their mates the poem turns a cramped hairpin bend and retreats into 'failure', 'risk' and 'hypostasis'. Clive Scott writes that as the sonnet is

a form whose ultimate shape is largely predicted, the act of writing can be an act of self-inscription into form, or of clothing the self with form to the self's fit, the creation of a coincidence of self with form. The small dose of the unpredictable in the sonnet, principally located in the rhyme-scheme of the sestet, provides that margin of negotiation, that opportunity for a final fitting, which can guarantee a perfect convergence of verse design and verbal being.[43]

What Larkin arranges for in the sestet of 'To My Wife', however, is a 'clothing of self with form' to the *form's* fit. This is a 'final fitting' which is awkwardly *un*fitting, like morning dress which gapes or sags, or both in different places; taking the 'opportunity' of the 'unpredictable' sestet he turns it into the end of choice.

The year before he wrote 'To My Wife', at the end of his tether and of his engagement to Ruth Bowman, Larkin had complained bitterly to a friend that it was 'sufficient for me to choose something to dislike it. If we part I shall be tormented by remorse at not having married. If we marry I shall spend my life kicking myself... [I am] in a very narrow, very steep, very dark place'.[44] Larkin's poem comprehends this particular type of situation and that ambiguity Empson describes as having

one meaning which is the answer of the puzzle, but while you are puzzling the words have possible alternative meanings, and even to those who see the answers at once the alternatives are in a way present as being denied.... [P]eople, often, cannot have done both of two things, but... whichever they did, they will still have lingering in

---

[43] Clive Scott, 'Engendering the Sonnet, Loving to Write/Writing to Love: Louise Labé's "Tout aussi tot que je commence à prendre" ', *The Modern Language Review*, 92: 4 (October 1997), 842–50 (p. 844).

[44] Letter to J. B. Sutton, 18 June 1950, in *SL*, pp. 164–5 (p. 165).

their minds the way they would have preserved their self-respect if they had acted differently[45]

Empson's ambiguity, as Larkin understands, is not merely an enumeration of different meanings, but a product of the ways in which these meanings interfere with and impinge upon one another. Dante Gabriel Rossetti wrote that 'A Sonnet is a moment's monument'; what 'To My Wife' sets in stone is the 'dead deathless hour' when the alternatives to marriage are most vividly present as most emphatically denied, and the octave's spread of past temptations haunts the sestet's single choice and just-married chooser.[46] The ambiguity of 'hypostasis' is another matter. The stanza-break switches the effect of ambiguity from variety to specification: Larkin's poem describes some other version of the Movement's Empsonian 'narrowness', as its polysemy closes in like the cross-hairs on a target. Only this word (of course) could have had exactly this combination of semantic and acoustic properties, making its choice feel, as choices can, like painting yourself into a corner. In a famous passage, Paul Valéry sketched the predicament of a poet at the end of the line:

> Je cherche un mot (*dit le poète*) un mot qui soit:
> féminin,
> de deux syllabes,
> contenant P ou F,
> terminé par une muette,
> et synonyme de brisure, désagrégation;
> et pas savant, pas rare.
> Six conditions—au moins![47]

Like Larkin's poem, which points 'To My Wife' as surely as Woolf's novel leads *To the Lighthouse*, Valéry's steep list of 'conditions' steadily whittles down his options as it enumerates the 'properties' of this word, which—akin to Larkin's hypothetical 'Wife'—is absent but essential to the structure which

[45] *Types*, pp. 43, 66.
[46] 'The Sonnet', in D. G. Rossetti, *Poems*, ed. Oswald Doughty (London: J. M. Dent, 1957), p 212.
[47] Paul Valéry, 'Tel Quel: Autres Rhumbs: Littérature', in *Œuvres*, ed. Jean Hytier, 2 vols (Paris: Gallimard, 1957–60), II, 672–82 (p. 676). 'I'm looking for a word (*says the poet*) a word which would be: | feminine, | of two syllables, | containing P or F, | ending with a mute e, | and a synonym for breakage, disintegration; | and not learned, not out of the ordinary. | Six conditions, at least!' (My translation.)

defines it, like the increasingly highly-specified answer to a riddle. Poems
in riddle form, Morrison argues, were part of the 'academicism and ration-
alism' of the Movement; 'the pleasure which they provide is...cerebral—
they are intellectual puzzles rather than emotional mysteries'.[48] Yet whilst
the conventional riddle-poems of Thom Gunn and John Wain recall what
Empson called the element of 'puzzle interest' in his own poems, Larkin's
riddles sound out the emotional depths of their form.[49]

A riddle, after all, is just a statement describing a subject in a number
of oblique ways, without naming it. In 'The Building', Larkin's description
of a hospital—which never so much as whispers the word 'hospital'—pits
the riddle's usual requirement to work out an unknown answer against
the hopes, born of fear and euphemism, that we won't have to face what
we already know. Like many riddles, it begins with a series of teasing claims
and qualifications: the building is comparable to a 'hotel', but 'what keep
drawing up | At the entrance are not taxis'; it is 'like an airport lounge' but
its inhabitants 'Haven't come far'.[50] And like a riddle, it leads to an answer
which is obvious when you've got it:

> All know they are going to die.
> Not yet, perhaps not here, but in the end,
> And somewhere like this. That is what it means[51]

In 'To My Wife', the poem's slide into claustrophobia came from Larkin's
awareness of the place and the process of choice in the sonnet's sestet, so that
writing the poem became a suppressed metaphor for tying the knot; here,
the complicated unease of a hospital visit is brilliantly figured by the riddle's
forward momentum and refusal to come to terms even as it approaches the
end. Guessing what might happen when you've just gone in for tests really
does feel like contemplating a riddle you're trying, but not entirely wanting,
to solve, for fear that what turns up will be what Larkin elsewhere terms 'the
solving emptiness | That lies just under what we do'.[52] As he wrote from hos-
pital in one of his last letters, 'of course they are looking for something, and

[48] Morrison, *The Movement*, p. 119.
[49] Empson, 'Note on Notes', in *The Gathering Storm* (London: Faber and Faber, 1940), repr. in *CP*,
pp. 112–13 (p. 112).
[50] 'The Building', *LCP*, pp. 191–3 (p. 191).
[51] *LCP*, p. 192.   [52] 'Ambulances', in *LCP*, pp. 132–3 (p. 132).

I bloody well hope they don't find it'.[53] 'To My Wife' had a different dynamic,
giving things away first so as to climax with an anticlimax, encouraging our
familiarity to breed with his contempt; the poem turned Emily Dickinson's
easy riddle into an allegory for marriage:

> The Riddle we can guess
> We speedily despise—
> Not anything is stale so long
> As Yesterday's surprise—[54]

Once you're a wife you've stopped playing hard to get. Larkin marks with a
cruel stanza-break and rhythmical hitch the moment of disillusionment:

> No future now. I and you now, alone.
>
> So for your face I have exchanged all faces

The last line of the octave drags its feet down the aisle, the repetition of 'now'
and the tired syntax slowing it to a stagger, so that it's almost unable to bring
itself to utter the final two syllables, 'alone', which will then slide assonantly
over the stanza-break to 'So'. 'So', meaning 'in this way': the exchange of
vows takes place in the sonnet's *volta*, its about-face, which is prolonged into
a blank pause, trying not to look as life turns a corner. Far from constituting
a mere 'framework', a poetic form is, as Eliot noted, 'not merely such and
such a pattern, but a precise way of thinking and feeling'.[55] Larkin's art, in
both these poems and elsewhere, lies in thinking about and feeling for what
the forms of poems can say about knowing and guessing and choosing.

   This sensitivity to form, rather than any 'Empsonian' imitation or echo,
is what allies Larkin to Empson. Amis remarked that Empson's poetry had
'showed that strict forms were all right. Not only all right, but a great help.
And that rhyming was all right'; a large part of the helpfulness of these fea-
tures is that they can assist with the articulation of helplessness and of being
not all right (but not all wrong either).[56] Larkin's poetry follows Empson's
in being what Peter McDonald calls 'a drama of form', attentive to 'the

[53] Letter to Kingsley Amis, 21 November 1985, in *SL*, pp. 757–9 (p. 758).
[54] Emily Dickinson, poem 1222, in *The Complete Poems of Emily Dickinson*, ed. Thomas H. Johnson (Boston: Little, Brown and Company, 1960), p. 538.
[55] T. S. Eliot, 'The Possibility of a Poetic Drama', in *The Sacred Wood: Essays on Poetry and Criticism* (1928; repr. London: Faber and Faber, 1997), pp. 60–70, (p. 63).
[56] Cited in Clive James, 'Kingsley Amis: A Profile', *New Review* (July 1974), 27.

ways in which…the rhythms of lines, the comings and goings of sound, the demands and revaluations of rhyme…perform their own transformations on the writing self'.[57] What Everett writes of Larkin's 'framing devices' is perhaps even better said of his attention to this staging: it 'is a matter of internal lineaments as well as external boundaries, a matter which may start as formal technical device but certainly does not stop there: poetic form in any good poet unites technique to metaphysics'.[58] This is because, as Angela Leighton puts it,

form spans the whole spectrum of meanings from body to soul, from thing to figure, poem to parts…It runs the gamut, as Raymond Williams observes, from 'the external and superficial to the inherent and determining'.[59]

Picture-frames, windows, doorways and photograph-albums may limit and restrict our views through Larkin's verse, but the framings of his poetic form frequently demonstrate, as we read on, how these limits are shaped.

So that in 'Wires', as in 'To My Wife', enclosure is a process of limitation as well as a limited location:

> The widest prairies have electric fences,
> For though old cattle know they must not stray
> Young steers are always scenting purer water
> Not here but anywhere. Beyond the wires
>
> Leads them to blunder up against the wires
> Whose muscle-shredding violence gives no quarter.
> Young steers become old cattle from that day,
> Electric limits to their widest senses.[60]

At the end of the first stanza, the reader inexperienced in this poem will hurry over the stanza-break, to discover what does lie 'beyond the wires' and at the end of the sentence, and find out that what's there is a sting; the syntax sends you back smarting, to reconsider the preposition as a noun (taught, now, that a preposition is all the noun you'll get). The rhyme recedes, hurt, from the blank, the transfixing exact rhyme 'wires' / 'wires' fading; the rhyme-words become

---

[57] 'Beside Himself' [review of Robert Lowell, *Collected Poems*], *Poetry Review*, 93 (2003–4), 62–70 (p. 64).

[58] Everett, *Poets in their Time*, p. 251.

[59] Angela Leighton, 'Elegies of Form in Bishop, Plath, Stevenson', *Proceedings of the British Academy* 121 (2002), 257–75 (pp. 257–8).

[60] *LCP*, p. 48.

more distant one from another, until we can almost forget that our final 'sense' of the poem, its last word, was set in train eight lines ago when the word 'fences' was first plotted, and that our 'widest senses' are now no longer shaped by or match the 'widest prairies' we remember from the beginning. Because its effects are achieved on a formal level, 'Wires' lets us feel in the broadest sense what Adam Phillips describes as the process by which 'our first fears turn into habits of evasion, and out of these habits an identity is cast.'[61] After the first reading, we'll approach not only that 'beyond', but also this poem, differently; remembering that there's something to be careful of, we'll pay an altered kind of attention. What the poem's form gives us is therefore not simply a metaphor for, but also an example of, the way in which we experience the world. As Empson writes of George Herbert's 'I gave Hope a watch of mine',

one can accept the poem without plunging deeply into the meaning, because...the movement is so impeccable as to be almost independent of the meaning.[62]

The 'impeccable movements' of Larkin's verse mean that his 'habits' of versification, like those created and written about by Empson, can at once form part of the texture of his poems, and stand slightly aside from—though never as mere containers for—his meaning. Larkin's poems often dwell on lives or events 'whose ultimate shape is largely predicted', but only 'largely'; patterns which 'something hidden from us chose', and, 'habit for a while, | Suddenly...harden into all we've got' not by prior decree but through learned custom, thoughtlessness, or cowardice.[63] Poetic form, as something chosen and then followed, adapted, sometimes a forgotten ground bass, and sometimes grindingly coercive, is particularly suitable for articulating the subtle strains and unspoken tensions involved in such predicaments. Empson's 'Aubade' offers a template for balancing two imperatives; 'To My Wife' was not just about getting married, but about all kinds of choice; 'Wires' is about limitations in all senses.

Asked in an interview whether he'd ever been to the United States, Larkin replied:

A writer once said to me, If you ever go to America, go either to the East Coast or the West Coast: the rest is a desert full of bigots. That's what I think I'd like: where if you

---

[61] Adam Phillips, *Houdini's Box: On the Arts of Escape* (London: Faber and Faber, 2002), p. 54.
[62] *Types*, p. 144.   [63] 'Dockery and Son', in *LCP*, pp. 152–3 (p. 153).

help a girl trim the Christmas tree you're regarded as engaged, and her brothers start oiling the shotguns if you don't call on the minister. A version of pastoral.[64]

Larkin's arch last sentence shows him to be a good reader of Empson's *Some Versions of Pastoral*; not only because his poems can be found so frequently 'putting the complex into the simple', as Empson's definition runs, but because the 'version of pastoral' he sketches here adds a complex development, and another archetype, to Empson's idea of the pastoral hero, the 'free and independent mind' John Haffenden summarizes as 'Satan-pagan-arriviste-fool-rogue-criminal-child-critic'.[65] At first glance, Larkin's poetic persona, replying to dull social invitations, submitting to 'the toad *work*', tracing the paths of suburban railways and marriages, liking the sound of 'a desert full of bigots', is a long way from Empson's freewheeling outlaw-critic, who heads the 'Cult of Independence'.[66] But that would be to forget that Empson himself is a critic who ended his first book of criticism warning against critical analysis:

many works of art give their public a sort of relief and strength, because they are independent of the moral code which their public accepts and is dependent on; relief, by fantasy gratification; strength, because it gives you a sort of equilibrium within your boundaries to have been taken outside them, because you know your own boundaries better when you have seen them from both sides. Such works give a valuable imaginative experience, and such a public cannot afford to have them analysed... The object of life, after all, is not to understand things, but to maintain one's defences and equilibrium and live as well as one can; it is not only maiden aunts who are placed like that.[67]

Larkin's poems are not these works of art, quite, for he has a different relationship with boundaries, and his writing, as a consequence, offers a quite differently 'valuable imaginative experience': that of an inability to see them from both sides, but a long time spent sitting on the fence, wondering. All of Larkin's gestures towards an 'Elsewhere' are made, very firmly, from this side of the fence: what's 'Beyond it all' and 'Beneath it all'; the 'Beyond' of 'Wires'; 'attics cleared of me! Such absences!'; what's 'Sent out of sight'; 'That vase.'; what's 'out of reach'; 'what something hidden from us chose'; what

---

[64] *RW*, p. 70.

[65] *Some Versions of Pastoral* (1935; repr. Harmondsworth: Penguin, 1995), hereafter *Pastoral*, p. 25; *AM*, p. 394.

[66] *LCP* p. 89–90; *Pastoral*, p. 157.   [67] *Types*, p. 285.

is 'Nothing, and is nowhere, and is endless'; what 'will happen, soon'; whatever 'We shall find out'.[68] The fantasy is of approach, not accomplishment, and these gestures occur almost without exception at the ends of poems; they are finishings, not beginnings, and don't propose to 'analyse'. In this way the shapes of Larkin's poems, as Eric Griffiths notes of Peter Robinson's rhymes,'feel for a reality beyond our representations just by attending to the reality *of* our representations'.[69] Form, as Leighton writes, 'recalls what it shuts out, and partly takes the shape of what it throws into relief'; Larkin's attention to form is an attention to this charged boundary, and to the poetic plots—like his sketch of an American dream—which articulate its edges.[70]

This is because his work has what Empson (who had it himself) praised as 'the capacity to accept a limitation... unflinchingly...[,] to conceive... a form as a unit of sustained feeling'.[71] A great part of what Larkin takes from Empson—from his poetry *and* his criticism, his reading as well as his writing—is a sense that the limits and choices and falterings of experienced life can properly fit and be figured by the limits and choices and falterings of poetic form. As Larkin wrote of Ogden Nash's wonky couplets, his writing demonstrates a belief that 'let-down rhymes and wait-for-it metrics are perfect stylistic equivalents for the missing chairs and slow burns of which civilized life is composed'.[72] Ricks claims that 'though Larkin's convictions are classical, his impulses are romantic', but this comes close to separating head from heart and form from content in a way which recalls the early critics of the Movement.[73] It was a division which Larkin explicitly denied and complicated: ' "passion & reason, self-division's cause", seems very naïve to me: the split in me at any rate comes between what I admire & what I am.'[74] Larkin's poems are both calm and exasperated because they don't articulate any frustration that words cannot adequately express feelings or ideas; what they articulate is the frustration that lives cannot adequately accommodate

[68] *LCP*, pp. 42, 48, 49, 116, 119, 137, 153, 165, 197.
[69] Eric Griffiths, 'Blanks, misgivings, fallings from us', in *The Salt Companion to Peter Robinson*, ed. Adam Piette and Katy Price (Cambridge: Salt, 2007), pp. 55–82 (p. 70).
[70] Leighton, 'Elegies of Form', pp. 269, 272.
[71] *Types*, p. 59.
[72] 'Missing Chairs', in *RW*, pp. 134–141 (pp. 134–5).
[73] Christopher Ricks, 'Philip Larkin: "Like something almost being said" ', in *The Force of Poetry* (Oxford: Clarendon Press, 1984), pp. 274–84 (p. 278).
[74] Letter to J.B. Sutton, 11 August 1948, in *SL*, pp. 148–9 (p. 149).

desires. What occupies him is that aspect of pastoral which Empson described as expressing 'the waste even in a fortunate life, the isolation even of a life rich in intimacy', so when the forms of his poems sag, give out, give in, they're giving up on life but upholding a contrasting faith in the efficacy of literary shape to convey that very resignation.[75] The last of Empson's Pastoral figures is Lewis Carroll's Alice, overturning the dinner-table, showing that

the gentleman is not the slave of his conventions because at need he could destroy them; and yet, even if he did this, and all the more because he does not, he must adopt while despising it the attitude to them of a child.[76]

Larkin's 'version of pastoral' turns this freedom on its head, freely and conventionally; he adds to Empson's gallery the figure of the maiden aunt.

Which is not to say that the boundary and the equilibrium are, as Empson writes elsewhere, 'safely placed'; we don't always know where we are.[77] Larkin's 'Here' takes the form of a train journey to what's 'out of reach':

> Fast-shadowed wheat-fields, running high as hedges,
> Isolate villages, where removed lives

> Loneliness clarifies. Here silence stands
> Like heat. Here leaves unnoticed thicken,
> Hidden weeds flower, neglected waters quicken,
> Luminously-peopled air ascends;
> And past the poppies bluish neutral distance
> Ends the land suddenly beyond a beach
> Of shapes and shingle. Here is unfenced existence:
> Facing the sun, untalkative, out of reach.[78]

Lineation, which fooled 'young steers' in 'Wires', plays similar tricks on readerly expectation here. Is 'Isolate' an archaic adjective, or a verb? 'Lives': verb or noun? Until we pass the stanza-break, we hesitate; later, too, the possibility of misreading 'poppies' as a possessive noun, the blueness of the leaves of a poppy-field, pulls us into hearing the next line's 'Ends' as a sudden intransitive inversion, in which the land ends itself. We read on but have to keep correcting our altering position, thinking back to how we've just made sense

[75] *Pastoral*, p. 12.   [76] *Pastoral*, p. 233.   [77] 'Reflection from Anita Loos', in *CP*, p. 85.
[78] 'Here', in *LCP*, pp. 136–7 (p. 137).

or got it wrong, or how things looked last time we went this way. 'Recently', wrote Larkin, at twenty-six, 'I've had a sense of one's character pulling one along roads already judged worthless or wrong'.[79] 'Here' hinges on and takes its shape from just such a prospective and retrospective shunt and drag. Balancing momentum against inertia, as the poem's great twenty-five-line sentence rounds the curve, its lines' and stanzas' articulations grate against its syntax, and we hear, and so feel, and if we have been here before recognize, a jolt, a fault on the line; a set of points, perhaps, more noticeable for having been felt previously, for

whenever a receiver of poetry is seriously moved by an apparently simple line, what are moving in him are the traces of a great part of his past experience and of the structure of his past judgements.[80]

---

[79] Letter to J. B. Sutton, 11 August 1948, in SL, pp. 148–9 (p. 149).   [80] Types, p. 16.

9

Boys on the Move

Karl Miller

Almost all of the Movement writers of the Fifties and early Sixties are now dead. But their story is still alive. To turn to their poems and novels, and to their letters, to the annals of their bid for authority in 'the kingdom', as the country would continue to be known to the *de facto* leader of the group, Kingsley Amis, is to be aware of a past which is both far and near.

In 1953, Amis wrote to offer his friend John Wain a mostly favourable view of his novel *Hurry on Down*, to appear to offer him the baton of leadership, and to predict, lightly or perhaps euphorically: 'With you as general, the boys could move right into control.'[1] A few years earlier Hartley Shawcross had been euphoric in the House of Commons about the election of a Labour government: 'We are the masters now.' This master was knighted in 1945, but by 1953 Labour's boys had lost power. The boys referred to by Amis were the Movement writers who were about to enjoy what mastery they were able to command, and the kingdom would one day gain a Sir Kingsley. 'Movement' was a name for the group that took on under-meanings. Up the road, on their motorcycles, came Thom Gunn's 'Boys'. They were 'On the Move'. 'One joins the movement in a valueless world,' wrote Gunn in the poem of that name. Among the under-meanings, perceptible to some but not much

---

[1] KA to JW; 6 November 1953, *The Letters of Kingsley Amis*, ed. Zachary Leader (London: HarperCollins, 2000).

evident in Gunn, was that of a certain social mobility. And there was mobility, too, in the politics of the Movement.

About a year before the receipt of Kingsley Amis's letter, John Wain came to Cambridge to speak to the Doughty Society, run by F. R. Leavis's pupils at Downing College. I have a memory of his writing to mention that he'd be recognizable at the station by the flashing of his eyes, eager for a sight of Little Downing, as Leavis's Cambridge could be called. Little Downing was a sort of movement, and was initially treated by Movementeers—who had something to learn about Leavis—as a possible source of friendship and support.

On 20 February 1955, he sent me his opinion of a juvenile piece, 'Notes on Agreement and Elegance', which I'd published that month in the *Twentieth Century* ('A Cambridge Number'), and in which I'd been trying to write like Leavis and Henry James. The piece was laboured and pretentious, and John's letter to that effect did him credit. It had none of the condescension for which he was occasionally blamed, and was written to be of some use and in a generous spirit:

Please, Karl, could you put it a bit more *clearly* next time? After finishing the essay, I realised (i) that it had taken me a long time, (ii) that the reason why it had taken me a long time was because I had to keep slowing down over sentences like, 'he activates his conversance with the society he moved in as a type of the socialite into a hard evaluation of it.' I don't mean that this is *obscure*—it's hypnotic. The force of it doesn't reach me until I translate it into, 'You might have taken him for a socialite, accepting the surface values of his society, but no, he was strictly judging it by standards beyond its own.'

The socialite in question was Henry James. John sent me his good wishes, having explained that he didn't feel he was being 'either interfering or in the smallest degree condescending'. 'I address you in the persona of the "plain" man who is going to *read* what you write, asking you on all our behalf to simplify the manner so that we can come at your matter the sooner.' This call for plain speaking was at the heart of Movement attitudes.

In 1968, I brought out a Penguin anthology, *Writing in England Today: The Last Fifteen Years*, a mingling of fiction and verse, and of criticism, that copious common pursuit of the period. The Movement contribution was paraded, but there was plenty of attention to writers remote from or unfriendly to the Movement, not all of them due to live out their lives as commoners. Waugh, Golding, Sybille Bedford, V. S. Naipaul and the young Heaney were there, as was Wain's friend from his Reading University days, Frank Kermode.

A religious strain, pro-God and post-God, was ascribed to some of these writers, together with a commitment to, and nostalgia for, the industrial working class. The Movement consisted largely of middle-class unbelievers, and was less responsive to and less familiar with the working class than its reputation, and the tactical disparagements popular with its enemies, originally suggested.

Some of the writing of 'the last fifteen years', as presented in the anthology, showed the immediate post-war period as a hopeful, though hardly blissful time, for all the austerity laid on the nation. This is not a view which is countenanced in most current accounts of the period, some of them by writers then unborn: the accounts in question give the sense that, with the country spent from war, in hock and under rationing, the Empire gone, the novel dead, spirits were low. This is not how I remember the time, and is not what appears in the rich and lively writing of the time. Many felt released, and ready to try again.

In supportive style, the introduction to the anthology summarized Movement aims: 'Many of the writers who rose to prominence during the Fifties were identified with a new sobriety and with a taste for comedy and iconoclasm; they were tired of the international, experimental avant-garde and of mandatory modernity; they were tired of the romantic individualism, the religiosity, the martyred sensitiveness that had been favoured by writers during the war; they were sceptics; and they were democrats. An implicit stage-direction of their collective comedy: "Exit the hero." ' These aims were in a sense satellite to Wain's plea for plain speaking. They could be considered one of the periodic reversions to a domestic clarity and candour which have long overtaken obscurantist or euphuistic excess. If Movement writings could be alleged to lack theoretical depth, they are certainly not without theoretical interest. Theirs was a theory which was thoroughly exemplified, critically and creatively, resting as it did, quite literally, on chapter and verse—on the production and examination of 'words on the page', as the saying used to go. They were like Leavis in supposing that theory should be so grounded, and in being therefore supposed untheoretical. The Movement performance did not have everything that literature can give, but it was a clearing of the air which deserves to be thought more than ephemeral and rather more than a clearing of the air.

The stance adopted by these often, but not always, polemical writers, and shared at first and in part with Leavis, involved an attack on a privileged upper class of the so-called 'cultivated' and on bohemian and metropolitan shams blamed by such opponents on Bloomsbury. Donald Davie read this as an assault by the provinces on the metropolis (to which Amis fundamentally belonged). It was also read, or misread, as was Leavis at one point, in a way that suggested a fight on behalf of a more equal society, and of the sort of people—'high-rise flat dwellers, office workers and factory robots and unassimilated multiracial minorities'—who would later be seen by Q. D.Leavis, Leavis's wife, as incapable of coming up with anything worthy of the traditions of the English novel.[2] The English countryside had died, she thought, and the English novel which had thrived on it was about to do the same.

John Wain should have been in the anthology, and so should the admirable Scottish poet Norman MacCaig, who started as a surrealist of a kind (an Apocalyptic) and moved to a practice appreciably close to that of his Movement contemporaries in the south, who took longer than they should have done to acknowledge his talent. Geographical proximity has been a factor in the formation of coteries and *cénacles*, and the Movement was no exception, with its limited number of early locations in the South of England and South Wales. Kingsley Amis was an English patriot who spent several years in Swansea largely liking the Welsh, while insisting on Swansea's Dylan Thomas as a disgrace to literature; but he could seem to agree with the historian Hugh Trevor-Roper in being able to do without the Scots—what with their linguistically-challenged dialect verse. MacCaig, of course, wrote fluent English, and individual Scots were let into the group: G. S.Fraser, who had moved to London, was allowed to be a Movement backer.

Wain was busy and incisive in the assertion of control that accompanied its aims. His star fell as Kingsley Amis's continued to rise, and their falling-out—with Wain accused of snubs and condescensions, among other errors—became an aspect of the group's melting away. Each tended to make light of the affinities between them, which others noticed and enlarged on.

Hurry on Down and Amis's *Lucky Jim*, which appeared soon afterwards, in 1954, are alike in the jokes they tell and in many of their *bêtes noires*: Wain and

---

[2] *Q. D.Leavis, Collected Essays*, 3 vols., ed. G. Singh (Cambridge: Cambridge University Press, 1983), p. 325. Randall Stevenson's *The Last of England? (The Oxford English Literary History*, Vol. 12: *1960–2000:* (New York: Oxford University Press, 2004), p. 4) discusses Mrs Leavis's opinion, and goes on to condemn Movement writers as mild and safety-seeking.

Amis were like the later Leavis in their propensity for insult and aggression. Both of their novels take an interest in what was called by critics 'rescue by millionaire'. Wain's Charles Lumley does a succession of dirty jobs but is not subdued to the condition of the lower orders. He appears to 'get' the upper-class girl he has been pursuing; Lucky Jim, too, gets lucky. Hurry on up? enemies may have asked.

Both in his novel and in his memoir *Sprightly Running* of 1962 Wain's angers are apt to communicate a phobic attitude to class. Lumley is a desolate man, irritable and complaining in his down-and-up endeavour to get 'out of the net' of the middle-class way of life he is heir to and entrapped by. *Under the Net* by the Movement affiliate Iris Murdoch, that far from angry, indeed sprightly, Irish-seeming comedy of London flat-dweller life, came out the year after *Hurry on Down*: it alludes to rescue by millionaire, but is not concerned in any major way with class or with entrapment; it carries the remark that theory should be shunned and that we must try to 'crawl under the net' of the particular.[3]

In Wain's novel, front teeth are threatened. A millionaire's son is a 'brainless lout'. Lumley is ferocious in his truculence towards many comers. When a man in grey suede shoes (a Movement badge of dishonour) says hello to him, Lumley inquires of the girl he is eventually to get: 'Will you excuse me while I take this gentleman outside and throw him down the lift shaft?' Lumley's wrath does not spare the lower orders: 'a succession of more or less mentally deficient girls from the village' troops by.[4]

This weird truculence seems related to the trapped, unhappy adolescence chronicled in *Sprightly Running*, where a longing for an unspoilt English-novel countryside encounters the louts and deficients pouring out of a new nearby Staffordshire housing estate. Wain was bullied at school to a degree which must be rare even among memoirists, and it is possible to detect an element

---

[3] *Under the Net*, p. 91. The novel has features of the Movement comedy of manners, and a dash of the camaraderie which the virtually all-male Movement writers sometimes went in for; it also has a romantic tendency. In a letter to Philip Larkin of 29 September 1979, Kingsley Amis associated with Iris Murdoch 'a defective sense of other people' (Leader (ed.), *Letters of Kingsley Amis*). He did not say what this might have done to the people in her books. In this one, the first-person narrator is both author and character, both author and other. An imaginary male someone else is vividly present in this narrator (and could well be vividly performed by the Irish actor of recent years, Dylan Moran).

[4] *Hurry on Down* (London: Secker & Warburg, 1953), see p.73, 204, 105, 189.

of release in the plain-spoken energy of his novel, of *Sprightly Running*, and of his enthusiastic account of his hero *Samuel Johnson* (1974), in which the reader is told that 'it is a law of nature that any adolescent regards his original setting of birthplace and family circle simply as a trap to be got out of'.[5] So Samuel Johnson left Lichfield, while later making his peace with it, and John Wain plunged into a fiction of escape and retaliation and into a full-blown literary career. His memoir has a long central chapter about the eccentric scholar Meyerstein, with his harrowing erudition and gruesome unrequited attachment to Oxford University, which is among the most satisfying and sympathetic of his writings. At this stage of his career, it might have been said that kindliness would sometimes break in. 'All the houses were alike, and yet each was unique and lovable to the people who lived in it,' reports scornful *Hurry on Down*, and there's a poem of his in which he speaks, in the same comradely vein, of the willingness to trust that the restaurants we go to won't poison us.[6]

The memoir is at pains to tell the difference between Wain and Amis:

My vision of life is more extreme than his, both darker and brighter; his work is based on a steadying common sense, a real hatred of imbalance and excess; mine, by comparison, is apocalyptic. In his view, I over-write, giving way too easily to the purple patch and the rhetorical flight; to me, he seems too much content with one level tone. And of course he is a much more finished writer than I shall ever be.[7]

The passage, which makes Kingsley Amis blander than he ever was, then refers to 'the so-called "Movement"'. Was there such a group, Wain may want us to ask, or did journalists invent it, as they did the adjacent category of 'angry young men', with whom John in his ire, and much to his indignation, was sometimes confused? The book inveighs against literary journalists, though the author had started to earn his living by behaving as one. At that stage, they were all charlatans.

His BBC Third Programme magazine *First Reading* showcased Movement writing and was 'handled pretty roughly; it was some months before the "metropolitan literary world" forgave me for thinking Amis a good novelist,

---

[5] See John Wain, *Samuel Johnson* (New York: Viking Press, 1974), p. 34.

[6] *Hurry on Down*, p. 172. The restaurant thought occurs in a love poem, collected in *Weep before God* (1961), which begins: 'This above all is precious and remarkable, | How we put ourselves in one another's care, | How in spite of everything we trust each other.'

[7] John Wain, *Sprightly Running* (London: Macmillan, St. Martins Press, 1965), p. 205.

Alvarez a good critic, and Larkin a good poet'.[8] Even the benevolent V. S. Pritchett bore arms in the war that had broken out. Pritchett was a man of the old world who might have been thought both Bloomsbury and not, and might also have been thought both Movement-compatible and not. But he was put off at first by the sight of the boys on the move. Others too were put off. As an editor who published their work—in the *Spectator*, the *New Statesman* and the *Listener*—I well remember what was said against them in their early days. They were teddy boys. They were lower-class. They didn't know Latin or Greek, or French. Bloomsbury rose again in reproof, from its comparatively recent past. The opprobrium was also aimed at Leavis and his 'disciples'. He was an upstart who displayed 'the acrimony of the learned' and who 'hated literature'. His dislike of the London literary world was aggravated by the arrival there of writers who had once shared his dislike. Meanwhile the Movement was itself opprobrious.

For the ill-feeling of the time and place—a sizable thing, in its way—these writers were some of them (including myself as their Scottish abettor) partly responsible. Kingsley's collected letters are a formidable achievement, a big black box of comedy and critical insight, but one that must have frightened elderly survivors of the war that was waged: open it, these veterans may have worried, and all the ill-feelings and rude words of the world would fly out. I don't think that the group's sympathizers were fully able to take the measure of his relentless limiting judgements—they were the air they breathed. Not all of these writers, though, as I say, were like that. D. J. Enright's ironies were relatively gentle beasts, gentle with partners in subversion and with their enemies. But was there a partnership?

At the declaration of this war, Movement writers were so called by themselves as well as by metropolitan literary journalists. It was as much a movement as any remotely similar confederacy of writers has been. Movements disagree internally. They come to an end. They disclaim their own existence. Writers don't take easily to behaving as team players, and take easily to running each other down. But the Movement's internal differences didn't stop it from being a movement, and it has remained one even after it ceased to be one. It shouldn't be pictured as an exhausted imperium, as a minitype of the bygone British Empire. The struggle continues. The debate they began about

[8] Ibid., p.169.

the meaning of meaning, and of plain speaking and common sense, has gone on, and has come and gone, ever since. What is worth stressing is not that these writers fell out or dispersed, but that there were internal differences almost from the first. Dispersal enacted what was in some degree inherent. Thom Gunn's departure for California illustrates this. His co-option by the Movement was welcomed by his new associates, but they were not his partners: he knew few of them well, and his early poetry was as much a dissent from as an acceptance of the values of the group. His early poetry was more military at moments than the Movement, for all their active-service metaphors. It spoke of heroes, of toughs and over-dogs, of 'brute purpose'. It seems fitting that he and Donald Davie should later have become friends in California, Davie counting as equally ambivalent from the first in relation to these values. His book *Purity of Diction in English Verse*, published in 1952, was said by him, when it was reissued in 1966, to have had the makings of a Movement manifesto. It is more abstruse than manifestos generally are, yet successfully conveyed that modern poetry might at times resemble that of the eighteenth century, and reveal a subordination of metaphor to statement, or at least effect an adjustment in the balance between the two. But his own elegant and accomplished poems were always more mysterious than plain-spoken, and further action in the history of his engagement with the group lay ahead.

He wrote a politely dissenting review of my poor old 'Notes on Agreement and Elegance', but that did not prevent us from working together. A decade later, I printed in my Penguin anthology his beautiful poem 'Or, Solitude', and read into it a meaning linked to what some saw as his departure from the Movement. The poem, first published in the *New Statesman* on the last day of 1965, opens with

> A farm boy lost in snow
> Rides his good horse, Madrone,
> Through Iowan snows for ever
> And is called 'alone'.

And the last stanza springs a surprise:

> The metaphysicality
> Of poetry, how I need it!
> And yet it was for years
> What I refused to credit.

I told myself then that the poem was beyond paraphrase, that the Movement had once been hospitable to paraphrase, and that the sudden literal, and surely autobiographical, statement at the close was, in a sense, a Movement sense, at odds with the Symbolist poem that precedes it. I received a letter from Donald (25 July 1968) which commented on my Introduction, pointing out, a little acidly perhaps, that 'Or, Solitude' was the subtitle given by Wordsworth to his poem about Lucy Gray. This was a difficult time for him, anticipated, conceivably, in the poem. He was in the 'agony' of an episode of student revolt at Essex University, where he'd been serving as Chairman of the English Department, an episode that belonged to a different world from the one in which the Movement had been convened, and he was about to 'leave the country'. I had just printed in the *Listener* a letter from a former colleague which alluded to Donald's authoritarianism and 'black spleen', to 'the wing of madness', and to his 'chosen role as a latterday Augustan poet'.

Davie told me: 'Your reading of that poem isn't the reading that I give to it (mine is more "impersonal"), but we both know that once a poem is in the public domain the author's reading of it has no more authority than anyone else's, and yours is a legitimate reading which will henceforth colour my own.' The letter proceeds to Movementize me, in virtue of my editorial activities: 'our "generation of the fifties" is a much tighter unity, more rigorously conditioned so as to stand together, than I've wanted to believe. You were right & I was wrong: the moral and imaginative universe of Black Mountain, which now commands the pop-intellectualism of the '60s, cannot be reconciled with the universe that you and I, and Enright & Osborne, and Amis & Larkin, inhabit.' And perhaps he had, in the letter, re-Movementized himself: having tasted other pastures, he wants here to belong to the generation of the Fifties. This was not, needless to say, his last word on the subject—the subject he'd politely said I had been right about: he was to continue to review his sense of the Movement.

The last stanza of the poem still doesn't yield, for me, a wholly or chiefly impersonal meaning. But 'the boys who knew it best' or 'best expressed it' and are 'gone from the land'—'to Boston' or, like Gunn and Davie, 'Out West'—remain inscrutable. I don't now know how to relate them to the boys who moved into control in the Fifties, or how far a break with Movement principles should be inferred from the need expressed here for the meta-physicality of poetry—which is seen both as a belief that the poet used to reject and as the range that the boys in the poem used to ride. What does seem plain enough is that this is not the kind of poem that was prescribed in Robert Conquest's *New Lines* anthology of 1956.

Movement purists who swore by paraphrase might have been nonplussed by the poem, and may have viewed it as a defection or declension. A similar case may have been posed by the endings which Larkin provided for some of his later poems, in which the camera pulls back from immediate concerns and stares, for instance, into a blank and endless sky, and which Kingsley Amis could be heard objecting to. Metaphysicality, poeticality, or rhetoric was no doubt suspected.

The complexities of Movement practice, not to be exaggerated but visible from scratch, have been elided in subsequent attacks on it, as in the recidivist avant-gardism of recent years, in which Larkin is denied the stature of an important poet and he and his fellows are said to be timidly retentive, set against innovation and inquiry. The Movement was shamefully old, as well as shamefully new, in the eyes of detractors, when its boys went into action. Old and new are apt to coincide, and did so then. Over the fifty years that followed, the kingdom has been urged to be modern, to change— Samuel Johnson might have thought it prone to innovation. There were Movement writers who shared Johnson's distrust as they grew older, came to share Johnson's distrust of innovation, but were all for the new broomstick Margaret Thatcher.

10

'I thought I Was So Tough': Thom Gunn's Postures for Combat

Alan Jenkins

Denying the existence of the Movement, or denying that, if it existed, one had any part in it, seems to have started almost at the same time as the Movement itself. Perhaps the fact that—as Ian Hamilton and others have pointed out—like the Sitwells, it now seems to belong as much to the history of publicity as of poetry has something to do with this. Donald Davie, for example, remembered 'nothing so distastefully as the maidenly shudders with which I wished to know nothing of the machinery of publicity even as I liked publicity and profited from it'.[1] For his part, Thom Gunn evinced no maidenly shudders in denying (in an autobiographical essay of 1978) that the whole business had anything to do with *him*:

It was around the time of the original publication of [my first] book, 1954 or perhaps a little earlier, that I first heard of something called the Movement. To my surprise, I also learned that I was a member of it.... What poets like Larkin, Davie, Elizabeth Jennings, and I had in common at that time was that we were deliberately eschewing Modernism, and turning back, though not very thoroughgoingly, to traditional resources in structure and method. But this was what most of the other poets of

[1] Donald Davie, cited by Ian Hamilton, in 'The Making of the Movement', in *A Poetry Chronicle: Essays and Reviews* (London: Faber and Faber, 1973), p. 130.

our age (even many Americans) were doing in the early fifties...The whole business looks now like a lot of categorizing foolishness.[2]

It may well have been in 1954 that Gunn first heard of the Movement, since that was when most people first heard of it: in a leading article in the *Spectator*, where Gunn's first book, *Fighting Terms*, had been reviewed the week before. Both review and article hailed a new generation of novelists and poets, apparently united by a common approach and an eagerness to break with their literary predecessors. For that tiny part of the reading public who read new poetry, however, the Movement was defined by two anthologies: *Poets of the 1950s*, edited by D. J. Enright (1955) and *New Lines*, edited by Robert Conquest and published in 1956. *New Lines* included eight poems by Thom Gunn: about the same number as by each of the other eight contributors to the volume. So, to the extent that the Movement was *New Lines*, Gunn was in it and of it. Notwithstanding, in a later interview he made his point again, more forcefully: 'my contention is that the Movement didn't really exist: what we had in common was a period style.'[3]

By the time of these remarks, the Movement virtues as promoted by the *Spectator* ('sceptical...robust...ironic') and by Robert Conquest in his introduction to *New Lines* ('submits to no great systems of theoretical constructs nor agglomerations of unconscious commands...free from both mystical and logical compulsions...empirical in its attitude to all that comes...a refusal to abandon a rational structure and comprehensible language...a negative determination to avoid bad principles')[4] were beginning to look a bit threadbare. But Gunn might have felt more justified than some in distancing himself from the pack, both at the time and subsequently. He had been the youngest of the *New Lines* poets and, by the late 1970s, had travelled the farthest: both from the Englishness that was the Movement's spiritual home and from its 'period style'. Born in Kent, educated in London and Cambridge (England), Gunn was always quick to acknowledge how much his adopted home town of San Francisco and, more broadly, California had to offer an adventurous, open-minded, educated gay man in the late 1960s

[2] Thom Gunn, 'My Life Up to Now', in *The Occasions of Poetry: Essays in Criticism and Biography*, ed. Clive Wilmer (London: Faber and Faber, 1982), p. 174.

[3] Thom Gunn, 'An Anglo-American Poet: Interview with Jim Powell', in *Shelf Life: Essays, Memoirs and an Interview* (London: Faber and Faber, 1994), p. 219.

[4] Robert Conquest, Introduction to *New Lines: An Anthology* (London: Macmillan, 1956), p. xv.

and 1970s—especially one eager to throw over English caution and inhibition and embrace hedonistic sensuality, mind-expanding drugs and 'countercultural' freedoms. As a homosexual man working in American universities from the early 1950s on, though, he had perhaps been exposed to greater personal and professional risk than those of his fellow-poets who spent their working lives in universities or libraries or publishing houses in London or Oxford—or even Hull.

This willingness to experiment in ways of living had its counterpart in Gunn's poetic development. His first two books announced a poet of rugged iambic pentameter, full rhyme and elaborate extended metaphor. His move to America saw him starting to experiment, not altogether happily, with syllabics and half-rhymes. Then, more or less simultaneously with his first LSD trips, he began to write poems based on tentative free-verse rhythms, observation of everyday San Francisco street life and loose-limbed epiphanies in Golden Gate Park or leather bars in the Castro. Not that he rejected his birthright or his beginnings, personal or artistic. His life, he once wrote, insisted on continuities, between England and America, teaching and writing, metrical and free verse. Insofar as many of his strongest later poems were metrically regular and stanzaic, this is true; but the reality was more complex, and the poetry it gave rise to more uneven, than that calm retrospect implies. Both the shapes and textures of Gunn's poems were to undergo a drastic overhaul, to make room for possibilities learned from Americans such as William Carlos Williams, Gary Snyder, Robert Creeley, and Robert Duncan.

Gunn's delight in these poets was real enough, and not merely structural or aesthetic. What they taught him about opening up in form and feeling issued in a relaxation of manner and a cheerful new emphasis on inclusion, integration and wholeness. But, gratifyingly attainable as these may have been to the mature, Californian, 'Anglo-American' Gunn, they are far from what we hear in the work of the young man whose earliest poems are, as James Campbell puts it, full of 'violent tension and contradiction'. For example:

> Suspended taut between two equal fears
> I was like to be torn apart by their strong pull
>
> ('The Secret Sharer')

Or:

> Lie back. Within a minute I will stow
> Your greedy mouth, but will not yet to grips.

> 'There is a space between the breast and lips.'
> Also a space between the thighs and head,
> So great, we might as well not be in bed
>
>   ('Carnal Knowledge')

Or even:

> Whether he poses or is real, no cat
> Bothers to say: the pose held is a stance,
> Which, generation of the very chance
> It wars on, may be posture for combat.

In his comments on this, the final stanza of 'Elvis Presley', Campbell catches the faltering and uncertain touch of Gunn's earliest attempts to deal with America in his poetry (and perhaps his earliest dealings with America as well). 'Something', Campbell writes, 'of the shock that must have been caused by Elvis's first appearances is present here, but not the background against which he posed and wielded his guitar. The context of the poem is not recognizably American; it is composed of the violent tension and contradiction typical of the Gunn of the period. The use of 'cat' as an item of hip talk jars. It is a poem by an English poet living in and observing America, but not yet at home there.'[5]

But nor was Gunn entirely at home in 1950s England—even, as a poet, in its 'period style'. That style, we recall, depended on 'eschewing Modernism and turning back...to traditional resources, in structure and method'. For all the New Lines poets, Gunn included, that meant eschewing the Modernist techniques of Eliot and (perhaps) Pound; in or around 1950 these were the only Modernist poets whose work was widely or readily available in England. (Gunn himself has described how he first encountered Williams, and even Wallace Stevens and Marianne Moore, only once he had moved to America. By 1978, he had come to regard Pound, the arch-Modernist, as a great poet and a great exemplar. Pound's Cantos was the work which—so he wrote in response to a TLS questionnaire in 1984—had exercised an enduring influence on his own sense of poetic form, as 'the work no longer necessarily enclosed: they start with "And" and never end'.[6] He had come to see Pound's

---

[5] James Campbell, 'Thom Gunn, Anglo-American Poet', in Agenda 37:2–3 (Autumn–Winter 1999), p. 71; the title of the issue as a whole is 'Thom Gunn at Seventy'.

[6] Thom Gunn, Times Literary Supplement, 27 April 1984, p. 462.

disciple Basil Bunting as a great poet as well, and to deprecate the way Bunting's reputation had, he felt, been overshadowed by the baleful influence of Philip Larkin: 'sour' and 'suburban' Larkin, a poet, Gunn wrote, 'of minute ambitions who carried them out exquisitely',[7] which some might think faint praise.) 'Traditional resources in structure and method' meant, for Gunn as for Larkin, Davie, Jennings *et al.*, rhymed, metrical stanzas and conventional prose syntax.

For most of the others, it also meant the diction and tone of polite educated speech. Here and there, in a poem by Larkin or Kingsley Amis, we hear the idiom of 'the ordinary bloke' (as discussed elsewhere in this book by Colin McGinn), a language that was new to poetry, at least, and a subject matter that was newly and perhaps shockingly ordinary as well. (This is what a poem in thrall to the Movement such as Anthony Twaite's 'Mr Cooper' principally has in common with Larkin's 'Mr Bleaney': a shared conviction that pub toilets and cheap bedsits are material out of which poems can be made, and the idiom proper to them an appropriate language for poetry.) But the dominant note is that of the Oxbridge bloke, marinaded in the English poetic tradition, literary criticism, and even philosophy. And there was sufficient sameness in the stance of the *New Lines* poets—restrained, rational, deflationary, and self-deprecating—for A. Alvarez, in the introduction to his own anthology, *The New Poetry* (1962), to have taken a line or two from each of them and constructed a just-about-believable 'representative Movement poem'. This was, of course, unfair. Alvarez's levelling or flattening-out was achieved only at the cost of nuance and implication in even the flattest or most level-seeming line of, say, Philip Larkin's. But in most of these respects Gunn's contributions seem not to belong in the company they are made to keep.

His poems of this period are extremely 'literary'—but in the sense that they attempt an impassioned identification with earlier writers (Shakespeare to Byron to Stendhal), rather than versified literary history or literary politics *à la* Davie or John Wain. They draw shamelessly on folklore and what Larkin called the 'myth-kitty'; and their language is far removed from the ironic poise of a D. J. Enright or the reasonable, pubbable register—not so much a man speaking to men as a chap speaking to chaps—of early Larkin or Amis. Gunn's models were Donne rather than Empson, Yeats rather than

---

[7] Gunn, *Shelf Life*, p. 225.

Graves, and Auden perhaps more than anyone. ('Who could escape that large
and rational talent?' asked Robert Conquest,[8] though it was the violently
irrational Auden of *The Orators* and the homosexual subtext who left his mark
on Gunn.) Most of these features are audible in 'Tamer and Hawk':

I thought I was so tough,
But gentled at your hands
Cannot be quick enough
To fly for you and show
That when I go I go
At your commands.

Even in flight above
I am no longer free;
You seeled me with your love,
I am blind to other birds—
The habit of your words
Has hooded me.

As formerly, I wheel
I hover and I twist
But only want the feel
In my possessive thought
Of catcher and of caught
Upon your wrist.

You but half-civilize,
Taming me in this way.
Through having only eyes
For you I fear to lose,
I lose to keep, and choose
Tamer as prey.

'Tamer and Hawk' appeared in *Fighting Terms* (1954). In that year Gunn also
took up a creative writing fellowship at Stanford University, where he stud-
ied under Yvor Winters. The poem was written, however, while Gunn was
still an undergraduate at Cambridge, and it bears out his contention that his
chief teachers at this time were Shakespeare and Donne, and his chief passion,
Yeats. There is something Yeatsian in the aristocratic metaphor—falconry
has never exactly been a pastime of the ordinary folk. Gunn alludes in pass-

[8] Conquest, Introduction to *New Lines*, p. xviii.

ing to Yeats's own poem 'The Hawk': 'I will not be clapped in a hood | Nor
a cage, nor alight upon wrist | Nor have I learned to be proud | Hovering
over the wood | In a broken mist | Or tumbling cloud'. Shakespeare shows
in the precision of 'seeled', a technical term in falconry, meaning to close the
eyes of the bird by stitching up the eyelids as part of the taming process, and
in its play on the more commonplace 'sealed', as in stamped, stuck together
or imprisoned. But it is Donne who sponsors the conceit, and the poem's
relish for the paradoxes of falling in love: the willing submission to another,
the loss of freedom that is experienced as freedom, the relinquishing of self-
possession in the greater cause of possessing and being possessed.

Catcher and caught, tamer and prey, terms that are, for this once, both
opposites and coterminous; not 'fighting terms' but terms of agreement and
complementarity, each fulfilling the other. And all because of the first sur-
render, which happens in the very first line, the surrender of an anterior sense
of self—a self now rendered wonderingly surplus to requirements by this
new, more commanding reality: 'I thought I was so tough'. Here, uniquely,
toughness is abashed and yields to tenderness. Elsewhere in this first volume of
Gunn's, toughness is the keynote. Though its master-theme is love, its master-
narrative is love as a battleground or a military action, a series of skirmishes
between combatants armoured in self-possession but exquisitely vulnerable to
self-doubt, uncertainty and confusion. Engagement can end in betrayal, ban-
ishment or even death. All this emotional violence is expressed in a confident,
sinewy language, the kind of thing Donne meant when he referred to his own
words' 'masculine persuasive force'. 'Suddenly', said Gunn, speaking of the
period between 1951 and 1953 when many of these poems were written,

everything started to feed my imagination. Writing poetry became the act of an exist-
entialist conqueror, excited and aggressive.... What virtues the collection possesses,
however, are mostly to be found in an awareness of how far I fell short of being such
a conqueror. Proust and Stendhal as well as Shakespeare and Donne had taught me
to watch for the inconsistencies of the psyche. The image of the soldier recurs in the
book, as it does I suppose throughout my work. First of all he is myself, the national
serviceman, the 'clumsy brute in uniform', the soldier who never goes to war, whose
role has no function; whose battledress is a joke. Secondly, though, he is a 'real' sol-
dier, both ideal and ambiguous, attractive and repellent; he is a warrior and a killer,
or a career man in peacetime.[9]

---

[9] Gunn, 'My Life Up to Now', *The Occasions of Poetry*, p. 173.

Gunn, born in 1929, was 10 at the outbreak of the Second World War. He had plenty of opportunity to see real soldiers in the streets of London, or moving about the countryside to which he was temporarily evacuated. At the age of 19 he became a soldier himself, a 'joke' one, doing National Service, which had been introduced for all eligible males of 18 or over in 1947. This was also a time, he has said, of denial about the fact that he was attracted to men, of acting 'straight', of determined experiments with girls. In an uncollected poem, 'The Soldier', dating from the late 1940s or early 1950s, we only just glimpse the eponymous hero before he disappears in a hail of metaphors (for penetration and being penetrated), rhymes or half-rhymes 'groping and stumbling' towards the final couplet's Metaphysical grimace:

> You'll make fine eating then,
> Flesh gone, and the worm in.

But the most famous or most often anthologized of his early poems to employ Gunn's master-narrative is 'The Wound', in which the speaker is both Achilles and the self who dreams he was Achilles: both an internalized soldier, then, and a divided self—divided by the wound that opens wide at the thought of another man's, 'my friend Patroclus" death. This is not Homer's Achilles but Shakespeare's in *Troilus and Cressida*, petulant and at least plausibly homosexual, unmanned by inaction. In a much later poem, 'The Corporal', Gunn is able unambiguously to recall his ambivalent feelings for the 'real soldier', the warrior-killer, 'attractive and repellent':

> Half of my life I watched the soldiers
> And saw mechanic clerk and cook
> Subsumed beneath a uniform.
> Grey black and khaki was their look
> Whose tool and instrument was death.
>
> .   .   .   .   .
>
> I saw them radiate from the barracks
> Into the town that it was in.
> Girl-hungry loutish Casanovas,
> Their wool and webbing grated skin
> For small forgettings as in death...

The natural soldier without a role, meanwhile, the 'career man in peacetime' who is also one such 'girl-hungry loutish Casanova', is the

speaker in the best of Gunn's early poems, 'Lofty in the Palais de Danse'.
(Most English towns in the 1950s still had a *palais de danse*, a dance-hall
popular as a courting-place for the young and, typically, lower-paid;
not as glamorous as a nightclub. This one is in the Midlands or the
north of England—the girls are factory or mill-girls. Lofty is a common
English nickname for an unusually tall man—or, used ironically, for a
very short one.)

> You are not random picked. I tell you you
> Are much like one I knew before, that died.
> Shall we sit down, and drink and munch a while—
> I want to see if you will really do;
> If not we'll get it over now outside.
> Wary I wait for one unusual smile.
>
> I never felt this restiveness with her:
> I lay calm wanting nothing but what I had.
> And now I stand each night outside the Mills
> For girls, then shift them to the cinema
> Or dance hall ... Like the world, I've gone to bad.
> A deadly world: for, once I like, it kills.
>
> The same with everything: the only posting
> I ever liked, was short. And so in me
> I kill the easy things that others like
> To teach them that no liking can be lasting:
> All that you praise I take, what modesty
> What gentleness, you ruin while you speak.
>
> And partly that I wouldn't if I could
> Be bed-content with likenesses so dumb.
> Passed in the street, they seem identical
> To her original, yet understood
> Exhaustively as soon as slept with, some
> Lack this, some that, and none like her at all.
>
> You praise my strength. The muscle on my arm.
> Yes. Now the other. Yes, about the same.
> I've got another muscle you can feel.
> Dare say you knew. Only expected harm
> Falls from a khaki man. That's why you came
> With me and when I go you follow still.

> Now that we sway here in the shadowed street
> Why can't I keep my mind clenched on the job?
> Your body is a good one, not without
> Earlier performance, but in this repeat
> The pictures are unwilled that I see bob
> Out of the dark, and you can't turn them out.

Lofty has been un-gentled by his loss. Nothing so strange, you might think, about his need to find a girl, to replace 'one I knew before, that died'. But 'that' instead of the expected 'who' signals something not quite right in his mental state. We sense, as does Lofty himself, that his search is doomed to failure; it has become its own compulsion. His muscles may be in good shape but he is emotionally adrift, perhaps even—or so the lack of affect in his speech sug-gests—in deep trouble; it may even be that the lack of affect *is* the trouble.

The poem is in the first person, but is not a personal utterance; it is a brilliant impersonation. By the time Gunn wrote it he had himself fallen in love with Mike Kitay, a slightly younger American man also studying at Cambridge, with whom he was to share the rest of his life (this liking, at least, was lasting). But in any case it would be a mistake to read Gunn's 'tough' early poetry, dominated as it seems to be by a psycho-sexual wound, agonistically, as the tortured compensation of a self divided against itself and its own desires. Karl Miller, a good friend of Gunn's at Cambridge, remem-bers him there as enjoying the company of other young poets and actors, at the centre of an intellectual–theatrical milieu that valued high spirits, play-fulness and play-acting. 'The time was the Fifties', Miller writes:

The war had not been forgotten. Homosexual relations were part of university life, as in the past, but were still, for some, anxious and clandestine. Gay had yet to dawn; the word had yet to be relieved of its old sense of a pleasure-loving demi-monde and had yet to sup-plant the word 'queer'... The period preoccupations in question which could be encoun-tered in other places besides Cambridge, may be summarised as an interest in manliness, which meant, in Thom's case, an interest in 'brute purpose', in toughness as opposed to sensibility, self-pity and the soul, in the panache of the biker, or of Brando....

This taste for histrionic masculinity formed part of a Cambridge where the newly Lawrentian teachings of Leavis were found supportive...and where an excellent the-atrical scene...was by no means averse to shows of sensitivity and effeminacy, or indeed to shows of denial and disclaimer on the subject. The game that was played reflected the ambivalence to be noticed within the individual sex life—tough went

with tender, active with passive...The game was played by homosexual and hetero-
sexual people alike. The tough person might belong to either persuasion, or to both,
and might prove on acquaintance to be as tender as the next man.'[10]

The Nietzschean side of D. H. Lawrence could, of course, make fairly sin-
ister common cause with a propensity to 'histrionic masculinity' and an
interest in military uniforms. It certainly seems to in 'Lines for a Book', from
Gunn's second volume, *The Sense of Movement* (1957):

> I think of all the toughs through history
> And thank heaven they lived, continually.
> I praise the overdogs from Alexander
> To those who would not play with Stephen Spender.
> Their pride exalted some, some overthrew,
> But was not vanity at last; they knew
> That though the mind has also got a place
> It's not in marvelling at its mirrored face
> And evident sensibility. It's better
> To go and see your friend than write a letter;
> To be a soldier than to be a cripple;
> To take an early weaning from the nipple
> Than think your mother is the only girl;
> To be insensitive, to steel the will,
> Than sit irresolute all day at stool
> Inside the heart...

And so on. (The reference is to Stephen Spender's poem 'My Parents': 'My
parents kept me from children who were rough | Who threw words like
stones and wore torn clothes'.) Gunn has joked about the 'Yeatsian–Sartrean
fascist' who wrote *The Sense of Movement*, and we hear something like an only
part-joking will-to-power here. But he is unequivocal about his actual left-
wing sympathies, at this time and subsequently. Both of his parents were
socialists, he recalled. The general election of 1945 saw Winston Churchill
dismissed from office as Prime Minister and the Labour leader Clement
Attlee elected in his place by a huge majority. 'When I was at school, at
the time of the 1945 landslide most of us were Labour...When I went to

---

[10] Karl Miller, from an unpublished talk delivered at a University of London Graduate School
of English conference to mark Gunn's seventieth birthday (1999).

Cambridge, in 1950, we were still all socialists then.'[11] It seems that Gunn never even so much as flirted with the attitude of queasy pro-Germanism that Philip Larkin expressed in a letter to his friend J. B. Sutton at the outbreak of the war. 'If there is any new life in the world today', Larkin wrote, 'it is in Germany. True, it is a vicious and blood-brutal kind of affair—the new shoots are rather like bayonets...Germany has revolted back too far, into other extremes. But I think they have valuable new habits. Otherwise how could D.H.L. be called Fascist.'[12]

Larkin was found medically unfit by the military in 1940, and by 1947 was no longer eligible for National Service. But Gunn was too young to be, in James Fenton's phrase about Larkin, 'wounded by unshrapnel'—to feel any shame or regret at not having fought, or some unsatisfied hankering for action. His interest in powerful masculinity, in the brute purpose of the Trojan warrior or the English squaddie was rather, according to Karl Miller, 'pursued for its subversiveness at a time when anti-fascism could be regarded by some as a feature of the post-war conventional wisdom, of the complacencies of the peace. What they were up to was in part a youthful game, which was intended by some as a small shock to the system, as it had yet to be called'.[13]

In other words, he only does it to annoy, because he knows it teases. We can concede the plausibility of this without thinking that it tells the whole story. The poems of *Fighting Terms* are, of course, being poems, all words and no action—though they sometimes strain energetically towards it. But this is 'action' not in the military sense—desire is not so much for an actual fight as for the unarmed combat of sex, and perhaps the authenticity to be found there. It is still strong in The *Sense of Movement*, but in these poems it is filtered through the Existentialism fashionable at the time, and the teachings of Leavis and Winters. As Gunn says:

[11] *Thom Gunn in Conversation with James Campbell* (London: Between the Lines, 1988), p. 20.

[12] Anthony Thwaite (ed.), *Selected Letters of Philip Larkin, 1940–1985* (London: Faber and Faber, 1992), p. 36; quoted by James Fenton in 'Philip Larkin: Wounded by Unshrapnel', in *The Strength of Poetry* (Oxford and New York: Oxford University Press, 2001). Larkin's father, the City Treasurer of Coventry, admitted no such reservations in his enthusiasm for the organizational efficiencies of the Third Reich, and kept a picture of Hitler on his office wall. By 'D.H.L.' Larkin is referring familiarly to Lawrence.

[13] Miller (see above, n. 10).

I was very influenced by [F. R. Leavis]... He was not, probably, a very likeable person, but he had a very interesting view of literature, seeing it as a part of life...Literature is not like a fine wine that you taste and judge by comparison with other wines. You compare a book to a person, for example, or to an action. That was what later attracted me about another slightly different critic, Yvor Winters. He too considered a poem as an action. And it is, of course.[14]

Of course, it is and it isn't. It is a writing-action or (by extension) a speech-act. It can also be a pretend action, the putting on or acting out of a pretend self: a pose. It can, as so many of Gunn's early poems do, interrogate a pose, expose it for what it is. At Cambridge, Gunn continued,

I was trying to develop certain thoughts. They amounted to a rather crude theory of what I called 'pose'...The theory of pose was this: everyone plays a part, whether he knows it or not, so he might as well deliberately design a part, or a series of parts, for himself. Only a psychopath or a very good actor is in danger of becoming his part, however, so one who is neither is left in an interesting place somewhere in between the starting point—the bare undefined and undirected self, if he ever existed— and the chosen part. This is a place rich in tensions between the achieved and the unachieved.[15]

Or, you could say, between the acted and the unacted, or un-acted-on. In *The Sense of Movement* Gunn's earlier chosen parts, those of would-be lover or soldier with his show of masculinity, are replaced by an 'I' who insists on being what he chooses: who attempts to define himself through action and the will. Or, through his own 'part' in another sense. Gunn insists that he was, when writing these willed and will-heavy poems, unaware of the Shakespearean sense of the word *will*: the penis; that instead he intended a Romantic, Existentialist, Yeatsian wilfulness, self-creating, self-delighting, and self-affrighting. But it was, he conceded, 'very much a male kind of will, a penis-like will'.[16] Hence his motorbike boys in 'On the Move', 'the self-defined, astride the created will'; hence the unsettled motorcyclist's aplomb. 'My human will cannot submit | To nature, though brought out of it'; hence 'to be insensitive, to steel the will' in 'Lines for a Book'; and 'the deliberate human will' Gunn celebrates in his poem to Yvor Winters. (Gunn's Christian name as recorded on his birth certificate was William; he later changed this

---

[14] *Thom Gunn in Conversation with James Campbell*, p. 22.

[15] Gunn, 'Cambridge in the Fifties,' in *The Occasions of Poetry*, pp.161–2.

[16] *Thom Gunn in Conversation with James Campbell*, p. 30.

by deed-poll—an act of will, and of Will—to Thomson William, later shortened to simply Thom. Thomson was his mother's maiden name.)

A part or a pose, an impersonation, a posture or imposture: all are ways of avoiding the direct expression of feeling. The will, in these poems, is expected to master the emotions: that is the point of it. In 'The Wound' it is not thought itself but '*rage* [at his noble pain]' that causes the wound to break open. All of Gunn's work of his Movement or *New Lines* years turns away from feeling as if from something not to be trusted, from the 'bare undefined and undirected self' where emotion might be thought to reside. Form, rather than a discipline for emotion, becomes a way of refusing entry to it; rigid stanzaic and metrical patterns become, like the soldier's uniform, self-protection, shield and disguise, or, like the biker's leather jacket, 'donned impersonality'. The relation is made explicit in a late poem, 'Clean Clothes: A Soldier's Song'. After a day spent 'drenching' a heavy uniform with sweat, the soldier looks forward to 'A change into | Dry clean clothes that renew | The anonymity which holds me in one piece':

> So after bath or shower
> For fully the first hour
> They touch my skin
> Like cool hands in a park at night
> Impersonal and light
> Withholding me from self, and regiment, and kin.

Predictably, perhaps, the American poetry that later made such an impact on Gunn was a poetry of the outward gaze, a poetry of perception and engagement with the external world. Under its influence his own 'American' poems, even as they bear witness to a romantic immersion in experience, in the life of the senses, stand back from that experience the better—or so is Gunn's instinct—to describe it. Much of this work bears witness also to a deep change in his conception of the poem, from the poem as action to the poem as process: a process as much of moral discrimination (which belief Gunn owed to Williams and Winters) as of existential or aesthetic discovery. This, clearly, is one development out of Modernism just as the apparently rawer self-laceration of a John Berryman or a Robert Lowell (or for that matter a Philip Larkin: see his poem 'Love Again') is another. There is yet another, which at first glance looks like the exception that proves Gunn's rule. Robert Duncan, he wrote, 'noticed the continuity between Modernist and Romantic long before most of the critics did: the specific life of his home-circle came from his connecting the Romantic admiration for impulse with the theory of "open form" that he, following Charles Olson, found suggested by the practice of Pound and the later W. C. Williams'.[17]

With Romantic 'impulse', spontaneity, and the open form of Pound, Olson and Duncan we are a long way from Eliot's 'no *vers* is truly *libre* for the man who wants to do a good job', and from his definition of poetry (which surely appealed to Gunn) as 'not a turning loose of emotion but an escape from emotion', not an expression of personality but an escape from it.[18] Yet in them Gunn seems to have found and approved something beyond or prior to personality. Speaking, again, of Duncan he extols the 'primordial, titanic, unaccountable spirit in poetry, beyond measure',[19] and this, too, seems both to precede and to negate personality and personal emotion.

From this perspective, eschewing Modernism, for the young Gunn, was much more a matter of preferring pre-Modernist models for verse than of antipathy to Eliot's insistence on the 'impersonality' of art—which in fact suited him very well. It was in opposition to a debased version of the primordial, unaccountable spirit in poetry, beyond measure, that Eliot began his great adventure of verbal precision and ironic deflation 'in or about' 1910.[20] And it was in opposition to an even more debased version of it, made popular by the poets of the New Apocalypse, that the poets of the Movement, Gunn included, saw themselves 'turning back to traditional resources in structure and method'—Modernism itself being by then a thing of the distant past. In thus turning back, Gunn was also turning his back: not just on the already remote Eliot and Pound, but on the vatic pretensions and torrid emotionalism in such plentiful supply throughout the Neo-Romantic 1940s. And saying goodbye to all *that* was for him much more than conformism to an emergent consensus, commitment to a 'period style', or peer-group pressure; it was a personal necessity.

He was to turn his back on the so-called 'confessional', too, and had no time for Berryman, Lowell, or Plath. Exploring the ballad-like qualities in

---

[17] Gunn, *Shelf Life*, p. 131.

[18] T. S. Eliot, 'Tradition and the Individual Talent', *The Sacred Wood* (London: Methuen, 1920).

[19] Gunn, *Shelf Life*, p. 132.

[20] 'In or about December 1910, human nature changed,' Virginia Woolf, 'Mrs Bennett and Mr Brown' (1924), in Peter Faulkner (ed.), *A Modernist Reader: Modernism in England 1910–1930* (London: Batsford, 1980), p. 113.

the poems of Thomas Hardy, even as Gunn acknowledges Hardy's 'mastering obsession' as loss and 'regret for the past', he writes: '[Hardy] particularly records his own losses as only important because they are a part of other people's losses. It is never the poetry of personality: nothing could be further from him than the Confessional poetry that was all the rage in the US and England a few years back.' Hardy's first person speaks as a 'sample human being, with little personality displayed and with no claims for uniqueness—with as little distinguishing him beyond his subject matter, in fact, as distinguishes the personages of the Ballads beyond their actions'. And his poems—even the 'Poems of 1912–13'—belong to a 'reflective mode' that is 'essentially impersonal, essentially non-confessional. It is concerned with its subject to the extent of excluding the speaker's personality, even when his emotion is the subject (as it often is)—for he sees his emotion as one which anybody in his situation would be able to feel'.[21]

This seems to me misleading both about Hardy and confessional verse. But it is richly suggestive to read in connection with Gunn's moving late elegies for friends who have died of AIDS, poems which, while they show all the discipline of the early verse, and for all their calm and unflinching truthfulness about the effects of the disease, carry a charge of personal emotion that is unprecedented in his work: though it is certainly also emotion 'which anybody in his situation would be able to feel'. It becomes even clearer why, for him, it was so essential that Hardy should be an 'impersonal' poet when we read what is perhaps the finest of Gunn's later poems, and one of his most personal, also an elegy—this time for Ann Charlotte Thomson, the adored mother who committed suicide when Gunn was 15 and whose name he later adopted. ('She was everything to him... He was her, almost', as Gunn's brother, Ander, put it years afterwards.) For what happens when one's situation or emotion is such that, far from 'anybody' being able to feel it, it seems unique to oneself, and literally unspeakable?

As the shrewd reviewer in Delta's ' "New Movement" Supplement' of 1956 put it, 'The main interest of all [Gunn's] work is loss of life, not in a personal, but in a social sense, or rather in the former only through the latter... The theme that something has interfered to disrupt the right working of life appears in a variety of traditional images but also occurs as a bad world

[21] Gunn, 'Thomas Hardy and the Ballad Tradition', in The Occasions of Poetry, pp. 93–102.

which interposes, vitiatingly, into even the most private experience…'.[22] Something had interfered, all right: but this something was a trauma so private and painful that it had to be kept at bay by a generalizing or abstracting or archaizing style, a poetry of un-feeling or toughened detachment whose every resource in structure and method interposes to keep the 'bad world' at an unrevealing distance. Gunn and his brother had discovered their mother's body, as the latter recalled: 'We pushed the door open with great difficulty because it had a bureau and several other things lying against it… And there she was lying on the floor with a gas poker rigid over her face and a rug over her mouth. And the place was full of gas… Rigor mortis had set in, and we turned the gas off and opened all the windows. It was terrible, really.'

It was to be forty years before Gunn stopped dreaming of his mother ('I am made by her, and undone', he wrote in another late poem), and fifty before he could write this particular primal scene—write it out of himself, in the truest sense. When he did it was not to free verse or 'open form' models he turned but to Thomas Hardy, the great master of highly disciplined, deeply personal emotion. 'The Gas Poker' is un-Hardyesque in only one respect; as Gunn told James Campbell in 1999: 'Finally I found the way [to write about it] was really obvious: to withdraw the first person. Then it came easy, because it was no longer about myself.'[23]

> The children went to and fro
> On the harsh winter lawn
> Repeating their lament,
> A burden, to each other
> In the December dawn,
> Elder and younger brother,
> Till they knew what it meant.

[22] Peter Thirlby, 'Thom Gunn: Violence and Toughness', *Delta*, No 8 (Spring 1956), p. 17.
[23] *Thom Gunn in Conversation with James Campbell*, p. 19.

11

In and Out of the Movement: Donald Davie and Thom Gunn

Clive Wilmer

When I interviewed Donald Davie for the BBC programme *Poet of the Month* in 1990, I contrasted the neat, witty, neo-Augustan quatrains of his first book, *Brides of Reason* (1952), with the fractured, open-form psalms of what was then his latest, *To Scorch or Freeze* (1988). Could he, I asked him, account for the difference?

Well [he replied], I'm a restless person, rightly or wrongly; I don't like doing again what I've done once. Of course, over and above that, there's the pressure of experience. I mean, outside of poetry and writing, you have experiences which turn you into a significantly different person, and plainly the styles that you work out when you're a young man ... well, they *shouldn't* still be serving you when you're middle-aged. It would seem to me that, if they were, it would mean that you'd been at a standstill in your psychological development. Indeed ... I would say that those of my contemporaries who rather notably have *not* changed from first to last are the ones who need to explain themselves.[1]

Prominent among these contemporaries, it emerged in conversation afterwards, was Philip Larkin, and though it could be argued that there are

---

[1] Clive Wilmer, *Poets Talking: 'Poet of the Month' Interviews from BBC Radio 3* (Manchester: Carcanet, 1994), pp. 50–1.

important differences between *The Less Deceived* (1955) and *High Windows* (1974), not to speak of the dramatic change of direction following *The North Ship* (1945), it is undoubtedly the case that Larkin created his distinctive mode— the tone, the qualities of versification, the range of subject-matter—in the early 1950s and kept to that mode for the rest of his life. Indeed, one wonders if it might not have been his dependence on it that blocked his creative powers in his last decade. Larkin's particular manner and the steadiness of his attachment to it were to become hallmarks of what we think of as 'Movement poetry', so Davie's dissatisfaction with it and the restlessness of his own approach might be thought indicative of *his* artistic character—and therefore of his development away from an early identification with the Movement. Davie was at the outset an enthusiastic admirer of Larkin's work. Reviewing *The Less Deceived* in 1956, he found it 'about the most important novelty in the British poetic scene since the end of the war', praising it for its 'unassuming commonsense' by contrast with the 'turbulent expressiveness' of the Neo-Romantics.[2] In most respects he remained a staunch admirer, but he could never be happy with what he took to be (as I understand it) a sort of complacency in a poet of whom he was otherwise not a little envious. The provincialism, xenophobia, and philistinism of the role Larkin so consistently played, as well as his dependence on irony: these exasperated Davie, not least perhaps because he struggled to resist the same reflexes and prejudices in his own background and make-up. With the publication of Larkin's *Oxford Book of Twentieth Century English Verse* in 1973, Davie's impatience with his erstwhile friend exploded in a review.[3] By 1993, when Larkin's *Selected Letters* appeared, he had come to the depressing conclusion that Larkin had chosen 'not to be a man, but to remain ... a discontented adolescent'. He found the letters 'hateful and disgraceful', though he clung 'to the conviction that there was more to [Larkin] than this volume even allows us to guess at'.[4]

Behind Davie's quarrel with Larkin is a still more complicated quarrel with himself—with the poet who had so happily identified with the Movement. Of the nine contributors to the first of Robert Conquest's *New Lines* anthologies (1956), Davie was probably the most sure that it existed as something more than a journalistic PR operation, though he did accept that part of its value

---

[2] [Untitled review], *Irish Writing*, 34 (Spring 1956), p. 62.
[3] 'Larkin's Choice', *The Listener*, 29 March 1973, pp. 420–1.
[4] 'Letters from Hull', *PN Review* 89, 19.3 (January–February 1993), pp. 4–5.

lay in promoting the careers of its members. This, he argued, was nothing to be ashamed of, provided the members believed in what they were doing.[5] But there is a certain irony in the fact that the contributor he was closest to by the end of his life, Thom Gunn, consistently denied that the Movement had ever existed. Of all the *New Lines* contributors, moreover, Gunn must have seemed at the outset the most distant from Davie: Gunn the Romantic individualist, the rebel against respectable society, and, later on, the drug-taking gay liberationist. Davie, by contrast, was for social cohesion, self-restraint, and responsibility; he believed in the old Tory values of family, nation, and, after a longish period of agnosticism, church. What Gunn saw as the reactionary pronouncements of Davie's later years were capable of infuriating him, committed as he was to a more experimental view of society. Davie's attempt to justify his distaste for a poetry that expresses homosexual feeling openly was especially problematic, yet the respect Gunn felt for Davie was such that he could declare 'that something that was in my mind the whole time I was writing [the elegies for AIDS victims in *The Man with Night Sweats*] was: how can I prove him wrong?!'[6] Part of the secret of the two men's friendship, I would judge, is that, unlike Larkin, Gunn did change with the years, learning from some of the things that Davie learnt—outstandingly, from American poetry and an American kind of openness to the outside world—and sometimes even prompted to them by Davie. He once described Davie as a literary explorer, who goes abroad 'to bring news back to the English … tidings of his discoveries'.[7] The conceit is a striking one for many reasons. In its generosity and acknowledgement of debt, it is characteristic of Gunn, though the idea of the poet as adventurer is more obviously applicable to himself.[8] Nevertheless, it is plainly the bringing *back* that is important.

---

[5] See Blake Morrison, *The Movement: English Poetry and Fiction of the 1950s* (Oxford: Oxford University Press, 1980), p. 4. (Hereafter 'Morrison'.)

[6] Gunn [interviewed by Clive Wilmer], 'The Art of Poetry LXXII', *Paris Review* 135 (Summer 1995), p. 180. Davie had complained that the overt homosexuality of Gunn's later work entailed 'the sacrifice … of any profound resonances from periods earlier than the eighteenth century': *Under Briggflatts: A History of Poetry in Great Britain, 1960–88* (Manchester: Carcanet, 1989), p. 180.

[7] 'Nightingales Sang for me Once', presented by Michael Schmidt, BBC Radio 3, 1984.

[8] Davie makes this point himself in the poem 'To Thom Gunn in Los Altos, California', calling Gunn a 'Conquistador' and wondering, as they stand at the edge of the world, 'What am I doing [here], I who am scared of edges?' *Collected Poems*, ed. Neil Powell (Manchester: Carcanet, 2002), 346–7. (Future references to this book will be in the form 'DCP 346–7' and cited in the text.)

Both men lived for at least part of their lives in the United States, but where for Gunn expatriation was not an issue—he wanted to stay in California but saw no need to change his nationality—for Davie it was an expression of his relationship with England. His intermittent fury with his homeland was the anger that comes of love. So when Davie translated from Russian and Polish, advocated the literatures of those languages, praised *avant-garde* American poets as temperamentally different from himself as it was possible to be, and insisted on the necessity for the poet to know and love the non-literary arts, he was preaching to the likes of Larkin and Kingsley Amis, who seemed to him to have wilfully narrowed their sensibilities. Unlike Larkin and Amis, Gunn was happy to listen to these sermons: openness to the unfamiliar was part of his motivation and subject-matter. When he wrote of Gary Snyder that he was 'like most serious poets...concerned at finding himself on a barely known planet, in an almost unknown universe, where he must attempt to create and discover meanings' he was, as he more or less admitted to James Campbell, in some sense describing himself.[9]

By his own account, Gunn first heard of the Movement from John Wain, whom he met when Wain was giving a talk at Cambridge, where Gunn was at the time an undergraduate:[10]

He was extremely nice to me and had read some of my poems in a Cambridge maga-zine. He said, There are some other chaps up in London who are writing like you, we must all get together...I wasn't quite sure who these other chaps were...The big joke about the Movement was that none of the people had ever met each other and certainly never subscribed to anything like a programme. There were a few chance resemblances, but they were pretty chance.

At around the same time, according to Blake Morrison, he went to Oxford to meet Elizabeth Jennings, whom he admired.[11] He had perhaps seen some-thing of himself reflected in Jennings's work: the combination of exact for-mality and intensely personal but contained emotion without dryness or ironical reflection—qualities that set the two of them apart from the rest of the Movement. In any event, Gunn's memories of the Movement are not

[9] *Thom Gunn in Conversation with James Campbell* (London: Between the Lines, 2000), p. 56. (Hereafter, Campbell.) The quotation is from the essay on Gary Snyder in Gunn, *The Occasions of Poetry: Essays in Criticism and Autobiography*, ed. Clive Wilmer (London: Faber, 1982), p. 43. (Hereafter, *Occasions*.)

[10] Gunn [in conversation with Ian Hamilton], *London Magazine*, Nov. 1964, pp. 69–70.

[11] Morrison, p. 40.

entirely accurate and may reflect a retrospective distaste for a career move that did not entirely suit his self-image. For however much Gunn doubted the existence of the Movement, it is the case, as Morrison has shown, that he benefited from its associations in publishing and publicity. Nor was it the case that the poets never met each other. Gunn himself had met only Jennings and Wain in those early days, but the other eight poets knew one another quite well—in some cases, very well—and nurtured the relationships. Gunn was unable to do the same for the simple reason that, in 1954, not long after the appearance of his first book *Fighting Terms*, he left Britain for the United States and soon decided to stay there.

Born in 1929, Gunn was significantly younger than the other Movement poets. Larkin and Davie, for instance, were born in 1922. Gunn was lucky to have been published so early but, though he shared much with the others, he also had things in common with nearer contemporaries whose work was to create the climate of the Sixties: A. Alvarez, Geoffrey Hill, Ted Hughes, and Sylvia Plath. He belonged to the National Service generation, while Amis, Conquest, and Davie, as older men, had served in the war.[12] As late as 1962, in a review of Alvarez's Penguin anthology *The New Poetry*, Davie expressed disquiet at the violence and irrationality Gunn and Alvarez seemed to be encouraging. No doubt he was thinking of such poems of Gunn's as 'The Beaters', 'Market at Turk', 'The Corridor', and 'The Monster'—poems in which perversity and fetishism seemed to play a part—to say nothing of Gunn's celebrations of bikers in such poems as 'On the Move' and 'Black Jackets'.[13] Davie took these new developments to be a reaction against the Movement and its concern, as he understood it, with a common language and civic responsibility. *The New Poetry*, he wrote,

might have been designed to illustrate how a poetic programme less than 10 years old, which called for a return to rational order and control, has been overturned from within its own ranks, by writers like Gunn and Alvarez who dwell instead upon the pain and violence of psychic disturbance.[14]

---

[12] Morrison, p. 89.

[13] 'Market at Turk' (GCP 58), 'The Corridor' (GCP 85–6), 'The Monster' (GCP 96–7), 'On the Move' (GCP 39–40), 'Black Jackets' (GCP 108). GCP = Thom Gunn, *Collected Poems* (London: Faber, 1993)—future references to the book will be cited in the text in this form. 'The Beaters' was not reprinted in *Collected Poems*; it appeared in Thom Gunn, *The Sense of Movement* (London: Faber, 1957), pp. 36–7.

[14] 'Reason Reversed', *New Statesman*, 4 May 1962, p. 640.

Where Alvarez was concerned this was clearly prophetic and Davie understood only too well why an anthology mainly of British poets like himself had to begin with the American 'Confessional' poets, Robert Lowell and John Berryman.[15] (A later edition was to include Sylvia Plath and Anne Sexton as well.) Gunn's poems had undoubtedly anticipated the change of direction Alvarez was promoting, but as Davie was later to discover, Gunn disliked the flagrant exhibitionism of Plath and Sexton quite as much as he did.

For the most vivid exemplification of what it is that identifies Gunn as anything but Confessional, it is necessary to jump ahead to a poem in his last book, 'The Gas-Poker'.[16] Gunn's mother, to whom he had been exceptionally close, committed suicide when he was 15, and he and his younger brother found the body. Here, it might be thought, was the perfect subject for a Confessional poem: raw anguish with all taboos broken. But it was not until Gunn was nearly 70 that he managed to write a poem on the subject, and when he did so, he made the verse form and rhyme scheme as elaborate as possible and used the third person to tell his story.

This approach was not out of keeping with Movement poetry, maintaining as it does a respect for the reader and the need to contain emotion. Indeed, as is shown by his elegies in *The Man with Night Sweats* (1992), Gunn's poetry is usually most moving when most controlled (GCP 461–88). As some of his free verse demonstrates, such control need not be metrical, but strict metre was an option he retained throughout his career. His instinct for it was both confirmed and instructed by the man under whom he studied in California. Yvor Winters was a stoical humanist whose main compendium of criticism is called *In Defense of Reason*. In Winters's moral urgency and his sense of American history, Gunn found an equivalent to F. R. Leavis, whose lectures at Cambridge had captivated him and influenced most of the poets of the Movement. It helped that Winters was also a poet himself and, as Gunn soon came to believe, a very fine one. Studying under Winters and befriending some of his followers, Gunn participated in a current of American poetry that had something in common with the *New Lines* poets. Like most of them, Winters was in reaction against residual Romanticism and the excesses of Modernism; he preached a return to orthodox metre and the value to poetry of rational argument. But

---

[15] For the word 'Confessional' as applied to these poets, see M. L. Rosenthal, *The New Poets: American and British Poetry since World War II* (New York: Oxford University Press, 1967), pp. 25–7.

[16] *Boss Cupid* (London: Faber, 2000), pp. 10–11.

in important ways, he differed from these younger British contemporaries. Sanity for Winters was not the default condition of human life; it was something that needed constant maintenance. And by sanity he meant as much the state of civilization as the mental condition of the individual. So the reason he defended against its Romantic enemies was rather more than a matter of common sense; it was an intellectual discipline with deep roots in Western thought. In consequence, Winters was not an ironist and did not warm to the *vers de société* aspect of much Movement poetry. He had, moreover, begun his career as a follower of Ezra Pound and William Carlos Williams, and his conscious and calculated reaction against Modernism was coloured by such early attachments. For all his deliberate Classicism, moreover, Winters remained a Romantic by temperament—hence his lasting attachment to the verbal and imaginative extravagance of Hart Crane—and it is significant that, early on in Gunn's time as his student, Winters urged him to read Williams and Wallace Stevens 'without delay'.[17] Winters recognized the power of such work, but poetry for him had to do something more than evoke or create experience. Gunn profoundly agreed with Winters about this; for both of them, the poem was first and foremost 'an attempt to understand'.[18]

Davie had been acquainted with Winters's work a good deal longer than Gunn. He had read *In Defense of Reason* in the late 1940s and written Winters a fan letter. A valuable correspondence had ensued.[19] There are signs of Winters's influence in Davie's early poetry, and he is cited at key moments in the early critical books, notably the first of them, *Purity of Diction in English Verse* (1952). In 1950 Davie reviewed Winters's anthology of poets who had studied under him, *Poets of the Pacific*, and applauded some Movement-like qualities in the Americans, especially praising them for renewing a 'poetry of statement, openly didactic but saved by a sedulously noble diction, from prosiness'.[20] I doubt, however, if Enright or Amis or even Larkin most of the time could be praised for 'sedulously noble diction'. Gunn on the other hand could, and so occasionally could Davie himself.

[17] *Occasions*, p. 176.

[18] Gunn in *Viewpoints: Poets in Conversation with John Haffenden* (London: Faber, 1981), p. 37.

[19] See *The Selected Letters of Yvor Winters*, ed. R. L. Barth (Athens, Ohio: Swallow Press, 2000). The book includes letters from Winters to both Davie and Gunn. One letter of 1958 (p. 376) gives Winters's response to Philip Larkin's 'At Grass', which Davie had clearly encouraged him to read.

[20] *The Poet in the Imaginary Museum: Essays of Two Decades*, ed. Barry Alpert (Manchester: Carcanet, 1977), pp. 3–5.

Gunn's reading of Williams and Stevens is hardly felt in his poetry until his third book, *My Sad Captains*, in 1961. But as early as 1954 there are signs that the anti-Romantic manner was not intrinsic to his purposes. When I first heard him read in 1964, he introduced a poem from *Fighting Terms*, 'Captain in Time of Peace' (GCP 30), as typical of the Movement. I presume he meant unconsciously, aware that there was much in *Fighting Terms* that exemplified the spirit of the age. The poem in question is anti-heroic, yet it alludes to the possibility of wilder virtues, and many other 'soldier' poems in the collection aspire to the heroic without any shade of irony. In his dream poem 'The Wound', for instance, the 'clumsy brute in uniform' of 'Captain in Time of Peace' is transformed into Achilles raging at the death of Patroclus (GCP 3):

> I was myself: subject to no man's death:
> My own commander was my enemy.
> And while my belt hung up, sword in the sheath,
> Thersites shambled in and breathlessly
> Cackled about my friend Patroclus' death.

This is closer to late Yeats than it is to any poet of the Movement, but even those poems that exhibit the Movement manner can present a contrast in their attitudes. 'Lofty in the Palais de Danse' shares something with Amis in cynical seducer mode, but the alarming existential anxiety of Gunn's poem has disturbing implications that leave Amis's poetry far behind (GCP 9–10). 'For a Birthday', also Movement-ish in tone, explicitly repudiates what one thinks of—perhaps unjustly—as Movement values. 'I have reached a time when words no longer help,' he tells his lover, and concludes (GCP 32):

> All my agnostic irony I renounce
> So I may climb to regions where I rest
> In springs of speech, the dark before of truth:
> The sweet moist wafer of your tongue I taste,
> And find right meanings in your silent mouth.

In suggesting that language has its limitations, Gunn implies that a poem is more than 'a statement in words about a human experience', to borrow a formulation of Winters's.[21] In renouncing agnostic irony, he is not necessarily renouncing agnosticism. (Gunn usually called himself an atheist.)

---

[21] *In Defense of Reason* (London: Routledge, 1960), p. 11. Winters's book was first published in the United States in 1943.

He *is* repudiating the frame of mind for which commonsensical scepticism becomes an excuse for not taking ethical or metaphysical risks.

Gunn's willingness to take on large metaphysical themes is immediately apparent in *My Sad Captains* (1961), which begins with 'In Santa Maria del Popolo', a poem about 'Saul becoming Paul' in a painting by Caravaggio (GCP 93–4). Though this could never be called a religious poem, it poses what might be called a religious question: how as human beings are we to confront nothingness? Gunn's previous collection, *The Sense of Movement* (1957) had suggested an interest in Existentialism, especially that of Jean-Paul Sartre. The influence here is rather Albert Camus. The first half of *My Sad Captains* is in some respects a continuation of *The Sense of Movement* (1957), but rather as the humanism of Camus's novel *La Peste* modifies the insights of his earlier *L'Etranger*. In both cases, the sense of living for the moment 'in a valueless world' (GCP 40) has to give way to a consciously chosen moral path. In terms of their style and method, however, the poems are still compatible with the Movement, and it is in the second half of the book that the radical change takes place. It consists of fourteen nearly flawless poems in syllabic verse. This was an experimental medium: that is to say, line-length is not determined by the feet or accents of orthodox metre but by arbitrary syllable-counts—usually seven or nine to a line. Gunn frequently commented that he had adopted this device as a way of learning to write in the wholly unstructured rhythms of free verse,[22] which he was to do for the first time in a book of captions to photographs by his brother: *Positives* (1965).[23] I am not wholly convinced he was right about this. The syllabic poems have a distinctive structure which discovers the tensions of poetry in what is otherwise lineated prose. Their prosaic qualities are crucial to their subject matter, in which Gunn seems to stumble on small perceptions, casual observations acquiring significance through being thus exhibited. The first of the group, 'Waking in a Newly-Built House', is an extended metaphor for the new method (GCP 115):

> Calmly, perception rests on the things,
> and is aware of them only in
> their precise definition, their fine
> lack of even potential meanings.

---

[22] '[U]sing syllabics was a way of teaching myself free verse rhythms.' *Campbell*, p. 45.
[23] Thom and Ander Gunn, *Positives* (London: Faber, 1965).

These syllabic poems are unimaginable without the precedents of American Modernism, being closely related to Williams's work in free verse and, in a rather different sort of syllabic arrangement, to Marianne Moore. They answer exactly to Davie's plea, in his essay 'Remembering the Movement' (1959), for a poetry in which 'outward and non-human things [are] apprehended crisply for their own sakes'.[24] Gunn's concern for such things owes something to Existentialism. Davie, by contrast, had begun to adopt a religious vocabulary, calling on the contemporary poet to 'regain his faith in a world outside man, bodied against him as something other with its own structure and its own modes of being open to him to discover'.[25]

The syllabic poems in *My Sad Captains* were published in magazines between 1960 and 1961. The date is not without interest. According to Gunn's partner, Mike Kitay, Davie, and Gunn first met in 1961 or thereabouts, and it was during the later 1950s and early 1960s that Davie's impatience with the Movement became apparent. This is not to suggest that Gunn and Davie influenced each other, though they may have reinforced each other's instinct for moving on.

But Davie was never ashamed to acknowledge his involvement with the Movement. The identification was not without vanity: if the Movement was important, then so was he. But to leave matters there would be to trivialize. There is a note of self-deprecation in his characterization of himself in 'Homage to William Cowper', a poem that must ante-date the Movement, as 'A pasticheur of late-Augustan styles' (DCP 8). As the manifesto aspect of his *Purity of Diction* implies, he wanted a revival of such styles, with their assumption of a common language and appeal to the common reader. He knew from the start, however, that the conditions of the past cannot apply in the present. In 'T. S. Eliot: The End of an Era' (1956) he announced that

---

[24] 'Remembering the Movement' (1959), reprinted in *With the Grain: Essays on Thomas Hardy and Modern British Poetry*, ed. Clive Wilmer (Manchester: Carcanet, 1998), p. 202. (Hereafter, WTG.)

[25] 'Common and Uncommon Muses', *Twentieth Century* (Nov. 1957), p. 468. This article is, in effect, a review of Frank Kermode's *Romantic Image* (1957), which stands with Davie's *Articulate Energy* (1955) as the major post-war challenge to Symbolist orthodoxy. Morrison, pp. 268–9, argues that the use, in both Davie and Tomlinson, of 'the phrases "bodied against" and "bodied over against" suggests that both . . . were familiar with the philosophy of Martin Buber, who in the "I consider a tree" of *I and Thou* uses the phrase *Er leibt mir gegenüber* ("It is bodied over against me and has to do with me").'

he wanted a kind of poetry that was different from that of Eliot and the Symbolists and more like that of the later eighteenth century.[26] But that he had written the essay at all was testimony to his sense of Eliot's importance. He knew perfectly well that

> history cannot be rewritten, that there can be no question of putting the clock back: the post-post-symbolist poetry I look for may be more in harmony with pre-Romantic poetry, it can never be the same. There cannot be a conspiracy to pretend that the symbolist revolution never happened.

Eliot was a post-Symbolist and his career was by this time effectively over. The post-post-symbolists, therefore, were contemporary poets, notably those in the Movement. Many of these poets were calling, as others have done since, for the rediscovery of a native English tradition, running from Hardy to themselves by way of Edward Thomas and Robert Graves. Such a tradition would bypass Anglo-American Modernism. For Davie, this was mere sentimentality and would doom English poetry to insignificance. He never thought of the Movement as a reaction. It was Modernism by other means, a second *rappel à l'ordre*. He agreed with John Wain 'that the task before the poets of the 'fifties is not further exploration, but rather "consolidation" of gains made by Eliot and Pound, Auden and Yeats'.[27] In consequence, his sense of what poetry could do in the modern age was bound up with the Movement.

There is an important contrast with Gunn here. Risk, that key value in Gunn's poetry, was not an option for those, like Davie, who had played their part in the war and, in disenchanted early adulthood, learnt of Hiroshima and the concentration camps. 'At Dachau Yeats and Rilke died' (DCP 35), wrote Davie, as if to say that a risk-taking rhetoric in the poet was as much to blame as the speeches of Adolf Hitler. And indeed, many of the Modernists, Yeats and Rilke among them, had flirted with forms of right-wing extremism, while Pound, a key enthusiasm of Davie's, had considerably more than flirted. I am far from wanting to suggest that Gunn took these matters lightly—many poems suggest the opposite—but that at that crucial juncture in history, the end of the Second World War, an age-difference of seven

---

[26] 'T. S. Eliot: The End of an Era' (1956) in Davie, *Modernist Essays: Yeats, Pound, Eliot*, ed. Clive Wilmer (Manchester: Carcanet, 2004), p. 23–4.

[27] 'Augustans New and Old', *The Twentieth Century* (Nov. 1955), p. 465.

years made for a contrasting approach to them. In an early poem of Davie's, 'Creon's Mouse', the mythical King of Thebes justifies his condemnation of Antigone with a sober critique of Romantic idealism (DCP 17):

> If too much daring brought (he thought) the war,
> When that was over nothing else would serve
> But no one must be daring any more.
> A self-induced and stubborn loss of nerve.

A few years later 'Rejoinder to a Critic' poses the question 'How can I dare to feel?' It responds with reflections on Hiroshima underpinned by a further question: 'How dare we now be anything but numb?' (DCP 67–8). The poem is from Davie's second collection *A Winter Talent* (1959), the title poem of which concludes with this fine stanza (DCP 65):

> What though less sunny spirits never turn
> The dry detritus of an August hill
> To dangerous glory? Better still to burn
> Upon that gloom where all have felt a chill.

There is a paradox to this dazzling passage, which one also encounters with Larkin. It suggests that Davie sees himself as a poet of low temperature: dry, ironical, bookish, cautious with regard to impulse and not given to violent passions. And yet how passionate it is! In later years, Davie's style came to be more unbuttoned. When in one such poem he protests that

> A man who ought to know me
> wrote in a review
> my emotional life was meagre

one might at first sympathize with the reviewer, yet close reading of Davie's work and the poem in question suggests that his protest is justified (DCP 180). The numbness and aversion to risk are the responses of a vulnerably emotional person who has counted the cost of feeling intensely. Like the persona of Winters's poem 'The Slow Pacific Swell', a man who really knows the sea will have learnt its terrors as well as its majesty and will therefore be inclined to keep his distance from it:[28]

> A landsman, I. The sea is but a sound.
> I would be near it on a sandy mound,

[28] *The Collected Poems of Yvor Winters* (Manchester: Carcanet, 1978), pp. 125–6.

And hear the steady rushing of the deep
While I lay stinging in the sand with sleep.
I have lived inland long. The land is numb.
It stands beneath the feet, and one may come
Walking securely, till the sea extends
Its limber margin, and precision ends.
By night a chaos of commingling power,
The whole Pacific hovers hour by hour.
The slow Pacific swell stirs on the sand,
Sleeping to sink away, withdrawing land,
Heaving and wrinkled in the moon, and blind;
Or gathers seaward, ebbing out of mind.

This may be Davie's source for the word 'numb'. It is hardly a matter of timidity.

The Movement poets, including Gunn and Jennings, share a distaste for emotional display, whether of the rhetorical kind which characterized the Forties or the emotional *déshabille* of the Confessional Sixties. English reserve, that proverbial quality sometimes thought to be coldness, had triumphed during the Second World War, and there was world-wide admiration for the stoical solidarity of Londoners during the Blitz and of the British in general at home and abroad. The reticence, sobriety, and modest good humour of Movement poetry are a tribute to that reserve, especially in so far as the poets aim at a common language, eschewing both the vatic pronouncements of the visionary and the wilful obscurities of the *poète maudit*, the Neo-Romantic and the Modernist. Larkin, Jennings, and Davie all in their different ways revive the use of the first person plural in their poetry—what 'we' think, do or say is a more significant matter than the language or insights of isolated individuals[29]—and a similar concern in late Augustan poetry provides Davie with the substance of his *Purity of Diction*. In the anthology that followed from that book, Davie has this to say of Samuel Johnson:[30]

This man who, as critic, insisted on the necessity for common sense to control the flights of the imagination, was the same whose imagination so peopled his solitude that he implored his friends' company in the middle of the night. The man whose

[29] The first person plural pronoun in Movement poetry is admirably discussed in Morrison; see esp. pp. 120–1.

[30] Introduction to *The Late Augustans: Longer Poems of the Later Eighteenth Century*, ed. Donald Davie (London: Heinemann, 1958), pp. xxii–xxiii.

vivid emotional life is recorded in his private prayers, whose tender susceptibilities led him to maintain for years a household of waifs and strays and unfortunate eccentrics, is the same whose verses observe disciplines equalled in strictness only by Pope's. And this is not paradoxical. For it is the mind which knows the power of its own potentially disruptive propensities that needs and demands to be disciplined...

Davie understood those needs and demands only too well and his need for control in his poems is the mark of it. But should the emphasis fall on the restraint and self-discipline involved or on the turbulent emotions withheld but implied? As the culture veered through the Sixties and Seventies towards more overtly personal and emotional sorts of discourse, Davie to some extent followed it. In the Fifties even Gunn, for all his independence, had accepted the limitation: of his bikers in 'On the Move' he had written, '*One* is always nearer by not keeping still' (GCP 40; my italics), a usage he came to dislike.[31] But by 1977, in a poem called 'In the Stopping Train', Davie could write of 'the man going mad inside me' (DCP 337), and his transition from the common language of men to 'confessions' of private woe was surprisingly seamless.

The journey went by way of a poem first published in 1960 and selected for *New Lines 2* (1963): 'To a Brother in the Mystery' (DCP 118–19). 'This poem,' he tells us, 'arose out of a visit to Southwell Minster, and a reading of Nikolaus Pevsner's *The Leaves of Southwell*. But the relationship explored in the poem is in some sort that between myself and Charles Tomlinson' (DCP 607). In other words, like a great deal of Davie's Movement poetry, it is a poem about poetry enlivened by the employment of an extended analogy: for sculpture, read poetry. And yet what the poem has to say about matters other than poetry seems in this case to exceed the requirements of the moral. Pevsner's little book effectively proves that the wonderfully unified leaf-decoration of the Minster's thirteenth-century Chapter House must have been carved by at least two different artists.[32] His preoccupation with these beautiful carvings and his willingness to confer major status on works of decorative art may be taken as prophetic. It was one of several post-war indications that

---

[31] See *Campbell*, p. 29. For a comparison of Larkin's 'we' with Gunn's insistence on distinctive selfhood, see my article 'The Later Fortunes of Impersonality: "Tradition and the Individual Talent" and Postwar Poetry', in Giovanni Cianci and Jason Harding (eds.), *T. S. Eliot and the Idea of Tradition* (Cambridge: Cambridge University Press, 2007), pp. 60–4. This passage also touches on Gunn's dislike of Confessional poetry.

[32] *The Leaves of Southwell* (London and New York: King Penguin, 1945).

foreshadow a revival of John Ruskin. The *oeuvre* of the polymathic Victorian critic is voluminous and Davie was not especially well-read in it, but there is much in his work to suggest that Ruskin was as much as Johnson a model for his critical philosophy. Ruskin was a thoroughgoing realist with a passion for art that records the external world, who believed that we approach an understanding of the world by paying close attention to its material facts. It is through the richness and harmony of nature, according to Ruskin, that we may come to know God and his purpose for us. Especially important for him is the representation in Gothic sculpture of natural particulars—birds, fruit, and leaves. '[A]ll great art,' he says, 'is the expression of man's delight in God's work, not in *his own*.'[33] All great art, therefore, has for Ruskin—quite as much as it does for Winters or Leavis—a moral significance. Some compelling pages of Davie's book *Ezra Pound: Poet as Sculptor* (1965) suggest that Pound's substantial but largely unacknowledged debt to Ruskin was the source of Davie's interest.[34] There can be little doubt that he was alerted to this connection by the poet he addresses in 'To a Brother in the Mystery'.[35]

In 1958 Charles Tomlinson had published his first full-scale collection, *Seeing is Believing*, in the United States, and in a review the following year Davie identified it as 'a landmark' in English poetry.[36] Tomlinson had not yet found a British publisher and the American connection suggests much greater interest across the Atlantic than in the United Kingdom, a fact which Davie lamented. The reason is not far to seek: the sensibility that inhabits Tomlinson's pages has learnt its poetic language from Americans—from Pound, Marianne Moore, Wallace Stevens, and William Carlos Williams, none of whom had yet made much of a name in Britain. Though it falls outside my immediate interests here, it should also be noted that Tomlinson like Davie was learning as much from poems in other languages as he was from British or American poets. Davie's translations of Boris Pasternak and Tomlinson's

---

[33] *The Works of John Ruskin*, ed. E. T. Cook and Alexander Wedderburn (London: George Allen, 1903–12), 39 vols., 7. 263 (italic in original). (Hereafter, *Ruskin*.)

[34] *Ezra Pound: Poet as Sculptor* (London: Routledge, 1965), pp. 168–81.

[35] Ruskin is an important influence on Tomlinson's poetry. See particularly the poem 'Frondes Agrestes' in *Seeing is Believing* (Oxford: Oxford University Press, 1960), p. 31, which must have been in Davie's mind when he wrote 'To a Brother in the Mystery'. *Frondes Agrestes* is the title of a selection from Ruskin's *Modern Painters* and means 'gathered [or selected] leaves'.

[36] New York: McDowell, Obolensky, 1958. Davie's review is reprinted in WTG, pp. 192–8. Tomlinson had previously published two short collections.

of Antonio Machado, for example, were fundamental to the changes their poetry underwent in the early Sixties.[37] This is not to say that they write in (so to speak) a foreign tongue. Tomlinson quite as much as Davie is steeped in British poetry, has an English manner and sounds uncomfortable when, for instance, he tries to improvise in the style of Williams. Paradoxically, their reading in foreign poetries seems to have had the effect of leading them back to vital traditions of English that for much of the twentieth century had gone unnoticed, except in the United States. Davie's surprising but (as it has proved) durable reading of *The Pisan Cantos* connects Pound's attention to natural particulars—to the wasp, for instance, in Canto 83—with an unexpected 'lineage': 'Coleridge, Keats, Ruskin, Hopkins—[not] the sort of family tree that Pound draws up for himself.' The wasp 'retains its otherness as an independent form of life; it is only by doing so that it can be a source of comfort to the human observer'. What is 'outside the human mind' can alone ' "take us out of ourselves" when we observe it and try to enter into its life.' And he goes on to speak of Pound's 'tenderness' and his 'capacity for sympathetic identification with inhuman forms of life'.[38] *Seeing is Believing* belongs to the same sensibility and implies a rejection of what Davie calls 'an imperious, appropriating attitude towards the perceived world', whether in post-Symbolists such as Eliot or in his own contemporaries.[39]

Ezra Pound: Poet as Sculptor was published in 1965, but Davie had clearly been working on the book for many years before that. It is impossible not to guess that Pound quite as much as Pevsner suggested the sculptural metaphor in 'To a Brother in the Mystery'. As I have implied, the role of sculpture is more than merely illustrative. In a radio talk, 'Two Analogies for Poetry', Davie had already talked of sculpture as providing a model for the composition of poetry. For Walter Pater, he had reminded his listeners, 'All art constantly aspires towards the condition of music' because in music 'matter and form' are indistinguishable.[40] But what if poets were to take sculpture

[37] *The Poems of Dr Zhivago*, translated with a commentary by Donald Davie (Manchester University Press, 1965); *Castilian Ilexes: Versions of Antonio Machado*, translated by Charles Tomlinson and Henry Gifford (Oxford: Oxford University Press, 1963).

[38] *Ezra Pound: Poet as Sculptor*, p. 177.

[39] Ibid., 173.

[40] ME, p. 47–52. For the Pater quotation, see his essay 'The School of Giorgione' in *The Renaissance: Studies in Art and Poetry* (London: Macmillan, 1900), p. 135. First published as *Studies in the History of the Renaissance* (1873).

instead of music as their model—as Pound (Davie's book argued) already had? Sculptors have to engage with materials—especially, in this argument, stone or wood—which pre-exist the creative act. Carving is thus inherently an engagement with otherness.

Davie had also been looking at Robert Browning, another of Pound's masters. The metre of 'To a Brother in the Mystery' is clearly derived from Browning's use—in *Sordello* and 'My Last Duchess'—of a conversational syntax that cuts across the grain of the pentameter couplet. The tension between verse-form and syntax, registered most forcefully at the line-ending, generates a powerful expressive energy. In the past Davie had had to apologize for a style 'too neat and self-possessed' ('Method. For Ronald Gaskell', DCP 37) and, though he had good reason for not allowing a 'disordered mind' to show in his structures, he now admitted an element of disruption, though the disruption derives from the subject-matter rather than any disturbance in the author. Davie was almost certainly thinking of Pound's advice that the poet should 'compose in the sequence of the musical phrase, not in sequence of a metronome', so that the metre seems to sustain the natural movement of the language rather than impose itself upon it.[41] Browning, moreover, is especially noted as the author of dramatic monologues spoken by artists— 'Fra Lippo Lippi', 'Andrea del Sarto', and 'Pictor Ignotus'—in which there is an implied analogy between painting and the poet's own activity. But the analogy remains implicit, allowing us to enjoy and learn from the poems simply as poems about painting or about Italy or about the characters Browning has dreamt up out of hints in Vasari. And so it is with Davie's poem. Though sculpture here is primarily a vehicle, it is also something that seriously concerns him. The life of the poem springs from his sense of the skill and resourcefulness of stone-carvers and from a care for their subject-matter and materials. It is, that is to say, as much a poem about 'leaves and stone' as it is about writing poetry.

It was in this period—between the review of Tomlinson and this poem about their friendship—that Davie wrote 'Remembering the Movement'.[42] In this brief article, for the first time, he drew together the limitations he detected in the poetry he and his friends had been writing. In particular, he

[41] The quotation is from Ezra Pound's Imagist manifesto, collected in 'A Retrospect', *Literary Essays of Ezra Pound*, ed. T.S. Eliot (London: Faber, 1954), p. 3.
[42] WTG, pp. 199–203.

missed 'an idea of poetry as a way of knowing the world … apprehending it, learning it'—words which anticipate Gunn's praise of Gary Snyder; he spoke, as we have seen, of 'the striking absence from "Movement" poetry of outward and non-human things apprehended crisply for their own sakes'. Davie related this failing to an excessive concern in Movement poems for the relationship of the poet with the reader: a concern which revealed itself in 'the inert gestures of social adaptiveness' that lubricated their language— such phrases as 'no doubt' and 'of course' and 'I suppose'. It accounts, too, for their ironical tone: 'ironical in a limited way, defensive and deprecating, a way of looking at ourselves and our pretensions, not a way of looking at the world'.

'To a Brother in the Mystery', as it draws to a close, discusses these very issues, though apparently in terms of medieval stone-cutting. Here, to put it crudely, the sculptor's medium (stone) stands for the poet's medium (language), both media seen as equally intractable. Like Davie in his soon-to-be published *Events and Wisdoms* (1964) and Tomlinson in *A Peopled Landscape* (1963), the two sculptors seem to have been influencing each other, the Davie-figure with his talent for 'human incident', the Tomlinson-figure with his 'godliness in leaf'—a striking phrase, to which we will need to return.

> We infect
> Each other then, doubtless to good effect …
> And yet, take care: this cordial knack bereaves
> The mind of all its sympathy with leaves,
> Even with stone. I would not take away
> From your peculiar mastery, if I say
> A sort of coldness is the core of it,
> A sort of cruelty; that prerequisite
> Perhaps I rob you of, and in exchange give
> What? Vulgarity's prerogative,
> Indulgence towards the frailties it indulges,
> Humour called 'wryness' that acknowledges
> Its own complicity. I can keep in mind
> So much at all events, can always find
> Fallen humanity enough, in stone,
> Yes, in the medium: where we cannot own
> Crispness, compactness, elegance, but the feature
> Seals it and signs it work of human nature
> And fallen though redeemable. You, I fear,

Will find you bought humanity too dear
At the price of some light leaves, if you begin
To find your handling of them growing thin,
Insensitive, brittle. For the common touch,
Though it warms, coarsens. Never care so much
For leaves or people, but you care for stone
A little more. The medium is its own
Thing, and not all a medium, but the stuff
Of mountains: cruel, obdurate, and rough.

The last sixteen of these concluding lines are indebted to two passages in Ruskin. The first is in *Modern Painters*, where Ruskin suggests that lovers of 'precious mountain substance' in Renaissance Italy may have had 'hearts of Stone' and cites a poem of Browning's in evidence.[43] Increasingly Davie wanted to argue that the values that count in democratic society or even in decent human relations are not necessarily those that count in art: hence what looks like praise of cruelty here, the cruelty representing, in effect, the passion for language which, in the poet, must always come first—before all other loyalties or attachments. At the same time, our buildings are 'expressive of [our] nature', as Ruskin puts it in *The Stones of Venice*; the necessary *imperfection* of Gothic art, he claims, is an acknowledgement that we are *fallen*. Perfection is inevitably limited and can only be achieved by dehumanizing the artist; *ergo*, the artist's humanity finds expression in his falling short.[44] As we have seen, Davie's earlier poetry was arguably 'too neat and self-possessed', and too anxious to be on good terms with his fellow-human, the reader. The ' "wryness" that acknowledges | Its own complicity' is unmistakably the reflex of irony he attacks in 'Remembering the Movement', while 'the common touch [which], | Though it warms, coarsens' is the habit of 'social adaptiveness': the assumption that it is the poet's business to address an audience rather than a subject. Here again, Browning and Ruskin may have provided prompts: in a letter to Ruskin justifying his supposed obscurity, Browning insisted that 'A poet's affair is with God,—to whom he is accountable, and of whom is his reward'.[45]

Though Browning and Ruskin were religious men, I don't think Browning was making a religious pronouncement. It was rather to say that the poet's

[43] *Ruskin*, 6.447, 450. The Browning poem is 'The Bishop Orders his Tomb in St Praxed's Church'.

[44] *Ruskin*, 10.180–269. For Ruskin's doctrine of imperfection in art, see especially pp. 184–204.

[45] Quoted in *Ruskin*, 36.xxxvi.

business was a matter of truth, not of easy communication. If the matter is challenging, let the poem be difficult. Poets do not *address* their readers; their readers *overhear* them. I find it hard not to infer, however, that Davie took something more from Browning than Browning was fully aware of. Why '*godliness* in leaf'? In an argument between Davie and Alvarez published in 1962, Davie makes his case for Tomlinson's 'leaves and stone', Alvarez by contrast for an extremist poetry driven by crisis, both personal and political. The two of them, says Davie at one point, agree in being 'infidels'. Their agreement, he goes on,

leads us naturally to suppose that the only grounds for poetry are therapeutic and social. Of course, in the history of poetry down the centuries…the grounds for poetry have frequently been religious or…ontological. It does seem to me increasingly—though it's embarrassing for me to admit it because of my own agnosticism—we may be selling the pass on poetry from the start when we don't allow that it may have metaphysical or religious sanctions. This is what I mean by respecting the otherness, the being of a tree, a stone wall, a landscape. Even if there were a social breakdown there would still be a poet with a tree in front of him, a poet with a stone wall in front of him.[46]

Davie had come to believe that a poetry which cares only for the human and not for the full richness of the world is unable in the end to assign a just value to anything. Over time he came to the view that reverence for otherness was tacit acknowledgement of a transcendent source, to which (as in Ruskin) art offered praise. This was not a conclusion that Gunn could have subscribed to, but his evident distaste for ingratiating rhetoric, combined with his calm attention to mere things, for Davie singled him out as a kindred spirit.[47]

The best-known of Gunn's syllabic poems is 'Considering the Snail' (GCP 117). The fame of this fine poem is probably due to its inclusion in the 1962 selection of poems by Gunn and Ted Hughes that was for many years an 'A' level set text.[48] It provided teachers with an opportunity to compare Hughes's poems about animals with at least one poem of Gunn's. Such a comparison, indeed, is not without its value. Gunn was at the time a

[46] 'A New Aestheticism? A. Alvarez talks to Donald Davie', *The Review*, 1 (April–May 1962), p. 19.

[47] See Davie, 'The Rhetoric of Emotion', WTG, pp. 324–30.

[48] Thom Gunn and Ted Hughes, *Selected Poems* (London: Faber, 1962).

champion of Hughes's work and it is not impossible that Hughes's success with animal subjects influenced him.[49] Nevertheless, 'Considering the Snail' is much more urgently a response by Gunn to his own earlier work:

> The snail pushes through a green
> night, for the grass is heavy
> with water and meets over
> the bright path he makes, where rain
> has darkened the earth's dark. He
> moves in a wood of desire,
>
> pale antlers barely stirring
> as he hunts. I cannot tell
> what power is at work, drenched there
> with purpose, knowing nothing.
> What is a snail's fury? All
> I think is that if later
>
> I parted the blades above
> the tunnel and saw the thin
> trail of broken white across
> litter, I would never have
> imagined the slow passion
> to that deliberate progress.

The context this poem needs can be provided by 'On the Move', the lead poem of Gunn's previous book. 'On the Move' quickly became—and no doubt remains—Gunn's most famous poem, largely because it brings the 1950s myth of the American biker into the orbit of formal poetry. As with 'Elvis Presley' from the same volume, Gunn succeeded in combining a subject from popular culture with the complex refinements of metaphysical poetry. But as often happens when a poem becomes iconic, the author soon found himself at odds with it.[50] As a result, he returned to its subject again and again, always modifying, complicating and humanizing it. He most explicitly did so in his 1970 volume *Moly*, in a poem about surfers called 'From the Wave', echoing 'On the Move' in its very title (GCP 198–9).

[49] See e.g. Gunn's review of Hughes's *Lupercal* in *Poetry*, 97.4 (January 1961), pp. 269–70. Gunn persuaded Robert Conquest to include Hughes in *New Lines 2* (1963). 'Considering the Snail' first appeared in print in 1960.

[50] See Gunn's objections to the poem in *Campbell*, p. 29.

'Considering the Snail' has the same theme as 'On the Move': the relation of will to energy. Gunn has chosen to embody those forces in a creature, proverbially slow, which we tend to regard as passionless. A snail is not a natural focus of human sympathy. It is here that Gunn most clearly meets the demands that Davie as critic was currently making for poetry. The attention to an object outside the ordinary scope of human feeling—we might compare Pound's wasp—is interrogated first for its own sake. But the more intensely the poet attends to what is outside him, the more exactly does his own condition move into focus. And so, in a creature that in terms of velocity, scale, body-temperature and consciousness is wholly alien to himself, the speaker is surprised to detect or infer such familiar characteristics as desire, power, purpose, fury and passion. The tone is also fascinating. In the hesitancy of its jagged enjambments—'green | night', 'He | moves', 'across | litter'—it owes something to Williams, while the quizzical tone may remind us of Marianne Moore: 'What is a snail's fury?' On first reading, one is not sure if the question is meant to be funny, and much the same may be said for lines in Moore. Gunn is undoubtedly in earnest, but the possibility of humour does no harm to an exploration of otherness. Nothing could be further from the ironies that Davie found so smug.

Looking back on the Movement and its works, now roughly fifty years on, its main achievement now strikes one as largely a matter of literary hygiene. This may sound like damning with faint praise, but clearing the Augean stables was a hero's task, and the Movement would have made no impact if the poems written under its banner had not included some great ones. There are poems by Gunn and Davie that fall into that category, but neither of them can quite be seen to exemplify the Movement, especially when one considers their full careers. The poet who unambiguously does is Philip Larkin, who of all the poets of the post-war era remains the most widely admired. No modern poet more subtly captures the inflections of ordinary speech within the constraints of demandingly complex stanzas, and where the tears of things are concerned, he belongs in the company of Wordsworth, Tennyson, and Hardy. What is more, that Larkin has a popular constituency does not seem—as it does in John Betjeman's case—to undermine his canonical status.

At the same time, where Larkin's work as a whole is concerned, it is hard not to sympathize with Davie's exasperation. There is something narrow about his sensibility: not just the provincialism, but the ready defeatism and the resistance to all forms of literary adventure. Gunn was too good a judge of poetry not to recognize Larkin's greatness: 'a wonderful poet,' he says in one interview, 'but a bad influence', and in another:[51]

Larkin, however good he is, is set against rhetoric—rightly perhaps—and set against daring. Daring is just what young poets ought to be making use of when they're trying themselves out, when they're trying their wings in the first place. One of the troubles, I think, with British poetry right now is that the example of Larkin is holding people back... You've got to make your mistakes. Think of your mistakes in any aspect of life: how terrible to lead a youth without mistakes! You're going to learn nothing.

Larkin's loathing of pretentiousness, as Gunn saw it, was a kind of timidity, and some element of risk was for Gunn essential to life. In this he might be thought at odds with Winters and Davie—there was nothing numb about either his life or his work—but it was not quite so simple as that. As is clear from his one important poem about poetry, 'To Yvor Winters, 1955', Gunn saw Winters's stoicism as itself a form of courage. And as we have seen from 'The Slow Pacific Swell', the perspective of the 'landsman' depends on vivid and passionate sensuous perceptions with memories of both ecstasy and danger. Davie in much of his work, especially the early poems, is an apologist for what he calls (with reference to Larkin) a 'poetry of lowered sights and patiently diminished expectations'.[52] His own patience, though, was to prove limited and he began to react against such evident selling short of a great art. In the mid-1960s and 1970s, he opened himself to improbable influences: not only to Pound and Eliot, but to Charles Olson, Edward Dorn and other heroes of the *avant-garde*. He and Gunn soon came to the conviction that the greatest English poem of the later twentieth century was Basil Bunting's *Briggflatts*, the last great monument of Modernism. There was something hugely admirable to Gunn in a person who, by nature conservative and academic, might have settled complacently into a nostalgia for the late Augustans or declared the so-called native English tradition his modernizing outpost. Instead, in his late sixties he was writing *To Scorch or Freeze*: Christian poems, but experimentally modern in manner and, in outlook, challenging to those who look for safety in religion. When Davie died in 1995, Gunn paid tribute to him in a poem: an experimental piece that has fun with their differences but captures

---

[51] *Campbell*, p. 24; Wilmer, *Poets Talking*, p. 7.   [52] WTG, p. 76.

Davie's virtues exactly and, in doing so, unconsciously registers the author's own: both of them inclined to consolidate, but more importantly, both willing—Davie despite himself—to take risks.

To Donald Davie in Heaven

I was reading Auden—But I thought
you didn't like Auden, I said.
Well, I've been reading him again,
and I like him better now, you said.
That was what I admired about you
your ability to regroup
without cynicism, your love of poetry
greater
than your love of consistency.

As in an unruffled fishpond
the fish draw to whatever comes
thinking it something to feed on

there was always something to feed on
your appetite unslaked
for the fortifying and tasty
events of reading.

I try to think of you now
nestling in your own light,
as in Dante, singing to God
the poet and literary critic.

As you enter among them,
the other thousand surfaced glories
—those who sought honour
by bestowing it—
sing at your approach
Lo, one who shall increase our loves.

But maybe less druggy,
a bit plainer,
more Protestant.[53]

[53] *Boss Cupid*, pp. 59–60.

12

Donald Davie, The Movement, and Modernism

William H. Pritchard

As a poet-critic and a thinker about poetry, Donald Davie used the word 'modernism' confidently ('There is no doubt about Robert Graves; no Modernist, he') but did not occupy himself with breaking new ground in clarifying it—his interests were in something other than achieving a good definition. As a poet and critic whose impulses and inclinations as an artist were formative of the directions taken in his criticism, Davie's relation to Modernism can be approached in two ways: either by looking at how his poetry came to terms with, accommodated itself to, or repudiated the principles and practices of Modernist forebears, particularly Yeats, Eliot, and Ezra Pound; or by inspecting his voluminous criticism of these and other Modernist poets in order to suggest his contribution to literary discourse— his right to the title accorded him by Christopher Ricks as the best literary critic in the post-Eliot–Leavis–Empson world. My emphasis will be on the latter approach and will begin by considering his relation to the Movement and its opposition—at least in the work of its most famous members, Philip Larkin and Kingsley Amis—to Modernism.

The story begins in 1956, when Robert Conquest's anthology *New Lines*, appeared. Davie was one of the contributors, thus becoming however briefly a member of the Movement even as he began to detach himself from the group. *New Lines* was reviewed the year after it appeared by Charles Tomlinson in *Essays in Criticism* (7 (2): 208–17). 'The Middlebrow Muse', was a lively attack on the anthology, deploring the 'unconscionable amount of self-regard' shown by many of its contributors, and finding it a sure sign of 'lack of genuineness'. The only good word Tomlinson had to say for any of the poets was to call Thom Gunn more 'promising' than Robert Conquest, and to regret that D. J. Enright and Donald Davie should have shown up as 'fellow-travelers' in this band of brothers (and one sister, Elisabeth Jennings). Tomlinson found Davie 'the least representative chosen poet here', whose recent work seemed to be developing away from his earlier manner—that manner to be observed in his poem 'Remembering the Thirties', one of the poems Conquest included, whose 'heavy iambic swat' to Tomlinson's ears was too pronounced to be sustained over its twelve quatrains. Generalizing about the poets in *New Lines*, Tomlinson said 'they show a singular want of vital awareness of the continuum outside themselves, of the mystery bodied over against them in the created universe, which they fail to experience with any degree of sharpness or to embody with any instress or sensuous depth'.

Davie responded, in the Critical Forum of the magazine's next issue (7 (3): 343), to Tomlinson's charge that ten years ago (in the 1940s) the average level of poetry was vicious while at present, as in *New Lines*, it was merely dull. His defence was minimal indeed, claiming that when the poor or minor poetry of an age is dull rather than vicious, then the poetic tradition is in a healthy state. Although he thinks many of Tomlinson's criticisms of the *New Lines* contributors are just, the 'cultural phenomenon they represent as a group' should not be disparaged. This somewhat contorted attempt to say the least for the anthology and its members, of which he was one, is brought out when juxtaposed, as it was, with D. J. Enright's response to the Tomlinson review. Enright called it 'second-generation vulgarisation which today passes as healthy literary criticism' and said it 'confidently aped Leavisian and Lawrentian gestures, the blank assertion of authority with little behind it except the "right" phraseology and the O.K. names (including even Laforgue, that old Anglo-Saxon invention)' (7 (3): 344). Doubtless part of Davie's much more pacific handling of Tomlinson had to do with his having been Davie's pupil at Cambridge; more deeply it reveals at how early a stage he had become acutely uneasy in being associated with the Movement writers.

Further items testified to his dissociation from the group, such as a 1957 review of Enright's second book of poems, in which Davie found disconcerting an attitude he called 'common-mannerism', an element in the Movement particularly to be detected in Kingsley Amis's critical writing. In Enright's poetry it showed itself in the way references to traditional culture, Oriental or European, were elevated only to be torn down again 'with snarls of disgust'. Davie deplored how impatience with cultural pretentiousness was turning into impatience with culture itself; this he finds 'a very ugly phenomenon'.[1] ('Ugly' is not a commonly used word in aesthetic criticism and here it rings with moral disapproval.) Two years later Davie wrote a glowing review of Tomlinson's *Seeing as Believing* (*Essays in Criticism*, 9 (11): 188), which had been published, with the help of Hugh Kenner, by Kenner's American publisher, MacDowell-Obolensky. Here Davie threw down the gauntlet by insisting that since Tomlinson's models are mainly French and American rather than English, 'he refuses to join the silent conspiracy which now unites all the English poets from Robert Graves down to Philip Larkin, and all the critics, editors, and publishers too, the conspiracy to pretend that Eliot and Pound had never happened'. He went on to add Marianne Moore and Wallace Stevens—presences detectable in Tomlinson's book—as other American poets whose work should have altered the English poetic tradition. One could not find in F. R. Leavis any stronger—or is it any more fantastic?—notion of a conspiracy that united all English poets, critics, and publishers under the same sinister motive. I'm sure Davie did this with deliberate swagger and overstatement, but it is overstatement such as his criticism would continue to thrive on. He hadn't of course then read some future Larkin poems, notably 'White Major', about which Barbara Everett would artfully point out their trafficking with Mallarmé.[2] But what about not mentioning Auden (is he or is he not in the 'conspiracy'?), a poet who surely did not pretend that T. S. Eliot never happened and who was attacked by Graves for his Modernist irresponsibilities? It must have been heady for Tomlinson, reading the review, to imagine himself as single-handedly bucking a conspiracy most recently embodied in *New Lines*.

---

[1] Donald Davie, 'Common-Mannerism' *Listener* (Spring, 1957), reprinted in *The Poet in the Imaginary Museum*, ed. Barry Alpert (New York: Persea Books, 1977).

[2] 'Philip Larkin: After Symbolism', in Donald Davie, *Poets in Their Time* (London: Faber and Faber, 1986).

Finally, as epitaph, there is 'Remembering the Movement',[3] a short prose reflection in which Davie buried the thing almost before it happened. His poem 'Remembering the Thirties' was about English writers from twenty years before; 'Remembering the Movement', if it might to the unwary sound like an affectionate trip down memory lane, was anything but. Its major gist is that 'we' sold out ignobly to—in particular it seemed—knowing readers of magazines like *Essays in Criticism*, readers of the 'high-brow élite' Davie and his friends were catering to. It was those believers in Leavisian 'minority culture', Davie claimed, whom Movement poets were all too ready to woo and placate. As with the stance taken in his review of Tomlinson's poems, Davie was concerned to make out the very worst case that could be made for the tough-minded (so they thought) no-nonsense Movementeers. Not a bit of it, he declared: 'Ours was writing which apologized insistently for its own existence, which squirmed in agonies of embarrassment at being there in print on the page at all.' 'We were deprecating and ingratiating', he charged—as if self-deprecation weren't a perfectly usable human attitude for a poem to display, or as if 'ingratiation' weren't basic to the technique of any poem. (I am thinking of Kenneth Burke's useful definition of literary style as 'ingratiation'.) Davie notes how frequently 'almost' or 'no doubt' or 'perhaps' or 'of course' occur in Movement verse, gestures that might, one would think, reasonably occur in poems spoken by an 'ordinary' person. Whether such gestures justify the charge of 'craven defensiveness' Davie brings against them and against the behavior these poets showed in interviews and other publicity, is a question to be asked.

'Remembering the Movement' is significant, not as a balanced assessment of Davie's sometime associates, but for its announcing two principles that would figure largely in his later thinking and writing about predecessors and contemporaries in the poetry scene. The first was his linking the self-deprecating 'defensive' nature of Movement poetry—its amounting to what he called an act of 'private and public therapy'—with the absence in it of what presumably is a real world outside the poet's head: the absence, in Davie's words, of 'outward and non-human things apprehended crisply for their own sakes'.[4] There is a relation between this homage to the non-human

---

[3] Donald Davie, *The Poet in the Imaginary Museum*, ed. Barry Alpert (Manchester: Carcanet Press. 1977), pp. 72–5.

[4] Ibid., p. 74.

and the wish or hope he had expressed three years earlier at the end of his extremely tendentious criticism of the third of Eliot's *Four Quartets*, 'The Dry Salvages'. This was a wish for—in contradistinction to the symbolist principles on which Eliot composed the *Quartets*—a different sort of poem, 'more in harmony with what was written in Europe before symbolism was thought of'. This would be poetry 'which stands on its own feet...as an independent creation, a thing to be walked round, and as satisfying from one standpoint as another'.[5] It sounds, as if such a hope were linked with the one, expressed in the Movement remembrance, for 'outward and non-human things apprehended crisply for their own sakes'. What's interesting is that the two styles Davie hopes poetry will move away from are, on the one hand, Eliot's Modernist verse that does not try to pretend Mallarmé or Laforgue never existed; on the other, the revisionist common-mannerism of the Movement vernacular. Did he change his mind over the three years, or is there a contradiction here? Or is it, most likely, that both Eliot's powerful and intimidating achievement—which can't be a useful model or influence on Davie's own poetry—and the Movement verse he's concerned to dissociate himself from, were equally to be fended off?

The other principle, indeed obsession, that announced itself in 'Remembering the Movement' was enunciated in its final paragraph containing a sweeping extension of the charge of self-deprecation Davie had brought against Movement writers. This charge could be made about the procedures of most English and a great many American twentieth-century poets. It was being practised blatantly by Auden and Empson—the 'it' being what Davie called 'the manipulation of "tone"', 'tone' being placed within quotation marks. Even such a Modernist as William Carlos Williams, who tried to keep his eyes on 'things' rather than on the reader, was also guilty of, in Davie's strong language, 'the excruciating tone of the *faux-naif*', a tone (and this time the quote marks have been removed) to be found in Williams's American followers as well.

When 'Remembering the Movement' was collected in *The Poet in the Imaginary Museum*, Davie added a brief postscript: 'The occasion for this piece determined its tone. The anger—with myself, as well as with others—is designedly unbuttoned and topical.' A curious way to speak about one's anger, as 'designedly unbuttoned', suggesting that it was more a matter of

---

[5] Davie, 'T.S. Eliot: The End of an Era', in *The Poet in the Imaginary Museum*, p. 41.

strategy than the eruption of outraged feelings. Some years later in an interview, he was asked by Millicent Dillon whether he thought the 'personal voice' she heard in his criticism had to do with his being British rather than American. Davie answered by again using the word 'unbuttoned'. 'A degree of unbuttoned trenchancy, sharpness, a frank avowal of a personal reaction,'[6] he said, was more common in British than in American criticism, and he had detected in himself of late increasing sharpness and impatience. It is as if the designedly unbuttoned tone had grown into second nature, where it was impossible to distinguish sincere occasional impulse from habitual procedure. At any rate, this matter of tone continued to raise Davie's hackles. 'The Rhetoric of Emotion', an essay of 1972 concerned partly with praising Thom Gunn's *Moly* poems for treating inflammatory subjects with coolness—with an absence of tone—ends in a moment of unbuttoned (designedly unbuttoned?) trenchancy by lashing out at 'our fussiness about "tone" (most baleful and most insular of all I. A. Richards's bequests to us.)'.[7] It will be recalled that in *Practical Criticism*, Richards defined tone as the speaker's relation to his audience, 'his sense of how he stands towards those he is addressing'. On the surface it looks as if, forty years after Richards's work, Davie found a preoccupation with tone to issue mainly in 'fussiness'; such a preoccupation was 'baleful' because of its 'insular' propensities, as if to fuss as any poet might about such matters was to convict yourself of being a Little Englander, one who thinks of poems as rhetorical efforts at wooing an audience, rather than as something more admirable, impersonal, done 'for itself', whatever that might be.

After Davie's death in 1995 there was an outpouring of essays about him by various hands, mostly published in the magazine *PN Review* he edited for some years with Michael Schmidt and C. H. Sisson. Schmidt's Carcanet Press has since brought out four important collections of his essays, most of which had gone out of print, and an enlarged volume of his *Collected Poems*. The essay volumes are *A Traveling Man* (2003) and *Two Ways Out of Whitman* (2000), collections respectively of his pieces about the eighteenth century and about American writing, both edited by his widow Doreen Davie. Two further

---

[6] 'Talking to Millicent Dillon', in *Trying to Explain* (Ann Arbor: University of Michigan Press, 1979), p. 34.

[7] Davie, *The Poet in the Imaginary Museum*, pp. 242–8.

collections deal with twentieth-century poets: the first, *With the Grain* (1998), reprints his book on Hardy and his essays on a number of recent English poets, notably Basil Bunting; the second, *Modernist Essays* (2004), take up one or another aspect of the work of Yeats, Pound, and Eliot. These last two volumes were edited and introduced by Clive Wilmer, a critic who makes the strongest case for Davie's achievement as, in Wilmer's words, 'the indispensable thinker about poetry of the later 20th century'. Wilmer concludes his introduction to *Modernist Essays* (p. xiii) by claiming that, for Davie, 'the stature of the three great Modernists seemed to him indisputable but, especially in the case of Eliot, he was never quite at peace with them'. Of course, one hastens to add, with whose poetic achievement was Davie *ever* at peace? The temperamental sharpness he confessed to in the interview, the trenchancy of personal response at which he consistently aimed, precluded being simply 'at peace' with what another poet had written, certainly when the poets were twentieth-century predecessors whose status as 'major' was generally agreed upon. Not totally so of course, particularly with Pound: we remember Robert Conquest's attack on that poet's 'bullfrog' reputation,[8] as well as various comic derogations of Pound and Eliot shared by Amis and Larkin in their correspondence. But it was not just these three Modernist predecessors about whose achievement Davie was ambivalent. Perhaps the most unexpected book he produced in his career was *Thomas Hardy and British Poetry*, in the introduction to which he claimed that the most 'far-reaching influence' on British poetry of the last fifty years (he was writing in 1972) was not Yeats, nor Pound, nor Eliot, but Hardy—'an influence both for good and ill'.[9] Yet even with that warning, a reader like myself who came to the book looking for illumination as to why and where Hardy was a great poet rather than a far-reaching influence, was disappointed. After two chapters in which a number of his poems are taken up, sometimes briefly and adversely, the verdict passed is that Hardy's 'engaging modesty and decent liberalism' was in fact a 'selling-short of the poetic vocation'. Hardy was not 'radical' enough, did not, as a great poet must, go to the roots, and Davie found it unfortunate that so many of his British successors (of whom the Movement poets were surely

[8] 'Ezra Pound', in Robert Conquest, *The Abomination of Moab* (London: Maurice Temple Smith, 1979), pp. 236–56.

[9] Davie, *With the Grain: Essays on Thomas Hardy and Modern British Poetry* (Manchester: Carcanet Press, 1998), p. 23.

central ones) followed his cue. Accordingly the remainder of the book took partial, sometimes sceptical, looks at Larkin, at Amis, at Auden, and at John Betjeman; along with sympathetic appreciations of lesser-known names like Roy Fisher and Jeremy Prynne. The finest piece of critical appreciation Davie bestowed upon Hardy occurs not in the book but in a separately published essay—one of his very best—'Hardy's Virgilian Purples'.[10] Even there though, the appreciation was qualified, in a later postscript he wrote to it in which he said that Hardy's 'European' allusion to Virgil showed that the poet at his best proceeded in a manner not wholly different from Pound's or Joyce's or Eliot's. But in the years since the essay, Davie noted, recent books and essays on the poet were 'still impelled by a wish to prove that Hardy provides a viable insular alternative to the international "modern movement" '. 'I am quite out of sympathy with that endeavour', was his ominous concluding declaration. Surely the shaft is most clearly directed at Larkin's championing of Hardy as such an alternative to the 'international'.

Davie's relation to Modernism as it showed itself in Yeats, in Pound, and in Eliot, is discussed by Clive Wilmer in his introduction to *Modernist Essays* and will be developed here. Of the five essays Davie published on Yeats, by far his most important ones were written early in his career, in the middle 1960s, and focus on Middle Yeats—the Yeats of 'A Prayer for My Daughter', 'Easter 1916', and other poems from *The Wild Swans at Coole* and *Michael Robartes and the Dancer*. Visionary Yeats of the 'great' period Davie more or less ignores, except to discuss 'Blood on the Moon' as a 'fascist' poem. His interest is in Yeats the craftsman who alludes in his poems to Ben Jonson and finds the Renaissance rather than the Romantic poem something to emulate. Wilmer says that in the early essays Yeats is seen from a 'movement-ish perspective' and celebrated for his insistence on the importance of craftsmanship. But 'craftsmanship' is surely not an exclusively Movement concern, and Davie's best critical perceptions about Yeats can hardly be accounted for by any common aim 'Davie and his associates' (Wilmer's words, p. xiv) shared. Rather, as in the following brilliant commentary on 'Easter 1916', we see him at his most rewarding when he takes up the poem's third section:

> Hearts with one purpose alone
> Through summer and winter seem

---

[10] Ibid., pp. 3–19.

> Enchanted to a stone
> To trouble the living stream.
> The horse that comes from the road,
> The rider, the birds that range
> From cloud to tumbling cloud,
> Minute by minute they change;
> A shadow of cloud on the stream
> Changes minute by minute;
> A horse-hoof slides on the brim,
> And a horse plashes within it;
> The long-legged moorhens dive,
> And hens to moor-cocks call;
> Minute by minute they live:
> The stone's in the midst of all.

My ancient copy of Yeats's poems has its margins filled with the attempt to paraphrase that third section. Davie seizes upon the problem—or the marvel—of these lines and comments thus:

> At this point, in fact, 'Easter 1916' goes past the point where exegesis can track its meaning. The imagery of stone and birds, rider and horse and stream, has a multivalency which discursive language cannot compass—and this accrues to these images simply because of the beams which fall upon this poem out of other poems in the same collection. Because Yeats holds and keeps faith in the discursive language, for instance by the sinewiness of his syntax, as his contemporaries Eliot and Pound do not, a moment like this when perceptions pass beyond the discursive reason is poignant in his poetry as it cannot be in theirs, and we do not dream of grudging him the right to acknowledge his defeat and to retire baffled before it, as he does in the last section of the poem.[11]

It may be recalled that 'Easter 1916' is a poem the never-at-a-loss for words Harold Bloom found 'puzzling', although, or perhaps because, it possessed a 'clarity of [its] rhetoric' that made it unlike other Yeats poems.[12] Davie's point about the third section is that it marks a moment when 'clarity' is precisely not the word for its effect on a reader. Wilmer quotes a remark Davie made in reviewing Hugh Kenner's *The Pound Era*, to the effect that Kenner was excellent in showing 'how words on the page, as they come off the page,

[11] Davie, 'Michael Robartes and the Dancer', in *Modernist Essays: Yeats, Pound and Eliot*, ed. Clive Wilmer (Manchester: Carcanet Press, 2004), p. 125.

[12] Harold Bloom, *Yeats* (New York and Oxford: Oxford University Press, 1970), p. 314.

work upon us as we read'. The praise may be directed even more strongly at Davie's own procedures in exploring the question of 'What does it feel like to read X' rather than 'What does X *mean*, how should it be interpreted'.[13] The payoff for such exploration may be seen in his remarks about that third section of 'Easter 1916'.

But for all the salience of his commentary on Middle Yeats, Davie's real engagement with Modernism over the years can be seen in his writings on Eliot and on Pound. His first book on Pound, still a notable piece of criticism, appeared in 1964 when Davie was campaigning for a poetry that recognized a world outside the mind as real and available to be saluted in language. In his chapter on the *Pisan Cantos*, he quotes the 'Brother Wasp' passage ('When the mind swings by a grass-blade | an ant's forefoot shall save you | the clover leaf smells and tastes as its flower') to note that neither Yeats nor Eliot could have written it:

In fact, what lies behind a passage such as this . . . is an attitude of mind that is incompatible with the symbolist's poet's liberation of himself from the laws of time and space as those operate in the observable world. In order to achieve that liberation the poet had to forego any hope or conviction that the world outside was meaningful precisely insofar as it existed in its own right, something other than himself and bodied against him.[14]

He would extend and elaborate the difference between symbolist and non-symbolist poetry in 'Pound and Eliot: A Distinction' where he complicates his usual procedural question ('What does it feel like to read X') by considering how, in the opening of 'Burnt Norton' as in many other passages in *Four Quartets* and in 'Prufrock' as well, 'we have hardly begun reading before we find the poem talking about itself, appealing to the reader with the question: 'So far as you've gone the experience of reading this poem is rather like this, isn't it?'[15] Whatever reservations about the symbolist practice Davie may have had, his demonstration of how it works in the *Quartets* is permanent criticism, as is his treatment of that poem in the essay 'Anglican Eliot'. There he presents us with a bipolar poem, one extreme being the symbolist, Mallarméan, musical, non-discusive one; the other, an extreme prosaicism that also aspires to say something about the condition of England at war.

---

[13] Davie, *Modernist Essays*, p. xv.
[14] Davie, *Studies in Ezra Pound* (Manchester: Carcanet Press, 1999), p. 147.
[15] Davie, *Modernist Essays*, p. 87.

Why should a poet aspire to incorporate, or try to incoporate, such tension in a poem? Davie's conclusion is one of his most memorable formulations, as he supposes such a situation

might come about if a poet compelled by temperament as well as history to school himself in the ironic reticences of Henry James on the one hand and of Jules Laforgue on the other, should find himself wanting to speak to and for a nation which conceives of itself as cornered into a situation which is wholly unironical because not in the least ambiguous. For such a poet (who may be wholly imaginary) I should feel affection as well esteem.[16]

Again, Davie's criticism at its best, as in these remarkable essays on Eliot, gets its energy and audacity from never being at peace with its subject, by always worrying it one more time.

The worrying, of course, went on longest in relation to Pound, through twenty-some essays in addition to the books, and it's not possible here to praise highly enough the interest of these writings, even for the reader unconvinced of Pound's greatness as a poet. Part of Davie's authority as a critic of Pound is his willingness to write off whole sections of the Cantos— like the John Adams and Chinese ones—as unredeemable, and although he struggles hard to make the post-Pisan 'Rock-Drill' and 'Thrones' sections more available, the strain is palpable. So even in an address to the converted, lecturing at a London conference on Pound studies in 1977, he refer to 'us', the exegetes, 'industriously annotating out of Sir Edward Coke Canto 107, without noticing that the English language is in that canto handled with none of the sensitivity that would make those labours worthwhile'.[17] This unwillingness to pass off everything in the long poem as masterly distinguishes him from Hugh Kenner, even though Davie acknowledged more than once that serious study of Pound began with Kenner.

At the close of his address to the Pound conference, he rallied the troops by calling the assembly an act of homage to a great poet and also 'a patriotic demonstration against suffocating insular coziness', one of his perhaps too frequent hits at Little Englandism. Eight years later, in a piece entitled 'Pound's Friends' he insisted that whatever satisfactions and dissatisfactions The Cantos provide, and though they will remain caviar to the general

[16] Ibid., p. 168.   [17] Davie, Studies in Ezra Pound, p. 269.

yet there they sprawl, a labyrinthine ruin (to put the case at its worst) plumb in the middle of whatever we understand by Anglo-American Modernism in poetry. Anyone may be excused for deciding that life is too short for coming to terms with *The Cantos*: but if we make that decision we thereby disqualify ourselves from having any opinion worth listening to, about the poetry in English of this century.[18]

Here is the Davie 'unbuttoned trenchancy' at its extreme, the gauntlet thrown down most provocatively. If in his later years he mellowed in some respects, as in his 70th birthday interview when he indulged in a moment of nostalgia for the Movement, he never wavered in his advocacy of Pound. There's no doubt in my mind that the attachment has much to do with Davie's feelings about his own father, and the matter is made explicit in something he wrote at the end of his life, his last word about Pound titled 'Son of Ezra' published in the year of Davie's death in 1995. He begins with a military analogy, noting that his father was an NCO and like all NCOs both loyal to his superior officer and most fiercely critical of him. Davie speculates that what first drew him to Pound was 'the voice of the NCO in his mess: a voice stroppy and irreverent, yet devoted to authority'.[19] 'It is this voice that offends others by just so much as it appeals to me', he announces, raising the ante more or less to Davie against the world, certainly the world of English letters. In the final paragraph to the essay, he notes its elegiac tone and declares that he would like his own life in writing to be 'considered in the light of Pound's'. His own best stab at explaining this allegiance 'would have to use fuzzy or loaded words like "heroic" and "adventurous", even— or particularly—"magnanimous" '. 'If in my chosen trade I was looking for authority, he more than anyone embodied it.'[20] In other words Davie had something to live up to, 'the stroppy and irreverent voice' of the non-commissioned officer he heard in his poetic father, Pound, and perhaps in his real father, the Barnsley–West Riding one.

Having touched on Davie's relations with the Movement and with his three giant Modernist predecessors, what about the critical attitudes he took or didn't take toward some of his British and American contemporaries? It would be naive to expect that any poet can assume disinterested or 'object-ive' attitudes towards his practising colleagues, but Davie's championing or

[18] Ibid., p. 349.   [19] Davie, *Modernist Essays*, p. 229.   [20] Ibid., p. 241.

marking down of a fellow poet nearly always emanates from a critical prin-
ciple he makes explicit. This distinguishes him from such a critic as Helen
Vendler who, especially on the basis of his later poems, admitted Davie
into the lists of those she has praised, but who has consistently refused to
formulate any criteria that would explain her preferences for X rather than
Y. By contrast, Davie follows the example of Yvor Winters, for whom criteria
were everything. There is as well the example of T. S. Eliot who, in *The Sacred
Wood* and with Aristotle in mind, spoke of intelligence 'swiftly operating the
analysis of sensation to the point of principle and definition'.[21]

One of his key principles had been announced in 'The Rhetoric of
Emotion' when he spoke against 'the baleful and insular matter of "tone"' as
all-important determinant of a poem's virtue. Five years later he published
an important article on Basil Bunting, the first of a number on the poet. In
'English and American in *Briggflatts*',[22] Davie sought to account for Bunting's
being ignored by English readers of contemporary poetry, just as, he finds,
the American 'objectivists' like Louis Zukofsky, George Oppen, and Lorine
Niedecker are ignored by American readers. He proposes that in England
at least, readers 'have got used to being cajoled and coaxed, at all events
sedulously *attended to* by their poets'. For this he blames, in part, teachers in
English classrooms who persuade children that reading a poem is 'a matter
of responding to nudges that the poet, on this showing debased into a rhet-
orician, is supposedly at every point administering to you'. John Berryman,
whom Davie calls 'at times a very affecting writer indeed', does so 'nudge and
cajole and coax his readers, in a way that one can be sure Americans such as
Oppen and Zukofsky are offended and incensed by'. Davie is on the side of
those Americans, and the Englishman, Bunting, who share the 'wholesome
conviction' 'that a poem is a transaction between the poet and his subject
more than it is a transaction between the poet and his reader'. So the good
reader is conceived as someone who merely sits in on or listens to a 'transac-
tion' that he is not a party to, rather than someone manipulated by suasions
of the poet as rhetorician.

I find this a strange argument and perhaps it should be taken as one
(another one) of the extravagant formulations Davie has made throughout
his career, with the hope of jolting complacent readers into entertaining

[21] T. S. Eliot, *The Sacred Wood* (London: Methuen, 1920), p. 11.
[22] Davie, *With the Grain*, pp. 275–83.

a new thought. But suppose we take it seriously and see to what extent it justifies or rationalizes Davie's preferences among his English and American contemporaries. No disputing tastes of course, yet to this reader Davie's seem extremely odd ones, especially in relation to poets he—at least in his criticism and reviewing—has little or no time for. Among his American contemporaries, as is evident from their names above, Oppen and Zukofsky are given good marks; Charles Olson and other Black Mountain poets such as Robert Creeley receive some attention, respectful if not wholly favourable. Davie's enthusiasm for Ed Dorn, who joined him for a time during Davie's years at the University of Essex, is patent, and he also admires Samuel Menashe. Of poets in the generation that preceded him, he has good words for Winters and Allen Tate and not-so-good words for William Carlos Williams, who should have been in the 'good' Modernist group with Pound and the Objectivists, but whose poems Davie mainly can't abide. This we may call the positive side; on the other one—not so much a negative as an under-described side—can be grouped the 'confessional' poets Lowell and Berryman, to whom Davie's responses were mixed; the sometimes confessional, surely rhetorical appeals of Jarrell and Theodore Roethke; and Elizabeth Bishop, however one would describe her. Then there is the triumvirate of American Formalist masters—Richard Wilbur, Anthony Hecht, and James Merrill—whom Davie completely ignores.

There are different though related ways to understand his relation to American poets of the last century. One of them has to do with the spirit of place. Davie first encountered America, as it were, when as a postwar student at Cambridge he discovered Yvor Winters's *In Defense of Reason*, wrote to Winters, and over the course of reading Winters's criticism and letters, learned, he said, much about poetry, particularly poetic rhythm and metre. A year spent teaching at Santa Barbara in 1958 futher extended his American 'side', which would be seriously developed in the ten years he spent teaching at Winters's university, Stanford, 1968–78. Davie's America was very much the far West (he also spent a term in the 1950s at Grinnell College in Iowa); later would come the ten years at Vanderbilt preceding his retirement and move back to England. Except for one semester at Smith College, he neglected the Atlantic seaboard—the New York/Boston axis where so many poets taught and flourished. My sense is that his attraction to Winters's poetry, and later to the very different but equally unfashionable, by academic 'Eastern' standards, work of the Objectivists, Olson, and Dorn, had to do as much as anything with an adventurous desire *not* to cast his vote for poets—like Wilbur, Hecht, Merrill, just to name three—who were at peace with old-fashioned English verse in traditional forms, no matter how freshly and inventively they used those forms.

Yet as anyone will immediately ask, how can admiration for Yvor Winters's poems and critical principles square with the seventy-five or so pages that conclude Davie's *Two Ways Out of Whitman*, containing celebrations of Zukofsky, Oppen, Carl Rakosi, Olson, Dorn, with even a friendly nod to, of all people, John Ashbery? They don't square with admiration for Winters, anymore than they do with the pages from this volume devoted to rescuing Allen Tate from oblivion. In 1977, interviewed by Dana Gioia and asked about his association with the Movement, Davie rather wistfully looked back and then around him in America, for some contemporary movement 'in which variously talented but serious writers clung to their little things in common for a while'.[23] He thought that would be a good thing to have happen; it might do something to make the landscape less 'eclectic' and might give poets something to focus on. The Black Mountaineers, he said, were such a movement, but that, like the English one, was history.

Davie's eye was able to find no rallying ground by which sense could be made out of the American—or English—poetic scene in the final decades of the last century; perhaps because of this his celebrations of individual talents have something overblown and under-criticized about them. I noted this way back in 1971 in reviewing a volume of essays, *The Survival of Poetry* (edited by Martin Dodsworth), that led off with Davie on the Black Mountain group. I found him to be 'advertising' rather than criticizing the product when he claimed that for those poets it would not do to 'dissect' specimen poems in a manner of 'the graduate seminar class which spends a happy hour winkling out the symbols and the ambiguities from a dozen lines of Robert Lowell or Allen Tate or Ted Hughes'.[24] This special treatment, and pleading, was evident in Davie's willingness, in this essay and others collected in *Two Ways out of Whitman*, to make large quotation with minimal commentary seek to do for a more critical presentation of the poet's work. In 'Two Kinds of Magnanimity', for example, he casts a cold eye on Charles Olson's poems,

[23] Davie, *Trying to Explain*, p. 207.
[24] 'The Black Mountain Poets: Charles Olson and Edward Dorn', reprinted in Donald Davie, *Two Ways Out of Whitman*, ed. Doreen Davie (Manchester: Carcanet Press, 2000), p. 162.

'marred as they are on nearly every page by solecisms and gaucheries, by arbitrary coarseness in diction, punctuation, syntax, lineation'.[25] After which he proceeds to make the case for Olson nonetheless.

The moral seems to be that when Davie put himself to 'positive' appreciation of the underdog, the underappreciated, he denied himself the right to quarrel with the writer in question, as if to say X has enough detractors already, why should I heap on further adverse commentary? But without such quarrelling, so important a feature in his criticism of Modernist predecessors, his recommendations of Zukofsky, Oppen, and the Black Mountaineers offer little, to these eyes, in the line of pertinent criticism. One finds something similar happening with regard to the Whitman who figures in the title of his writings about American poetry. The title essay, 'Two Ways out of Whitman' pays stimulating and sceptical attention to then recent work by William Carlos Williams and Theodore Roethke, neither of whose 'way' in the volumes to hand Davie finds satisfactory. But the only piece that deals with the great precursor directly is the shortest one in the volume, a 1968 *Guardian* review of a selection of Whitman's work edited by Donald Hall. Titled 'Coming to Terms with Whitman', that is exactly what this five-paragraph review *doesn't* do—or does only in the most casually assertive manner. For after noting Yvor Winters's charge that Whitman as sage was 'profoundly and dangerously irresponsible' (Winters had gone so far as to argue that Hart Crane's suicide was the inevitable consequence of his taking Whitman and Emerson seriously), Davie executes a striking turnabout. Calling Whitman a confessional poet who must be allowed the right to be irresponsible, he notes that articulate British readers of the poet refuse to make this concession, then states in a new paragraph:

We shall have to learn to do so. For reluctantly and with embarrassment I record for what it is worth my own testimony: reading *Song of Myself* in this selection I found myself reading a great poem, invigorating and liberating.[26]

He adds that after this 'undeniable' experience, his ideas about poetry and morality will have to undergo a change, at which exciting and surprising point the review ends. He was never to return to Whitman again in print, and as for his ideas about poetry and morality undergoing a change, I fail to see that this portentous vow was ever followed.

---

[25] Davie, *Studies in Ezra Pound*, p. 254.   [26] Davie, *Two Ways Out of Whitman*, p. 63.

Twenty years later, in 1987, he began a review of *The Collected Poems of William Carlos Williams* by declaring 'Williams is the most embarrassing poet in the language, surpassing even Whitman'.[27] Davie never changed his mind about Williams and was impervious to the efforts of two critics he greatly admired—Hugh Kenner and Charles Tomlinson—on the poet's behalf. Aside from allowing a few early Williams poems to have merit, like 'The Widow's Lament in Springtime' and 'To Waken an Old Lady', Davie treated Williams as Modernism's Dumb Ox, calling his most famous poem, 'The Red Wheelbarrow', a 'trivial and self-preening squib'[28]—something that surely needed saying. With Williams, Davie didn't need to act as advocate—the poet had plenty of advocates and followers—so was free to provide vigorous and useful demurs and acceptances toward a number of Williams's poems, by way of assessing an achievement more 'precarious and perverse' than Black Mountaineers and Objectivists would admit. This, however, does not mean that we need accept his invitation to admire certain of Williams's followers—Robert Creeley and Ed Dorn for example—more than Williams himself.

Finally let me return briefly to this congeries of the Movement, Modernism, and Donald Davie. And to England, the history of whose poetry from 1960 to 1988 he treated in his volume *Under Briggflatts* (Carcanet, 1989). This odd and in many ways unsatisfactory book is nonetheless full of interest. In this his last polemic, though he denied in the preface it was a polemic, he proposed to commemorate and promote certain British authors as 'however modestly, canonical'. He also admits that his judgements are disputable, although he had not come by them lightly. Accordingly I will dispute, beginning with the title. What does it mean? That British poets have written, or should have written under the aegis of Basil Bunting's poem? Or that *Briggflatts* towers above all other poetry written during the past thirty years? (The latter seems to have been the case, since he would later call Bunting 'the master of us all'.) For an uninstructed reader like myself who finds that though there are attractive effects in the twenty pages of *Briggflatts*, Peter Dale's judgement that the poem is 'tediously dominated by the simple sentence' is incontrovertible. What I should call, without demonstrating it, Davie's overvaluation of Bunting goes hand in hand with an undervaluing of Movement writers—a final putting of them in their place. On the evidence of *Under Briggflatts*, that

---

[27] Ibid., p. 64.   [28] Ibid., p. 68.

place in the history of poetry in Great Britain is not a significant one. Messrs Conquest and Wain are mentioned, but not for any poetry they have written. Elizabeth Jennings and John Holloway are absent; so, more questionably, is D. J. Enright except for a tiny mention in a footnote. Kingsley Amis appears once, in the course of Davie's discussion of a Tony Harrison poem whose 'combination of formality with coarse sentiment' recalls Amis.

That leaves Larkin and Gunn. The former is acknowledged to be, along with Seamus Heaney and Ted Hughes, the only British poets to command a 'public' rather than a 'following'. (Davie calls Auden and Betjeman 'special cases'.) On the evidence of his pages about Larkin in this volume, having a public is nothing to celebrate. In the book on Hardy, Davie devoted a chapter to landscapes in Larkin's poetry, with 'Water' and 'The Whitsun Weddings' as notable examples. *Under Briggflatts* contains nothing comparable, but does contain the following about Larkin: 'The career, as distinct from the poetry (some of which will surely endure), calls out for sensitive and searching study.'[29] The enduring qualities of Larkin's poetry are nodded at in a parenthesis: evidently it doesn't demand—or Davie refuses in this history to give it—sensitive and searching study. Why this refusal to commemorate at least by singling out what in Larkin's verse will endure? The answer is, I'm afraid, that Davie sees Larkin less as a poet than as a portent of the English reading public's diminished expectations. If Larkin's subject matter was inevitably 'lowering' ('lowering' is a word John Wain used about R. S. Thomas's poetry), Davie cautions that to write in such a 'sweetly formal way' and to 'set up that way of working as a norm runs the risk of overvaluing a suave melancholy, the poignantly managed dying fall'. He adds, 'it is a risk to which admirers of Larkin, that poet of very "lowering" apprehensions are particularly prone'.[30] It seems then that Larkin's public has been seduced by 'tone', by a rhetoric that ministers to admirers who were unable to appreciate (although Davie doesn't say this explicitly) the more impersonal, sterner transactions between the poet and something outside him—the non-human. In the pages where Larkin figures in *Under Briggflatts*, I find but a single reference (and that parenthetical) of positive commemoration, that to Larkin's great poem 'The Explosion'.

---

[29] Davie, *Under Briggflatts: A History of Poetry in Great Britain 1960–1988* (Manchester: Carcanet Press, 1989), p. 220.

[30] Ibid., p. 148.

I conclude with Thom Gunn with whom Davie felt a kinship. 'There is no one of my contemporaries I respect more', he declared about Gunn in a *PN Review* salute on the poet's sixtieth birthday. It was partly their shared admiration for Yvor Winters; partly a matter of them having both taken up residence, for many years, in California. Davie once referred to Gunn as the 'scrupulous expatriate', and he would not have minded being so named himself. After Davie's death, Gunn in an interview called him 'consistently supportive, very kind to me'. But also 'very against queers', and Gunn understood him to have said, reviewing *The Passages of Joy*, that unlike Gunn's earlier books, 'Davie couldn't admire *Passages of Joy* because it advocated homosexuality'. Actually what Davie had said, extravagantly, in the review and in *Under Briggflatts*, was that Gunn's commitment to 'Gay Liberation' was such as to alienate him from the seventeenth-century English poets whom he had so fruitfully drawn on in his earlier work. In making 'experience' the true test of worth, rather than any anterior moral idea or principle, Gunn had sacrificed 'resonances' from pre-Enlightenment poets. But, Davie added, 'it could always be maintained that the objectives of Gay Liberation were objectives so obviously just and overdue' that 'the sacrifices of such resonances and continuities was a small price to pay'.[31] It could be maintained, though Davie didn't exactly maintain it; yet he singled out for praise the 'chaste' diction of two poems from that volume, 'Expression' and 'Night Taxi'.

Gunn said in the interview that part of his next volume, *The Man with Night Sweats*, was written to show Davie that 'what I hoped he would admit was good poetry could be written out of this kind of sexuality'. And in conversations subsequent to the volume, Davie admitted Gunn had made a point. And though, Gunn added, he thought Davie's own point of view was 'strangely ridiculous, Davie was not a ridiculous man—he was a good thinker and a good critic'.[32]

[31] Ibid., pp. 180–1.

[32] Quoted in Peter Hennessey, *Outside the Lines: Talking with Contemporary Gay Poets* (Ann Arbor: University of Michigan Press, 2005).

13

How It Seemed Then: An Autobiographical Anecdotal Essay

Anthony Thwaite

When I first began to write poems and to read them voluntarily, in 1945, coming up to the age of 15, I fairly rapidly adopted a large and contradictory number of influences: Rupert Brooke, T. S. Eliot, David Gascoyne, George Barker, Henry Treece (a sort of Dylan Thomas-and-water, before I discovered Thomas himself), Hart Crane. At the same time, I discovered earlier poets: Blake, Langland, George Herbert.

When I arrived at Oxford, to take up the scholarship in English I had won in December 1948, the year was actually 1952. I had, in a sense, messed about for three years, doing my compulsory army service—partly in Libya—and rather desperately getting the qualification in Latin that was necessary for Oxford entrance in those days. But I had also been copiously writing poems, and reading voraciously. The first poems I published in Oxford were full-blooded, full-throated George Barkerisms. At the same time, I had certainly read the poets who are usually cited as among the immediate influences on the Movement: Edwin Muir, Robert Graves, William Empson. At school in Bath, in 1948, a young English master arrived for a term or so, a man called

Fowler, who was besotted with Empson, and I remember puzzling with him through 'Invitation to Juno':

> Lucretius could not credit centaurs;
> Such bicycle he deemed asynchronous.
> 'Man superannuates the horse;
> Horse pulses will not gear with ours.'

This was a couple of years before John Wain's famous essay in *Penguin New Writing*,[1] which is usually seen as the beginning of Empson's influence. At Oxford in 1952 there was a good deal of fascination with Empson; you can see it in Al Alvarez's poems then, in some of George MacBeth's, and in some of Jonathan Price's. You can see it, too, in some of the Cambridge poetry of the early 1950s. In *Isis*, the Oxford student weekly, I reviewed *Cambridge Poetry 1951–52*, edited by Thom Gunn—probably the first occasion I'd come across Gunn's name.[2] The anthology included stuff like this, from a poem called 'Artifect' by P. J. Head:

> Beam resolution needs two walls of will.
> Not any random ground bears rows of bricks;
> Too wet or dry brings rot. Who cannot kill
> His plaster has for ceiling roof of sticks.

At the same time, there was enthusiasm for much more 'romantic' flavours. In my first term, in October 1952, Dylan Thomas came to the Poetry Society and read to a packed Rhodes House: about 600 people. He put on what I later learned was his usual display—half-drunk, very funny, a great performer, but also, interestingly, reading a lot of poems by other people: Hardy, Yeats, William Plomer, Henry Reed (Reed's marvellous parody of Eliot, 'Chard Whitlow'). George Barker (whom I first read in 1947, and first met in 1948) came on another occasion, at my invitation, when I was secretary of the Poetry Society, and his sardonic, slightly menacing manner was powerful.

But in Oxford in the early 1950s, I was also aware of alternative lines. In my *Isis* review of *Poetry from Cambridge* I thought I noticed something else:

It is something which I can grace with no more fresh a name than *Neo-Augustan*, and that is a superficial, snap-judgment label, for it applies only to a cleanness of diction

---

[1] 'Ambiguous Gifts', *Penguin New Writing*, no. 40, 1950.
[2] 'The New Leanness', *Isis*, 29 April 1953.

and a spare coolness of form which English poetry has not had...since the best of
Pope and Dryden, or before that the sinews and muscle of Donne.

My review is dated 29 April 1953, so you might think that I had been reading
Donald Davie's *Purity of Diction in English Verse*, published in 1952, but I don't
think I was even aware of the book. I may have read some of Davie's poems
in the journals, but nothing had stuck in my head.

So what was the 'feeling in the air' in 1952, 1953? I think it was a lot more
various than people nowadays imagine. The monumental figure on the liter-
ary scene in Oxford at that time was an American graduate student, Donald
Hall, a few years older than everyone else (born 1927); a large man, with a
solid, confident presence. He'd been at Harvard, won the Newdigate Prize
in Oxford in the summer of 1952 with an early-Robert Lowell-like poem
called 'Exile', and talked knowledgeably and intimately about 'Tom' Eliot
and 'Cal' Lowell and 'Dick' Wilbur. He selected those who were going to be
the Fantasy Poets—the slim pamphlets printed on a hand-press by Oscar
Mellor, a painter who lived a few miles outside Oxford, near Eynsham. The
first Fantasy Poets pamphlet had been published not long before I arrived
at Oxford: it was by Elizabeth Jennings, whom I met in my first few weeks.
She was a recent graduate of St Anne's, working on the issue desk in Oxford
Public Library. She was like a Botticelli angel—so lovely, so pure. And that
was true of her poems, too.

Against that, I ought to set my first memory of Geoffrey Hill, whom I also
met during my first term, at a rather drunken party in St Edmund Hall, to
which I had been invited by someone with whom I had just been doing a
fortnight's compulsory Territorial Army camp. This man, Bob Lunn, said to
me, at some late point in the evening: 'Anthony, you're a poet, aren't you?
Read us a poem.' So I fetched out of a pocket some recently composed some-
thing, and read it. No sooner had I finished than, on the other side of the
room, a tall dark young ploughboy stood up, swaying slightly, and began to
recite, from memory:

> Against the burly air I strode,
> Where the tight ocean heaved its load,
> Crying the miracles of God...[3]

---

[3] The opening lines of 'Genesis', the first poem of Hill's *For the Unfallen: Poems, 1952–1958* (London:
André Deutsch, 1959).

This was the 20-year-old Geoffrey Hill, from Keble College. As Larkin wrote of Amis on their first encounter: 'For the first time I felt I was in the presence of a talent greater than my own...' Geoffrey's Fantasy Press pamphlet was published a week or so later.

The young-poet population of Oxford at that time was rather remarkable. Apart from Donald Hall, Elizabeth Jennings, and Geoffrey Hill, there were Al Alvarez, George MacBeth, Jonathan Price, Alan Brownjohn, Jenny Joseph, Alistair Elliot, Adrian Mitchell (later to become a 'pop' poet), and several others, including Edward Lucie-Smith, soon to be one of the eminences of the 'Group'. There was for a time Adrienne Cecile Rich (later dropping the 'Cecile'), a graduate student from America who had already published a first book, with an introduction by Auden, in the Yale Younger Poets series, and whose second publication was a Fantasy Press pamphlet. As I've already hinted, simply listing these names shows what a variety of types and styles there were.

As far as Cambridge is concerned, we became increasingly aware of Thom Gunn, who indeed was invited to Oxford by Don Hall almost as if he were a sort of official delegate from Cambridge. We liked and admired his poems even before his Fantasy Poets pamphlet was published in 1953, and then his Fantasy Press book *Fighting Terms* in 1954. A poetry magazine in Oxford, edited by George MacBeth, J. S. Bingham, and myself, called *Trio*, first published several of Gunn's poems, and later an enthusiastic review of his pamphlet.

But of the other names cited in the 1954 *Spectator* articles by Anthony Hartley and by J. D. Scott—in particular 'In the Movement' by the anonymous Scott—I didn't actually lump them together. Some names I didn't know at all. Elizabeth Jennings I knew, but she wasn't I think mentioned in either the Hartley or the Scott articles. Kingsley Amis—well, initially just one poem I had read in the little magazine *Outposts* while I was still at school in 1949: a poem called 'Masters', rather Audenesque, but so remarkable that on the strength of it I asked him in 1953 to travel from Swansea to take part in an Oxford University Poetry Society brains trust, held early in 1954, just after the publication of *Lucky Jim* in January that year: in other words, I had invited him several months before that famous book was published. Robert Conquest: I do remember writing him a fan-letter in, I think, 1951, when I was a sergeant doing my army service in British-administered Libya—I had read and liked a poem of his on Hart Crane published in the *Listener*, and he replied genially; but I think I knew nothing else about him. John Holloway:

nothing. D.J. Enright: I saw his poems here and there in magazines, but I didn't, then, much respond to them: a bit loose and baggy, I thought. Later, in 1955 and 1956, when we were both teaching in Japan, I got to know and like and admire him; but not in 1952–3. John Wain: I don't remember his own poems at that time, though I must have read some.

As for Philip Larkin, I read, in the *Spectator*, such poems as 'Wires' and a few others in 1953; and an undergraduate at Corpus Christi, Graham Bury, urged me to read the novel *Jill* (his 'Oxford' novel, published by the Fortune Press in 1946). He also told me this man Larkin had published a little pamphlet called *XX Poems*, which I duly ordered through Blackwell's bookshop in Oxford, paying four shillings and sixpence for it. I was very impressed. (It goes for about £2,000 these days. There were only a hundred copies.)

But I didn't immediately link these people together. In the summer of 1953, the publisher Peter Owen brought out a very miscellaneous anthology called *Springtime*, edited by G. S. Fraser and Iain Fletcher. Somehow or other—perhaps because I was literary editor of *Isis* at the time—a Peter Owen rep. put a copy of this 'Anthology of Young Poets and Writers' in my hands, and I inserted into *Trio* no. 4 (Summer 1953) the following anonymous piece:

This anthology is a collection of poems, translations and poetic-prose by British writers under an arbitrary 30. Among them are three well-known Oxford writers: Elizabeth Jennings, A. Alvarez and Donald Hall. Other particularly promising contributors are Kingsley Amis, Thom Gunn, Philip Larkin and John Wain. The introduction, an expanded version of which was given as a talk by Mr Fraser to the O.U. Poetry Society, classifies the contributors under six main headings: the 'Empsonians' have a distinct lead over the others, in both quantity and quality, and it would seem that the editors, realising this, tried to make a representative balance by including some freer work which stands up rather badly to comparison.

The book is worth buying, however, as an interesting forecast of possible trends during the next five or ten years, and as an opportunity to read several accomplished poems by the seven contributors mentioned.

Fraser and Fletcher's six introductory headings were: Academics (Davie), Empsonians (Alvarez, Amis, Gunn, Wain), Neo-Decadents (Thomas Blackburn), Naked Sensitives (Iris Orton), Sophisticates (Ithell Colquhoun, Arthur Boyars, Margaret Crosland, Erik de Mauny, Michael Harari) and Regionalists (Sydney Goodsir Smith, Robin [sic] Garioch, Tom Scott, and— presumably because he was living in Belfast at the time—Philip Larkin).

When, about a year later, I read the Anthony Hartley and J. D. Scott pieces in the *Spectator*, I didn't have any sort of blinding revelation. Indeed, I was a bit irritated by, and contemptuous of, 'In the Movement', as I demonstrated in a facetious letter published the following week, 8 October 1954:

Sir, I was interested to read 'In the Movement,' the *Spectator*'s first literary leading article. It seemed to have the importance of a White Paper in a field where previous remarks merely had the nature of, say, inter-departmental memoranda. For some time one had noticed these Civil Servants (let us put them in the Ministry of Literary Education) industriously worrying themselves into planning a new, an entirely and radically new, School. Everything looked splendid on paper. True, there was a lot of previous neglect and mismanagement to put right: Mr Macspaunday's attempt to merge the YCL with the public school system had failed shabbily, and even worse was Mr N. Apocalypse's Anglo-Welsh Free School (a great deal of flowery language, but so *little* learned). But now (we were told) here was a new chance—a chance to mould the young men of Britain into a 'new toughness' (as one eminent Under-Secretary put it), a chance to make them 'sceptical, robust, ironic' and, above all, 'anti-wet.' A headmaster, Mr William Empson, had been chosen, and several notable assistants, such as Mr Robert Graves and Dr F. R. Leavis. The first pupils had even been enrolled, and the telephone was busy between one Min. of Lit. Ed. colleague and another: 'Shall we take T. Gunn and D. Davie?' 'Certainly; just the sort we're looking for.' 'What about B. or W.?' 'My dear chap, certainly not: I happen to know that neither of them went to Oxford and Cambridge Council School, and what could we possibly do with them without that? I hate, for one thing, to contemplate what the Ministry Press (The Reading Fantasy) would think of them.'

And then your White Paper was published. A strange document, tentative in some places, assured—perhaps even to the point of complacency—in others. There was appropriate humility about what the School had achieved ('It is not very much'), but plenty of emphasis that the whole project was 'interesting.' And the peroration, if one can speak like this of such a sober report, was masterly in its rhetoric: 'a part... of that tide which is pulling us through the Fifties and towards the Sixties.' If it had been the Head's Speech on Speech Day, and if there had been any parents there to listen to it, and if, listening, they had understood it, they would certainly have clapped like mad.

But one thing does seem rather extraordinary to me, and I speak as one who has had a little experience of this sort of education myself. I've had the good luck to speak to two or three of these young chaps who (the Ministry says) are at the School, chaps like young Gunn and Wain; and all of them deny that they've been there, or are there now, or intend to go. This is very odd, more odd than the absence of a teaching staff. And yet the Ministry goes on publishing Progress Reports, and even a White Paper like your own, all of them telling about the keen team spirit of young Gunn, etc. You know, sometimes I can't help wondering whether the School even exists at all. Or would that be putting the men at the Ministry out of a job?

Yours faithfully,
ANTHONY THWAITE
Christ Church, Oxford

If this outburst at what looked like opportunism needs a bit of footnoting today, perhaps I should point out that by 'B' or 'W' I almost certainly meant Bernard Bergonzi and Gordon Wharton, at that time young non-university poets. Bergonzi later became a distinguished critic and academic. I don't know what eventually happened to Wharton, but a little later he published a good Fantasy Press booklet and, in 1957, a collection of eighteen poems, *Errors of Observation*, from the University of Reading School of Art—an outfit which also published early books of poems by Amis and Wain: hence my silly joke about 'the Ministry Press (The Reading Fantasy)' in my *Spectator* letter. It was Wharton who produced what I think of as the classic Movement line, full of flat portentousness, in a villanelle called 'Paradise Lost':

The knives and forks are washed and put away.

If in this piece I seem to have sounded blasé, or in any way contemptuous of all this 1950s stuff, it hasn't been my intention. It was for me a lovely time, a time when I wrote like a man possessed, when in 1953 my own Fantasy Press pamphlet was published (the one after Thom Gunn's), when in 1954 and 1955 all the London literary periodicals published my poems, when I made my first broadcasts, when I was (I felt) on the edge of something big. Soon I fell in love, in 1955 got married and went with my wife to teach in Japan, and for two years almost—but not quite—detached myself from English literary life.

It was in Tokyo, late in 1955, that my pre-publication subscriber's copy of Larkin's *The Less Deceived* arrived. Reading this book did, I suppose, in some sense change my life. For the next ten or so years many of my poems were influenced by Larkin. In July 1958, back in England, working as a young BBC radio producer, I met Larkin for the first time, and we became friends. Involved as I was with him for the rest of his lifetime, as radio producer, as editor and correspondent, then as one of his chosen literary executors, and finally as his posthumous editor, it is, I know, almost inevitable that my link with Larkin has been made much of, as a matter of discipleship. (I remember being approached in 1973, when I was putting in a stint as a 'visiting professor' at Kuwait University, by a young Kuwaiti in full splendour of traditional robes and head-dress, who earnestly inquired: 'Is it true, sir, that you may be described as a disciple of Philip Larkin?' I felt I'd been transported back to Biblical times.) But I hope the earlier parts of this memoir show that the literary atmosphere in which I grew up, from 1945 onwards, doesn't give itself to simple characterization. Even now, in my late seventies, in my imagination George Barker and Philip Larkin can, and do, co-exist.

14

New Lines in 1956

Eric Homberger

New Lines, Robert Conquest's anthology of younger poets, was published in June 1956.[1] His selection of contributors and forceful introduction seemed a statement of 'new bearings' in English poetry. *New Lines* was understood at once as marking a watershed, a change of sensibility. Of course, sensibility changes, and there have been plentiful shifts of taste and tone during the half-century since the publication of Conquest's anthology. The passion for formal structures, the most traditional aspect of *New Lines*, has not quite shaped the future. But the anthology does what it set out to do, and with such confidence, that it is hard to see how we can make sense of English poetry in the twentieth century without it. John Press described *New Lines* as 'arguably the most influential anthology of contemporary poetry that has appeared since the end of World War II'.[2]

[1] Robert Conquest (ed.), *New Lines: An Anthology* (London: Macmillan, 1956). Conquest substantially weighted the contents towards Oxford poets: Elizabeth Jennings, John Holloway, Philip Larkin, Kingsley Amis, Conquest, and John Wain, adding Thom Gunn, D. J. Enright, and Donald Davie from Cambridge. *New Lines* was reprinted in 1956, 1957, and 1962. Further references in the text. Conquest's *New Lines—II* (London: Macmillan, 1963), with a 16-page introduction, was a more representative survey of British poetry, adding sixteen contributors to the original nine in *New Lines*. Only one poet, John Holloway, failed to make the cut. He was the one poet of the original nine on whom Larkin was not keen. See Larkin to Conquest, 14 April 1955, Thwaite (ed.), *Selected Letters of Philip Larkin 1940–1985* (London: Faber & Faber, 1992), p. 239.

[2] John Press, 'Robert Conquest', in Thomas Riggs (ed.), *Contemporary Poets*, 7th edn. (London: St. James Press, 2001), p. 196. Press published an admiring review of *New Lines* in *London Magazine*, 3 (October 1956), pp. 71–7.

New Lines was understood in 1956, and since, to be a 'Movement' anthology. And the story of that new thing in English letters hangs on the role played by two journalists, and their magazine, *The Spectator*. Anthony Hartley announced in *The Spectator* in August 1954 that there was a 'new movement' in contemporary poetry.[3] 'We are now', he confidently wrote, 'in the presence of the only considerable movement in English poetry since the Thirties'. Hartley identified a common tone among the younger poets: they were cool, analytical, dissenting, suspicious of rhetoric. Their work embodied a 'liberalism distrustful of too much richness or too much fanaticism, austere and sceptical'. Something of a poet himself, Hartley had known Larkin, Amis, and Wain at Oxford. He joined the staff of *The Spectator* in 1953, at the age of 28, as assistant to J. D. Scott. In addition to a regular routine of reviewing new plays, and some general cultural journalism, he also wrote about new poetry. Hartley clearly hoped to become a player in the 1950s literary scene, rather grandly offering to help Amis place his poems with Faber & Faber. Whether his article in *The Spectator* was a concerted puff, at the instigation of the poets themselves (most of whom he seemed to know), we cannot say.[4] In 1954 several of the *New Lines* contributors were writing for *The Spectator*; some were old Oxford acquaintances; some were in fairly informal contact. 'Then Hilly and Bruce and I went to London', Amis wrote to Larkin, 'and I met the Spectator lot who all seemed very decent.... Then we went and saw Tony Hartley and John [J. D.] Scott in a pub... and then Hartley and Hilly and I went and saw Ken Tynan and his wife, but I was so pissed I could hardly speak'.[5]

Just over a month later Hartley's boss, J. D. Scott, literary editor of *The Spectator*, published an unsigned summary of the new spirit among younger writers, titled 'In the Movement':

---

[3] Anthony Hartley, 'Poets of the Fifties', *The Spectator*, 27 August 1954, pp. 260–1, and a letter in reply by Bernard Bergonzi, 3 September 1954, p. 280. Hartley was reviewing Fantasy Press publications by Gunn and George MacBeth, and Fantasy pamphlets by Davie and Jonathan Price. Rather unhelpfully, the same title ('Poets of the Fifties') was used when Hartley reviewed *New Lines* on 20 July 1956.

[4] Larkin thoroughly deplored the literary tipsters on the review pages like Hartley and G. S. Fraser who were 'very stupidly crying us all up these days: take my word for it, people will get very sick of us... UNLESS they produce some unassailably good work, I think the tide will turn rapidly & they will be rapidly discredited. I'm sure I don't care.' Larkin to Patsy Strang, 9 October 1954, in Thwaite (ed.), *Selected Letters of Philip Larkin*, p. 230.

[5] Amis to Larkin, 14 March 1954, in Zachary Leader (ed.), *The Letters of Kingsley Amis* (New York: Talk Miramax/Hyperion, 2001), p. 376.

So it's goodbye to all those rather sad little discussions about 'how the writer ought to live', and it's goodbye to the little magazine and 'experimental writing'. The Movement, as well as being anti-phoney, is anti-wet; sceptical, robust, ironic, prepared to be as comfortable as possible in a wicked, commercial, threatened world.[6]

The letters pages of *The Spectator* hummed throughout October with sarcasm, dissent, and measured agreement with the idea that there was something new going on among the younger writers, and that it mattered or was a Good Idea. As labels go, this one has had an unusually long run.[7]

The idea of 'The Movement' preceded *New Lines* by several years. Wain's 1953 *First Reading* broadcasts on the BBC, and G. S. Fraser and Ian Fletcher's anthology, *Springtime*, published in the same year, assembled the *dramatis personae*. 'There's no doubt, you know', Amis wrote to Larkin in 1954, 'we are getting to be a movement, even if the only people in it we like apart from ourselves are each other.... I don't give a pinch of shit for old Al's "stuff", nor Davie's, nor old John Barry Wain's really much'.[8] D. J. Enright's *Poets of the 1950s* (1955) was a parallel project, involving many of the contributors to Conquest's anthology. All this makes it certain that *New Lines* in 1956 did not launch the 'Movement'. Nor did Conquest openly embrace the idea that there was a new thing on the poetry scene. He was guarded, and ambivalent about signing on to someone else's bandwagon. As we shall see, his introduction to the anthology suggests something like a balancing act between rival conceptions of what these writers were doing, and what they stood for.

In a memoir of Larkin published in 1982, Conquest says his first draft of the introduction contained an attack on the 'Movement', a word then used to signify 'cerebral sub-Empsonian work like that of Al Alvarez'.[9] The swipe at Empson survived into the published text. In the critical terminology of the mid-1950s, 'Empson' often served as a code-word for 'intellectual', or at

[6] 'In the Movement', *The Spectator*, 1 October 1954, pp. 399–400. John Dick Scott was literary editor of *The Spectator* between 1953 and 1956. During the war Scott had been Assistant Principal at the Ministry of Aircraft Production. He later went on to work in the Cabinet Office as an official war historian, co-authoring *The Administration of War Production* with Richard Hughes (1955). He published four novels between 1947 and 1963.

[7] Blake Morrison, *The Movement: English Poetry and Fiction of the 1950s* (Oxford: Oxford University Press, 1980).

[8] Amis to Larkin, 14 March 1954, in Leader (ed.), *The Letters of Kingsley Amis*, p. 375.

[9] Robert Conquest, 'A Proper Sport', in Anthony Thwaite (ed.), *Larkin at Sixty* (London: Faber & Faber, 1982), p. 33.

least the idea of intellectual poetry. Conquest wanted the rigour and 'intellectual framework' of 'Empsonianism' but preferred it with the 'flesh of humanity, irony, passion or sanity' (p. xvii). The absence of the 'necessary intellectual component' of poetry in the 1940s led, Conquest wrote, 'to a tendency to over-intellectualise. Some years ago Mr. John Wain advocated the methods of Mr. William Empson in poetry.... And soon a number of young poets were following Empsonian and similar academic principles and often producing verse of notable aridity' (p. xvi).

That Wain and Amis had been working in an Empsonian vein may have persuaded Conquest to tone down the attack. It was a circumspection which he later regretted, since it might have steered critics away from automatically associating his anthology with the 'Movement'. The draft introduction, he wrote, 'was sent to all the contributors. I remember that while Kingsley Amis wanted it tougher Larkin would have preferred it milder.'[10] By temperament Conquest was with Amis, with all guns blazing, but he went along with Larkin's reservations. 'Tougher' *chez* Amis is suggested by a passage in a letter to Larkin, taking no prisoners on the question of meaning in poetry: 'What I think about poetry is that... it has got to be *instantaneously comprehensible* if anyone at all is going to read it these days. No use this 'difficult simplicity' lark; no use being clear after one reading. Got to be clear *line by line*, see?'[11] And 'milder' probably carried with it Larkin's dislike of aggressive public attacks on other poets: 'I certainly don't think attacks on other people help a "movement": the way to attack bad work is to produce good yourself: that's about all you can do.'[12]

The Introduction to *New Lines* deserves a closer look. In his contribution to this book Conquest affirms that politics was not a factor in his selection of poets. But it is hard as a reader to detach the politics from our response to the anthology. Conquest's political itinerary from an 'open' member of the Communist Party while at Oxford to an 'extremist right-winger', as he was described by Denis Healey,[13] is indeed a familiar one. I think

---

[10] Ibid.

[11] Amis to Larkin, 19 April 1956, in Leader (ed.), *The Letters of Kingsley Amis*, p. 466. See also Amis to William Van O'Connor, ibid., 21 January 1958, p. 525.

[12] Larkin to Conquest, 10 June 1955, in Thwaite (ed.), *Selected Letters of Philip Larkin*, p. 243.

[13] Along with Conquest, Healey was a member of the Communist Party while at Oxford in the late 1930s. His description of Conquest is quoted from Andrew Brown, 'Scourge and poet' [profile of Conquest], *The Guardian*, 15 February 2003.

Conquest would reject the idea that he had ever been a fulminating Red. At different times he told interviewers that he was never an especially committed member of the Party, that by enlisting in the army in 1939 he demonstrated his rejection of the Party's line that it was an imperialist and capitalist war, and that he became seriously anti-communist in 1944 while serving as liaison officer with the Bulgarian forces fighting under Communist control.[14]

Of his career on the right there is less uncertainty. While putting *New Lines* together, Conquest was a high-flier in the Information Research Bureau of the Foreign Office, combating Soviet propaganda.[15] There is in the Introduction to *New Lines* a contempt for totalitarianism, all teleological systems, and utopianism. He argues in effect that history inoculated the poetry of the 1950s against the temptations of totalitarianism—whether of political tyranny or absolutist religious systems. He suggests that the poetry of the 1950s 'submits to no great systems of theoretical constructs nor agglomerations of unconscious commands. It is free from both mystical and logical compulsions and ... is empirical in its attitude to all that comes' (p. xv). With Orwell as Conquest's patron saint,[16] what mattered in the end was 'reverence for the real person or event' (p. xv).

Conquest's Introduction to *New Lines* should be read in another context, that suggested by his 1957 attack on the work of Charles Williams. Conquest fits Williams into a mould which was standard fare in Cold War polemics—the engaged writer corrupted by the 'ideological straightjacket' of a 'closed and monopolistic system of ideas and feelings'.[17] In Williams's case, it was religion which was the author's straightjacket. Two terms dominate the essay:

---

[14] Zachary Leader, *The Life of Kingsley Amis* (London: Jonathan Cape, 2006), pp. 288–9.

[15] Conquest is mentioned once in Frances Stonor Saunders, *The Cultural Cold War: The CIA and the World of Arts and Letters* (New York: The New Press, 1999), pp. 420–1. A future biographer will doubtless find much of interest in Conquest's work at the FO, a topic which has remained stubbornly below the radar of scholarship on the Cold War.

[16] Of all the contributors, Conquest was the strongest admirer of Orwell, while Amis felt the most ambivalence, shading off into animus. See his summary of his changing attitudes to Orwell in a letter to M. G. Sherlock, 5 April 1967, in Leader (ed.), *Letters of Kingsley Amis*, pp. 710–11. See among Amis's early thoughts about Orwell 'The Road to Airstrip One', *The Spectator*, 31 August 1956, pp. 292–3; and his discussion of Orwell in *Socialism and the Intellectuals*, Fabian Tract No. 304 (January 1957).

[17] Robert Conquest, 'The Art of the Enemy', *Essays in Criticism*, 7:1 (January 1957), pp. 42–55. There were hostile letters from Valerie Pitt, Patricia Meyer Spacks, A. O. J. Cockshut, Alec Craig, and a reply from Conquest in 7:3 (July 1957), pp. 330–43. Further citations in the text.

totalitarianism and terrorism.[18] 'I would call any system of ideas which is self-consciously complete and final (except as to details to be discovered within it nor by its own methods), and which is regarded as suitable for imposition on the whole human race, as in emotional effect totalitarian' (pp. 43–4). The savage treatment meted out to barbarians in 'Taliessin through Logres', whipped and enslaved to force their conversion to Christianity, reminded Conquest of the 'impulse to power and cruelty' of Hitlerism and Stalinism. There is no attempt here to defend Williams, as Pound was defended by the advisory jury of the Bollingen Prize in 1949, with a sharp distinction between 'poetic achievement' and other things. Conquest is a subtle reader of Williams, and does not stint praise for the poet's real achievement, but the closed system of the poet's thought and beliefs, his 'tendency toward terrorism' and a distinct undercurrent of sado-masochism proves a decisive basis for a negative evaluation. New Lines stands as the product of a different mind-set, one which G. S. Fraser described as humanitarian and liberal.[19]

Are the politics of the New Lines poets, as they have unfolded, a necessary part of the history of the anthology? It could be argued that they belong to a different story, though one which has its cultural dimension: the broad right-ward shift of intellectuals in the 'Anglosphere' over the course of the second half of the century. Conquest, Davie, Amis, and Larkin (whose political views Conquest described as being of the 'traditional far right' and 'reactionary in the broadest sense', though certainly not fascist[20]), proudly regarded themselves as reactionaries who hated the changes which were transforming England. Larkin described the Modernisms he detested, whether perpetrated by Parker, Pound, or Picasso, as 'irresponsible exploitations of technique in contradiction of human life as we know it'.[21] Amis told a Conservative Political Centre summer school in 1968: 'I am . . . a tremendous supporter of righteous and well-thought-out inequality. I am all for reinforcing that and

[18] Conquest was alone among the New Lines poets in understanding the political significance of these heavily-loaded terms. Hannah Arendt's The Origins of Totalitarianism (1951) was among the most widely discussed, if not most influential, books of the decade. See Elisabeth Young-Bruehl's discussion of the book and its critical reception in Hannah Arendt: For Love of the World (New Haven and London: Yale University Press, 1982), pp. 250 ff.

[19] [G.S. Fraser,] 'Poets of Moderation', TLS, 13 June 1956, p. 424. This review was published anonymously, but the reviewer is identified on the TLS digital archive.

[20] Conquest, 'A Proper Sport', pp. 37, 38.

[21] Philip Larkin, All What Jazz: A Record Diary 1961–68 (London: Faber & Faber), p. 17.

having an elite.'[22] As for Davie, there is so much to choose from.[23] As 'men of the right' they had lots of company in postwar Britain. But Conquest was dead right about the big things—the Terror, Ukrainian starvation, Stalin, the Gulag, Vorkuta, Kirov. Battle honours, indeed.

In the introduction to *New Lines* Conquest sets out a division between the healthy in 1950s poetry, and the 'vicious taste' which was so powerfully revealed in contemporary writing. Taking a stand on behalf of integrity, honesty, and rational structure, and rejecting the indiscriminate enthusiasms and other literary misdemeanours of the 1940s, the spirit of *New Lines* was calculatedly combative. 'It was not a balanced or judicious piece,' wrote Conquest. 'Nor was it intended to be—it was a provocative showing of the flag, or trailing of the coat.'[24] Tendentious anthologies often overstate their case. Showing the flag catches the eye, and sets the ball rolling in terms of publicity. But it is rare, perhaps, for an editor to set out the bearings of a new movement so comprehensively in terms of moral, emotional, and even physical well-being. There is an unmistakable Lawrentian and Leavisite dimension to the *New Lines* project. Other tastes, other aspirations for poetry, are dismissed with scorn. That too has the feel of true Leavisism. Yet a certain decorum is maintained: none of the guilty men are personally named, though there is little doubt of whom the editor (and presumably the contributors) disapprove: the poets who are devoted to 'images of sex and violence' and those who are promulgators of 'diffuse and sentimental verbiage' (p. xii). In 1956 Leavis was an unavoidable presence in the Introduction to *New Lines*.

The influence of the arch-Modernist Ezra Pound and echoes of some aspects of Poundian doctrine appear in Conquest's introduction. The

---

[22] Kingsley Amis, *Lucky Jim's Politics* (CPC pamphlet No. 410, July 1968), p. 17.

[23] The tang of Davie's reactionary views is no less sharp. See his *Trying to Explain* (Manchester: Carcanet New Press, 1980). From his earliest writings there is a fondness for right-wing cultural and political overstatement: thus, notoriously, his assertion that 'the development from imagism in poetry to fascism in politics is clear and unbroken' (*Purity of Diction in English Verse* (London: Chatto & Windus, 1952), p. 99). This is a good example of the kind of teleological thinking which Conquest scorned in the introduction to *New Lines* and elsewhere. Robert Von Hallberg draws attention to Davie's 'liberalism' (of the Lionel Trilling kind, 'based on certain habits of mind' rather than social justice, etc.) in 'Donald Davie and the "Moral Shape of Politics" ', in George Dekker (ed.), *Donald Davie and the Responsibilities of Literature* (Manchester: Carcanet Press, 1983), pp. 74–94.

[24] Conquest, 'A Proper Sport', p. 33.

publication in 1954 of T. S. Eliot's edition of Pound's literary essays did much to reintroduce what Eliot called 'the *least dispensible* body of critical writing in our time' to British writers and critics.[25] Even Pound-averse sceptics—and the moving spirits behind *New Lines* were deeply sceptical—found themselves echoing, sometimes unwittingly, Pound's critical dicta and emulating his polemical edge. As *capo* of the Imagists, a central instigator of Vorticism, and a contributor to Wyndham Lewis's *Blast* (1914, 1915), Pound knew a thing or two about literary gang warfare and sharp-edged polemics. But he also wrote as teacher, mentor, schoolmaster, and disciplinarian, addressing the 'candidate', 'neophyte', and 'freshman' (pp. 5, 6). This was a role which Conquest did not seek, yet one can sense a convergence of views, a shared body of literary values, between the young Foreign Office hot-shot and the poet holding court at St Elizabeth's Hospital. Conquest's side-swipe at Auden's tendency to 'turn abstractions into beings in their own right' in the *New Lines* introduction (p. xviii) is the legitimate heir of Pound's warning to 'Go in fear of abstraction'. Pound deplored the prolix, the verbose and the abstract and cautioned against expressions such as ' "dim lands of *peace*". It dulls the image. It mixes an abstraction with the concrete. It comes from the writer's not realizing that the natural object is always the *adequate* symbol' (p. 5). He did not name the author of the offending image, but the line is from 'On a Marsh Road', a little-read poem by Ford Madox Ford.[26]

Pound sharply excommunicated the 'viewy' in poetry, advice which the *New Lines* poets took to heart. Though often writing nature poems and 'place' poems, they do not embrace the natural world with ardour. Rather the opposite. They approach nature with a cautious, rather cerebral distrust. Amis set his face against 'swooning wilderness' in 'Against Romanticism' (pp. 45–6). It was a note shared widely among other contributors:

[25] *Literary Essays of Ezra Pound*, edited with an Introduction by T. S. Eliot (London: Faber & Faber, 1954), p. xiii. Further references in the text. English reviews of this volume were quite hostile: see Tomlinson, Davie, and others reprinted in Eric Homberger (ed.), *Ezra Pound: The Critical Heritage* (London: Routledge & Kegan Paul, 1972), pp. 422–34. Holloway and Wain (who had visited Pound at St Elizabeth's) were notably more sympathetic in reviews of *Thrones* in 1960 (*Pound: Critical Heritage*, pp. 453–6, 463–4). Davie's convoluted and unresolved struggle with Pound may be traced through his many essays and reviews on Pound, and in *Ezra Pound: Poet as Sculptor* (1964) and *Ezra Pound* (Harmondsworth: Penguin Modern Masters, 1975).

[26] Ford Madox Ford, *Collected Poems*, with an Introduction by William Rose Benét (New York: Oxford University Press, 1936), p. 199. Ford was quite fond of the epithet *dim*, as in 'these dim, thronged streets' (p. 130) and 'your sweet, dim face' (p. 167).

It is the association after all
We seek, we would retrace our thoughts to find
The thought of which this landscape is the image,
Then pay the thought and not the landscape homage.

(Jennings, 'A Way of Looking', p. 6)

What can a poem do with a landscape? What
Extract that pure philosophies cannot?

(Conquest, 'Anthéor', p. 75)

...like a spectacled curator showing
The wares of his museum to the crowd,
They yearly waxed more eloquent and knowing
To moderns who devoutly hymn the land.
So be it: each is welcome to his voice;
They are a gentle, if a useless band'.

(Wain, 'Reason for Not Writing Orthodox
Nature Poetry', pp. 83–4)

Insisting on the contrast between the 'genuine and healthy' (p. xi, 'healthy' repeated on p. xiv) and the poetasters of the 1940s with their 'diffuse and sentimental verbiage' (p. xii), Conquest is Poundian in emphasis. Pound, too, inveighed against 'rhetorical din, and luxurious riot' (p. 12). The defence Pound made of literature itself, that it 'has to do with maintaining the very *cleanliness* of the tools' and that it also serves to maintain 'the *health* of thought outside literary circles' (pp. 21, 22, emphasis added), suggests how Conquest in *New Lines* was largely within the mainstream of early Modernism—not least as set out by Pound in 'How to Read', a long essay published in the *New York Herald Tribune*, in January 1929 (*Literary Essays*, pp. 15–40). Of course 'The Movement' was, as David Lodge pointed out, an 'aesthetically conservative force, consciously setting itself against Modernist experimentation'.[27] But the air of twentieth-century writing was so profoundly disturbed by the language, aesthetic ideas, and combativeness of Modernism *circa* 1914–30, that even avowedly anti-Modernist formations struggle to purge its styles, tones and approaches, or some of them. 'The Movement' was more successful in this than many other twentieth-century English literary movements, but the traces remained.

---

[27] David Lodge, obituary of Sir Kingsley Amis, *The Independent*, 25 October 1995, p. 16.

Needless to say the differences between Pound's language and Conquest's were profound. Pound's interest in the sound and music of verse has no parallel in Conquest. Conquest's advocacy of the 'empirical', his rejection of ideology and all such 'great systems of theoretical constructs', and his belief in the desirability of 'rational structure and comprehensible language' (p. xv) swerve decisively away from Pound's thinking about either the structure or language of poetry.

New Lines made quite a stir. Behind the contemptuous tone of some of the reviews, and the spirit of ill-will and tetchiness which has usually marked the reviewing of contemporary poetry in England, the reservations expressed about the volume were both serious and thoughtful. G. S. Fraser's was the first review to appear, on 13 June 1956, and was the most temperate in language.[28] These are careful craftsmen, he wrote, who speak to us in a reasonably confident tone; their poems are reflective rather than lyrical. He found a liberal, humanistic temper of mind in *New Lines*; there were no traces here of the radical or the reactionary. (He was not the only critic to note the decent liberalism of the anthology.) The review was titled 'Poets of Moderation' and picks up a theme from D. J. Enright's introduction to *Poets of the 1950s*: 'Our new poets are… "moderate", and of course moderation lacks the immediate popular appeal of the extremes—whether of cynicism or of sentimentality.'[29] This too was a theme of Charles Tomlinson's: 'Moderation is the poetic watchword of the fifties.'[30] The poets of the decade, Enright argued, embodied a 'chastened common sense'. Fraser agreed—with reservations. His strongest doubt about the *New Lines* project was expressed in how little Conquest's contributors seemed to live in the poetic imagination. These sceptical, pragmatic poets were in danger of working too safely within the limits of their aspirations.

Stephen Spender's review of *New Lines* appeared in the *New Statesman and Nation* on 7 July.[31] Among the poets of his generation, he was the most active

---

[28] [Fraser,] 'Poets of Moderation', *TLS*, 13 June 1956, p. 424.

[29] D. J. Enright (ed.), *Poets of the 1950s* (Tokyo: Kenkyusha, 1955), p. 13. There was much overlap in contributors, but among the seventy-eight poems selected by Enright, only thirteen also appeared in *New Lines*.

[30] Charles Tomlinson, 'Rock Bottom', *Poetry* 89:4 (January 1957), pp. 260–4. He was reviewing Enright's *Poetry of the 1950s*.

[31] Stephen Spender, 'New and Healthy', *New Statesman and Nation*, 7 July 1956, pp. 20–1.

in the 1950s as a man of letters and literary journalist, and often assumed the mantle of spokesman and defender of the 1930s generation. In a reflective look back at the Spanish Civil War on the twentieth anniversary of its outbreak, Spender argued that there remained 'a pure and uncontaminated essence of the "Cause"'.[32] This kind of writing, which enabled the horrors of the war, and particularly the role played by the Communists, to be subsumed within a larger and honourable purpose, was precisely the kind of sentimental leftwingery which Orwell attacked in *Homage to Catalonia* (1938), and which Conquest loathed. In more than twenty books unmasking Soviet lies and mystifications, Conquest scornfully attacked the dupes and fellow-travellers who for whatever ulterior reasons went along with Stalinism. It is easy to understand why Spender, the living embodiment of the romantic myth of the 1930s, became defensive when he came under attack by younger writers. He took Donald Davie's 'Remembering the "Thirties"' (*New Lines*, pp. 70–2) as an intended personal attack. (Davie pointed out in the November 1956 issue of *Encounter* that Spender misread the poem.) Spender held off replying to Davie for two months, and then omitted him when he reviewed *New Lines*.[33] There were things Spender liked in *New Lines*, but there was too much dead wood, and the collection overall lacked freshness. At best, he wrote, 'there is a serious search for reality, without the meretriciousness of the Kitchen Sink. Its best are Philip Larkin and John Holloway, who have subdued the most subtle and insidious of the leftover devils of the Twenties and Thirties—intellectual pretentiousness.'

Anthony Hartley returned to 'The Movement' in a review of *New Lines* in *The Spectator* on 20 July 1956. Aware of his own (and J. D. Scott's) over-simplifications, he nevertheless launched once again into the cultural shorthand of generations, movements, influences, and ideologies as dozens of reviewers had done before, and uncounted dozens would do after. Trying to sound like an insider, trend-setter, and knowledgeable critic-judge, Hartley conveys, rather, a growing boredom with 'The Movement' ('I have spoken of many of these poets elsewhere so shall not talk about them in detail'). It is time for

---

[32] Stephen Spender, 'Looking Back on Spain', *The Spectator*, 13 July 1956, pp. 57–8.

[33] Stephen Spender, 'Notes from a Diary', *Encounter*, 7:3 (September 1956), pp. 52–3. Davie's reply appeared in *Encounter*, 7:5 (November 1956), p. 70. John Sutherland mentions Spender's review in *Stephen Spender: The Authorized Biography* (London: Viking, 2004), pp. 385–6, without shedding much light on his uneasy relations in this period with the younger poets.

the tight-lipped virtues and strict discipline he touted in 1954 to loosen up. 'A reversion to dynamic romanticism is what is wanted.'[34]

Neither Fraser nor Spender could claim to be of the generation of the *New Lines* poets, or even to be poets working in the contemporary mode; but David Wright could make that claim. In 1956 he was in his mid-thirties (as was Enright and Holloway), and had published two books of verse. He had appeared alongside Larkin in several wartime anthologies of poetry. A South African poet who fell deaf at the age of 7 from scarlet fever, he was—according to Ted Hughes—a fairly nasty piece of work. Hughes wrote to Lucas Myers sometime in the early 1960s of running into Wright at a pub.

He had read my book—Lupercal—in proof, because he was one of the judges for the Poetry Book Society choice (which was given to Peter Levi). He said he didn't like my book—'too American'—and so downed it, he 'thought it oughtn't to be encouraged'. This to my face—enough of a draught of that sad circle for me. The other judge was J. C. Hall, who had attacked the Hawk in the R[ain]. What a dim muddy glow there is lighting this goldfish bowl of the English intelligentsia...They are damply steaming compost of bile, saliva, & disintegrated copies of Penguin New Writing.[35]

Larkin was of a similar mind. After the publication of his attack on *New Lines* Larkin dismissed Wright as a 'deaf cunt'.[36]

Every sentence of Wright's review was dripping with distaste[37], and it was hard not to suspect that Spender, editor of *Encounter* since 1953, had used Wright as a proxy. It was comeuppance time, and Wright shifted between a cudgel and a rapier in his attack on the poets. He thought they collectively lacked ambition. Some of the weaknesses of the poetry of the 1940s ('muddled, confused, sentimental, muse-happy') were also evident in *New Lines*. He particularly deplored the contributors' 'frightened, welfare-state mentality' and the 'attitude of positively enormous resentment, very like that of the Teddy-boy'. He was unimpressed by Conquest's 'hesitating vagueness and

---

[34] Anthony Hartley, 'Poets of the Fifties', *The Spectator*, 20 July 1956, pp. 100–1. See the letters in reply: 27 July, pp. 142–3, and 5 August, p. 179.

[35] Ted Hughes to Lucas Myers, in Christopher Reid (ed.), *Letters of Ted Hughes* (London: Faber & Faber, 2007), pp. 156–7.

[36] Larkin to Conquest, 5 October 1956, in Thwaite (ed.), *Selected Letters of Philip Larkin*, p. 266.

[37] David Wright, 'A Small Green Insect Shelters in the Bowels of My Quivering Typewriter', *Encounter*, 7:4 (October 1956), pp. 74–8. Conquest replied in the December 1956 issue, p. 69.

extraordinarily negative attitude' and quoted Pound and Yeats against the adulation of the mediocre in *New Lines*.

Charles Tomlinson set out his case against the 'Movement' in a hostile review of Enright's *Poets of the 1950s* in *Poetry*. He was scornful precisely of the moderation which G. S. Fraser praised: 'one is tempted . . . to feel that moderation is becoming an excuse for lack of ambition among English poets'. The 'confident lowbrowism' and rejection of 'grander themes' by Amis, along with Larkin's dismissal of the 'myth-kitty' and dislike of allusions to other poets, were proof, in Tomlinson's eyes, of an 'inadequate sense of civilized values' in the work of these poets. There was a need in poetry, he concluded, of

le pain spirituel, amor intellectualis Dei, even if it expresses only delight in the shapes, colours, and textures of the created universe. Such spiritual realities the poets of the fifties seem all too willing to forgo, in their compromise of moderation with the world as they find it.[38]

Tomlinson's review was the longest notice of *New Lines*, and perhaps the most predictable.[39] The cerebral distrust of nature, so distinctive a quality of the anti-romanticism of the *New Lines* poets, seemed to Tomlinson no victory at all; it was a failure of nerve. The secular caste of mind in *New Lines*, which Fraser noted, gave Tomlinson a sense of the desiccation of these poets. 'They seldom for a moment escape beyond the suburban mental ratio which they impose on experience.' In the aftermath of his review it was revealed by D. J. Enright that Tomlinson had wished to be a contributor to *New Lines*, implying that his criticisms were little more than the sour grapes of a disappointed poet. A number of his poems had been submitted to Conquest by Donald Davie (who had been Tomlinson's tutor at Cambridge in the previous decade). Conquest turned them down. Tomlinson denied any knowledge of the submission.

Tomlinson's rejection of *New Lines* was complete but it's hard not to feel that nine pages in *Essays in Criticism* attacking a poetry anthology was somewhat excessive. It was clearly not a moment for British understatement.

---

[38] Charles Tomlinson, 'Rock Bottom', *Poetry*, 89: 4 (January 1957), pp. 260–4.

[39] Charles Tomlinson, 'The Middlebrow Muse', *Essays in Criticism*, 7:2 (April 1957), pp. 208–17. Replies in *Essays in Criticism*, 7:3 (July 1957), pp. 343–5 (Davie, Enright); 7:4 (October 1957), p. 460 (Tomlinson). Conquest's rejoinder, 'New Critics and New Lines', appeared in *Essays in Criticism*, 8:2 (April 1958), pp. 225–7.

He deplored everything Conquest's anthology stood for. He disliked the tone, the way these poets pandered to popular culture (Wain's lyrics suggested Sinatra's 'croon-songs'), and there was too much 'sex-in-the-head' in Conquest's poems; Enright was a journalist in verse; Larkin was 'old-maidish' and guilty of 'intense parochialism'. These poets seemed quite indifferent to tradition: 'one can only deplore Mr. Larkin's refusal to note what has been done before 1890 in the ironic self-deprecating vein by Laforgue and Corbière and to take his bearings accordingly' (p. 214). ('And who's Corbière?' Amis asked Larkin. 'Is this some new character or a jesting/punning reference to someone I already know?'[40])

Some of the themes of these reviews comfortably crossed the Atlantic. Hayden Carruth in *Poetry* noticed in *New Lines* 'a certain aridity of imagination, a failure of response'. These British poets 'believe in control, clarity of feeling, austerity of technique, a strict abhorrence of excess. They share their retreat, in other words.'[41]

The reviews of *New Lines* suggest a perspective upon the contributors which we have lost—the liberalism and moderation of these poets. Reviewers found their work to be cerebral, careful, humanistic, moderate, sceptical, ironic—and above all *moderate*. Wherever they were headed politically, in 1956 they were not taken to be reactionaries. There is in Conquest's anthology no swaggering neo-imperialist verse, none of the ruralism and nature-worship of the Georgians. Nor were the contributors men or women of the avant-garde. In their eyes, Modernism was passé. (They look to me quite a lot like the England of Eden, Macmillan, and Gaitskell, but without the politicians' illusions about national greatness.)

The accusation of provincialism made by Tomlinson omits much: military service in the war, the encounter with foreign languages; and also the broadly internationalist perspective of a decolonizing power. Davie embodied the paradox: a restless, wide-ranging cultural interest which went hand-in-hand with ill-tempered and reactionary cultural polemics. Holloway's lectures, delivered in Chicago in 1965, and published as *Widening Horizons in English Verse* (1966), ended with a suspicion that centuries of 'widening hori-

[40] Amis to Larkin, 20 December 1954, in Leader (ed.), *The Letters of Kingsley Amis*, p. 416. Pound's 'Irony, Laforgue, and Some Satire' (1917) and 'The Hard and Soft in French Poetry' (1918) were included in the 1954 *Literary Essays*.

[41] Hayden Carruth, '2,000 Poems, Mostly Good', *Poetry*, 91:2 (November 1957), pp. 124–33.

zons' had now come to an end; and he later edited the *Oxford Book of Local Verse* (1987). Yet at Cambridge in the 1960s his seminars on Modernism were probably the best on offer in Britain. He was an anti-provincial voice in an English faculty over-laden with those who scarcely concealed their dislike for Modernism.[42] Gunn, Enright, and Conquest in their different ways were the very opposite of provincial in their intellectual interests and view of the postwar world. That leaves us with Amis and Larkin. These are not cautious, moderate welfare state men either. As revealed in biographies by Andrew Motion, Eric Jacobs, and Zachary Leader, and with the hefty selected letters of Larkin edited by Anthony Thwaite and Leader's Amis letters in hand, we can see these men as quite far from the 'moderate' *New Lines* which the reviewers described. They are men bursting with passions and prejudices. Transcendence, the vatic, the high-flying 'poetic imagination' were not their game.

[42] In Cambridge in the late 1960s Holloway was the supervisor for my doctoral dissertation on Ezra Pound. In 1990 he opposed an honorary Cambridge degree for Jacques Derrida. That was one 'widening horizon' too far.

15

'Fond of What He's Crapping On': Movement Poetry and Romanticism

Michael O'Neill

In a letter to Philip Larkin of 9 May 1949, Kingsley Amis discusses his response to Scott Fitzgerald's *The Great Gatsby* (characteristically rechristened 'The gatsby'). Amis admires the 'climax of the thing' as 'horrible and moving and profound'. His only complaint is that Fitzgerald 'seems a wee bit fond of what he's crapping on—or rather (because that on its own wouldn't matter) fondof fockof fond of it through gullibility not through deliberate yielding, if I can make myself clear'.[1] The restless switch between registers here shows an agile intelligence at work. 'Fond of what he's crapping on' is acute in its undeceived way, but it prompts the question: why was Fitzgerald, the most idealizing of post-Romantic ironists, drawn to what repelled him? Thinking about that is partly what drives Amis to intensify 'fondof' into 'fockof'. He is mocking a typographical error ('fondof'), but his execration also has the seeming effect of instructing Fitzgerald to 'fuck off' for not telling Tom Buchanan, Daisy, and the rest so to conduct themselves. Amis is not content with saying

---

[1] *The Letters of Kingsley Amis*, ed. Zachary Leader (2000; London: HarperCollins, 2001), p. 204.

that the author was ambivalent. He pushes further, arguing that Fitzgerald's reason for being ambivalent was not as impressive as it might have been: he was 'fond of' what he disliked and exposed 'through gullibility not through deliberate yielding'. Its analytical edginess showing a distinct ethical preoccupation, that last phrase would almost slot into a Movement poem.

Amis underestimates Fitzgerald's ability to express Nick Carraway's simultaneous attraction and repulsion. But his interest in mixed-up responses is relevant to the ways in which Movement poets react to Romantic poetry. At times they seem more than 'a wee bit fond of what [they're] crapping on'. For Donald Davie, 'Romantic was for me and my friends the ugliest imputation that could be thrown at anyone or anything, a sentence of death from which there was no appeal.'[2] Yet many poems by Davie and other Movement poets spend a surprising amount of energy adjusting themselves to the possible claims of the Romantic, as examples, especially from Robert Conquest's two anthologies, New Lines (1956) and New Lines—II (1963), will reveal.[3] The very discarding of Romantic 'singing robes' in a Movement poem such as Jonathan Price's 'A Manner of Speaking' (NL2, pp. 44–5) involves trying them on:

> 'Where are these poets' hearts?' a reader cries.
> Not withered, but not worn upon the sleeve
> Of singing robes. Some things they choose to leave
> To bards who wield their pens between their thighs.
>
> Acknowledged legislators, too, you find
> Despairing over some poetic flower:
> 'So-and-so should be writing at this hour,
> Mankind hath need of him.' He needs mankind.

After the obligatory swipe at Dylan Thomas, the probable pen-between-thighs-wielder of the first stanza,[4] Price adroitly weaves together allusions

[2] 'Eliot in One Poet's Life', Mosaic 6 (Fall 1972), p. 231; quoted in Blake Morrison, The Movement: English Poetry and Fiction of the 1950s (Oxford: Oxford University Press, 1980), p. 154.

[3] New Lines: An Anthology, ed. Robert Conquest (London: Macmillan, 1956), hereafter cited parenthetically with relevant page numbers as NL1, and New Lines—II: An Anthology, ed. Robert Conquest (London: Macmillan, 1963), hereafter cited parenthetically with relevant page numbers as NL2.

[4] Compare the lines, 'A candle in the thighs | Warms youth and seed, and burns the seeds of age', from 'Light Breaks Where No Sun Shines', Dylan Thomas: The Poems, ed. with intro. and notes Daniel Jones (London: Dent, 1971). For an account of 'The Movement's reservations about Thomas', see Morrison, The Movement, pp. 145–56 (quoted phrase is on p. 145).

to Shelley's *A Defence of Poetry* and Wordsworth's sonnet to Milton, even as
he debunks their vatic authority (Milton dwindles to 'So-and so', Shelley's
'unacknowledged legislators' have become would-be literary grandees).
The poem's rejection of a 'Ventriloquism' dependent on 'echoes of a liter-
ary shade' is artfully aware of the Romantic tradition. Opposition to 'faked
passion' cannot, the poem half-concedes, be the sole preserve of a single
school. Indeed, if you denigrate 'faked passion' in poetry, you must believe
in something like 'the true voice of feeling', in Keats's phrase, an archetypal
Romantic ideal and one which Keats prefers to 'the false beauty proceeding
from art'.[5]

Such a 'false beauty' is one which Romantic and Movement poets alike
are lured by and mistrust. Movement poetry is suspicious of labels, seeking
to reconnect itself to what Robert Conquest calls 'the central tradition of all
English poetry, classical or romantic'. Yet the 'tradition' is summed up for
Conquest by Coleridge's remark: 'poetry is the blossom and the fragrancy
of all human knowledge, human thoughts, human passions, emotions, lan-
guage' (*NL1*, p. xv).[6] Conquest champions a poetry that yokes thought to
feeling, and is prepared to examine 'the poetic process itself' (*NL1*, p. xvi): a
distinctly Romantic interest.[7] This fascination with 'poetic process' is among
the features of Movement poetry that most strongly declare a continuity
with Romantic poetry. It occurs implicitly in the opening of Davie's 'Tuscan
Morning' (*NL2*, p. 91), 'Presences are always said to brood'. In fact, as 'are
always said' indicates, the statement is by no means offered as incontestable,
and the poem's three five-line stanzas debate the continuing relevance of

---

[5] Quoted from *The Oxford Authors: John Keats*, ed. Elizabeth Cook (Oxford: Oxford University Press,
1990), p. 493. This edition is used for quotations from Keats's letters (and some poems), and is
referred to parenthetically in the text as 'Cook'.

[6] For Coleridge's words, see *Biographia Literaria*, ed. James Engell and W. Jackson Bate (2 vols.,
Princeton: Princeton University Press, 1983), 2. 26. An editorial footnote on the same page suggests
that Coleridge 'is recalling Wordsworth in the Preface to *Lyrical Ballads* (1802): "Poetry is the breath
and finer spirit of all knowledge; it is the impassioned expression which is in the countenance of
all Science."' In the 'Introduction' to *NL2* Conquest writes: 'Our own situation has looked worse,
superficially, than that which the *Lyrical Ballads* were designed to remedy' (p. xxix): further evi-
dence that the Romantics were by no means thought of in antagonistic terms by a chief repre-
sentative of the Movement.

[7] In support of this contention, see my *Romanticism and the Self-Conscious Poem* (Oxford: Clarendon,
1997).

'Presences', evoked with a mixture of ironic detachment and disturbance in the first stanza:

> Presences are always said to brood;
> And in the Boboli gardens just at noon
> Toad-like Silenus squats inside a shade
> While Michelangelo's giants cannot break
> The curtain of their element, the haze.

With Davie's typical angularity, the poem goes on to intimate that to dwell on the achievement of the past might be to ignore the significance of the here and now, a significance suggested by the poem's final stanza:

> High noon of the Renaissance was in Rome,
> This was the Tuscan, Brunelleschi's morning,
> The guidebooks say. What have renaissances
> To do with noon? It is the edge of light
> Goes cleaving, windless presence, like a ray.

Yet Brunelleschi is associated with the 'morning' of the 'Renaissance'; to that degree, he serves as an exemplary precursor, anticipating the impulse to make it new which finds expression at the poem's close. Thanks to the sharp enjambment and keen stresses, the last two lines themselves 'go cleaving', a present-tense illumination. They bring into being a 'windless presence' that seems to have little to do with the 'High noon of the Renaissance'. At the same time, this epiphanic 'presence' is itself the heir of the opening 'Presences'; the weight of cultural history fascinates Davie even as he seeks to offload it. The poem's refusal to settle into the rhymes that it seems throughout to be on the verge of finding deftly mimics its uneasy balance of feelings.

'Presences' haunt early Davie, probably brooding on the Yeatsian 'Presences' who, in 'Among School Children', 'break hearts' (53) by virtue of their apart-ness, their aesthetic fixedness.[8] For Davie, the word connotes not only such fixity but also a sense of abiding value, and this complex sense is simultan-eously yielded to and debated in his 'A Head Painted by Daniel O'Neill': 'Yes, presences at home with presences | Can only brood and move us to repose; | Our broken-ness can burn across the air' (*NL1*, pp. 66–7). Like 'the edge of

---

[8] Quoted from *The Poems of W. B. Yeats: A Sourcebook*, ed. Michael O'Neill (London: Routledge, 2004).

light' in 'Tuscan Morning', 'Our broken-ness' has a power to 'burn' denied to 'presences'; and yet, as in 'Tuscan Morning', Davie advocates a posture of dissenting respect, in this case towards the beautiful head of the painting, concluding with this imperative: 'Be stilled, not daunted, by her steadiness.' The watcher is, so to speak, watched, steadied by the object's steadiness, stared into an exemplary mode of responding to the past. By analogy, as in 'Tuscan Morning', the poet enacts his response to a tradition that includes Romantic poetry.

Among the 'Presences' haunting these poems by Davie is Wordsworth's 'Ode: Intimations of Immortality', the poem that reduced Larkin to tears when he heard it read out on the radio. 'I was driving down the M1 on a Saturday morning: they had this poetry slot on the radio, "Time for Verse": it was a lovely summer morning, and someone suddenly started reading the Immortality Ode, and I couldn't see for tears. . . . I don't suppose I'd read that poem for twenty years, and it's amazing how effective it was when one was totally unprepared for it.'[9] Being 'totally unprepared' for the impact of a Romantic masterpiece is crucial here. Whether such a propitious openness ever exists in Movement poetry is questionable, though there are evidently moments when the ironist is persuaded to lower his guard. Davie, in a sense, is 'totally prepared' for the Wordsworthian phrasing that enters his poem—Wordsworth apostrophizes the child in the Immortality Ode thus: 'Thou, over whom thy immortality | Broods like the day, a master o'er a slave, | A presence which is not to be put by' (117–19)[10]—but Romanticism itself turns out to be 'A presence which is not to be put by' in Movement poetry, for all its intermittent attempts to do precisely that.

In 'Remembering the Thirties' (*NL1*, pp. 70–2) Davie writes with a knowing irony about knowing irony, as though he knew that he would produce a devastating critique of Movement poetry in his later essay, 'Remembering the Fifties'. The essay asserts with acerbic insight that 'In "Movement" poetry the poet is never so surrendered to his experience, never so far gone out of himself in his response, as not to be aware of the attitudes he is taking up.'[11]

[9] Philip Larkin, *Required Writings : Miscellaneous Pieces 1955–1982* (London: Faber, 1983), p. 53.

[10] Quoted, as are all poems by the Romantic poets where possible, from *Romanticism: An Anthology*, ed. Duncan Wu, 3rd edn. (Oxford: Blackwell, 2006).

[11] In Donald Davie, *The Poet in the Imaginary Museum: Essays of Two Decades*, ed. Barry Alpert (Manchester: Carcanet Press, 1977), p. 74.

The comment may be right, but it need not imply the worthlessness of the poetry. 'Remembering the Thirties' exemplifies the best Movement poetry's refusal not only to sloganize, but also to settle for comfortable ironies. Ostensibly about the Auden generation, and that generation's quasi-mythic distance from the present, it turns out, self-reflexively, to be a poem about Movement poetry, too.

Davie's tone in his alternately rhyming, almost parodically clockwork iambic quatrains is smoother, more urbane than elsewhere; but if he assumes a pose and a poise, he proceeds to ruffle them. The first section considers the Thirties poets as mythic figures who cannot be taken seriously: 'what for them were agonies, to us | Are high-brow thrillers, though historical'. 'Agonies' are just one of history's changes of garments, one of poetry's once potent, now shopworn words: ' "the agonies, the strife of human hearts"?—why, Hollywood will do that for us', writes D. J. Enright in 'The Interpreters (or, How to Bury Yourself in a Book)' (*NL1*, pp. 60–2), quoting well-known lines from Keats's 'Sleep and Poetry' (123–4) in order, it would seem, to imply that Romantic 'agonies' are hackneyed. But if we think they are, then, in the case of both poems, the 'joke' is on us. In Enright's poem, the quotation from Keats serves as a touchstone of what poetry that sang 'of the merely real' would never overlook. In Davie's poem, we are told that 'The Devil for a joke | Might carve his own initials on our desk, | And still we'd miss the point, because he spoke | An idiom too dated, Audenesque'. 'Idiom', there, suggests that the 'Devil' suffers from writing in too restrictive a way, 'addressing only a coterie of personal friends and other poets', as Davie describes the predicament of 'most modern poets' (by which he appears to mean most twentieth-century poets) in *Purity of Diction in English Verse*.[12] The lines suggest the myopia afflicting the poet anxious to speak what he takes to be the speech of his time and indirectly describes Davie's complicated feelings about Romanticism, the point of which was easy to miss or simplify because of a sense that, in the title of one of Amis's poems in *New Lines*, it employs 'Wrong Words' (*NL1*, p. 44).

'Wrong Words' does not specify the identity of the 'poets in a silver age' whom it both sneers at and finally seeks to understand. But in their display of 'high words' these poets have much in common, from Amis's perspective

[12] (1952; London: Routledge and Kegan Paul, 1967), p. 17.

in other poems, with the Romantics. In fact, 'Wrong Words' points in the direction of a reluctantly sympathetic response to worn-out poetical fashions: 'Behind their frantic distortion', he writes, 'lies the dread, | Unforced, unblurred, of real defeats'. 'Frantic distortion' undergoes an assonantal subduing in 'Unforced' that brings into 'unblurred' focus 'real defeats'. The poem's shock is its sense that seeming opposites meet: the lines might be applied to the Romantics, or to Amis's generation, 'poets in a silver age'. In a similar way, 'Remembering the Thirties' is highly critical of its own ironies, even as it thrives on them. In the second section, Davie concedes that Thirties writers were every bit as 'deprecating' as their Fifties descendants; as he wittily notes, 'England expected every man that day | To show his motives were ambivalent', where 'ambivalent' rhymes expressively with 'Isherwood's ascent'. 'Yet irony itself is doctrinaire' is the point at which Davie rises above his mistrust of grand statement, and allows his poem to reconnect with the more heroic energies associated with the Romantic imagination. Any such reconnection is highly implicit and tentatively offered:

> A neutral tone is nowadays preferred.
> And yet it may be better, if we must,
> To find the stance impressive and absurd
> Than not to see the hero for the dust.

Davie's use of the passive voice in the stanza's opening line permits him to have things both ways; he does not wholly disavow his 'neutral tone', yet he hints at its limitations in the following lines. 'May be better' is itself hardly a ringing endorsement of the heroic, while 'if we must' is a phrase that grits its teeth; the stance is 'absurd' as well as 'impressive'; and the reworked cliché of the final line concedes that there is a good deal of 'dust' in the vicinity of the 'hero'. 'And yet', as the second line opens, the stanza clearly discerns the shortcomings of doctrinaire irony, and prepares the way for the shift to the 'idiom' of anthropology in the celebration of the poem's close:

> For courage is the vegetable king,
> The sprig of all ontologies, the weed
> That beards the slag-heap with its hectoring,
> Whose green adventure is to run to seed.

It is distinctly possible to see 'the vegetable king' as a figure for the bogeyman of the Movement, Romanticism, the Devil carving his initials on the poem's desk. Opposites meet. If 'hectoring' suggests shrillness, it also evokes the ghost of Hector. 'Whose green adventure is to run to seed', the poem's last line, is typically ambivalent: courage is 'green' in that its 'adventures' are fresh and new, but also in that those adventures involve an element of immaturity; if 'run to seed' means to grow unfit and lazy, it suggests as well the generation of new life.

The poem concerns itself with Davie's view of literary tradition, not just of the Thirties. Latent in it is the awareness that he spells out in a subsequent essay:

we must be glad to be compelled to recognize that we are all, like it or not, post-Romantic people; that the historical developments which we label 'Romanticism' were not a series of aberrations which we can and should disown, but rather a sort of landslide which permanently transformed the mental landscape which in the twentieth century we inhabit, however reluctantly. . . . It is not a question of what we want or like; it is what we are stuck with—post-Romantic is what we are.[13]

Davie's critical books of the 1950s, *Purity of Diction in English Verse* (1952) and *Articulate Energy* (1955), draw abundantly on Romantic poets by whom he is, in general terms, offended. Wordsworth, Coleridge, and Shelley all come out of the earlier book surprisingly well. The positive comments offered by Davie about all three appear, it is true, wrung from him. They emerge against the grain of an innate suspiciousness, and they apply only to poems ostentatiously selected as exceptions. Still, their number is considerable. Wordsworth lacks 'urbanity' and reveals 'a determined provincialism' (not entirely, one suspects, for Davie, a weakness), yet in 'The White Doe of Rylstone' he 'achieved . . . a pure diction, a speech of civilized urbanity which can "purify the language of the tribe"'. The chapter on Coleridge argues with more bravado than insight that 'the Romantics rebelled not only against the forms they inherited, but against all forms, form as such', before going on to praise 'Dejection: An Ode' as 'one of the great poems in the language . . . the voice which speaks it is impersonal and timeless, the voice of a language'. And Shelley, guilty all too often of 'licentious phrasing', was also 'the master of the familiar style', where the first definite article is distinctly eyebrow-raising.[14]

---

[13] 'Sincerity and Poetry', in *The Poet in the Imaginary Museum*, p. 144.
[14] *Purity of Diction*, pp. 114, 117, 126, 129, 137, 140.

What should one make of the fact that Davie, supposedly anti-Romantic, in fact devotes many pages to pointing out how well the Romantics wrote? Certainly, he radically subverts the stereotypes of literary periodization; his critical insights show the value for Movement poetry of Romantic poems, when those poems are freed, as they are in Davie's close readings in *Purity of Diction*, from caricature. Davie's 1966 Postscript to the book offers it as 'a common manifesto' for Movement poets, but if there was a hate figure against which Movement poets united, it appears to Davie in his Postscript not to be Romanticism so much as 'all the values of Bohemia'.[15] His admiration for 'Dejection: An Ode' shows in his quotations from it in the first stanza of 'Rejoinder to a Critic' (*NL1*, p. 67):

> You may be right: 'How can I dare to feel?'
> May be the only question I can pose.
> 'And haply by abstruse research to steal
> From my own nature all the natural man'
> My sole resource. And I do not suppose
> That others may not have a better plan.

The first time 'Dejection' is quoted, in lines 3 and 4 of the stanza, which quote lines 89 and 90 from Coleridge's poem, Davie uses quotation marks. The second time it is quoted, in the first three words of the stanza's fifth line, which quotes from line 91 of Coleridge's poem, Davie dispenses with quotation marks, as if to indicate how interiorized 'Dejection' has become. Coleridge's attempt to find refuge in 'abstruse research' finds an echo here in Davie's own suspicion of feeling. But just as Coleridge moves us by speaking of his wish to escape feeling, so Davie's rejoinder to criticism is fraught with division, as in the poem's concluding stanza (which apparently turns from Coleridge, the queller of feeling, to Donne as feeling's apologist):

> 'Alas, alas, who's injured by my love?'
> And recent history answers: Half Japan!
> Not love, but hate? Well, both are versions of
> The 'feeling' that you dare me to. Be dumb!
> Appear concerned only to make it scan!
> How dare we now be anything but numb?

[15] Ibid., pp. 197, 199.

The last two lines deliberately protest too much: the penultimate line rounds off repetition of a rhyme first found in the opening stanza ('man' | 'plan'), as if to say that its only interest is technical, but the sturdily iambic 'Appear' is made to scan so that we hear the imperative as advocating a stance rather than the poet's deepest feeling; the final line looks like a rhetorical question, but running below it is a more open-ended and Romantic-influenced enquiry: 'How might we dare to break out of numbness?'

Even greater interest in Coleridge and Romantic poetry is apparent in *Articulate Energy*, a work which asserts that 'For poetry to be great, it must reek of the human, as Wordsworth's poetry does' and which finds in Coleridge's poetry a pattern of 'fleeing in a circle, and being overtaken by the feelings from which the poet flees', a pattern that is applicable to Davie's own work. To select two further examples: Blake's 'A Poison Tree' receives praise for a subtle 'syntax' that is 'neither narrative nor propositional, but partaking of both'. And Davie doughtily defends Wordsworth, a presiding presence, from the strictures of Leavis and Empson; syntax in *The Prelude* 'presents what is really going on, meditation, not argument; and it is therefore authentic, not a play of misleading forms'.[16] The judgement asks to be set beside Davie's poem 'The Fountain' (*NL1*, p. 65), which takes its point of departure from another figure important for *Articulate Energy*, George Berkeley. Indeed, Davie accuses himself of playing lawlessly with an image used by Berkeley from the end of the latter's *Dialogues of Hylas and Philonous*, in which the trajectory of 'the water of yonder fountain' serves to illustrate how 'the same principles which at first view lead to scepticism, pursued to a certain point, bring me back to common sense'.[17] In the poem Davie finds that he has merely engaged in meddling with an image; debarred from Berkeley's convictions, 'We ask of fountains only that they play', a line wholly 'post-Romantic' (and even pre-Martian) in its Schilleresque sense (however muffled) of the aesthetic as a form of 'play'. The poem ends with a cordoned-off line, 'Though that was not what Berkeley meant at all', a downbeat snub to the poem's bravura, its self-admiring delight in 'Similitudes of surf and turf and shawl'. What is authentically 'post-Romantic' about the poem is its anxiety about its own

---

[16] Donald Davie, *Articulate Energy: An Inquiry into the Syntax of English Poetry* (1955; London: Routledge and Kegan Paul, rpt with postscript, 1976), pp. 165, 76, 84, 112.

[17] Quoted in Introduction to *The Poet in the Imaginary Museum*, p. xi.

authenticity. Indeed, its capacity to celebrate and question its own imaginative 'play' gives it much in common with Romantic poems that share Davie's confessed loss of 'confidence' in 'enlightened but still common sense'.

If Davie is productively convoluted in his response to Romanticism, Kingsley Amis, at first sight, seems robustly contemptuous, wishing less to put Romanticism by than to squash it flat. In 'Ode to the East-North-East-by-East Wind', Amis has Shelley in his sights, the Movement's favourite whipping-boy among the Romantics.[18] The poem addresses the wind, mocked descendant of Shelley's 'breath of autumn's being' ('Ode to the West Wind', line 1), in teasing, patronizing tones:

> Sometimes you pump up water from the ground;
>   Why, darling, that's just fine of you!
> And round Mount Everest—such fun!—you blow
>   Gigantic bits of rock about, for no
>   Reason—but every boy
>   Must have his little toy.[19]

This identifies the wind with childish bravado, exhibitionism, and irrational energy, all needing to be reined in by the adult Movement poet. The poet, in effect, mimics and mocks the 'I–thou' relationship which, according to Harold Bloom in *Shelley's Mythmaking* (1959), Shelley seeks to establish with all that lies beyond the self; bristling with ironic indulgence and putdowns, Amis has no time for the natural as a force demanding awe or reverence. For him, the wind, like the Romantic poets who exalt it, is a spoilt child.

And yet it threatens to take over the poem in the final couplet of the third stanza. Ostensibly jeered at for 'Telling the void of your distress, | Raving at emptiness', the wind brings into the well-ordered world of the poem two nouns—'distress' and 'emptiness'—that challenge the speaker's ironies as

---

[18] Amis may also, as Zachary Leader has observed to me, be thinking of Charles Kingsley's 'Ode to the North-east Wind', included in *The Amis Anthology*, chosen and ed. Kingsley Amis (London: Hutchinson, 1988). That is not to say that Amis is wholly mocking the Victorian poet; Kingsley's poem would, one imagines, be approved by Amis for its bluff, unShelleyan nationalism: 'But the black North-easter, | Through the snowstorm hurled, | Drives our English hearts of oak | Seaward round the world'. Indeed, the choice of this poem may be a calculated snub directed at Shelley, who is pointedly excluded from the anthology, an omission to which Amis draws attention in his Introduction, p. xv.

[19] Quoted from Kingsley Amis, *Collected Poems: 1944–1979* (London: Hutchinson, 1979).

too easily assumed. The final stanza sustains its attack on the wind as a fit 'theme' for 'Poetic egotists' who find reflected in its chaotic energy 'their hatred for | A world that will not mirror their desire'. But the tone shifts, even in that last line, which, despite itself, pays out a good deal of verbal rope to Romantic 'desire', hoping, doubtless, that it will contrive to hang itself. Instead, it gives way to a close in which urbane superiority falters: 'Silly yourself', writes Amis, 'you flatter and inspire | Some of the silliest of us. | And is that worth the fuss?' Echoing Auden's words from his 'In Memory of W. B. Yeats', 'You were silly like us', Amis provokes memory of the second half of Auden's line: 'your gift survived it all'.[20] He allows the wind to 'inspire' as well as 'flatter', and even if it affects 'Some of the silliest of us', we note the pronoun, 'us'. Amis might have been influenced by one of Larkin's parodies, 'a form of travesty in which nothing was altered but much added: "Music, when soft *silly* voices, that have been talking *piss* die, | Vibrates, like a..." '.[21] But it is worth noting that even here, as in many parodies, the effect is not wholly to annul the power of the original: 'Music' still 'Vibrates' in the lines, arguably the more so for having to compete with and overpower 'soft *silly* voices, that have been talking *piss*'.

Amis's own parodic response also finds itself obliged to get on speaking terms with its Romantic original, as occurs in other poems by him, such as 'A Song of Experience', which rewrites Blake to depict with circumspect approval the philandering of a salesman who 'found the female and the human heart', or 'The Triumph of Life', which borrows Shelley's terza rima to assert the wry irony that what survives of us are 'photographs', an art, for Amis, that always lies. Like Shelley's 'Ode to the West Wind', 'Ode to the East-North-East-by-East Wind' concludes with a question, a question which, like Shelley's, seems merely rhetorical. But, like Shelley's, it conceals a latent complication. 'Oh wind, | If winter comes, can spring be far behind?' (69–70) invites the answer 'no, it cannot', yet, given what has gone before, Shelley's final question also invites us to see the seasons metaphorically, an invitation which muddies the waters. Will the 'winter' of poetic dryness or political tyranny necessarily pass into the 'spring' of creativity and freedom? One hopes

[20] Quoted from W. H. Auden, *Collected Poems*, ed. Edward Mendelson (London: Faber, 1991).
[21] Kingsley Amis, *Memoirs* (1992); quoted from Andrew Motion, *Philip Larkin: A Writer's Life* (London: Faber, 1993), p. 58.

that it might, but cannot be sure that it will. Amis's laconic question, 'And is that worth the fuss?', seems to insist on the answer, 'no, it is not', until the reader asks both 'what do you mean by "that"?' and 'what "fuss"?' If the most obvious candidate as an answer to the second query is the 'fuss' made by the wind always about to 'rush off somewhere new', another possibility, following the concession that the wind inspires 'Some of the silliest of us', is that the 'fuss' refers to the poem itself. And 'that' would seem to mean 'that fact', the fact that the wind flatters and inspires 'Some of the silliest of us'. 'Fuss' is a typical Movement word, almost self-mockingly unliterary, quick to deflate anything too theatrical or declamatory. But, as in many of Amis's and the Movement's best poems, satire at the expense of another leads to irony at the expense of the self. The very title 'Ode to the East-North-East-by-East Wind' may have been intended, in its 'pedantic geography', to serve as a 'reproach' to the 'extravagant pantheism of Shelley's "Ode to the West Wind" '.[22] But, re-read after the wobble of feelings registered by the close, it begins to seem like a compass needle trembling between divergent directions.

Comparable tensions inform Amis's 'Against Romanticism' (*NL1*, pp. 45–6). The poem works in a mode one might call semi-allegorical. It features 'A traveller who walks a temperate zone', much like a Movement poet, about to find himself caught up in a net of Romantic temptations. The blank verse sustains its 'temperate' manner, but it also captures the appeal of all that is officially disapproved of by the poem: the 'ingrown taste for anarchy', 'Torrid images', the appeal of the senses. 'Over all, a grand meaning fills the scene', Amis affirms sardonically, presenting what, for him, is among the headiest and most seductive of Romantic lures. As in Pope's satires, the poem's imaginative energies do not, to the advantage of the poetry, completely defer to the super-ego's dictates. The Dunce who 'from the effluvia strong | Imbibes new life, and scours and stinks along' (ll. 105–6) and who is heedless of 'the brown dishonours of his face' (l. 108) in the mock-epic contests of *The Dunciad* is magnificent as well as merely ignominious in his indifference to appearance.[23]

[22] Morrison, *The Movement*, p. 169.

[23] Quoted from *The Poems of Alexander Pope: A One-Volume Edition of the Twickenham Text with Selected Annotations*, ed. John Butt (London: Methuen, 1963). For the strange appeal of the Dunces, see Emrys Jones's Chatterton Lecture, 'Pope and Dulness', *Proceedings of the British Academy* 54 (1968), pp. 231–63.

In Amis's poem, too, the longing for discipline and decency seems more than half in love with the unruly energies that it seeks to curb. The 'traveller' in the 'temperate zone' forestalls the response of many readers of Movement poetry when he 'Finds that its decent surface grows too thin'. 'Decency' is implicitly praised here, but it is also exposed briefly as a question of surfaces. What lies below the surface may be suspect, but Amis lends the temptations of the 'Romantic' enough verbal colour to make us hesitate before dismissing them as corrupt. The writing half-suggests that the Romantic derives from an illicitly subjective desire for thrills: the 'Torrid images' manifest themselves 'To please an ingrown taste for anarchy', for example, where the wording suggests a tug towards chaos that is wilful, self-absorbed. Yet if the phrase is 'aimed at Shelley',[24] matters complicate when one recalls that Shelley's most famous use of 'anarchy', in *The Mask of Anarchy*, is decidedly negative. For Shelley, 'anarchy' is a condition of misrule that masquerades as order and control. 'And he wore a kingly crown, | And in his grasp a sceptre shone; | On his brow this mark I saw— | "I am God, and King, and Law"'(34–7).

Indeed, Amis's text releases two forces at odds with a straightforward 'Against Romanticism' stance. The first is that the language does not always support the idea of a wanton subjectivity making all things the mirror of itself. At times the self is the seemingly passive object of overpowering forces: 'Something unperceived fumbles at his nerves', for example, or 'verbal scents made real spellbind the nose'. It can be argued that the 'Something unperceived' or the 'verbal scents' are the self's creation; but their power, at once 'fumbling' and 'spellbinding', bears witness to longings and desires which cannot (the poem's counter-argument implies) be banished by an act of will. In 'Church Going' (*NL1*, pp. 20–2) Larkin at once gainsays and builds on his confession that 'I've no idea | What this accoutred frowsty barn is worth', commenting that it is 'A serious house on serious earth', never 'obsolete, | Since someone will for ever be surprising | A hunger in himself to be more serious'. Doing so, he might almost be rewriting Amis's 'Something unperceived fumbles at his nerves'. Larkin recasts Amis's troubling *frisson* as a quasi-transcendental impulse, but in both poets, albeit with contrasting inflections, the Romantic, if interpreted as the pull of the hitherto 'unperceived', exercises a hold.

[24] Morrison, *The Movement*, p. 162.

'Against Romanticism' also makes one question whether the work of the Romantic poets themselves corresponds to what the poem seems to mean by 'Romanticism'. For Amis, Romanticism is discontent, desire, 'the brain raging with prophecy, | Raging to discard real time and place, | Raging to build a better time and place | Than the ones which give prophecy its field | To work, the calm material for its rage, | And the context which makes it prophecy'. These lines imply that Romantic 'raging' takes the form of petulant discontent with the here and now. One wonders who is in Amis's sights. He clearly is not remembering the accents of Wordsworth's recollections in *The Prelude*, where the poet recalls how his former revolutionary self looked for change

> Not in Utopia—subterraneous fields,
> Or some secreted island, heaven knows where!
> But in the very world which is the world
> Of all of us, the place in which in the end
> We find our happiness, or not at all.

(1805. X. 724–8)[25]

Wordsworth is describing a kind of anti-Utopian visionary politics, designed to be relevant to 'the very world which is the world | Of all of us'. Arguably, from a later perspective, such a politics seems to him flawed. Or it can also be contended that he empathizes with his youthful self. On either interpretation, the lines present a Romantic politics that is 'raging with prophecy', not in order to 'discard real time and place', but to transform 'the place in which in the end | We find our happiness, or not at all'. Amis's Romanticism risks being a target of straw, ignoring the degree to which Romantic prophecy intersects with 'real time and place'. Morrison suggests that the figure this section of the poem attacks is Blake.[26] If it is, one might retort to Amis that 'the voice of the bard' ('Introduction', line 1, *Songs of Experience*) in Blake, or the voice that launches prophetic denunciations in the longer poems, may wish to build a new Jerusalem, certainly, but that these voices are acutely aware of 'context', of the injustices and miseries that disfigure the Romantic poet's England.

[25] Quoted from William Wordsworth, *The Prelude: The Four Texts (1798, 1799, 1805, 1850)*, ed. Jonathan Wordsworth (London: Penguin, 1995).
[26] Morrison, *The Movement*, p. 162.

Does this mean that Amis's explicit anti-Romanticism is a form of political conservatism, even quietism, mistrustful of those who would rebuild society in accordance with an overarching 'grand narrative'? Not quite: in the lines quoted above, Amis manages to have his cake and eat it. If he objects to one mode of 'prophecy', his trailing clauses give house-room to another, one that is alert to the 'context' of prophecy, giving it 'its field | To work'. Breaking surface is a kind of updated, topsy-turvy Romanticism. In the poem's second paragraph, in fact, Amis recognizes, a shade ruefully, that 'complexities crowd the simplest things', and his homiletic mode still has commerce with 'visions': 'Let us make at least visions that we need'. Granted, the rhythm here is calculatedly dogged, while 'visions' is immediately undercut by the next line: 'Let mine be pallid'. Yet the white-out of Amis's negative Romanticism—conjuring a world 'free from all grime of history, | The people total strangers, the grass cut'—has little to do with any 'real time and place', and shapes an ironized post-Romantic Utopianism. In Shelley's transformed universe, 'None talked that common, false, cold, hollow talk | Which makes the heart deny the "yes" it breathes' (*Prometheus Unbound*, 3. 4. 153–4). In Amis's desired state, plurality and strangeness are the ideals needed; he wishes for a 'vision' that 'cannot | Force a single glance, form a single word', but this non-dictatorial desire is distinctly 'single' in inflection. Nor is the gap between the imposition of authorial will and the fear of single-mindedness the only inconsistency. If the desired flight from 'history' speaks volumes about a writer suspicious of a cultural march from the Byronic hero to the Fascist dictator, the wish annuls itself in the utterance. It may speak out of a Britain building itself as a Welfare State, but the 'grime of history' will not so easily be washed away.

The curving back to the 'temperate zone' at the end of the poem occurs after Amis has dispatched a variety of 'Romantic' follies—including the 'long, voluble swooning wilderness', 'frantic suns', 'a rout of gods', and 'the havering unicorn'—with firm disapproval and just a hint of wistfulness. When he asks that 'the sky be clean of officious birds | Punctiliously flying on the left', the poet may have in mind a soothsayer's auguries. Yet in a poem that invites Romantic allusion-hunting, it is hard not to think of Keats's 'gathering swallows twitter in the skies' (33) at the conclusion of 'To Autumn'. Inspired by the weather's 'temperate sharpness' (Cook, p. 493), Keats writes of his birds in a correspondingly 'temperate' manner. His swallows are not turned into symbols or projections of feeling, and yet they participate in a deeply imaginative response to being human, which is all the more powerful for being understated and avoiding overt sentiment. Amis's 'officious birds' cut Romantic birds down to size, dismissing them as so many props, poetic mumbo-jumbo. But as Keats's swallows fly, however accidentally, into Amis's poem, they remind us, in the midst of the twentieth-century poet's attack on Romanticism, of an unignorable Romantic achievement.

Romantic poetry, then, lives and moves and has its being in Movement poems in troubling, thought-provoking ways. When, in 'Something Nasty in the Bookshop' (*NL1*, pp. 46–7), Amis silently quotes Byron, the effect contributes to the poem's overall trickiness of attitude. 'Should poets bicycle-bump the human heart | Or squash it flat? | Man's love is of man's life a thing apart: | Girls aren't like that.' The stanza's third line is taken (with the comically ponderous substitution of 'man's life' for 'his life') from Julia's farewell letter to Juan in *Don Juan*, canto 1, stanza 194, a letter which is at once affecting and histrionic. 'My brain is feminine', writes Julia, 'nor can forget— | To all, except your image, madly blind' (1. st. 195), as if anticipating Amis's bluff sense of gender difference: 'And the awful way their poems lay them open | Just doesn't strike them'. Both Amis and Byron are superb mimics, a mimicry embodied, in Amis's poem, in the shuttling between attitudes mimed by his long and short lines, so that here the 'way their poems lay them open' is imitated by the rhythm's unguarded amiability. Both Amis and Byron manage to expose gender presuppositions through their acts of mimicry. Byron, one feels, is less teasingly infuriating than merely calling it as it all too often seemed to be in his society when he declares, 'Man's love is of his life a thing apart, | 'Tis woman's whole existence' (*Don Juan*, 1. 194). Amis adopts the Byron line (in both senses), but he does so mock-solemnly. Indeed, the whole poem succeeds by suggesting that its kidding, jokey phrases belong to a manner of speaking that wishes to do away with illusions and postures, but cannot escape awareness of playing a part. The poem's close punctures the speaker's seemingly illimitable male self-confidence, recalling, in the act of forgetting, 'those times | We sat up half the night | Chock-full of love, crammed with bright thoughts, names, rhymes, | And couldn't write'. Here what is squashed flat by the final short line is the arrogance of supposing 'We men have got love well weighed up'. 'Chock-full of love' is a phrase still snaffled by irony, but 'couldn't write' opens the poem out to feelings beyond the scope of its ironic style: indeed, 'And couldn't write' is a line that Amis could not have written without the example of Wordsworth's throwing in the verbal towel at the end of 'She dwelt among th'untrodden ways', an end which glimpses the limits of speech: 'But she is in her grave, and oh! | The difference to me' (11–12).

Elsewhere, for ancillary Movement writers such as Elizabeth Jennings or Thom Gunn, Romantic fires continue to burn, albeit in modes that play up rationalist control. Gunn moves towards an Existentialist commitment to 'movement in a valueless world' ('On the Move', *NL1*, pp. 31–3) that has much in common with Romanticism's stress on 'becoming'. For Gunn, 'Reaching no absolute' ('On the Move') seems itself to be an 'absolute', but the trajectory of his thought recalls Wordsworth's pursuit of 'something evermore about to be' (*The Prelude, 1805*, VI. 542). His sonnet 'Lerici' (*NL1*, p. 31), in effect, constructs for its own purposes two kinds of Romanticism: one, associated with Shelley, is passive and surrendering, the other, with Byron as its exemplary figure, is 'masterful', 'Squandering' rather than 'submissive'. If Shelley died 'Arms at his side', in Gunn's swiftly caricaturing sketch, Byron is one of the 'Others' who 'make gestures with arms open wide'. The rhyme, like the poem, makes of Shelley and Byron antitheses, and the Byronic penchant for 'gesture' leaves its impress on Gunn at this stage. His language seems to stamp itself on experience. When he seeks to empathize with the worshippers in his 'In Santa Maria del Popolo' (*NL2*, pp. 34–5), he sees them as producing 'the large gesture of solitary man, | Resisting, by embracing, nothingness'. That last line might describe the ethos of Byron's *Childe Harold's Pilgrimage*, and it is more profitable to read Gunn as post- rather than anti-Romantic.

Jennings's 'The Island' (*NL1*, pp. 1–2) offers a post-Arnoldian vision of human beings as 'islands'. Arnold's Victorian pessimism seems washed away by Movement trust in reason; his 'unplumbed, salt, estranging sea' ('To Marguerite—Continued', 24)[27] undergoes a soothing transformation in Jennings's image of 'Men' who 'steer | Self to knowledge of self in the calm sea, | Seekers who are their own discovery'. That last line might well describe many Romantic questers, but its formulaic patness lacks the note of anguish one associates with figures such as Manfred or Blake's Mental Traveller. Yet in a poem such as 'In the Night' (*NL1*, pp. 7–8) Jennings renders the schism

---

[27] Quoted from *The Poems of Matthew Arnold*, ed. Kenneth Allott, 2nd edn. ed. Miriam Allott (London: Longman, 1979).

between 'thoughts' and 'object' in a powerfully post-Romantic manner: 'my thoughts about it divide | Me from my object. Now deep in my bed | I turn and the world turns on the other side'. The rhythmic strength here, shown in the way that 'turns' takes an emphatic stress, compels belief in a 'world' brought into the poem by being located 'the other side' of the poem's lines. In so doing, 'In the Night' concedes a debt to the practice of Romantic poets such as Wordsworth, Coleridge, and Shelley when confronting the fear that reality will not conform to the dictates of pantheist or transcendental desire. When Jennings affirms, 'Something of me is out in the dark landscape', the very tentativeness of 'Something of me' reminds us of the scepticism that pervades Movement poetry when it ponders the relationship between the human and the non-human. Yet such scepticism, in part aimed at supposed Romantic nature-worship and the basis for later denigration from poets such as Hughes, reminds us, too, how the Romantics themselves unsettle the idea that Nature never betrays the heart that loved her. Coleridge's 'in our life alone does nature live' ('Dejection: An Ode', 48) is a line that resonates throughout second-generation Romantic poetry and beyond.

John Wain has no time, in 'Reason for Not Writing Orthodox Nature Poetry' (NL1, pp. 83–4), for 'moderns who devoutly hymn the land', and this dislike of nature poetry runs through the work of the Movement poets. In 'Here is Where' (NL1, pp. 47–8), Amis parodies then mocks this most Romantic of genres. His question 'What has this subject | Got to do with that object?' is meant to invite the answer 'Nothing at all', yet it opens up communication with those many Romantic poems that are forms of heterodox nature poetry, poems such as Shelley's 'Mont Blanc' in which the subject tussles to make sense of a near-unfathomable object. Wain himself settles for a modified post-Coleridgean 'love' of nature in his poem, scorn converting itself to affection in the clipped one-liners that his sub-Empsonian style favours: 'Simply,' he concludes, 'I love this mountain and this bay [. . .] | And where you love you cannot break away.'

One poet who cannot wholly break away from his Romantic forebears is Philip Larkin, as is now widely recognized. Donald Davie's 'Two Intercepted Letters', his elegy for Larkin, draws on Romantic parallels to convey his complicated feelings about the dead poet. 'What's said should be unsaid | Of Byron dead', ends the poem's first part, inviting us to substitute the modern poet's name. The close of Hazlitt's essay on Byron in The Spirit of the Age may be an influence here. Hazlitt writes:

We had written thus far when news came of the death of Lord Byron, and put an end
at once to a strain of somewhat peevish invective, which was intended to meet his
eye, not to insult his memory. Had we known that we were writing his epitaph, we
must have done it with a different feeling.[28]

Davie conceivably alludes to this famous change of heart. In post-Movement
guise, he had, after all, raised at best only two cheers for Larkin's poetry of
'lowered sights and patiently diminished expectations'.[29] But by bringing
Larkin into connection with Byron, he concedes that his judgement in *Thomas
Hardy and British Poetry* may itself involve a not wholly accurate diminishing.
Edna Longley opens her essay 'Poète Maudit Manqué' in the same memorial
volume with the comment, 'I think it is now more generally accepted that
Philip Larkin was a Romantic who covered his tracks,...an aesthete who
pretended to be a hearty ("Art, if you like").'[30] Longley alludes to 'Reasons for
Attendance', a poem which, for all its no-nonsense idiom, arguably descends
from Keats's 'Ode on a Grecian Urn'. Both poems chart dialectical voyages
between, in Larkin's terms, 'Sex' and 'Art, if you like'.[31] That throwaway 'if
you like' can only barely conceal the aesthetic purity of Larkin's vocation, his
commitment to 'What calls me', 'that lifted, rough-tongued bell | ...whose
individual sound | Insists I too am individual'. 'Individual' is still in touch with
the obdurate bloody-mindedness on show earlier in the poem ('to think the
lion's share | Of happiness is found by couples—sheer | ... | Inaccuracy, as far
as I'm concerned'), but it also hints at a more private, more fugitive selfhood
called into being and made possible by 'Art'. As if repressing this possibility as
soon as he senses it, Larkin goes on to assert that all 'Art', that 'rough-tongued
bell', can do is to toll him and other listeners back to their sole selves:

> It speaks; I hear; others may hear as well,
> But not for me, nor I for them; and so
> With happiness.

The remote allusion at work here and in previous lines to the last stanza
of Keats's 'Ode to a Nightingale' clothes itself in staccato, down-to-earth

---

[28] Quoted from *Byron: The Critical Heritage*, ed. Andrew Rutherford (London: Routledge & Kegan
Paul, 1970), p. 277.

[29] Donald Davie, *Thomas Hardy and British Poetry* (London: Routledge & Kegan Paul, 1973), p. 71.

[30] *Philip Larkin 1922–1985: A Tribute*, ed. George Hartley (London: Marvell, 1988), pp. 16, 220.

[31] Quoted from Philip Larkin, *Collected Poems*. ed. with intro. Anthony Thwaite (London: The
Marvell Press with Faber, 1988).

phrasing. For Keats's questioning whether he sleeps or wakes, Larkin sub-stitutes a final doubt concerning his and others' judgement and integrity: 'and both are satisfied, | If no one has misjudged himself. Or lied.' Yet, again, one notes that only a simplistic reading of Romantic poetry overlooks the fact that it concerns itself as much with 'truth' as 'beauty'. Moreover, the gruff suspicions voiced by the poem's end fight hard to keep at bay any hint of unqualified 'aestheticism', enthusiastically endorsed by Larkin in an early letter, in which he adduces the close of 'Ode on a Grecian Urn' as 'judging everything by its beauty'.[32]

Keats's supposed identification of 'truth' and 'beauty' (an identification urged, in fact, by the Urn, finally stirred into imagined speech) intrigued Larkin, even though he expresses his disillusionment with the idea in a let-ter of 1945: 'Keets was a silly Bum'.[33] Tentative, stubborn wishes to reconcile 'truth' and 'beauty' seek expression in many of his finest poems, including 'Church Going', a Movement poem *par excellence* precisely because of its dis-comfort with its own initial response of near-frivolous indifference. In the final stanza, the line 'A serious house on serious earth it is', quoted earlier in this essay, earned Amis's reproof for 'the inversion..., which makes me think of "A casement high and triple arched there was" and such bits of flan-nel'. Amis goes on, 'I'd say you've got to be extra careful, at the point when you ease your foot gently down on the accelerator, to avoid reminding the reader that "this is poetry".'[34] As Zachary Leader notes, Larkin ignored the criticism, along with other cavils.[35] But the comment shows the sensitiv-ity of Amis's allusive radar as he detects the influence of Keats's 'The Eve of St Agnes', line 208.

One may feel that it is by no means undesirable that, as Larkin eases his foot gently down on the accelerator, what comes to mind is a Romantic poem. The two lines stand in emblematic relation: Movement poetry attaining, through the art of its most distinguished practitioner, the status of 'A serious house on serious earth'; Romantic poetry in momentary comparison and contrast taking on the form of 'A casement high and triple-arched'. Larkin's 'serious house' dwells on 'serious earth'; his 'is' at the end of the line has a

[32] *Selected Letters of Philip Larkin 1940–1985*, ed. Anthony Thwaite (London: Faber, 1992), p. 56.

[33] *Letters of Philip Larkin*, p. 108. Larkin's misspelling of Keats's name is presumably a joke.

[34] *Letters of Kingsley Amis*, p. 399.

[35] Ibid.

Wordsworthian resonance, 'the figure presented in the most naked simplicity possible', as Wordsworth says of his use of '*was*' in the original version of 'Resolution and Independence'.[36] Keats's 'casement' is his poetry's favourite image for the possibility of an imaginative elsewhere (a topic explored by Larkin in 'The Importance of Elsewhere'), its triple arch pointing skywards. Yet he, more than any other Romantic poet, practised a 'poetry of earth' ('On the Grasshopper and Cricket', 9; quoted from Cook), while Larkin allows for a quasi-transcendent impulse in a phrase such as 'blent air'. There the poetic diction flirts with archaism but earns its keep. Taking us back to earlier poetic practices, it enacts the survival into the present of human 'compulsions', including the 'compulsion' to turn 'compulsions' into 'destinies'. In the *New Lines* printing, a typographical error underplays the post-Romantic restlessness at work in the stanza: the second line, wrongly, reads 'In whose blent air all our compulsions rest'; it should read 'In whose blent air all our compulsions meet'.[37] No more than is usually the case with the Romantics is Larkin seeking a final certitude. Rather, he finds an idiom that is at once of its time and in contact with a poetic tradition that includes the Romantics.

'How is it that you live, and what is it you do?' Wordsworth's question in 'Resolution and Independence' (126) trembles on the verge of self-caricature (Lewis Carroll would give it a nudge in 'Upon the Lonely Moor' that takes it over the comic cliff-edge), but Larkin commented with approval on Richard Murphy's application of it to his work, which sought, Murphy said, 'more and better answers to Wordsworth's question'.[38] In 'Church Going' Larkin puts a similar enquiry not only to himself but to his culture. He moves beyond 'the debunking, uninformed and awkward persona' of the poem's opening, unobtrusively expanding, like Wordsworth in 'Tintern Abbey', from 'I' to 'we'.[39] The 'hunger in himself to be more serious' which Larkin exemplifies in this poem is an appetite evident in many Movement poets, one that they often seek to satisfy through their fraught, exacting negotiations with Romantic poetry.

---

[36] Letter of 14 June 1802, quoted in *William Wordsworth: A Critical Anthology*, ed. Graham McMaster (Harmondsworth: Penguin, 1972), p. 86.

[37] For Larkin's awareness of the error, see his letter to Robert Conquest of 7 May 1957, *Letters of Philip Larkin*, p. 274. The error still occurs in the 1967 reprint of *New Lines*.

[38] *Letters of Philip Larkin*, p. 249 ('I thought the Wordsworth quotation was nicely chosen', Larkin wrote to Murphy).

[39] Morrison, *The Movement*, p. 230. For the movement from 'I' to 'we', connected to Larkin's ability 'to universalize the experience', see p. 229.

16

Elizabeth Jennings, the Movement, and Rome

Rachel Buxton

Elizabeth Jennings often sought to distance herself from the Movement. She queried not only its value to her as a poet—she remarks in a 1995 interview, for instance, that 'I thought for myself that I didn't do too well out of it'[1]— but also its very existence. Like many both at the time and since she considered it an 'artificial' grouping invented by 'systemizers and newshounds'.[2] Typical of this stance is her 1961 assertion that

When the most valuable qualities which poets share are clarity, honesty and formal perfection—qualities which we expect to find in all worthwhile poetry—it is not very surprising to find those poets developing away from the group, especially when they were rather uneasily huddled together in the first place.[3]

Certainly the publication of her third volume, *A Sense of the World*, in 1958, marked Jennings's divergence from that 'huddle'; much of the collection sits awkwardly alongside the predominantly secular and sceptical poems of the

---

[1] In Gerlinde Gramang, *Elizabeth Jennings: An Appraisal of Her Life as a Poet, Her Approach to Her Work and a Selection of the Major Themes of Her Poetry* (Lewiston, NY: Salzburg: Edwin Mellen Press, 1995), 93.

[2] Elizabeth Jennings, Introduction, *An Anthology of Modern Verse: 1940–1960* (London: Methuen, 1961), p. 11.

[3] Jennings, *Poetry To-Day* (London: Longmans, Green & Co., 1961), p. 12.

other Movement poets. But, just as certainly, Jennings shared with others in the grouping a little more than the 'clarity, honesty and formal perfection' that she claims here. If we step back to the late 1940s and early 1950s, to those years before her receipt of the Somerset Maugham Award in 1957, we find Jennings playing a central role in a thriving Oxford poetry scene, and can begin to appreciate how it was that she came to be associated with the Movement.

Jennings encountered Philip Larkin and John Wain at Oxford, and was later to become a close friend of Wain's; she also got to know Kingsley Amis, whom she first met in early 1948 at a lecture at Magdalen College on Court handwriting (she admits to brazenly copying his notes). The course was part of the preparation for the B.Litt. preliminary examinations which both of them were sitting, and which Jennings failed, blaming the fact that she was spending more time than was good for her study with her then-fiancé, Stuart.[4] She and Amis became good friends, drinking together, browsing record shops, listening to jazz, and going to the cinema.[5] Over the next couple of years, during which time she was copy-editing in London during the week but living with her parents in Oxford at weekends, she met fairly regularly with him, James Michie, and Peter Chettle; when she returned permanently to Oxford in 1950 to work in the City Library she also got to know other young poets then studying at the university such as Paul West, Donald Hall, Adrienne Rich, Geoffrey Hill, and Anthony Thwaite.[6]

Jennings and Amis exchanged poems in these years. Six of these were collected in *Oxford Poetry 1949*, edited that year by Amis and Michie; in his memoir Amis was to proclaim that 'the star of the show, our discovery, was Elizabeth Jennings'.[7] Jennings had in fact already had one poem, a fairly conventional love lyric entitled 'The Elements', published in the previous year's *Oxford Poetry*, but in the 1949 poems we see emerging the spareness of style and the coolness of tone which were to characterize her subsequent published work—take

[4] Amis succeeded in passing his exams though failed the thesis—see Zachary Leader, *The Life of Kingsley Amis* (London: Jonathan Cape, 2006), pp. 206–10; 248–9.

[5] Jennings, 'As I Am', unpublished autobiography, typed MS, Georgetown Special Collections, Elizabeth Jennings Papers (Group 2), Box 32, Folder 1, undated, p. 55. All passages from 'As I Am' reprinted with the permission of David Higham Associates, on behalf of the Estate of Elizabeth Jennings. All previously unpublished material in this essay © 2009 Estate of Elizabeth Jennings.

[6] Jennings, 'As I Am', pp. 61, 78–81; see also Jerry Bradley, *The Movement: British Poets of the 1950s* (New York: Twayne, 1993), p. 88.

[7] Kingsley Amis, *Memoirs* (London: Hutchinson, 1991), p. 109.

the poem 'Weathercock', which begins with the line 'A hard tin bird was my lover'; or 'Winter Love' which closes with the image of 'white skin shaken like a white snowflake'.[8] The Jennings poems selected for inclusion in the anthology accord readily with the editors' stated preference for hardness and precision, for the 'telegraph-pole and the rifle' over the 'amethyst and the syrup'.[9] More strikingly, we find in Jennings's 'Modern Poet' a distrust of the bardic and the Neo-Romantic which pre-empts the 'Better, of course, if images were plain' assertions of Amis's manifesto poem, 'Against Romanticism':

> This is no moment now for the fine phrases,
> The inflated sentence, words cunningly spun,
> For the floreate image or the relaxing pun
> Or the sentimental answer that most pleases.
>
> We must write down an age of reckless hunger,
> Of iron girders, hearts like plumb-lines hung
> And the poet's art is to speak and not to be sung
> And sympathy must turn away to anger.[10]

A few other events from the start of the following decade illustrate Jennings's continuing involvement in all things poetry. In 1951, she was introduced to John Lehmann during a talent-spotting visit of his to Oxford; shortly afterwards one of her poems, 'The Substitute', was included in his first *New Soundings* broadcast, on 9 January 1952.[11] Of perhaps more significance for our understanding of Jennings's association with the Movement was the arrival in Oxford of the painter and printer Oscar Mellor. In 1952 he published a short pamphlet of seven of Jennings's poems (including 'Weathercock' and 'Winter Love'); so successful was this that he went on to publish pamphlets of other poets, including Larkin, Amis, Gunn, Davie, and Holloway; he also put together the first full-length collection of Jennings's poetry, *Poems* (1953), and was later to publish both Gunn's and Davie's first full-length collections. And in the following year, 1954, Jennings further cemented

[8] Jennings, 'Weathercock', and 'Winter Love', *Oxford Poetry 1949*, ed. Kingsley Amis and James Michie (Oxford: Basil Blackwell, 1949), pp. 31, 35.

[9] Kingsley Amis and James Michie, Editorial, *Oxford Poetry 1949*, p. 3.

[10] Jennings, 'Modern Poet', *Oxford Poetry 1949*, 34. Reprinted with the permission of David Higham Associates, on behalf of the Estate of Elizabeth Jennings.

[11] Kate Whitehead, *The Third Programme: A Literary History* (Oxford: Clarendon Press, 1989), pp. 181–2. Other writers included in that broadcast were Henry Green, Lynette Roberts, James Michie, Vernon Watkins, Roy Fuller, Simon Broadbent, and James Price.

her association with these poets when, along with Wain and Amis, she leapt to the defence of Anthony Hartley, whose hostile review of Edith Sitwell's *Gardeners and Astronomers* and stated preference for 'our young academic poets, the University Wits (Kingsley Amis and Donald Davie, for example)' had provoked a furious rebuttal from Sitwell and a stormy exchange on the letters pages of *The Spectator*.[12]

Regardless of whether or not we agree with her that the Movement was an invention of 'systemizers and newshounds', it is clear that Jennings was an integral part of the poetry scene from which it was seen to have emerged. Although, as she insists, the Movement poets 'bear none of the typical signs of the usual so-called literary movement'—they 'have issued no manifesto' and 'share no ideological preconceptions or convictions'—the poets associated with the group were linked by more than the 'common aims' which she attributes to them.[13] Not only did Jennings share with them certain formal qualities, but, largely by virtue of being in Oxford during those decisive years, she also established some of the friendships and participated in the key networks of printers, publishers, and fellow poets, which led to the development of that group identity. Given some of the basic similarities in form and attitude (if not always in tone), and the parallels in friendships and publishing histories, it should be little surprise that she was included as one of the senior Movement members in both Enright's *Poets of the 1950s* (1955) and Conquest's *New Lines* anthology (1956).

Jennings's differences from the Movement began to become apparent in 1958, with the publication of *A Sense of the World*. Philip Larkin reviewed the collection for *The Guardian*, and opens his review with the sly observation that, 'As Maugham-award deportee, Miss Jennings would clearly be more at ease than at least one of her predecessors'.[14] The dig, of course, is directed at Kingsley Amis, who received the Maugham Award in 1955 for *Lucky Jim*,

[12] Anthony Hartley, 'Critic Between the Lines', *The Spectator*, 8 Jan. 1954, p. 47; Letter from Sitwell, *The Spectator*, 22 Jan. 1954, p. 96; Letters from Wain, Amis (posing as 'Little Mr. Tomkins') and Jennings, *The Spectator*, 29 Jan. 1954, p. 123.

[13] Jennings, Introduction, *An Anthology of Modern Verse*, 10.

[14] Philip Larkin, 'Reports on Experience', *The Guardian*, 5 Sept. 1958, p. 6.

and who wrote to Larkin a few days after hearing of his success to gripe about 'this deportation order from the Somerset Maugham Trust; forced to go abroad, bloody *forced* mun…the whole prospect fills me with alarm and depression'.[15] In order to fulfil the terms of the award—worth a substantial £400, but requiring the recipient to spend this sum on at least three months' travel or residence abroad—Amis reluctantly decamped to Portugal with his family, a trip made more bearable, it seems, by his decision to base his novel *I Like It Here*, complete with contemptuous take on 'abroad' (or, as he would say, on those who write about 'abroad'), on this enforced exile.

Contrast this with the attitude of Jennings, who was awarded the prize the following year for her second collection of poems, *A Way of Looking* (1955). She elected to spend her three months in Italy, travelling to Rome in April 1957 and remaining there for the majority of her stay, bar a side trip to Assisi and Florence and then two weeks in Paris on the way back to England. During this time she wrote many of the poems which are collected in *A Sense of the World*. Although she had travelled to the Continent before, including on holidays in Sorrento, Florence, and Venice in the early 1950s, it had never been for more than a fortnight at a time, and never alone. Yet while her letters home reveal that she left Heathrow feeling understandably apprehensive about what awaited her in a place where she knew no one, she was quickly 'at ease'—to use Larkin's phrase—in Rome. Indeed, so enamoured was she of the city that she returned often, and it grew to assume something of the status of a lodestar in her life; in an unpublished 1979 poem she refers to it as her 'second home'.[16] She wrote essay upon essay and poem upon poem—some, like the cluster in 1985's *Extending the Territory*, published, dozens not—about Rome and its significance to her. Such circlings around and tropings of a favourite subject are not unusual for Jennings; she was a prolific writer, with the tendency to dwell on a handful of themes in her work. Nevertheless, it is difficult to overstate the importance to her of Rome, both as a real place and as a

---

[15] Kingsley Amis to Philip Larkin, 28 March 1955, first part quoted in Eric Jacobs, *Kingsley Amis, A Biography* (London: Hodder & Stoughton, 1995), p. 200; second part in Zachary Leader (ed.), *The Letters of Kingsley Amis* (London: HarperCollins, 2000), p. 425.

[16] Jennings, 'A Sign-Post to Rome', handwritten MS, Georgetown Special Collections, Elizabeth Jennings Papers (Group 2), Box 8, Folder 11, notebook dated 1–28 May 1979. Reprinted with the permission of David Higham Associates, on behalf of the Estate of Elizabeth Jennings.

place part-remembered, part-imagined, onto which she could project her interests in art, relationships, and spirituality.

Although Jennings travelled repeatedly to Rome, including several lengthy visits in 1958 and 1959, it was that initial Maugham-sponsored stay in 1957 which proved the formative experience, and which determined the direction that much of her work would subsequently take. She begins her unpublished poem 'Three Months in Rome: In Memory of Somerset Maugham' with the acknowledgement that 'I owe you so much, almost everything'. It is a revealing poem, even if not entirely successful. Looking back on that time 'when I was young and wandered round | This place in wonder', she declares that

> ...Here was
> Faith made easy. All the doubts I'd known
> Vanished here. Belief rose up in stone
> And marble. Fountains poured wild waters and
> Cooled each piazza. Easter was a place
> And act to understand. (ll.7–12)[17]

The poem points to two things. First, it underscores the fact that, for Jennings, one of the great pulls of Rome was its significance as the home of Roman Catholicism—'a city made half of light | And half of the world's power' (ll.87–8), as she writes in 'A Roman Trio'.[18] Secondly, and perhaps more importantly for our understanding of the development of Jennings's oeuvre in the 1950s, it suggests that it was not until her extended stay in the city in 1957 that she was able to overcome many of her earlier uncertainties and ambivalences about Catholicism, and establish for herself the importance of her faith: 'All the doubts I'd known | Vanished here'. She makes similar claims in a draft of her unpublished autobiography. 'It is to Somerset Maugham that I owe the rediscovery of my religion', she writes, although she goes on to describe how she had in fact been attempting to live 'more fully and more faithfully' for a few months before then: 'since the January of

---

[17] Jennings, handwritten MS, Georgetown Special Collections, Elizabeth Jennings Papers (Group 2), Box 31, Folder 20, loose poem, undated. Reprinted with the permission of David Higham Associates, on behalf of the Estate of Elizabeth Jennings.

[18] Jennings, 'Roman Trio', *New Collected Poems*, ed. Michael Schmidt (Manchester: Carcanet, 2002), p. 181, first collected in *Tributes* (1989). All subsequent references to Jennings's published poems are from the *New Collected Poems*.

that year [1957], I had been trying to go to Confession more regularly, to be a better Catholic, and to abandon the horrible compromise which had made me pretend, even to friends, that I was not a serious Catholic'.[19]

Many discussions of Jennings and her relationship to the Movement begin with an assertion along the lines of Jerry Bradley's: that 'Jennings is unique in two particular ways: she is the Movement's only woman and its only Catholic'.[20] And such a statement certainly stands up to some scrutiny. Jennings was—to take the title of one of her poems—a 'Cradle Catholic',[21] born in 1926 into a Catholic family which, after moving to Oxford in 1932, quickly established itself within the small population of middle-class and professional Catholics in the city; the family attended the local Catholic church, St Gregory and St Augustine, and for a few years Jennings was enrolled at the Catholic school Rye St Antony. Catholicism was an integral part of her life, culturally and socially, throughout her childhood. However, as she makes plain in her unpublished autobiography 'As I Am', written in the late 1960s, her faith was also the source of much misgiving as she was growing up. She writes of 'suffering from severe religious doubts and difficulties' as a teenager, and of having 'built up a travesty of religion, a religion which denied all goodness and blessedness to the natural world';[22] she depicts just such an adolescent frame of mind in her poem 'Whitsun Sacrament':

> ... Where is peace now in our unrest—
> The childish questions in the throbbing mind,
> The new name, itching loins, the shaping breast? (ll. 11–13)[23]

By the late 1940s (by which time Jennings had finished her undergraduate degree in English at Oxford, and was living in London from Monday to Friday, working as a copy editor), she writes that 'I was paying little less than lip-service to my religion. ... I always went to Mass on Sundays and Feast Days, and I went to Confession and Communion at Easter and Christmas. This was really the bare minimum'.[24]

[19] Jennings, *Autobiography Vol. I, The Inward War*, handwritten MS, Washington University Special Collections, Elizabeth Jennings Papers, Box 12, Notebook I, undated. Reprinted with the permission of David Higham Associates, on behalf of the Estate of Elizabeth Jennings.

[20] Bradley, *The Movement*, p. 87.

[21] Jennings, *New Collected Poems*, p. 131, first collected in *Consequently I Rejoice* (1977).

[22] Jennings, 'As I Am', p. 24.

[23] Jennings, *New Collected Poems*, p. 103, first collected in *Growing Points* (1975).

[24] Jennings, 'As I Am', pp. 62–3.

Only the unreflective never doubt their faith, and it's evident from these and similar comments that Catholicism still occupied Jennings's thoughts throughout her teens and twenties, despite the fact that she was doing what she saw as 'the bare minimum'. Nevertheless, an awareness of the distance that she felt from her religion during these years allows us to see her early work, and its relationship to Movement poetry, more clearly and accurately. It also enables us to recognize the extent of the shift that took place in her work from 1957, as her faith deepened and stabilized. Her collections from *A Sense of the World* onwards contain increasing numbers of explicitly religious and theological poems, and an appreciation of Jennings's oeuvre demands an understanding of her Catholic faith. Yet although Jennings is rightly considered a Catholic writer, the trajectory taken by her poetry after the 1957 trip to Rome can all too easily obscure our view of the earlier work. During the late 1940s and early to mid-1950s, when Jennings was establishing herself as a poet, and, significantly, when the Movement grouping was becoming recognized, she was in fact writing and publishing no overtly religious poetry. Her poems from these years tend to fall into two categories: self-analysis and sense of place. Some of her more allegorical poems could be considered implicitly religious, but only one poem from this period—'Tribute', which is addressed to 'my test of life and gauge', and which ends with the lines 'you are that place where poems find room, | The tall abundant shadow on my page'[25]—is clearly religious, although even here God remains unnamed.

That Jennings had not been considered a religious poet during the early part of her career is apparent from the critical reception of *A Sense of the World*. In his review of the collection, for instance, Larkin remarks that, although 'the steady, calm, precise voice is unchanged',

What does seem new about this collection is the group of religious poems at the end. These, though not pictorial, are mostly studies of particular events and people…made with the dispassionate devotion of the Old Masters. Peguy and Claudel may be the signposts to the road Miss Jennings is taking next.[26]

The poems to which Larkin refers are the final eight of the collection, but the religious elements extend beyond this concluding cluster. The volume as a whole can be seen as a broadening of theme and subject for Jennings—it takes

---

[25] Jennings, *New Collected Poems*, pp. 10–11, first collected in *A Way of Looking* (1955).
[26] Larkin, 'Reports on Experience', p. 6.

as its epigraph Thomas Traherne's 'It becometh you to retain a glorious sense of the world', suggesting a reaching out towards and drawing into oneself of external experience. The collection certainly persists with some of the cool philosophical dissections and meditations which characterize *Poems* (1953) and *A Way of Looking* (1955), but whereas these earlier publications take emotional and intellectual states of mind as their typical subject matter, *A Sense of the World* explores and examines a physical world which has been seen and heard, touched and tasted—we have the boy listening to the 'sliding and suck of shingle' in a seashell ('The Child and the Seashell'), the sculptor who rubs 'the marble flakes between his fingers, | Pulling a splinter from his thumb' ('Piazza San Marco: The Mystics and Makers'), and pine trees which 'droop their dark' ('The Roman Forum'), such shadowy coolness contrasting with that 'battering daylight' of the Mediterranean from which the speaker of one poem retreats only to discover that, despite the silence and stillness of the church in which she finds herself, she 'cannot quite forget the blazing day':

> For me the senses still have their full sway
> Even where prayer comes quicker than an act. (ll.21–2)[27]

Throughout the collection the sensory impact of the outer world is seen to feed into and enrich the inner, contemplative world—as Jennings puts it in 'The Roman Forum', 'O and the heart is drawn to sense, | Eye and the mind are one'.[28]

Jennings wrote freely, prolifically, during that 1957 trip—she took her typewriter with her, and her correspondence and notebooks from these months reveal that, as well as writing plenty of formally-patterned poetry, she was experimenting with different forms and genres. She completed a radio script, 'Roman Easter: A Theme for Voices', which she hoped to have accepted by the BBC, as well as various essays and a series of 127 short prose meditations, or 'Pensées', and, while none of these apart from some of the poems and essays were published, *A Sense of the World* does demonstrate a widening and a ratcheting up of technical skill, including expertise in free verse and the prose poem.[29] However, the strongest of the poems from

---

[27] Jennings, 'San Paolo fuori le Mura, Rome', *New Collected Poems*, p. 30, first collected in *A Sense of the World* (1958).

[28] Jennings, *New Collected Poems*, p. 27, first collected in *A Sense of the World* (1958).

[29] It is unclear whether Jennings ever submitted 'Roman Easter' or the 'Pensées' for broadcast or publication.

this collection are those which, as well as being distinguished by technical proficiency, also make manifest Traherne's 'glorious sense of the world'—which manage to capture something of the idea that Jennings expresses in her poem to Maugham: that in Rome, for her, the spiritual found physical embodiment; 'Belief rose up in stone | And marble'.

'Fountain' is one of Jennings's best-known poems from *A Sense of the World*, and one in which an idea—that of power, of energy, held in check—is approached, given shape and form, through the physical, in the 'tumult' of a fountain.[30] She wrote the poem in Rome on Maundy Thursday 1957, and, in her introduction to a reading of it for the BBC's *Third Programme*, said that she would like to think that it 'stands by itself and justifies itself both as a crystallization of an experience *and* as an attempt to draw a general truth out of a particular occasion or subject'.[31] Both the poem's form and chosen image are appropriate to the ideas of power, authority, and discipline being expressed. The first two stanzas are in free verse, the opening lines murmuringly serene in their suggestion both of the sound of the fountain heard from some distance away, and of the imagined source of the water:

> Let it disturb no more at first
> Than the hint of a pool predicted far in a forest (ll.1–2)

The reader, who is addressed directly in the poem, is then invited to 'step closer', urged to 'come out of the narrow street and enter | The full piazza'—and here we shift from the soft assonances and alliterations of the opening lines to a place where 'the noise compels', and where we not only hear, but see, the fountain which is

> Too wild for the lights which illuminate it to hold,
> Even a moment, an ounce of water back (ll.20–1)

The poem has here moved from free verse into a loose iambic pentameter which works to channel the energy of the tumbling water, focusing its force, giving us a sense of power restrained, like Marianne Moore's 'sea in a chasm, struggling to be | free and unable to be'[32]—although Jennings doesn't keep rigidly to her metre but rather emulates the fountain's turmoil, its wildness,

---

[30] Jennings, *New Collected Poems*, p. 29.

[31] Jennings, Introduction, 'Poems by Elizabeth Jennings', *Third Programme*, BBC, 4 March 1958.

[32] Marianne Moore, 'What Are Years?' *Complete Poems* (London: Faber, 1984), p. 95.

its 'prodigality', in the switches between rising and falling, binary and ternary, feet:

> x / | x x / | x x/ | x/ |x x /
> Too wild for the lights which illuminate it to hold,
>
> / x x| / x |x / | x / |x /
> Even a moment, an ounce of water back (ll.20–1)

But as we stare at the fountain, at the contained energy, we perceive in it, says Jennings, 'an image of utter calm' (l.26). And the poem concludes by seeking to draw a wider meaning from this display of disciplined power, as Jennings employs what might be seen as that typically Larkinesque technique of beginning with an anecdote or a personal experience and then universalizing it, and implicating the reader in the conclusions drawn.[33] In 'Fountain' this is achieved through the opening out of the experience in the final lines of the poem. Here a collective 'we' is envisaged in a place beyond time,

> at the edge of some perpetual stream,
> Fearful of touching, bringing no thirst at all,
>
> .   .   .   .
>
> But drawing the water down to the deepest wonder. (ll.28–9, 31)

There are clear echoes here both of Frost's 'Directive' with its exhortation to 'Drink and be whole again beyond confusion',[34] and of the river flowing from the Garden of Eden which foreshadows those healing, life-nurturing waters which stream through the Old Testament and on into Revelation.[35]

In its concern with form, its gesture against chaos, and its drawing out of a general truth from a specific experience, 'Fountain' incorporates several of the features that we tend to associate with Movement poetry—but it is also a poem which, both in the influences it displays and in the changes to Jennings's poetry that it heralds, points to divergences from the Movement. That reaching beyond the quotidian to a timeless and affirming reality that we find at the poem's conclusion, for example, is something which Jennings

---

[33] For a discussion of this quality, see Blake Morrison, *The Movement: English Poetry and Fiction of the 1950s* (Oxford: Oxford University Press, 1980), pp. 125–6.

[34] Robert Frost, *Robert Frost: Collected Poems, Prose and Plays*, ed. Richard Poirier and Mark Richardson (New York: Library of America, 1995), p. 342.

[35] Genesis 2:10; Psalms 36:8; 46:4; Ezekiel 47:1–12; Joel 3:18; Revelation 22:1–2.

learnt not from Larkin but from Edwin Muir, who was the chief influence on Jennings's first full-length collection, *Poems* (1953). In *A Sense of the World*, however, she shows herself increasingly able, at least in poems such as 'Fountain', to realize what she perceives to be Muir's chief strength: that 'However abstract the ideas, the expression of them is always concrete; and, further, the vision is not complete till it is embodied in sensuous language.'[36] It is this same quality she values in the writing of Teresa of Avila, who provides the subject and title of the final poem of *A Sense of the World*: 'She is never at a loss for a comparison or a simile. Her whole approach to the spiritual life is a repudiation of the abstract.'[37]

'Teresa of Avila' is one of the strongest poems in *A Sense of the World*. Despite its being a prose poem, it is also—to borrow Larkin's metaphor—a clear signpost 'to the road Miss Jennings is taking next'. The poem is based on Teresa's conception of the Four Waters as she describes them in her *Life*. Here she figures the soul as a garden, with the four waters representing the four ways in which the soul can, as Jennings explains in her gloss on the *Life*, be 'purified, nourished and brought to fruition'—that fruition being mystical union with God.[38] The image of the 'perpetual stream' at the end of 'Fountain' should probably be seen in the context of this allegory. As with 'Fountain', the success of 'Teresa of Avila' is due in part to its form: as a prose poem, it avoids the flat endings and neat resolutions which can on occasion mar the tight stanzaic forms for which Jennings is best known (although her formal precision and composed elegance can, of course, work to supreme effect, as we see in poems such as 'Delay'); moreover, the assurance and control of language demanded by the prose poem form distil and concentrate the images. Take the description of Teresa, kneeling at prayer, metaphorically drawing up the first and second of the four waters—both drawn from a well, but the second made easier with the aid of a windlass and divine intervention:

Water from the well first, drawn up painfully. Clinking of pails. Dry lips at the wellhead. Parched grass bending. And the dry heart too—waiting for prayer.

Then the water-wheel, turning smoothly. Somebody helping unseen. A keen hand put out, gently sliding the wheel. Then water and the aghast spirit refreshed and quenched.[39]

---

[36] Jennings, *Every Changing Shape: Mystical Experience and the Making of Poems* (1961; repr. Manchester: Carcanet, 1996), p. 152.

[37] Ibid., p. 50.   [38] Ibid., 53.   [39] Jennings, *New Collected Poems*, p. 33.

The simple concrete images—'Dry lips', 'parched grass'—prove apt analogies for Teresa's spiritual state—'dry heart', 'aghast spirit'. But what ensures the poem's effectiveness is its success on an acoustic as well as a visual level. Recall Jennings's contention that, for Muir, 'the vision is not complete till it is embodied in sensuous language'; imagery is not in itself enough. 'Teresa of Avila' is carefully modulated throughout: not only do we have the aural tagging of those words which are key to the poem's development ('water', 'well', 'wheel', and 'waiting', for example), but the prose poem form allows Jennings to create her own internal rhythmic effects to reinforce the chosen imagery. Of course there is no regular metre here, but if we mark the stressed syllables in the passage then we can see, or more precisely hear, that many of the sentences end with a dactylic or trochaic fall ('painfully', 'well-head', 'bending', 'smoothly'). Then part way through the description of the drawing of the second water, just at the point at which Teresa receives divine assistance in her task, these falling feet are counterpointed by the iambic 'unseen'. The rise provided by the stress on 'seen', locked into place by the internal rhyme with 'keen' just two syllables later, works to lift the sentence—and indeed the following sentences also end on rising notes, suggesting the raising and refreshing of the parched spirit.

In her discussion of Anne Ridler's collection *A Matter of Life and Death* (1959), Jennings labels religion one of those 'difficult and dangerous subjects' which lends itself 'only too easily to mawkishness and triteness'.[40] In 'Fountain' and 'Teresa of Avila', Jennings seeks to avoid these dangers by searching out the appropriate image and the precise language in which to cloak the concept she is seeking to communicate—as she puts it in a later poem, 'Act of the Imagination', 'I need to cast around | And find an image for the most divine | Concepts'.[41] While she is not always successful in locating such an image for her work, her adoption of such an approach in *A Sense of the World* does mark a distinct and a conscious shift in her poetry, and we can attribute much of this shift to her trip to Rome. For it was here, as she writes in her autobiography, that she first realized the power of art as a means of comprehending, illuminating, and articulating spiritual mysteries, and this freed her to write the sort of poetry with which she was to become increasingly associated. She describes, for instance, visiting the Vatican galleries: 'To see

---

[40] Jennings, *Poetry To-Day*, p. 35.
[41] Jennings, *New Collected Poems*, p. 297, first collected in *In the Meantime* (1996).

Raphael's *Discourse on the Blessed Sacrament* and then to go to Communion in St. Peter's was a rare experience. So, day by day, I seemed to be discovering my religion as I ought to have learnt it as a child.'[42] The Manichean worldview which had coloured her earlier apprehension of Catholicism was replaced with a concept of embodiment, of incarnation, which opened her poetry up to the transcendent; which recognized and had confidence in the transforming power of language, of the metaphor and of the image. And accompanying this was an increasing appreciation of the parallels between mystic and poet, explored most fully in 1961's *Every Changing Shape* (which she first conceived of and began writing in Rome in 1957) but also finding expression in her poetry, perhaps most famously and most succinctly in her affirmation—in the poem 'Visit to an Artist', for David Jones—of 'art as gesture and as sacrament'.[43]

In the concluding pages of *Poetry To-Day* (1961), her survey of the contemporary poetry scene written for the British Council, Jennings reflects upon the doctrine of incarnation in relation to language, and specifically in relation to contemporary poetry. Drawing on Jacques Barzun's *The House of Intellect* she argues that, when applied to poetry, the concept of indwelling, of the word becoming flesh, affords a means of escaping abstraction and, by implication, impersonality:

Barzun speaks of 'incarnation' in connection with language; incarnation, taking flesh, implies a profound horror not only of abstractions but also of all that is impersonal. Much that confronts us today *is* impersonal . . . but our reactions, if we are truly human, must always be personal. Poetry, like Christianity, preserves, when it is in a healthy state, the sense of personality and the dignity of being human. . . . To write is to affirm; to write clearly is to express an implicit faith in the possibility and necessity of communication.[44]

It is perhaps no coincidence that Jennings employs the metaphor of health in this passage; Robert Conquest took just such an approach in his Introduction to the *New Lines* anthology five years earlier with his oft-quoted contention that 'a genuine and healthy poetry of the new period has established itself', and that the poets emerging in the late 1940s and early 1950s

[42] Jennings, 'As I Am', p. 120.

[43] Jennings, *New Collected Poems*, p. 45, first collected in *Song for a Birth or a Death* (1961).

[44] Jennings, *Poetry To-Day*, 55–6. See Jacques Barzun, *The House of Intellect* (London: Secker & Warburg, 1959), p. 232.

possess 'a certain unity of approach, a new and healthy general standpoint' as opposed to 'the sort of corruption which has affected the general attitude to poetry in the last decade'.[45] Jennings also adopts a line similar to Conquest's in her emphasis on writing 'clearly', and on the 'possibility and necessity of communication'. But there is an obvious difference between the Jennings passage and the Conquest Introduction: although both ascribe moral virtue to Movement poetry's formal qualities, Jennings is alone in situating those virtues firmly within a Christian context, arguing that the affirmation of poetry is an expression of faith. The comparison largely sums up both why Jennings was associated with the Movement and why she was increasingly seen as an anomalous figure within the group.

What would have happened to Jennings's poetry had she not won the Maugham Award and rediscovered her faith in Rome? Or, to consider it from another angle, would she ever have been deemed a part of the Movement if, from the outset, she had been publishing the profoundly religious poetry collected in, say, *A Sense of the World*, or *Song for a Birth or a Death*, or any of her later volumes? These are, of course, impossible questions, and any answers can only be supposition. Nevertheless, it is evident that the path that Jennings's poetry took was acutely influenced by two events which occurred fairly early in her life: first, her trip to Rome in 1957, and secondly, the mental breakdown she suffered in the early 1960s. Both of these saw her poetry take a sharp turn away from the typically secular, rational, Movement poem. And, just as the religious trajectory taken by Jennings's poetry after 1957 can impede our view of her earlier work, so too can the impression that we have formed of Jennings from her later, lonelier years obscure our appreciation of the sort of person she was, and the part she played in literary circles, in the 1940s and 1950s. That early Jennings is perhaps best captured by the image of her in her late twenties, an outgoing young poet with a fast-growing reputation, boarding that plane at Heathrow weighed down by none of Garnet Bowen's sourpuss cynicism, with three months of freedom and independence ahead of her, a typewriter in her luggage and £400 in her pocket, out to discover a new city, and a new way of seeing her world.

---

[45] Robert Conquest, Introduction, *New Lines: An Anthology* (London: Macmillan, 1956), pp. xi, xiv, xii.

17

New Lines, Movements, and Modernisms

Robert Conquest

'Modernism' is a vague and loose expression. But 'Movement' presupposes some sort of joint activity—or failing that at least some sort of agreed attitude. The 'Movement' as first met with was a journalistic coinage, a catch-phrase only later peripherally applied—by overspill—to desiccated verses then emerging to counteract what were seen as the excesses of the 1940s. No such overview united those I anthologized in *New Lines*, and my first draft of its introduction (still with me) had a paragraph specifically rejecting the Movement appellation. I left it out because it seemed not worth arguing about, especially as some contributions had a touch of it. We had, indeed, all been brought up on, and had digested, 'Modernism' of every type (that is to say a slice of enlightenment plus a tureen of pretension).

New Lines was just an anthology of poets I liked, regardless of sex or sexual orientation, let alone politics. We hardly cared or even knew about each other's views—let alone approving them. Few of the contributors had even met. The book's emergence came about in a way scarcely assimilable to any other involvement. Its first seed was sown when Dennis Enright, reviewing *Poems 1951*, praised one of my contributions, and I had, almost simultaneously, seen and admired a poem of Enright's. We wrote each other. And soon I visited him and his wife in Birmingham where he had a university job. Enright's writing is always a special trouble to literary assigners (and this in spite of his having been a close associate of Leavis). His poems were never in the least formal or formalist—or 'movementy'.

I should present some of my own credentials. A couple of my poems had appeared in 1937–8 in *Twentieth Century Verse*. In 1944–5 I won a PEN Prize for a 'Long Poem on the War'. This was 'For the Death of a Poet'—on that fine young poet I had known in the army, Drummond Allison, killed in Italy in 1943 (published in *The Book of the PEN, 1950*). After that, I had a number of poems in the *Listener*, *Tribune*, and elsewhere. I had got to know the others of that vintage.

As with Enright, it is easy to show that we did not fit the retrospective stereotype. One reader, Anthony Thwaite—then an NCO with the British Army in North Africa—wrote praising one of these poems of mine, called 'The Death of Hart Crane'. Its first lines ran

> At first his own effortless high tension
> Could match and move the edged electric city,
> While under the great bridge sloped the waves,
> Flat, tamed, shimmering with oil,
> Vestigial to the dying endless sea.

This alone ought to be enough to derail the old preconceptions.

In 1950 I was in the Foreign Office, and had lately spent a month or two at the United Nations in New York, becoming friendly with Alan Maclean, then Gladwyn Jebb's secretary. Back in London, he got a job at Macmillan and I soon met him again. They published a collection of mine—*Poems*—and then suggested an anthology, which became *New Lines*.[1] By now Dennis was living in Japan, where his *Poetry of the 1950s* was published. We had chosen the same poets, except that I had Thom Gunn as well.

When *New Lines* came out the comment I most valued (and still most value) was that of Julian Symons (who had edited *Twentieth Century Verse*). He did not wholly approve of *New Lines*. But he said the actual choice of poems was splendid. Perhaps the continued interest in *New Lines* is due to that? Perhaps not...

As Gunn and Davie both often said, we came together and went off in various directions—without regretting or disavowing our commingling. If

---

[1] *New Lines* (London: Macmillan, 1956).

we had anything in common it might be summarized in the following lines (composed specially for this volume), which are to be taken in a very latitudinarian way on how, on the whole, poetry should be—in what Gunn saw as the whole tradition from Chaucer through Auden.

> Neither too wet nor too dry,
> Neither too low nor too high,
> Neither too loose nor too tight,
> Neither too dark nor too bright,
> Neither too mad nor too mild,
> Neither too tame nor too wild,
> Neither too thick nor too thin,
> Neither too Out nor too In.

Nor did we (or I) think one could describe, even to this degree, how all poetry should be written. There were always fine poets of wild eccentricity like Stevie Smith or Emily Dickinson. We would have agreed with no less a product of classicism than Gibbon himself, who spoke of the alternative aims of poetry being to 'satisfy, or silence, our reason'.[2]

New Lines had made quite a stir, and gone into several editions. The jacket of *New Lines II* notes of its predecessor, 'No book in recent times has been met with such a huge volume of abuse.—*Observer*'. It became a rallying point, or a target, in the ensuing 'song-strife' standoffs of the time. Al Alvarez spoke of 'gang warfare' and some sharp blows were exchanged, but on the whole it is surprising how the decencies survived. The— notably non-movementy—verse magazine *Stand* once asked me for a couple of poems. One, called 'Breathings', started, 'Caught in the long wind, draperies...'. The other, more to the point, ran

> When verse seemed in need of improvement
> We sat down and started a movement
> > We foregathered in Hull
> > Working hard to be dull
> For we sure knew what being in the groove meant.

They used both (but I left the second out of my *New and Collected*). Still—indeed to this day—both *New Lines* anthologies were typecast by some as the

---

[2] Edward Gibbon, *The Decline and Fall of the Roman Empire*, Vol. 3 (New York: 1907), p. 193.

'Movement' incarnate. Which, I suppose, gave a certain cachet to the survival of the M word, little though any of us accepted, or accept, it. As an arch perpetrator, I was—and still to some degree remain—a fall guy for anti-movementeers on rampage. A writer of many books, on various subjects, I have often had bad or hostile reviews. But—except from the odd Western Stalinist—I've only once had one that consciously falsified a point about 'Movement' verse—as detectable by the use of an Amis-style slang phrase in a poem otherwise totally unmovementy, indeed romantic.

A common taunt was that we were philistine, and insular too. Six or seven poems in *New Lines* are set abroad. And even Larkin has, *in New Lines II*, one set in New Orleans. I once offered to meet his plane in that city, see him to a hotel and so on, so that he could make a local pilgrimage to the blues' historical milieu. This probably shaky enough project failed when he heard that Congo Square had been subsumed into a *Cultural Center*.

This transatlantic detour recalls a frivolous example—published in *The Listener*— of how these poets remained associated in one's mind:

Crossings

> Neither poet—Philip Larkin, Thom Gunn—
> Impinges much on the other one:
>
> And yet—I note in Gunn's earlier work
> A rather good poem called Market at Turk.
>
> Each is a San Francisco street:
> The phrase indicates the place they meet.
>
> Gunn chose the title (he told me once)
> For its faintly sinister resonance.
>
> —Well, in San Francisco the other day
> I found (I promise) Larkin at Bay.
>
> As a painting?—surely all of us find
> Landseer's the name that springs to mind.
>
> For a poem, though? Wordsworth? Hopkins? or Scott?
> I invite my readers to have a shot.

As I draft this piece, I receive from the Bodleian copies of my letters to Philip. The 800 pages will take some digesting (see my eventually forthcoming *Memoirs*). My first skim on anything relevant here finds what amounts to a double refutation of one major American 'critic's' line on Philip as a bad poet and a bad man.[3] Apart from his jokily-overdone reactionary poses, the ethical charge is based on his supposed addiction to 'pornography'—that is, to his liking for the 'girlie' magazines of the period, which were just inside or outside the law as it was then (no pudenda)...though in fact about as 'obscene' as what is found nowadays in bra advertisements. These were to be found in little shops in Soho. Leader, quoting my 'Literature in Soho', records how Amis and I, lunching there with Thom Gunn, noted how 'very decent' it was of Thom to accompany us on the usual look at the latest.[4] Nothing secretive there! Though Larkin, not wishing to be seen by curious Hull neighbours (if indeed such emporia existed so far north), would ask us to send him anything attractive. He recalled that enjoyable representations of the female nude were common to almost all other periods and cultures. In our exchange, I find a 'charming' girl in blue jeans, and a 'beautiful' ballerina posed by a swimming pool, plus pages of denunciations of 'disgusting' magazines, also sold there—though of course sharing amusement at striking sexual, but hardly erotic, grotesqueries.

It may be thought relevant that the same Larkinophobe critic defended Stanford University's purchase of Allen Ginsberg's personal archives for $1.2 million on the grounds that his personal life (including his membership in the North American Man/Boy Love Association) had nothing to do with his value as a poet. But Ginsberg's verses must rate high for activist obscenity, in which he openly revelled, enthusing about the insertion into the lower half of his excited body of various objects human and otherwise.[5]

Lionel Trilling noted how a demand excessively catered to in his time was for verse that advertised itself as being under high pressure. Some verse of that type may indeed be successful. But mere groaning and sweating and thrashing around, with adjectives to suit, simply begs for Enright's comment: 'the effects may be striking but they don't strike very deep'.[6] And this is, or can easily become, bad taste—Wordsworth's 'a degrading thirst after outrageous stimulation'.[7]

---

[3] Marjorie Perloff, 'What to Make of a Diminished Thing', *Parnassus* 19.2 (1994), pp. 9–30.

[4] Zachary Leader, *The Life of Kingsley Amis,* (London: Jonathan Cape, 2006), p. 320.

[5] See Mark Ford, 'The Dreams of Allen Ginsberg,' *The New York Review of Books* 54:14 (27 September 2007).

[6] D. J Enright, *Injury Time* (London: Pimlico, 2003), p. 157.

[7] William Wordsworth, 'Preface', *Lyrical Ballads, Volume I* (London, 1800), p. 6.

New Lines II included poets who had not previously made their mark. As I wrote in its Introduction, we wanted verse that was 'neither howl nor cypher'.[8] These are negatives: we took the positives for granted. In general *New Lines II* ranged a little more broadly (I was particularly glad to get Vernon Scannell, whose death as I write is a great loss to us all). Even so, there was some surprise that Ted Hughes was in it. Though I had always defended Dylan Thomas from Amis and others, I had to agree that Hughes was hard to fit into our general stance. But Thom finally said that at least I must admit he was as good as John Wain, who was being included again this time (saved by some echoes of Theodore Roethke). That did the trick. And when I asked Ted for some poems he sent some more formed than his usual—and when given the proofs, he very amiably tightened them up even further. (As to Thom's views, I cherish his horror of Ted's nuptial poem for the Duchess of York[9]—not perhaps his worst lapse!) Anyway I came round to the validity of a taste for Hughes *at his best*, even if—a different point—preferring Sylvia Plath *at her very best*.

Even in these exceptional cases, one problem with poetry is clear—that while even competence in most arts requires techniques of musical note, brushwork, etc.—verse has no such entrance ticket. And its critics often are in effect tone deaf. Kingsley Amis once wrote to me that, 'The trouble with chaps like that is they have no taste—I don't mean bad taste, just the mental organ that makes you say This is bloody good and This is piss is simply missing, and they have to orientate themselves by things like "importance" and "seriousness" and "depth" and "originality" and "consensus" (= "trend").'[10]

It was a prose writer, Anthony Burgess, who wrote, 'Art begins with craft, and there is no art until craft has been mastered.'[11] This is not to say that 'craft' is enough to produce art. One can have craft without art... though not vice versa. But in poetry—no doubt elsewhere in 'creative writing'—there is no technical apprenticeship. And it is widely held that craft is anyhow not necessary. Students try to produce verse minus such abilities, and

[8] Robert Conquest, 'Introduction', *New Lines II* (London: Macmillan, 1963), p. xxvii.

[9] Ted Hughes, 'The Honey Bee and the Thistle' (1986).

[10] 29 February 1984, in Zachary Leader (ed.), *The Letters of Kingsley Amis* (London: HarperCollins, 2000), p. 970.

[11] Anthony Burgess, 'A Deadly Sin—Creativity for All', *But Do Blondes Prefer Gentlemen?* (New York: McGraw-Hill, 1986), p. 101.

revel in it. That is to say that—except perhaps granting the exceedingly rare exception—they are no longer poets, are no longer makers. Worse than that, their highly touted academic sponsors no longer have an 'ear' for poetry. The crux, the main and major disjunction in all fields was when the artist took the decision to abandon the laity—as Larkin always said. The non-laity, that is 'academics', however 'knowledgeable', simply lacked the deeper necessity.

Many of those Larkin spoke for had, like him, university-type jobs. The most virulent attacks on academe are in the Larkin–Amis letters. I am not in a position to be too rough on the academicist literature. Apart from anything else I myself have only a minimal experience of the field. I was in 1958–9 a Visiting Poet and Lecturer in English at what was then the University of Buffalo (where, not having a University degree in English I could only 'teach' Freshman English and Graduate seminars—and 'Creative Writing'). Literature had long been beset by an excess of discussionizing ('eating the menu instead of the meal'). Some academic critics claimed to be the only ones competent to discuss poetry properly and indeed to prescribe its forms, methods, and contents. This is as if a claim should be put forward that only professors of ballistics should discuss football.

Critics have always been the more troublesome to the degree that they were systematic. No doubt, then and now, non-dogmatic criticism nevertheless contains a congeries of more or less unconscious assumptions. But that is not the same thing—just as those people are wrong who say that conscious and systematic political indoctrination is all right, since in any case we are subject to unsystematic indoctrination in the set of assumptions implicit in our society.

Which reminds me of our 'creativity'. And, as Anthony Powell put it, 'It is a rule, almost without exception that writers and painters who are always talking about being artists, break down at just that level.'[12] Also relevantly, Proust notes (of Saint-Loup), that it is a philistinism to judge the arts by their intellectual content alone, 'never perceiving the magic appeal to the imagination...found in things which he condemned as frivolous'[13]—thus narrowing the grasp of the arts by blocking its lighter side.

[12] Anthony Powell, *A Writer's Notebook* (London: Heinemann, 2001), p. 144 .

[13] Marcel Proust, trans. C. K. Scott Moncrieff, *Within A Budding Grove, Remembrance of Things Past* (*À la Recherche du temps perdu*), vol. 2. (New York: Modern Library, 1951), p. 44.

A taste for involved intellectualism in literature is often accompanied, or succeeded, by a taste for the most extreme irrationalism. But on second thoughts, it will be seen that this is natural; the two approaches both involve, in most cases, contrivance, in its shallowest sense. We think of art from the intellect as clear, arid, formal. Obviously, this is not always so; anything, however emotionalist, which is devised to suit a conscious scheme is intellectual, in this sense. Hysteria is the product of frigidity, not of passion.

The view of A. E. Housman (the most 'formal' of poets) was that poetry finds its way 'to something in man which is obscure and latent, something older than the present organisation of his nature, like the patches of fen which still linger here and there in the drained lands of Cambridgeshire'.[14] The rules of these profound and intricate unconscious activities are probably in practice unknowable. At any rate, if not unknowable, much of their working is at present unknown. If the vague, peripheral, and hypothetical knowledge we have is given the status of law we are worse off than before. This goes with an authoritarian attitude; and its products, because of the formality of their definition, are hard and less able to evolve. Such are the approaches we rejected. The extremists on both sides are missionary types: the one of a highly organized and ritualistic set of sacramental forms, the other of a theology of revivalist self-abandon. In either case, a sectarianism. As Paul Valéry wrote, 'Enthusiasm is not an artist's state of mind.'[15]

In his last book Enright quotes a Professor at the University of Wales, in a newsletter of the British Council's Literature Department: 'we no longer ask as our first question how good a work is', as a result of which 'a great many new texts' are available to 'tell us about the cultures'. As Enright puts it 'that's to say, literature doesn't matter'.[16] Only a theorist could produce such nonsense.

Some of the most impolite (though private) cracks out of what must be seen as 'our side' came from Larkin—though I have never been able to identify one of Larkin's targets as 'my Italian colleague R. Schrippa' (except that he wasn't Italian). One curious piece of evidence in the history of relations among these poets came when, in Larkin's will, it was seen that he had left

[14] A. E. Housman, 'The Name and Nature of Poetry' (The Leslie Stephen Lecture Delivered at Cambridge 9 May 1933), London: Macmillan, 1933.
[15] Paul Valéry, *Introduction à la Méthode de Léonard de Vinci* (Paris, 1895), my translation.
[16] D. J. Enright, *Injury Time*, p. 157.

his letters from Kingsley Amis, Robert Conquest, Barbara Pym, and Monica Jones to the Bodleian Library—letters from others to be returned to sender or destroyed (a troublesome legacy since that included those from his literary executors, but a rare insight into the mind of the old Archpoet). All of which reminds me of how different the poets of which we speak were, as well as their level of agreement, which, *on the whole* extended to much personal goodwill.

Enright was a friend for the rest of our lives. Larkin too and—with one short interruption—Amis. I was always on the best of terms with Gunn. Donald Davie was always a good friend. I stayed with him for several months at Stanford (and he with us in London)—visited him in Nashville and Exeter. I seldom saw Elizabeth Jennings—but I had a poem about her that began

> The superficial graces go
> And yet such grace remains
> About that bare iambic flow ...

Let me urge any serious reader to look through the actual poetry in the two anthologies before coming to any conclusions.

Thom Gunn once wrote me, much taken with the broad view, or stance, he saw in the last lines of a poem of mine called 'Galatea', where, after Pygmalion brings the statue to life,

> He still regards her with
> The whole intent of art—
>
> *With passion and reserve.*

That may be seen as one indication of the way in which our 'Poetry of the Fifties' is identifiable. Putting it not very differently over half a century later, one asks if it still stands up. And if, and to what extent, it has withstood various intervening outbreaks of anti-verse. Can we outline the views on poetry that still, or again, seem valid—and to need sustaining? It seems appropriate to give what amounts to something like a *New Lines*—or Neolinean—guide to pleasure in new poetry. Let's call this

A Tasting

> One should satisfy neither
> The emotional heavy breather
> Nor the uptight, unsexed
> Sniffer of dried text

Half seas over
Or ostentatiously sober
Themes served tartare
Or grilled till they char

Clashing with primary colours
Or nuanced to nothingness
Gross satiation
Or scrawny alienation.

On offer: the homey and wry
Or the slaughterhouse-steamy
Twisted simile-scraps
Or muddled news-clips

Evading coherence
Down a trickle of type-fonts
To sink without closure
In a flatland of posture,

Yes, above all the ones
Who, for whatever reasons
Hype their transcendence
One up on us peasants.

You'll drink to that? Well
Who'll be your clientele?
Only the strange lot
Who don't care what

It says on the label:
But seek deep, indefinable
Savours—much the same
In a wine or a poem.

It is rather surprising that *New Lines* is still on the agenda when all except myself from that anthology of more than half a century ago are no longer with us. To them let me comment:

To survive is not to surpass,
To outlive is not to outclass.

Far from it. But I am still proud of you, and of myself for presenting you at, I hope, your best.

LIST OF CONTRIBUTORS

Deborah Bowman is a Lecturer in English at Gonville and Caius College, Cambridge. She has written and broadcast on William Empson and other writers of the 1920s, and is currently working on a book about Empson and Practical Criticism.

Rachel Buxton is a Senior Lecturer in English at Oxford Brookes University. Her main research interests are Irish, British, and American poetry. Her monograph, *Robert Frost and Northern Irish Poetry*, was published by OUP in 2004; she is currently working on a co-authored critical introduction to Elizabeth Jennings for Manchester University Press.

Deborah Cameron is a sociolinguist who currently holds the Rupert Murdoch Chair of Language and Communication at Oxford University. Her main research interests are in the cultural history of language and the sociolinguistics of gender and sexuality. Publications include *Verbal Hygiene* (1995), *Good to Talk?* (2000), and *The Myth of Mars and Venus* (2007).

Terry Castle teaches at Stanford University and has written seven books, including *Masquerade and Civilization: The Carnivalesque in Eighteenth-Century English Culture and Fiction*, *The Apparitional Lesbian: Female Homosexuality and Modern Culture*, and *Boss Ladies, Watch Out! Essays on Women, Sex, and Writing*. She writes regularly for the *London Review of Books*, the *New Republic*, the *Atlantic Monthly*, and other magazines and journals.

Robert Conquest edited the *New Lines* anthologies. *Penultimata*, his seventh book of verse, is just out; other books include works of verse translation, criticism, biography, fiction, and history, inclucing *The Great Terror*. He is a fellow of the British Academy, the American Academy of Arts and Sciences, the Royal Society of Literature, and the British Interplanetary Society; and a member of the Society for the Promotion for the Roman Studies.

James Fenton is the author of *The Memory of War*, *Children in Exile*, and *Out of Danger* (poetry). *The Strength of Poetry* contains his lectures given when Oxford Professor of Poetry.

Eric Homberger is Professor Emeritus of American Studies at the University of East Anglia, Norwich. He was educated at the University of California, Berkeley, the University of Chicago, and at Cambridge. His first book, *The Art of the Real*, was a study of English and American poetry from the 1940s to the 1960s. He is the author of *The Historical Atlas of New York City* and other books about politics, culture, and society in New York City.

Alan Jenkins is Deputy Editor of the *Times Literary Supplement* (having previously been Poetry Editor, 1981–1990). He has written on poetry for various publications and taught in England, France, and the US. His book of poems, *Harm*, won the Forward Prize for Best Collection in 1994; his other collections include *The Drift* (2000), and *A Shorter Life* (2005).

Nicholas Jenkins teaches English at Stanford. He is the co-editor of three volumes of Auden Studies, has recently completed a book on Auden, and his reviews and essays have appeared in the *London Review of Books*, *Times Literary Supplement*, *New Republic*, *New Yorker*, and *New York Times Book Review*.

Zachary Leader is Professor of English Literature at Roehampton University. He is the author of *Reading Blake's Songs*, *Writer's Block*, *Revision and Romantic Authorship*, and *The Life of Kingsley Amis*, a finalist for the 2008 Pulitzer Prize in Biography. Among the books he has edited are *The Letters of Kingsley Amis* and *On Modern British Fiction*. He is a Fellow of the Royal Society of Literature and is currently at work on a biography of Saul Bellow.

Colin McGinn is Professor of Philosophy at the University of Miami and a Cooper Fellow. He is the author of some twenty books, among the most recent *Shakespeare's Philosophy* and *Sport*.

Karl Miller founded the *London Review of Books* and was its editor for many years. Before that, he was literary editor of the *Spectator* and the *New Statesman* and editor of *The Listener*. From 1974 to 1992 he was Lord Northcliffe Professor of Modern English Literature at University College London. His books include *Cockburn's Millennium*, *Doubles*, *Authors*, and two works of autobiography, *Rebecca's Vest* and *Dark Horses*. A study of James Hogg, *Electric Shepherd*, appeared in 2003.

Blake Morrison is Professor of Creative and Life Writing at Goldsmiths' College, London. He has written poetry, fiction, and libretti, but is perhaps best known for his two memoirs, *And When Did You Last See Your Father?* and *Things My Mother Never Told Me*. The poetry in his first two collections, *Dark Glasses* and *The Ballad of the Yorkshire Ripper*, won the Somerset Maugham, Dylan Thomas, and E. M. Forster awards. His most recent book is a novel, *South of the River* (2007).

Michael O'Neill is a Professor of English at Durham University and a Director of the University's Institute of Advanced Study. His books include *The Human Mind's Imaginings: Conflict and Achievement in Shelley's Poetry* (1989), *Romanticism and the Self-Conscious Poem* (1997), and *The All-Sustaining Air: Romantic Legacies and Renewals in British, American, and Irish Poetry since 1900* (2007). He is also the author of two collections of poems, *The Stripped Bed* (1990) and *Wheel* (2008), and he received a Cholmondeley Award for Poets in 1990.

William H. Pritchard is Henry Clay Folger Professor of English at Amherst College. His books include critical biographies of Robert Frost, Randall Jarrell, and John Updike and a memoir about teaching, *English Papers*. He reviews widely for various publications and has published four collections of essays, the most recent of which is *On Poets and Poetry* (2009).

Craig Raine is Fellow in English at New College, Oxford, and a poet, dramatist, critic, librettist, and novelist. He edits the arts tri-quarterly, *Areté*.

Anthony Thwaite, b.1930, after Oxford (1952–5) taught at Tokyo University. Since then he has been a literary editor (*Listener*, *New Statesman*, *Encounter*), and taught in universities in Libya, the USA, and England. As one of Philip Larkin's literary executors, he has edited Larkin's *Collected Poems*, *Selected Letters*, and *Further Requirements*; at present he is preparing a selection of Larkin's letters to Monica Jones. His own *Collected Poems* appeared in 2007.

Clive Wilmer is a Fellow of Sidney Sussex College, Cambridge. A poet himself, his most recent book is *The Mystery of Things* (Carcanet, 2006). He has edited two volumes of Donald Davie's prose, *With the Grain* (Carcanet, 1998) and *Modernist Essays* (Carcanet, 2004), and one of Thom Gunn's, *The Occasions of Poetry* (Faber, 1982). He is currently preparing a new *Selected Poems* of Thom Gunn.

INDEX